ANCIENT NAUKRATIS
Excavations at a Greek Emporium in Egypt

Part II
The Excavations at Kom Hadid

THE ANNUAL OF
THE AMERICAN SCHOOLS OF ORIENTAL RESEARCH

Volume 55

Series Editor
Nancy Lapp

Billie Jean Collins
ASOR Director of Publications

ANCIENT NAUKRATIS
Excavations at a Greek Emporium in Egypt

Part II
The Excavations at Kom Hadid

by
Albert Leonard, Jr.

with contributions by

Andrea Berlin and Morris Weiss

American Schools of Oriental Research

ANCIENT NAUKRATIS

EXCAVATIONS AT A GREEK EMPORIUM IN EGYPT

Part II
The Excavations at Kom Hadid

By
Albert Leonard, Jr.

Volume 1 in the Ancient Naukratis series
The Ancient Naukratis series is edited by
William D. E. Coulson
Albert Leonard, Jr.
Co-directors, Naukratis Project

Volumes in this series already published are:

Vol. 1 Ancient Naukratis: Excavations at a Greek Emporium in Egypt
Part I, The Excavations at Kom Ge'if, by Albert Leonard, Jr.
American Schools of Oriental Research

Vol. 2, Part I The Survey at Naukratis, by William D. E. Coulson
Oxford: Oxbow Books (Oxbow Monograph No. 60)

Vol. 3 The Tomb Chamber of Hsw the Elder: The Inscribed Material at
Kom El-Hisn I: Illustrations, by D. P. Silverman
Winona Lake: Eisenbrauns, 1989

Vol. 6 Greek Painted Pottery from Naukratis in Egyptian Museums, by Marjorie S. Venit
Winona Lake: Eisenbrauns, 1988

This volume has been published with the assistance of the
Provost's Author Support Fund of the University of Arizona

©2001
American Schools of Oriental Research

ISBN: 0-89757-025-1

Library of Congress Cataloging-in-Publication Data
Leonard, Albert.
    Ancient Naukratis : excavations at a Greek emporium in Egypt / by
Albert Leonard, Jr. ; with contributions by Andrea Berlin . . . [et al.].
        p.   cm. — (Annual of the American Schools of Oriental Research ;
v. 54)
    Includes bibliographical references (p. 361–374).
    Contents: v. 1. The excavations at Naukratis. pt. 1 : The excavations
at Kom Geif.
    ISBN 0-7885-0392-8 (cloth : v. 1, pt. 1 : alk. paper)
    1. Naukratis (Extinct city)   2. Excavations (Archaeology)—Egypt
—Naukratis (Extinct city).   I. Berlin, Andrea. II. Title.   III. Series.
DS101.A45 vol. 54
[DT73.N3]
    930 s—dc21   97–028045
    [932]   CIP

Printed in the United States of America
on acid-free paper. ♾

To William G. Dever
scholar, mentor, colleague, and friend

Who would dig [Naukratis] for [the Egypt Exploration Fund]? The first person to be approached had been Heinrich Schliemann, who responded enthusiasically to the suggestion that he should excavate Naucratis. The proposal was vetoed at once by Maspero: Schliemann would never do: he was tactless and quarrelsome, sought only publicity for himself and would alienate the authorities.

(Drower, 1985, 66)

Contents

Preface

The work of the Naukratis Project has been concentrated in the western Nile Delta, specifically in an area bounded by the sites of El-Barnugi in the north and Kom el-Hisn in the south. This area contains the ancient city of Naukratis (modern Kom Ge'if), which, according to the Greek historian Herodotus, was the first and only city in which the early Greek merchants were allowed to settle. The area also contains a number of other sites dating from Pharaonic through later Roman times. Unfortunately, little is known of these sites and their state of preservation. Indeed, the process of decay and modern encroachment has been so serious in the Delta that a resolution was passed at the Second International Congress of Egyptologists held at Grenoble, France, in September 1979, giving top priority to survey work in the Delta. Accordingly, the Naukratis Project has involved: 1) A survey of all ancient sites within an approximate 30 km area to the north and west of Naukratis in order to learn more about the environs of the city. Such a survey has assessed the character of the visible remains, the state of site preservation, and the extent of intrusions made by modern settlements and cultivation (Coulson 1996); 2) a program of excavation at the site of Naukratis based on modern excavation techniques and backed by an interdisciplinary support staff.

This report of the Ancient Naukratis series is divided into two volumes. The first describes the results of the excavation at the southern end of the ancient city at a mound within the village of Kom Ge'if (Leonard 1997). This, the second fascicle, details the excavations to the northeast of that village in an area known to both Sir William Flinders Petrie and local farmers as Kom Hadid.

Excavations were carried out almost simultaneously, and according to the same excavation methodology, at both Kom Hadid and Kom Ge'if during the 1982 and 1983 field seasons. This fact accounts for the degree of duplication in the Preface of both Naukratis fascicles since many of the same people and funding agencies were involved in both aspects of the project. The author believes that such duplication is necessary not only for the sake of completeness but also to facilitate use of each volume by the reader.

Because the details of the stratigraphy at Naukratis had been debated for almost a century, the strategy of our excavations in the South Mound at Kom Ge'if was to present first the maximum vertical exposure of the archaeological soils still extant between the rising ground water and the *sebakhin*-scarred surface of the ancient site. Then, after we had produced a clear understanding of the historical periods that were still preserved at Naukratis, we would direct our emphasis to the clearing of larger (horizontal) areas in an attempt to elucidate the type(s) of occupation represented by each chronological/historical phase in the life of the inhabitants of this famous emporium.

Excavation was conducted according to a modified "Wheeler-Kenyon" (balk/debris) method of excavation (Dever and Lance 1978; Seger 1971) that was specifically tailored to meet the particular problems of excavation in the Nile Delta. At Naukratis all archaeological excavation was done by the excavation team and volunteers under strict supervision by experienced field and square supervisors. The use of local labor was limited to tasks such as the removal of already-excavated soils, the washing of pottery, and the guarding of excavation areas. Our *gafir*, Mr. Ahmed Shehab Mousa, the local antiquities guard, provided immeasurable help in securing qualified people to help us in this respect.

The basis of our recording system is the Locus, defined simply as any three-dimensional entity encountered during the excavation process. Loci can be either artificial (a procedural device more commonly termed a probe), or they may be authentic (such as a wall, pit, soil lens, or floor). Occasionally a Locus will carry a "Point P" suffix (Locus XXXX.P), a device that is restricted to artifactual and ecofactual material found directly on a floor or surface, and is used to call attention to the association of that material to the floor/surface. Also used is a "Point One" suffix (Locus XXXX.1), which is used as a control when collecting the first 10 cm below such occupation surfaces.

The basic unit of our excavation system is the "pottery bag," which represents the specific material collected from a precisely recorded, three-dimensional entity and in that regard may be considered to be a mini-Locus (Seger 1971: 16). A pottery bag may be excavated as one Locus and on the basis of subsequent study be reassigned to another Locus, but it always remains intact and cannot be subdivided. Any suspicion of contamination in a pottery bag automatically reassigns it to the latest of the Loci under consideration, or to Topsoil. A typical pottery bag from our excavations might be recorded as "N.III.62.10," which stands for Naukratis, Field III (Kom Hadid), Area/Square 62, Bag 10. This will have been the tenth bag assigned during the excavation in Area 62, and that was assigned (or reassigned) to Locus 6210.

Artifacts (pottery, glass, coins) as well as ecofacts (bone, shell, soil samples) are all attached to an individual pottery bag so that if that bag is reassigned during the interpretive phase, all of the material culture will remain (and move) together. Ceramic artifacts other than sherds as well as other objects of material culture are assigned a Material Culture Number (MC#) sequentially as the excavation progresses in a given square. They are also tied to the recording of the pottery bag, but, since the numbers are assigned in the square notebook, there may be more than one MC#58 but there will only be one MC#58 from Area/Square 62—that from pottery bag N.III.62.29, which is assigned to Locus 6210.

The present volume, therefore, presents the second of the two-part final report on our excavations at the ancient city of Naukratis, specifically the work at Kom Hadid. Chapter 1, by the present author, attempts to describe the stratigraphy and supply interpretation for the excavations in the major areas of Kom Hadid. Although the interpretations are those of the author, their formulation was assisted by the fine stratigraphical eye of Cynthia Johnson-Romy who did much to put this material in order. Ultimately these chapters are based on the meticulous excavation done by an exceptionally dedicated cadre of volunteers and faithfully recorded by area/square and field supervisors. The Locus Summaries appended to each chapter reflect the work of many of the staff members and specialists. Chapter 2, based on the pottery from Kom Hadid, is the work of Andrea Berlin who joined us late in the study phase of our project, but whose scholarship and personality breathed new life into the publication process. Her work attempts to put the situation at Naukratis into the wider Egyptian and even Mediterranean perspective. Chapter 3, dealing with miscellaneous pieces of the material culture, is not intended to be the last word on these pieces but rather an attempt to present them in a manner in which others might make use of them in future research. Especially important has been the assistance and expertise on the animal bones and shells that David Reese has given to the Naukratis Project since its inception. Because David was not able to work with the shell material on site, the author made a series of sample cards of distinctive shells by which all field identifications were made (usually by Joanne Curtain and other Simon Fraser University students). Through the kindness of the Egyptian Organization of Antiquities, we were able to obtain these cards during our "division" and David was finally able to handle the shells that he had previously only been able to work with through photographs. In the study of the animal bones David was equally hampered since only a small percentage of the total sample (and that randomly selected) was allowed to us at the division. The fish bones from the project's part of the division were sent to Douglas Brewer and his help is also acknowledged here.

Finally, the author would like to take this opportunity to thank all of those who labored at Kom Hadid. I find it incredible that so much "good archaeology" was done in the constant face of extreme heat, continual dust, innumerable flies, omnipresent fleas, Halazoned water, tepid Tang, miserably redundant meals, extremely limited shower facilities, closely cramped quarters, constant sickness, and nocturnal leapings of the canal to the field toilets. Such strength reflects a dedication to a project that I have never experienced elsewhere. Surely, somewhere in the future, a cold Stella awaits us as our just reward.

* * *

The preliminary season of the Naukratis Project, funded by a Research and Development grant awarded by the Smithsonian Institution, was conducted during a three-week period in December 1977 and January 1978. The four excavation and study seasons (1980–1983) were funded by matching grants from the National Endowment for the Humanities. The author wishes to acknowledge the Endowment's continued support of the project. Matching funds were provided by the Graduate School and the College of Liberal Arts at the University of Minnesota, by the Social Sciences and Humanities Research Council of Canada, the University of Missouri-Columbia, Carleton College, the College of St. Catherine, Gustavus Adolphus College, Honeywell Inc., the 3H Industries in Sunnyvale (CA), and by private individuals. RCA, Inc. provided much of the computer hardware used in the field.

Co-directors of the project were William D. E. Coulson, University of Minnesota, who was in charge of the survey project from 1980–1983 as well as the soundings at sites within the survey area, and the present author, then at the University of Missouri-Columbia, who was in charge of the excavations at Kom Ge'if and Kom Hadid.

The Naukratis Project is indebted to the invaluable help provided by the American Research Center in Egypt and by its directors at the time of fieldwork, Paul Walker and Robert Wenke. Mme. Attiya Habachi from her desk in the Cairo office also provided many helpful suggestions. Assistance was also provided by many Egyptian officials: Ahmed el-Sawy, former Director General of the Egyptian Antiquities Organization, Hashem el-Alfy and Ibrahim Amir, former Chief Inspectors of the West and South Delta Inspectorates respectively, Youssef el-Gheriani and Doreya Said, former Directors of the Graeco-Roman Museum in Alexandria, Dia abu Ghazi, former Director General of Egyptian Museums, and Mohammed Mohsem and Mohammed Saleh, former Directors of the Egyptian Museum in Cairo. Inspectors assigned to the Naukratis Project by the Egyptian Antiquities Organization were Faten Abdel Halim, Sabry Taha Hassanein, and Adly Roshdy Amin. Thanks also go to the antiquities guard at Kom Ge'if, Ahmed Shehab Mousa, and his family for help and kindness and to Abdel Monem, mayor of the municipality.

The preparation of this manuscript was greatly assisted by a Research Grant from the National Endowment for the Humanities in 1990, and by several Small Grants awarded by the University of Arizona. Most site photography was done by the author, while most of the object photography was done by the late Duane Bingham, our project photographer. Pottery illustrations were drawn in the field by a number of volunteers who were supervised by Susan Osgood who, literally, drew hundreds of sherds herself. Each sherd was checked against its drawing by the author in the field and any errors are solely his. Pottery drawings were inked primarily by Cynthia Johnson-Romy assisted, in the later years, by Lois Kane and Kate Mackay. Much of the artwork for this volume was destroyed by nature in 1989. The ensuing chore of recreating illustrations from the original (in-field) pencil drawings caused considerable delay in the appearance of this volume. All plate layout was initially done by the author but assisted in the later stages by Lois Kane and Kate Mackay often working at the suggestion of Andrea Berlin. The author wishes to offer special thanks to Kate Mackay who has been especially helpful in the production of the final draft of this manuscript, and without whose diligence this volume would not have been possible.

The final manuscript on Kom Hadid was prepared before and without benefit of the comparative material from Tel Anafa (*Tel Anafa I, i–ii: Final Report on Ten Years of Excavation at a Hellenistic and Roman Settlement in Northern Israel*, by Sharon C. Herbert. Journal of Roman Archaeology Supplementary series No. 10, Parts 1–2.) which will be of great interest to readers of this volume. The author would also like to thank Sharon for her valuable suggestions during the final phases of the production of this manuscript.

Albert Leonard, Jr.
Tucson, Arizona 1998

The Excavation Staff

Director	Albert Leonard, Jr.
Field Directors	Cynthia Johnson-Romy
	James W. Rehard
	Jan M. Sanders
Area Supervisors	Mike Arwe
	Meg Miller
Photographer	Duane Bingham[†]
Conservator	Gayle Wever
Surveyor	Gerald W. Johnson
Artist	Susan Osgood
Balloon Photogrammetry	Gerald W. Johnson
	Christopher Loring
Geology	Cathleen Villas
Paleobotany	Julie Hansen
Physical Anthropology	A. Joanne Curtin
	Jeanne Hourston Wright
Core Drilling	John Gifford
Computer Project	Alden Arndt
EAO Inspectors	Adlu Roshdy Amin
	Faten Abdel Halim
	Sabry Taha Hassanein

Post-Seasons Study Staff

Floral Analyses	Patricia Crawford
Faunal/Marine Analyses	David S. Reese
Physical Anthropology	Brian S. Chisholm
Ceramics Analyses	Andrea Berlin

Project Consultants

Art/History	Bernard Bothmer[†]
Science	George Rapp, Jr.
Historian	Richard Sullivan[†]

[†]Deceased

List of Figures

Chapter 3

List of Plates

List of Tables

List of Abbreviations

ASL	above sea level
avg	average
cm	centimeter
Ch.	chapter
c.	circa
D.	diameter
E. A. O.	Egyptian Antiquities Organization
fm	from
frag(s)	fragment(s)
H.	height
HRC	Human Remains Catalogue
km	kilometer
lg	large
mm	millimeter
m	meter
MC#	material culture number
med	medium
n'd	necked
n.	note
NW	Northwest
pb	pottery bag
prox	proximal
SE	Southeast
sm	small
Th.	thickness
TN	Terra Nigra
ud	undistinguishable
v	very
W.	width
wh.	white

Chapter One

The Excavations at Kom Hadid (Naukratis Field III)

Albert Leonard, Jr.

Introduction

The two main foci of the Naukratis Project were the survey of ancient Naukratis and its environs and the excavation of what little remains of one of the most important international commercial centers in pre-Alexandrian Egypt. The survey portion of the project was directed by William D. E. Coulson (1996), while the excavation portion was directed by the present author.

Remnants of this ancient emporia are preserved (albeit very poorly) in the small village of Kom Ge'if, located 80 km southeast of Alexandria, a few miles to the west of the highway that connects the modern port to Cairo (fig. 1.1). For the sake of presentation, these remains can be divided into two main areas: the mound in the village Kom Ge'if (Leonard 1997), and the area northeast of Kom Ge'if and east of the lake that has filled the depression left by the work of the earlier excavators that is specifically known to the local villagers as Kom Hadid (Mound of Iron, fig. 1.2; pl. 1.1). Initially our attention had been drawn to Kom Hadid during the winter survey of 1977–78, because its surface was densely covered by lumps of a vitreous material that, at first, we interpreted as metal slag since the Arabic word *hadid* means "iron." However, in this area Sir William Flinders Petrie had encountered "eight to ten foot high slag heaps" (fig. 1.3), which he identified as the product(s) of a lime-slaking industry, fed by the limestone blocks that had originally come from the monumental entryway that had been added to the Great Temenos during the reign of Ptolemy II (Coulson and Leonard 1979: 155, and Coulson and Leonard 1981: 48). In 1980 the true nature of this glossy detritus was clarified when, during an on-site study of the material, Dean George Rapp, Jr. (Archaeological Laboratory at the University of Minnesota-Duluth) identified the material as "kiln waste" or "furnace product"— evidently the residue from a (still unlocated) ceramic industry in the neighborhood. Associated with his heaps of slag (that he recorded but evidently did not excavate), Petrie mentioned finding "large substructures of red baked Roman brick, some chambers of which . . . (exhibited) . . . many successive coats of painted frescoes" (Petrie 1886: 4); unfortunately no architectural evidence for such remains were visible during either the general area survey of 1977–78 or the intensive survey of Naukratis and its environs in 1980 and 1981.

With the hope that the tremendous quantity of furnace product on the present surface would indicate the location of an ancient kiln, as well as clarify Petrie's reference to the frescoed brick chambers, six squares (4.0 × 4.0 m) were opened at Kom Hadid during the 1982 season (fig. 1.4).[1] They were (in numerical order): Areas 48, 62, 63, 76, 130, and 144, but are discussed below in the approximate order in which they were opened. For the purposes of presentation, the work at Kom Hadid can be viewed as two separate operations: the excavations in the northern/northwestern part of the site (Areas 130 and 144), where indications of a wall were thought to have been detected during a sweeping of the general area prior to excavation; and near the top of the shallow *kom* (Areas 48, 62, 63, and 76)

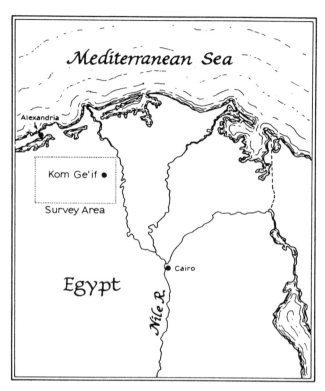

Fig. 1.1. Map of Egypt showing the location of ancient Naukratis and the area surveyed by the Naukratis project. (John Huffstut in Coulson and Leonard 1981b: 39, fig. 1).

in an area in which digging by the omnipresent *sebakhin* (local farmers) had produced fragments of lamps, terracotta figurines, and what appeared to be chunks of painted plaster.

Areas 130 and 144

On the northwestern edge of the mound, in the area that would later be excavated as Area 130 and Area 144, a ridge of soil had been noticed running north–south, apparently having been left by the *sebakhin* as being too firmly compacted to dig easily. Because the ridge was relatively straight, it was felt that the soil differentiation might represent the side of a mudbrick wall. In addition, building debris and detritus were visible on the surface here, and similar material covered the surface of the mound to the west (the future Area 144), a logical place for it to have fallen from the hypothesized wall. However, excavation in Areas 130 and 144 produced only mudbrick detritus, and no contiguous mudbrick was encountered. Work in these two areas was halted when labor was required for investigating Wall 7612/6212 in the center of the mound (see below). At one time a structure must have existed somewhere in the neighborhood of Areas 130 and 144, but unfortunately it could not be detected during our two small (and brief) soundings in the area.[2]

Areas 48, 62, 63, and 76

The four areas of excavation that were opened on the top of the low mound are presented below in the approximate order in which they were excavated (fig. 1.5; pl. 1.2). In general, the stratigraphy in these areas can be summarized, as can most of the stratigraphy at Kom Hadid, as a series of simple sediment and debris layers, occasionally interrupted by pits and animal burrows. The matrices of the debris layers all share building rubble as a common attribute.

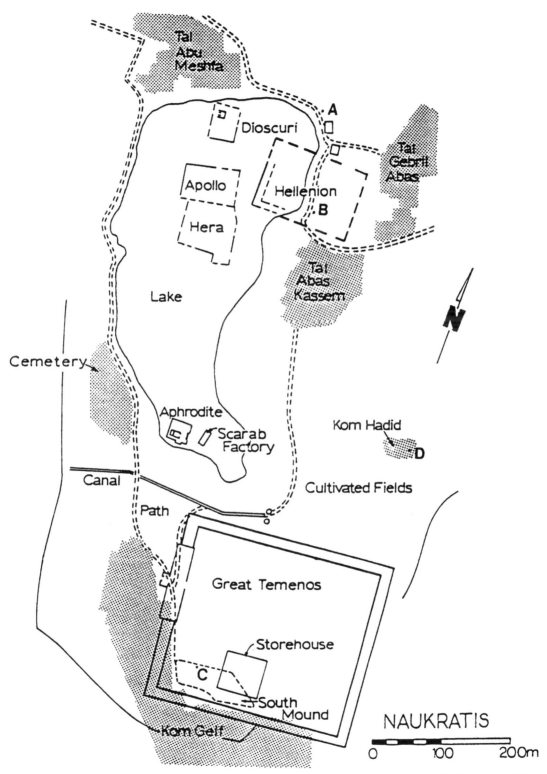

Fig. 1.2. Naukratis showing the relation of Kom Hadid to the South Mound at Kom Ge'if and to Petrie's "Great Temenos" (G. Johnson).

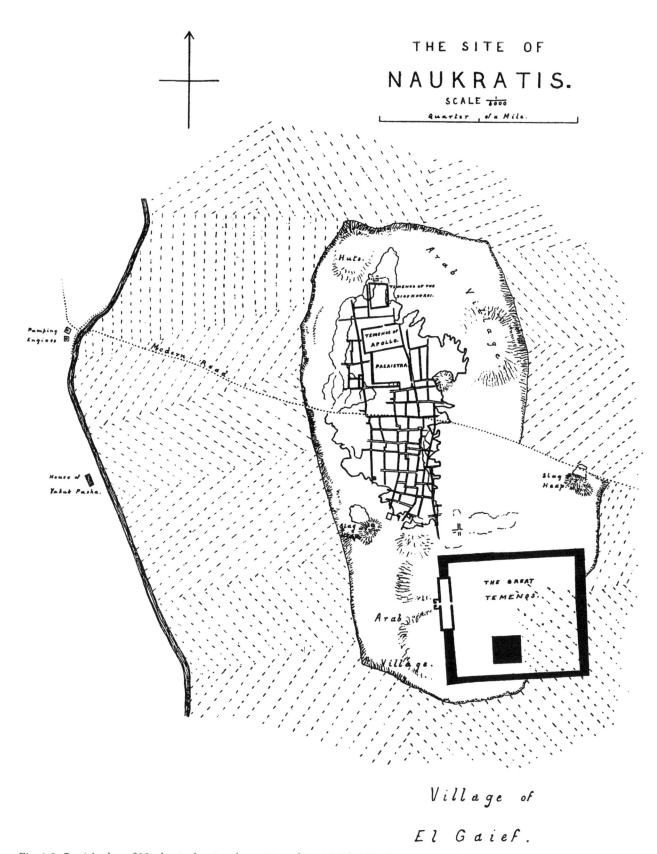

THE SITE OF
NAUKRATIS.

Fig. 1.3. Petrie's plan of Naukratis showing the position of Petrie's "slag heap" at Kom Hadid.

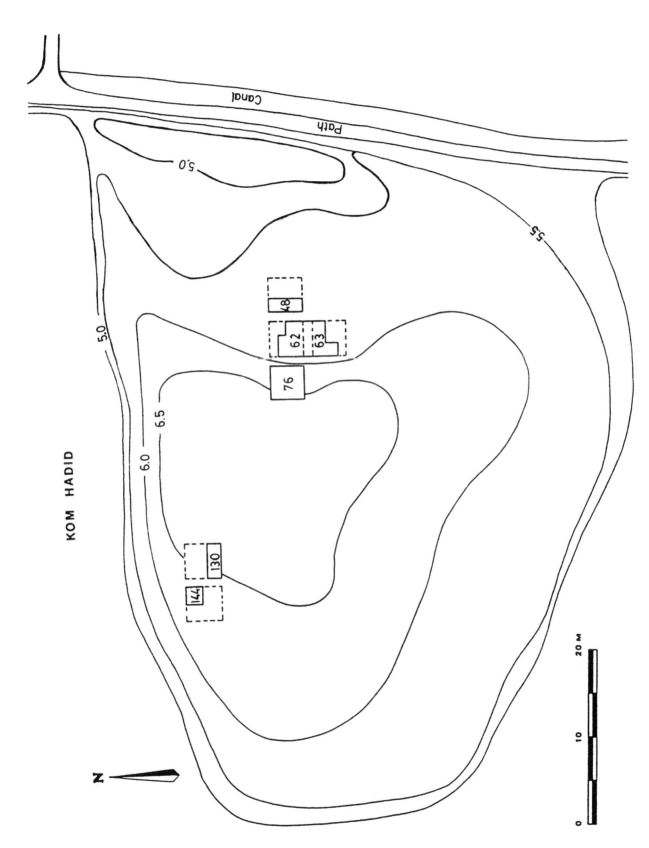

Fig. 1.4. Kom Hadid. Plan of the site showing the location of the excavation areas (J. Rehard).

Area 76

Area 76 was selected for excavation when an exposed concentration of sherds (Pit 7603) was noticed in an area where soil was being removed by the *sebakhin* in order to be deposited as fertilizer in the nearby fields. The surface of Area 76 sloped sharply downward from west to east, dropping as much as 80 cm across the four meter area (see especially the East Section drawing [fig. 1.6]); and much of this slope was the direct result of previous agricultural digging activity.

Our excavation was begun at the higher elevation with a probe (Locus 7602) through Topsoil 7601 that immediately exposed the full extent of Pit 7603. Pit 7603, containing an enormous amount of pottery mixed with pieces of faience and fragments of terracotta figurines (see Locus Summaries), had been dug into Sediment 7604, which consisted of building debris in the form of mortar, plaster, and fired brick fragments. Sediment 7604 covered another pit, Locus 7609, that was also filled with intact fired bricks and brick fragments, large sherds, painted plaster, and kiln waste. In turn, Pit 7609 had been dug into Sediment 7611, which was exposed but not excavated. Elsewhere in the square, below the level of Sediment 7604, Locus 7605 was encountered. As was the case with Sediment 7604, Locus 7605 also contained building debris and kiln waste, but much of the locus had been severely contaminated by much animal burrowing.

Debris layer 7606 was the first locus to be encountered that covered the entire east/west axis of the square (Sediments 7604 and 7605 had both been eroded or dug out toward the east). It was also relatively free of the animal burrowing so characteristic of Locus 7605. In fact, the only real distinction between Locus 7606 and Locus 7605 was the absence of the burrows. Cut into both Loci 7605 and 7606 was Pit 7610, the matrix of which consisted of at least three distinct components: kiln waste, pockets of ash, and decomposed particles of fired brick, a mixture that could have been the by-product of a burning or kiln operation. Unfortunately, animal burrows had also severely disturbed Pit 7610.

Beneath Sediment 7606 was Locus 7608, a debris layer that could be associated with the collapse of mudbrick Wall 7612 that extended into the square for about two meters from the east balk before disappearing into the south balk, forming a triangle of exposed wall surface in the southern end of the square (pl. 1.3).[3] Locus 7608 was the material formed by the deterioration of the upper portion of Wall 7612; the upper portion had slumped and covered the wall itself. Below Locus 7608, the next three debris layers (Locus 7613, Locus 7618, and Locus 7619) are considered to represent collectively the northward collapse of Wall 7612. In each descending layer the percentage of detritus and loose (but intact) mudbricks to the soil matrix increased noticeably. Removal of these layers and Pit/Trench Locus 7617, revealed eight intact courses of mudbrick in Wall 7612. Unfortunately, at this point the rising ground water was encountered. It is presumed that the wall continued below the present water table since neither a use-surface nor a foundation trench was encountered before water filled the bottom of the excavation area and forced us to stop digging (pl. 1.3).

Along the three uppermost preserved courses on the northern side of Wall 7612, a trench (Locus 7617) had been cut, evidently in antiquity. It was about 0.20–0.25 m wide at the top of the wall, tapering toward the wall and joining it beneath the third (from the top) preserved course of brickwork. At first Trench 7617 was considered to have been a foundation trench for Wall 7612; but this view was dismissed eventually as more courses of the wall were encountered below the bottom of Trench 7617, and also because the bricks above and below the bottom of Trench 7617 were of similar size, color, and composition. Trench 7617 was found filled with crushed kiln waste and many sherds, including some nearly intact small vessels, and may have been a robber's trench. Any suggestion as to what was robbed, however, would be pure speculation.[4]

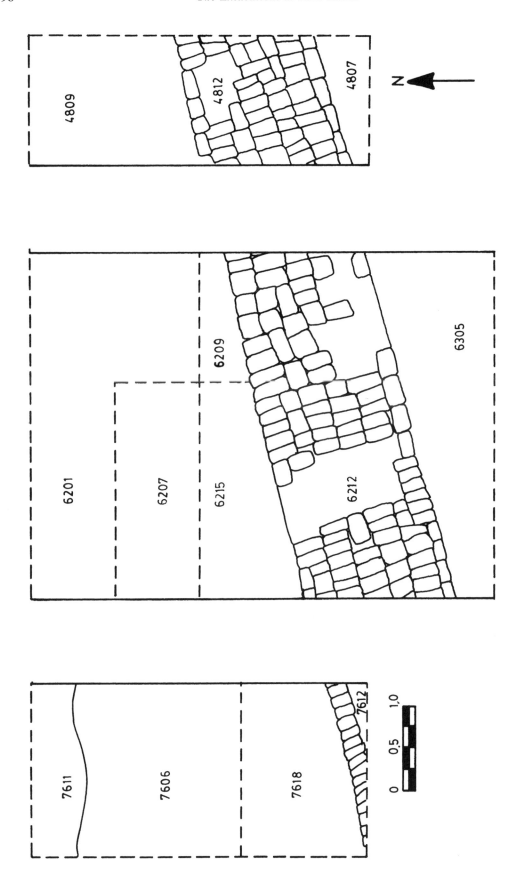

Fig. 1.5. Kom Hadid. Plan of east–west, mudbrick Wall 7612/6212/4812 (J. Rehard).

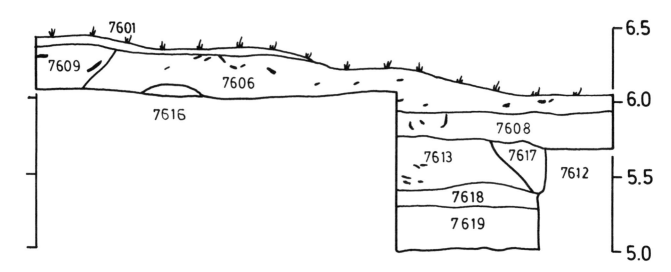

Fig. 1.6a. Kom Hadid. East Balk of Area 76 after the 1982 season of excavations (C. Romy-Johnson and J. Rehard).

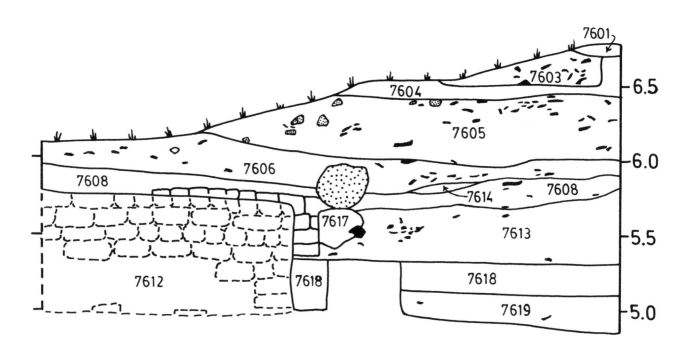

Fig. 1.6b. Kom Hadid. South Balk of Area 76 after the 1982 season of excavations (C. Romy-Johnson and J. Rehard).

Debris Layer 7613, into which Trench 7617 had been cut, consisted of building debris: mudbrick detritus and occasional pieces of plaster. It also produced a surprising array of items of material culture, such as bits of faience, terracotta figurine fragments, and an intact saucer lamp (see Ch. 3 #18), suggesting that this material may represent an intentional fill-deposit brought in from elsewhere (see Locus Summaries). Debris Layer 7618, beneath Locus 7613, produced mudbricks, painted plaster, and small fragments of a pebble-in-mortar pavement. More fragments of such a pavement were found in debris Layer 7619, just above the point where ground water was reached and excavation had to cease in Area 76.

As excavated, Area 76 can be considered to consist of two basic strata. The later (upper) stratum is characterized by the presence of soils rich in kiln waste or furnace product. Interestingly, kiln waste, combined with building debris, appeared in every layer above and including Locus 7606 (i.e. Loci 7601, 7603, 7604, 7605, 7606, 7609, 7610); but it appeared in only one other locus, the possible robber Trench 7617 that ran alongside Wall 7612. This suggests that at some point after the hypothesized stone facing had been removed from Wall 7612, Trench 7617 began to fill with kiln waste (probably encouraged and hastened by rain wash). The freshly defaced portion of Wall 7612 subsequently fell apart, resulting in the creation of Layer 7608 that covered and sealed Trench 7617.

The earlier (lower) stratum, consisting of the material beneath Locus 7608, appears to have remained free from any disturbance after the destruction of Wall 7612. From the debris found in Loci 7613, 7618 and 7619, it can be suggested that the large structure, of which Wall 7612 formed a part, had been provided with an aggregate pavement floor and had walls embellished with three-dimensional, painted plaster, possibly above a cut-stone veneer.

Area 62

The excavations described above exposed eight courses of a mudbrick wall and produced substantial evidence for elaborate architectural decoration in the southern portion of Area 76, but this work did not provide any evidence for the size of the wall or give any indication of the dimensions of the structure with which we were dealing. Therefore, excavation was initiated in Area 62, directly to the east of Area 76, in an attempt to trace the eastern extension of Wall 7612 that was recorded as Locus 6212 in this square. The bricks of this impressive wall were encountered at different levels across the excavation area,[5] suggesting one of the following hypotheses: the wall had been built in several phases; the upper courses of the wall had decayed at different rates; or, the top of the wall had been damaged severely by the *sebakhin*. The third hypothesis seemed to us to be the most plausible.

Wall 6212 was traced across the entire four-meter width of Area 62 (fig. 1.5), producing mudbrick Wall 7212/6212 with a minimum length of approximately seven meters. The length alone indicated that we were dealing with a substantial structure, but at that point we still did not have definite evidence for the width of the wall (pl. 1.4).

Area 63

Area 63 was the third of the four areas to be opened in an attempt to define Wall 7612 which had been partially exposed in the southeast quadrant of Area 76 and traced (as Wall 6212) across Area 62, situated immediately to the east. This work had uncovered the northern face of the wall, but its southern face had not been exposed because it ran into the southern balk across the entire width of Area 62 (fig. 1.5). To clarify the situation and to uncover the width of Wall 7612/6212, Area 63 was opened immediately to the south of Area 62 (fig. 1.4). For this reason excavation was conducted only in the northern 1.50 m of the square.

Because of the nature of this probe and the fact that the excavation of Area 63 was begun late in the season, Locus 6301 and Locus 6302, the upper two sediment/debris layers (open and most probably contaminated), were quickly removed to an elevation corresponding to the top of Wall 7612/6212. Surprisingly, this work did not produce any trace of the wall. However, when the 1.0 m balk that separated Area 62 from Area 63 was excavated to that level, both the top of the wall and its southern face were encountered beneath Debris Locus 6304 (pls. 1.5 and 1.6). Finally, it could be demonstrated that we were dealing with a wall that averaged c. 1.70–1.75 m in width.[6]

The loci excavated above the collapse of Wall 6212 (including debris Layers 6301, 6302, and 6304) all contained building debris, kiln waste, and a large quantity of pottery. Cutting into both Layers 6302 and 6304 was Pit 6310 that continued into Area 62 (as Pit 6310/6210), where it met the top of Wall 6212 at the east balk. A second intrusion, Pit 6308, containing a large quantity of kiln waste and fired bricks, had also been cut into Layer 6304. This is the same sequence of debris loci and pits that had been noticed elsewhere at Kom Hadid.

Layer 6305, interpreted here as the southward collapse of Wall 6212 in Area 63, consisted of mudbrick detritus, loose mudbrick fragments, and, again, a large quantity of pottery. Removal of a small section of Layer 6305 that had been deposited against the southern face of Wall 6212 revealed five courses of brickwork. Due to temporal considerations, excavation ceased in this area at an arbitrary level established within the matrix of debris Layer 6305, but Wall 6212 most probably continued deeper, as was indicated in the probe in Area 76.

Area 48

Area 48, the final area to be excavated at Kom Hadid, was opened in order to trace the eastern limits of the massive mudbrick Wall 7612/6212 that had already been uncovered in Area 76 and Area 62 (figs. 1.4, 1.5). It was also hoped that this work might present us with a corner, or second wall joining the main wall, which would give some definition to the structure. However, the huge mudbrick wall continued eastward in a straight line across the excavated portion of Area 48, and no other wall was encountered (fig. 1.5; pls. 1.6 and 1.7).

Because of temporal constraints, only the western portion (1.50 × 4.00 m) of Area 48 was excavated, but the following stratigraphy was observed. Beneath top soil, Locus 4801, a solid layer of mudbrick detritus, Locus 4802, covered the entire excavation area. Below this was debris Layer 4803 characterized by a dense admixture of kiln waste and fragments of fired brick. Also beneath Locus 4802 was Pit 4810, a loose fill of large chunks of kiln waste and fragments of brick rubble that could be equated with Pit 6210 in Area 62.

After the removal of sediment Layer 4805 (below Loci 4810 and 4803), Wall 4812 was encountered, the top of which had been partly disturbed by an animal burrow or robber trench (Locus 4806), forming a shallow channel along the northern edge of the wall. As exposed, Wall 4812 consisted of six or seven rows of irregularly laid mudbricks with an average width of c. 1.70 m. Removal of debris Layer 4808 to the north and Layer 4807 to the south of Wall 4812 enabled us to delineate three courses of the wall before excavation was terminated at an arbitrary level in both Locus 4808 and Locus 4807. Time did not permit further excavation.

The Structure at Kom Hadid

The building of which Wall 7612/6212/4812 had once formed a part, was a substantial structure with at least one room measuring more than nine meters on a side. Although we have no idea of the plan of the structure, it does not seem excessive to postulate the presence of a second story, based on the thickness of that wall. Finds from loci sealed by the collapse of the wall suggest that the structure had at one time been provided with a pavement of aggregate possibly embellished further with sections of *opus sectile* and/or *opus alexandrinum*. Its walls appear to have been decorated with lime plaster that had been painted in panels of solid color, stripes, and faux marble, inscribed with lines suggesting marginally drafted blocks of stone, and even sculpted into architectural moldings in the distinctive "Masonry Style" that was the vogue throughout the Mediterranean (Hellenistic/Campanian/Ptolemaic/Hasmonean) world of the second and early first centuries B.C.

In addition to the substantial size and elaborate decoration of the building, the frequency of fragments of faience bowls, molded lamps, terracotta figurines, *terra nigra* vessels and the stamped handles of imported amphorae bear further witness to the importance of the section (or suburb) of ancient Naukratis that is now known as Kom Hadid.

It is unfortunate that, because of the height of the water table in this area, only eight courses of the wall could be excavated, and that any occupation surface of the structure is presently below ground water and therefore inaccessible through conventional means of excavation.

Locus Summaries[7] Lists Area 48

Locus	Description
4801	**Description**. Top soil. Pale Brown (10YR 6/3). **Pottery Bag**. N.III.48.01.
4802	**Description**. Layer of Very Dark Grayish Brown (10YR 3/2) mudbrick detritus covering the entire square. Indurated upper-face may indicate use as a surface. **Pottery Bags**. N.III.48.02, 03, 08.
4803	**Description**. Layer of Brown (10YR 4/3) debris. Matrix is loose and porous with a high percentage of kiln waste and fired brick fragments. **Pottery Bags**. N.III.48.04, 09. **Material Culture**. *Animal Bone*: #1, 1st phalanx prox epiphysis (2×) and 1st phalanx (1×) fm lg mammal; #5, spine fm lg fish, rib shaft fragments and distal humerus and radius fragments fm med/lg mammal. *Faience*: #2, base [**Ch. 3, #34**][8]; #7, rim [**Ch. 3, #41**]. *Plaster*: #6, fragment of white lime plaster, with red exterior surface [**Ch. 3, #77**] (unillustrated).
4804	**Description**. Number not used.
4805	**Description**. Layer of Dark Brown (10YR 3/3) sediment soil with crushed kiln waste and fired brick fragments (also crushed?). This layer was cut into by Pit 4810 and disturbed by animal burrow Locus 4806. **Pottery Bag**. N.III.48.06. **Material Culture**. *Faience*: #4, ud fragments.
4806	**Description**. Rodent burrow filled with very loose Reddish Brown (5YR 4/3) soil matrix. Inclusions consisted of straw, kiln waste, and crushed fired brick particles (sand to granule size). Locus 4806 disturbed sediment Locus 4805 through which it had been cut. **Pottery Bag**. N.III.48.07.

Locus	*Description*

4807   **Description**. Debris layer of Dark Brown (10YR 3/3) soil/detritus deposited against the north face of Wall 4812 and the south face of Wall 4812. Locus 4807 was excavated only to a level sufficient enough to delineate the south face of Wall 4812.
Pottery Bag. N.III.48.10.
Material Culture.
Plaster: #8.

4808   **Description**. Thick layer of Very Dark Grayish Brown (10YR 3/2) debris/detritus touching the north face of Wall 4812. Matrix contained occasional mudbricks in secondary deposition. Locus 4808 was excavated only to a level sufficient to delineate the north face of Wall 4812.
Pottery Bag. N.III.48.11.
Material Culture.
Animal Bone: #10, tooth and mandibular fragments and complete metatarsus (III or IV) of *sus*, fragment of right scapular fm immature med mammal

4809   **Description**. Number not used.

4810   **Description**. Pit filled with a Brown (10YR 5/3), extremely loose and crumbly, soil matrix, with inclusions of large (cobble-size) fragments of kiln waste. Deposit is about 75% kiln waste with a few fragments of fired bricks also included. The sides of Pit 4810 were dish-shaped and the bottom was relatively flat. Locus 4810 is part of the same pit that was excavated in Area 62 as Locus 6210, and in Area 63 as Locus 6310.
Pottery Bag. N.III.48.05.
Material Culture.
Animal Bone: #3, prox 1st phalanx fm lg mammal (*equus*?).

4811   **Description**. Number not used.

4812   **Description**. Wall of Very Dark Gray (10YR 3/1), Dark Grayish Brown (10YR 4/2), and Dark Brown (10YR 3/3) mudbricks. The Wall is 1.70 m wide and 1.50 m of its length was exposed in Area 48. Average brick size: .32 × .14 × .10 m and six rows of bricks compose the width. The top of Wall 4812 had been disturbed along its northern edge by the rodent burrow excavated as Locus 4806. The Wall was not fully excavated. Only two courses of the wall were exposed in order to determine the limits of Wall 4812 and Wall 7612-6212 which are, in fact, the same wall.

Locus Summaries Lists Area 62

Locus	Description

6201 **Description**. Topsoil.
Pottery Bags. N.III.62.02, 06.
Material Culture.
Other: Terracotta: #8.

6202 **Description**. Compact, Dark Brown (10YR 4/3) debris layer, with pebble–cobble-sized fired brick, kiln waste, and occasional limestone inclusions.
Pottery Bags. N.III.62.03, 04, 10, 11, 18, 20, 41.
Material Culture.
Animal Bone: #12, axial fragment fm mammal, shaft fragments fm lg mammal; #14, fragments of canine/incisor fm med mammal (*sus*?), axial fragments from med mammal. Sample also included fragments fresh-water bivalve (Lamarck)
Stone: #7, small (c. 3.7 cm × 4.8 cm) cylinder of white limestone (weight? or gaming piece?).
Metal: #3, Copper coin, very poor condition, ud.
Faience: #13, ud fragments.
Other: Terracotta: #33, stamped amphora handle [**Ch. 3, #29**].

6203 **Description**. Compact layer of Dark Brown (10YR 4/3) detritus, slightly darker than overlying Locus 6202, with pebble–cobble sized kiln waste and both fired and mudbrick inclusions. This material probably represents debris from the collapse of Wall 6212.
Pottery Bags. N.III.62.05, 07, 12, 13, 42.
Material Culture.
Animal Bone: #4, three humerus (or femur) fragments fm lg. mammal; #17, fragments of humerus, long bone, and rib shafts fm med mammal, cranial and spine fragments fm fish, axial fragments and incisor fragments fm med mammal, and synsacrum fragment, prax, and humerus(?) fm med bird; #22a, distal humerus and fragment of scapula fm med bird, cranial fragments fm lg fish, scapula, long bone and pelvic (cut marks), fragments and 1st phalanx fm med (immature) mammal, rib shaft (2nd) fragment fm small mammal, distal metapoidal epiphysis fm *ovis/capra*, vestigal metapoidal fm *bos*(?), and possible calcaneus fragments fm med-lg mammal; #75, tibia (right) shaft fragment fm med mammal.
Shell: #6, fragments of *Bellamay* ; #18, spine fragment fm ud fish; #22b, fragments of fresh-water bivalve (Lamarck) and *Donax trunculus*, #24, complete *Donax trunculus*, fresh-water bivalve (Lamarck), and either *Helicella* or fresh water gastripod (*Lanistes carinatu*); #76, intact *Terebra* spp. (auger shell) from Red Sea.
Terracotta: #20, head of Aphrodite(?) figurine [**Ch. 3, #5**].
Stone: #19.
Metal: #21 and #25, ud lumps.
Faience: #16 rim [**Ch. 3, #38**].
Other: #5, kiln waste.

6204 **Description**. Canceled. Combined with Locus 6212 (wall).

6205 **Description**. Loose, Dark Brown (10YR 3/3) debris layer with high (75%) percentage of pebble–cobble-sized kiln waste and fired brick inclusions. The high concentration of kiln waste distinguishes this from associated loci and suggests that the locus could be a pit.
Pottery Bags. N.III.62.02, 15, 21, 23, 46.
Material Culture.
Animal Bone: #49, calcaneus fragment fm med/lg mammal (cut marks and puncture mark, canine); #83a, cranial animal bone and spine fragments fm lg fish, possible synsacrum and mandibular fragments fm med–lg mammal.
Shell: #83B, several *Donax trunculus*.
Terracotta: #82.
Faience: #85, ud fragments.
Metal: #11, Iron nail fragment.

Locus	*Description*
	Stone: #57, broken piece of gray and white marble veneer with traces of plaster adhering to inner face [**Ch. 3, #64a**].
	Plaster: #40, two similar fragments of lime plaster [**Ch. 3, #75**].
6206	**Description**. Combined with Locus 6212 (wall).
6207	**Description**. Compact, Dark Brown (10YR 3/3) debris layer with some pebble–cobble-sized kiln waste and fired brick inclusions. Similar to Locus 6203, but locus changed artificially when the top of Wall 6212 was encountered.
	Pottery Bags. III.62.16, 19, 22, 24.
	Material Culture.
	Animal Bone: #27, possible calcaneus fm (immature) med mammal; #34a, spine and cranial fragments fm fish, rib shaft fragments, metatarsal/metacarpal (immature?), petrous long bone and cranial fragments fm med/lg mammal; axial, tooth and long animal bone shaft fragments fm lg mammal (some with cut marks); #43, long animal bone shaft fragments fm lg. mammal, rib shaft fragments and carpal/tarsal fm (immature) mammal, incomplete molar/premolar fm *bos*(?), fragments of distal tibia and lg ud pelvic/cranial (with cut marks) fm med/lg mammal; vertebral and axial fragments fm (immature) med mammal; #47, quadrate and cranial fragments fm med fish, left scapula and carpal/tarsal fm med (immature) mammal.
	Shell: #31, #34b, complete *Helicella*(?); #35, complete Venus verrucosa; #44, examples of *Donax trunculus*, possibly fragments of fresh-water bivalve (Lamarck); #51, *Donax trunculus*.
	Terracotta: #26, feet of Isis-Aphrodite(?) figurine [**Ch. 3, #10**]; #37, fragment of miniature theatrical mask [**Ch. 3, #31**]; #48a, head of a figurine of a young male [**Ch. 3, #6**].
	Faience: #36, base [**Ch. 3, #35**]; #36a, rim [**Ch. 3, #50**]; #36b, body [**Ch. 3, #46**]; #36c, base [**Ch. 3, #51**]; #50, ud fragments.
	Metal: #38, ud lump.
	Stone: #41, 42.
6208	**Description**. Canceled. Combined with Locus 6212 (wall).
6209	**Description**. Relatively loose, Dark Brown (10YR 3/3) debris layer with occasional pebble-sized kiln waste and fired brick inclusions. Locus is similar to Locus 6207 but locus was changed when the top of Wall 6217 was uncovered next to it.
	Pottery Bags. N.III.62.14, 26, 30, 32, 33, 35, 39.
	Material Culture.
	Animal Bone: #54, #59, long shaft fragments fm med mammal; #62a, vertebra fragment of med mammal with cut (butchering ?) marks; #64, prox 1st phalanx epiphysis, distil tibia epiphysis, vertebral centrum fm immature med mammal, long shaft and axial fragment fm lg mammal, pelvic fragment fm med mammal (*sus* ?), maxillae fragment and maxillae/cranial fragments fm sm-med mammal; #66.
	Shell: #62b, intact *Donax trunculus*, fragments of *Aspatharia rubens* (or *Etheria elliptica*).
	Terracotta: #55; #28, fragment of figurine of a young male.
	Metal: #63 and 65, ud lumps.
6210	**Description**. Pit. Loose, building debris in a matrix of Yellow (5YR 5/4 and 10 YR 7/6) soil. Mudbrick fragments in a variety of colors with Dark Grayish Brown (10YR 4/2) predominating; crushed (pebble to cobble-sized) fired brick, and similarly-sized fragments of mortar. Infrequent kiln waste inclusions. This locus is basically conical in shape and cut into Locus 6306. It was possibly lined with the loose soil of Locus 6216.
	Pottery Bags. N.III.62.27, 29, 43, 48.
	Material Culture.
	Animal Bone: #53, ud fragment of fish, possible pelvic or scapula fragment fm sm mammal; #79, rib haft fragments (burnt?) and long shaft fragments fm med mammal, incisor fm *equus*(?) or *bos*(?), many alveolar fragments (probably *sus*) and molars (3×) and premolars (3×) fm *sus*.
	Terracotta: #52a, feet of Isis-Aphrodite(?) figurine [**Ch. 3, #9**].
	Plaster: #58, fragment of gray-white, lime (CaCo3) plaster with a design that appears to be part of a floral or vegetal pattern [**Ch. 3, #67**]; #78, two fragments of white, lime plaster. Exterior surface has been "beveled" as if part of a panel design (**Ch. 3, #76**).

Locus	*Description*
6211	**Description**. Canceled. Combined with wall Locus 6212.
6212	**Description**. Huge mudbrick wall, constructed of large (avg. 32 × 14 × 10 cm) bricks in a variety of colors ranging from Very Dark Gray (10YR 3/1) through Dark Grayish Brown (10YR 4/2) to Dark Brown (10YR 3/3). The wall is six rows wide (ca. 1.70 m) and survives at least five courses high (in Area 62) to eight courses high (in Area 76). Seems to have been laid without mortar, in several different levels (phases?), which accounts for it having been assigned several different locus numbers during the course of excavation. No other walls could be associated with it. This wall continued into Area 76 (Locus 7612) through Area 48 (Locus 4812), and across Area 62 into its south balk. This wall is so long and so wide that it probably does not represent a simple, domestic architecture.
6213	**Description**. Canceled. Combined with Wall 6212.
6214	**Description**. Canceled. Combined with Wall 6212.
6215	**Description**. Debris layer of Dark Brown (10YR 3/3) soil adjacent to Locus 6217, with compact, Dark Grayish Brown (10YR 4/2) mudbrick detritus including some loose mudbricks, pebble-sized kiln waste and bits of fired brick. **Pottery Bags**: N.III.62.36. 38, 47. **Material Culture**. *Animal Bone*: #69, alveolar fragment (1×) with tooth fragment fm *sus*, 2nd phalanxes (2×) lacking epiphysis fm med mammal with cut marks, distal radius and pelvic fragment fm med mammal, prox tarsus or metatarsus fm lg bird, metapoidal (1× lacking distal epiphysis) fm *sus*, possible fish spine fm lg fish. *Shell*: #70, fragments of fresh-water bivalve. *Faience*: #71, rim **[Ch. 3, #49]**.
6216	**Description**. Layer of loose, silty, Brown (7.5YR 5/4) soil without any detectable inclusions. Possibly formed the lining of Pit 6210. **Pottery Bag**. N.III.62.45 (no pottery).
6217	**Description**. Loose Very Dark Grayish Brown (10YR 3/2), "ashy" soil layer along the northern face of Wall 6212, and tapering away from it. Matrix included pebble-sized kiln waste and bits of crushed fired brick. During excavation the locus appeared to have been a foundation trench, but so many courses were exposed that it probably was not. **Pottery Bags**. N.III.62.25, 28, 37, 40. **Material Culture**. *Animal Bone*: #67, alveolar fragment and tooth root fragments fm sm/med mammal, maxilla fragment and long shaft fragment fm med mammal. Also human(?) radius. *Faience*: #68, ud fragments. *Stone*: #61, small piece of agate, white with red and orange veins.

Locus Summaries Lists Area 63

Locus	Description
6301	**Description**. Topsoil. **Pottery Bags**. N.III.63.01, 02. **Material Culture**. *Animal Bone*: #27. *Stone*: #1, several small pieces of gray stone veneer, including one blackened by fire (evidence of Petrie's lime-slaking activity ?); #24, chip of purple stone (not further identified); #25, red stone veneer **[Ch. 3, #64b]**. *Plaster*: #28, fragment of lime plaster consisting of a total of five layers representing at least two finished and color-decorated surfaces with associated make-up layers **[Ch. 3, #69]**; #79, fragment of lime plaster consisting of three coats **[Ch. 3, #68]**. *Glass*: #26, fragment of a blue-green glass plaque/ingot **[Ch. 3, #66]**.
6302	**Description**. Debris layer of Brown (10YR 4/3) soil/detritus with inclusions of kiln waste, mortar fragments, and bits of fired brick, and a large quantity of sherds. Locus 6302 is cut into by Pit 6310. **Pottery Bags**. N.III.63.03, 06, 16. **Material Culture**. *Animal Bone*: #5, astralagus and humerus distal (right) from med mammal (*equus* ?), 2 tooth fragments lophodont type (i.e. *equus*), fragments of incisor fm *sus*, rib shaft fragments, axial fragment and long shaft fragments fm med mammal, cranial fragment(?) fm fish; #14, long shaft fragments fm med mammal. *Shell*: #3, *Bellamaya, Donax trunculus, Lanistes carinatus*. *Terracotta*: #2, stamped amphora handle **[Ch. 3, #25]**. *Stone*: #4 and #13a, two small pieces of gray-white marble veneer, one of which is 1.3 cm thick, the other is 2.0 cm. *Plaster*: #13B, two fragments of decorated lime plaster **[Ch. 3, #74]**.
6303	**Description**. Pit filled with a Yellowish Brown (10YR 5/4) to Dark Brown (5YR 3/2) matrix containing inclusions of kiln waste and fired brick fragments. This locus was cut through by debris Layers 6304 and 6305. **Pottery Bag**. N.III.63.04.
6304	**Description.** Debris layer of Dark Grayish Brown (10YR 4/2) soil containing mudbrick detritus and a large amount of pottery. This locus is cut by Pits 6308 and 6303. **Pottery Bags**. N.III.63.05, 07, 08, 09, 10, 14. **Material Culture**. *Animal Bone*: #7a, many tooth fragments fm *sus* and herbivore, alveolar fragments, axial fragments, long shaft fragments, humerus epiphysis (complete) and vertebral fragments fm med mammal; #11, thoracic spine, humeri fragments, long shaft fragments, rib shaft fragment and axial fragment fm med mammal, 3rd phalanx fm *Bos*, distal radii fragments and ud fragments fm med/lg mammal, rib shaft fragments fm human(?); #17, spine fm med fish, tooth fragment fm herbivore-selenodont type, axial fragments, 2 mandibular fragments (left), possible cranial fragment and distal femur fragment fm med mammal; #22, molars (2×) fm lophodont (*equus*), maxillae fragments fm med mammal, axial fragment fm lg mammal with cut marks; #39. *Shell*: #7b, fragments of *Lanistes carinatus*; #9, fragments of fresh-water bivalve; #15, many fragments of land snail; #21, *Donax trunculus*, fragments similar to fresh-water bivalve and to fresh-water gastropod. *Terracotta*: #19, lamp **[Ch. 3, #21]**; #20, fragment of a miniature theatrical mask **[Ch. 3, #2]**. *Faience*: #12, rim **[Ch. 3, #55]**; #18, rim **[Ch. 3, #45]**. *Other*: #8, Mortar.
6305	**Description**. Debris layer of Dark Brown (10YR 3/3) soil mixed with mudbrick detritus and a large amount of pottery. Locus 6305 touches the south face of Wall 6212 and is interpreted as the southward collapse of that Wall 6212. Locus not completely excavated. **Pottery Bag**. N.III.63.11, 12, 15, 18. **Material Culture**. *Animal Bone*: #31, metacarpus (III ?) fm *sus*, humerus shaft fragment fm lg mammal (*bos*?), axial fragments fm lg mammal; #36, cranial and centrum fragments fm lg fish, alveolar and incisor/canine fragments fm *sus*, distal humerus fragment (possible *equus*), scapula (right) fragment (glenoid fossa) and long bone fragments

Locus	*Description*

(end lacking epiphysis) fm immature med mammal; #40, many teeth (whole and fragment) and many alveolar fragments fm *sus*, cranial fragments fm med/lg fish, tarsal fm med bird; #49, cranial and spinal fragments fm med fish, incisor and alveolar fragments and cranial fragment fm *sus*, axial fragments and mandibular(?) fragments fm med mammal, long bone shaft fragments fm bird, long bone end fragment (lacking epiphysis—possibly prox radius) fm immature med mammal, sacrum(?) fragment fm med mammal, many ud burnt fragments (some possibly mandibular/maxillary).

Shell: #32, fragments of land snail; #35, fresh-water bivalve; #48, several complete *Helicid* and complete *Donax trunculus*.

Terracotta: #43, fragment of drapery from figurine/plaque) [**Ch. 3, #14**].

Faience: #34, base [**Ch. 3, #36**]; and #50, base [**Ch. 3, #37**].

Metal: #41, Copper coin, poor condition, ud.

Stone: #44, segment of a white, limestone ring stand(?) [**Ch. 3, #62**].

Plaster: #47, ud fragments.

6306   **Description**. Wall? An alignment of about six Very Dark Gray (10YR 3/1) mudbricks, two rows wide and one course deep. This "Wall" is not perpendicular to Wall 6212, and the bottom of "Wall" 6306 is higher than the top of that Wall (6212). This locus may represent part of a later pavement or, even, a coincidental fall of a segment of bonded bricks.
Pottery Bag. N.III.63.17.

6307   **Description**. Canceled. Combined with Locus 6305 (originally assigned to a matrix beneath Locus 6306).

6308   **Description**. Pit of Reddish Brown (10YR 4/3-3/3) soil with quantities of kiln waste, mortar fragments, and decomposing fired brick fragments. This locus was not excavated as a single unit; it was merely exposed and defined. No pottery or **Material Culture** saved.

6309   **Description**. Sediment of sandy, Brown (10YR 4/3) soil containing frequent micaceous particles. This locus was not excavated as a single unit, but partially removed as Pit 6303. In fact, Locus 6309 may be part of Pit 6303 and Pit 6308 since it is positioned directly under both of these loci and it seems to follow a similar outline. The locus was not excavated completely. No pottery or Material Culture saved.

Locus Summaries Lists Area 76

Locus	Description

7601
Description. Topsoil.
Pottery Bags. N.III.76.01, 02, 15,17, 48.
Material Culture.
Stone: #3; #106, small alabaster(?) bead.
Other: Kiln waste: #1, #2.

7602
Description. Canceled. Combined with Locus 7603

7603
Description. Shallow pit of Dark Grayish Brown (10YR 4/2) soil with a very large concentration of sherds. The eastern portion of this locus had eroded away, but the western edge reveals that it had cut into Sediment 7604.
Pottery Bags. N.III.76.03, 04, 05, 06, 16, 20, 22, 50.
Material Culture.
Animal Bone: #6, maxilae fragment with 3 molars fm *sus*, cranial fragments fm med mammal; #12, incomplete molar, lophodont type (e.g. rhino, horse, etc.); #17, peturous fragment fm med mammal [burnt]; #32, tooth fragments fm *sus*, tooth fragment fm ud herbivore(?), long bone and fragments fm sm-med mammal; #40: #109, tooth fragments, distal tibia(?) and ud fragments fm med mammal (immature).
Shell: #14, complete *Murex trunculus*; #38, fragments of fresh water bivalve (*Lamarck*); #39, fragments fm fresh water bivalve (*Lamarck*).
Terracotta: #29, sherds of vessel with bichrome decoration **[Ch. 3, #33]**; #23, fragment of a plaque depicting architecture(?) **[Ch. 3, #17]**; #85, fragment of drapery from figurine/plaque **[Ch. 3, #13]**; #121, lamp **[Ch. 3, #19]**.
Faience: #8, ud fragments; #13b, rim **[Ch. 3, #42]**; #15, base **[Ch. 3, #60]**.
Metal: #16, iron nail. Preserved length 7.2 cm, width (at head) 1.6 cm Square, cross section (c. 1.0 × 1.0 cm below corrosion) may be the result of the action of the rust and black corrosion that is present. Completely mineralized; #31, fragment of copper alloy "pin." Preserved length 4.0 cm, width 0.5 cm; very active bronze disease and encrustation. Mineralized.
Stone: #41, small piece of fine-grained quartz sandstone with traces of calcareous cement adhering to it. Possibly used (secondarily) as a burnishing tool.
Plaster: #106, fragment of lime plaster decorated with vertical stripes **[Ch. 3, #73]**.
Other: Kiln waste: #5, 9, 15; Soil: #10.

7604
Description. Sediment layer of Dark Brown (10YR 4/3) soil with occasional bits of mortar and fired brick fragments. This locus had been cut into by Pit 7603.
Pottery Bags. N.III.76.07, 08, 12, 24, 25.
Material Culture.
Animal Bone: #42, tooth fragments fm *sus*, alveolar fragments fm med mammal (*sus*?), incomplete thoracic spine and cranial fragment fm med mammal; #48.
Plaster: #43, fragment (3.1 × 2.0 × 0.6 cm) of gray-white lime plaster decorated with light blue color **[Ch. 3, #78]**, unillustrated.
Other: Kiln waste: #22.

7605
Description. Sediment of Dark Yellowish Brown (10YR 4/4) to Brown (10YR 4/3) soil with building debris and kiln waste mixed into the matrix. Severely disturbed by animal burrows.
Pottery Bags. N.III.76.09, 10, 29, 30, 32, 53, 54, 55.
Material Culture.
Animal Bone: #21, complete, first phalanx fm lg ungulate, long bone shaft fragment fm ud bird; #59, long bone shaft fragment (tibia?, femur?) fm med/lg mammal; #66, distal humerus fm med/lg mammal (not *equus, bos,* or *cervis*); #113, possible prox radius fm med mammal (very eroded) and a wish bone(?) fm sm bird.
Shell: #19, #56, complete *Lanistes carinatus,* fragments fm fresh-water bivalve (Lamarck), one with human-made slit worked through to other side; #115, fragments of fresh-water bivalve (Lamarck).
Terracotta: #33, lamp **[Ch. 3, #20]**; #62 head of Harpokrates figurine **[Ch. 3, #3]**; #114, stamped amphora handle **[Ch. 3, #28]**; #158, fragment of a figurine of a young male wearing a himation(?) **[Ch. 3, #11]**.
Faience: #13a, rim **[Ch. 3, #39]**; #69, body **[Ch. 3, #48]**; #117a, rim **[Ch. 3, #59]**; #117b, rim **[#57]**.

Locus	Description

Metal: #18, Copper band (modern?).

Plaster: #111, Small fragment of three-dimensional architectural decoration [**Ch. 3, #83**].

7606   **Description**. Debris layer of Dark Brown (10YR 4/3) to Yellowish Brown (10YR 5/4) soil mixed with kiln waste and small fragments of fired brick. Locus 7606 is very similar to Locus 7605, the distinction being merely the absence of the animal burrows that were found in Locus 7606.

Pottery Bags. N.III.76.13 (contaminated), 14 (contaminated), 19, 23, 36, 37.

Material Culture.

Animal Bone: #26, long bone and axial fragments fm med mammal (one with cut marks), cranial fragments fm fish(?); #47, molar and premolar fm *sus*, alveolar and long bone fragments (humerus?) fm med mammal; #77, axial fragment (probably pelvic) with cut marks and epiphysis fm ud mammal; #81, distal humerus fm med bird, cranial bones (quadrate?) fm med fish, axial fragments, humerus shaft fragment, and long bone shaft fragments fm med mammal (some with cut marks).

Shell: #30 complete *Donax trunculus*, complete *Ostrea edulis*, fragments fm fresh water bivalve (Lamarck).

Terracotta: #29, fragment of molded grapes(?) [**Ch. 3, #12**].

Faience: #27, rim [**Ch. 3, #43**]; #37, ud fragments.

Metal: # 28, Copper alloy coin(?), mechanically cleaned by electrochemical reduction with NaOH and aluminum foil. Almost completely mineralized, ud; #80, Copper "pin." Preserved length 5.0 cm, width 0.5 cm. Mineralized.

Other: Soil: #44.

7607   **Description**. Canceled. Combined with Locus 7605.

7608   **Description**. Layer of Very Dark Grayish Brown (10YR 3/2) to Dark Brown (10YR 3/3) soil/mudbrick detritus with occasional limestone fragments and intact mudbricks, and a large quantity of potsherds. Locus 7608, probably representing collapse from Wall 7612, covered the top of Wall 7612 and sealed Pit/Trench 7617.

Pottery Bags. N.III. 76.26, 28, 31, 33, 42, 43.

Material Culture.

Animal Bone: #49, #60, fragments of fresh-water bivalve, fragments of long bone fm lg mammal; #64, short bone fragments fm med mammal (burnt), tooth fragment *sus*; #68, thoracic spine fragments, axial bone (pelvis?), fm med mammal, immature with cut marks; #91, maxillae fragment with molar and premolar fm *sus*, cranial bone (quadrate ?) fm med fish, axial and long bone shaft fragments fm sm-med mammal, fragments of carpal or tarsal animal bone(?) and astralagus fragments fm lg mammal; #96, maxillae fragment (right) with two molars fm *sus*, humerus shaft fragment fm med-lg mammal, 1st or 2nd phalanx immature med mammal, rib shaft fragment fm med mammal, long bone shaft fragment and distal tibia (tarsus) fm immature bird(?).

Shell: #58, fragment fm *Murex trunculus*; #63 and #67, fragments of fresh-water bivalve (Lamarck); #93, complete *Ostrea edulis*.

Terracotta: #88, head; #52 feet of Isis-Aphrodite(?) figurine [**Ch. 3, #8**]; #70 [**Ch. 3, #23**] and #92 [**Ch. 3, #24**], stamped amphora handles; no #, pot-stand, inscribed before firing [**Ch. 3, #32**].

Faience: #57, ud fragments; #98, rim [**Ch. 3, #58**].

Metal: #50, Bronze coin, poor condition, ud. Mechanically cleaned by electrochemical reduction with NaOH and aluminum foil.

7609   **Description**. Pit of Dark Brown (10YR 3/3) soil with a heavy concentration of fired brick fragments. Bits of limestone and pieces of painted plaster were also in the matrix, as were numerous large sherds, especially amphorae fragments. Pit 7609 was covered by Sediment 7604 and cut into Sediment 7611.

Pottery Bags. N.III.76.27, 47, 58, 62, 78.

Material Culture.

Terracotta: #61 [**Ch. 3, #26**] and #168 [**Ch. 3, #30**], stamped amphora handles; #124, bowl with plaster inside; no #, imported (two-part) amphora toe [**Ch. 3, #22**].

Plaster: #51, several large fragments of white lime plaster decorated with either a fugitive blue or red pigment [**Ch. 3,#79**], unillustrated.

Other: Kiln waste: #53; Brick: #55.

Locus	*Description*

7610   **Description**. Pit filled with multiple layers of a very loose and light weight matrix comprised of ash and kiln waste representing sequential deposition. Colors vary from Gray (5YR 5/1) to Light Gray (10YR 6/1) to Pinkish Gray (5YR 6/2) to Gray (7.5 YR 5/0). Pit 7610 cut into Sediment/Debris 7605 and 7606 and, as Locus 7605, had been disturbed by animal burrows in one area.
Pottery Bags. N.III.76.35, 51, 52, 56.
Material Culture.
Animal Bone: #73, lg humerus fm lg bird; #108, thoracic certebra fm bird(?), pelvic fragment fm med/lg mammal.
Faience: #79, ud fragments.
Stone: 71 (water-worn pebble), no #, small (c. 3.0 × 3.0 cm) cylinder of white limestone (weight or gaming piece?); #107 green conglomerate.
Other: Kiln waste: #74; Soil: #72.

7611   **Description**. The top of a sediment of Brown (7.5YR 4/4) soil exposed by removal of Pit 7610 which had cut into Locus 7611. Locus 7611 was not excavated, only the top was uncovered. No pottery collected.

7612   **Description**. Wall constructed of c. 28 × 10 × 12 cm mudbricks which vary in color from Dark Brown (10YR 3/3) through Very Dark Brown (10YR 3/1) to Dark Grayish Brown (10YR 4/2). Only one row of Wall 7612 is located in Area 76 and that row defines the northern face of the wall. At least eight courses of Wall 7612 were uncovered intact, but ground water was reached (and excavation was halted) before either the lowest course of the wall or a foundation trench could be uncovered. Loci 7606, 7608, 7613, 7618, 7619 were all interpreted as representing collapse from Wall 7612. A trench, Locus 7617, had been dug along the northern face of Wall 7612 (perhaps a robber trench to remove facing from the wall?). No surfaces could be associated with Wall 7612. This wall was subsequently exposed more fully in Areas 62, 63, and 48 where it was determined to be six rows wide, with an average width of 1.70 m.

7613   **Description**. Layer of Dark Grayish Brown (10YR 4/3) soil and mudbrick detritus with a few intact mudbricks, some kiln waste, and numerous sherd, that has been interpreted as the northward collapse of Wall 7612. Locus 7613 had been cut by Pit/Trench 7617.
Pottery Bags. N.III.76.34. 38, 41, 44, 45, 46, 59, 61, 64, 65, 70.
Material Culture.
Animal Bone: #84, cranial bone fm fish, alveolar fragments (mox or mandible) and rib shaft fragment fm med mammal; #89; #102, ud fragment (possibly axial) fm med-lg mammal with puncture mark from tooth of a carnivore(?); #103, cranial fragments fm med fish, distal femur and long bone shaft fragment fm bird, molar (crown only) fragments of *sus*, long bone fragments, vertebral fragment, axial mandibular(?), rib shaft and axial fragments fm med mammal; #119, #126, many cranial and long bone shaft fragments fm med mammal, sternal fragment fm bird; #129, complete caracoid fm med bird; #142, fourteen maxillae fragments (one with three premolars) fm *sus*(?), ulna shaft, sternal fragment, and distal femur fm med bird, fragments of rib shaft, acetabulum and fragment (pelvic?, calcaneus, ulna (immature, with deep cut marks).
Shell: #75, fragments of *Cerastoderma*, complete *Bellamaya*; #90, fragments of fresh-water bivalve (Lamarck), *Donax trunculus*, *Donax trunculus* and *Cerastoderma*; #94, #123, shell similar to *Glycymeris glycymeris*; #128, complete *Donax trunculus*.
Terracotta: #101, phallus; #145, unguent jar; #146a, head of a Harpokrates plaque [**Ch. 3, #4**]; #146b, two (non-joining) pieces of a plaque [**Ch. 3, #15**]; #104, wheelmade saucer (trefoil) lamp [**Ch. 3, #18**]; no #, potstand, inscribed before firing [**Ch. 3, #31**].
Faience: #76, ud fragments; #95, rim [**Ch. 3, #54**]; #125a rim [**Ch. 3, #44**]; #125b, rim [**Ch. 3, #40**]; #140a, rim [**Ch. 3, #53**]; #140b, rim [**Ch. 3, #56**]; #140c, base [**Ch. 3, #52**] ; #140d, body [**Ch. 3, #47**].
Metal: #87, copper head of an iron pin. Preserved diameter 1.3 cm, thickness 0.5 cm; #122, bronze coin, ud. Mineralized.
Stone: #97, 120; #139, small chip of basalt, fine grained black; #144, small (c. 6.0 × 4.5 × 3.8 cm) fragment of pebble mosaic (unillustrated).
Plaster: #99, ud fragments.
Other: Soil: #134.

7614   **Description**. A thin scree of Dark Reddish Brown (5YR 3/2) debris consisting of soil, kiln waste, and crushed fired brick, deposited over the sloping portion of debris Layer 7608.
Pottery Bag. N.III.76.40.

Locus	*Description*
7615	**Description**. Canceled. Combined with Locus 7613.
7616	**Description**. Sediment of Reddish Brown (5YR 4/3) soil exposed by removal of Pit 7609. This locus was excavated only enough to define its top; and it is possible that it may simply reflect the remains of a large animal burrow. **Pottery Bag**: N.III.76.57.
7617	**Description**. Trench-like pit of Dark Grayish Brown (10YR 4/2) debris consisting of soil mixed with kiln waste that had been dug along the northern face of Wall 7612. The matrix was loose and contained many large sherds and a few nearly intact vessels. In Area 62, this trench (Locus 7617) was traced as Pit/Trench 6217 along the face of Wall 6212 Locus 7617 may have been a robber trench dug to remove a possible stone facing on Wall 7612. **Pottery Bags**. N.III.76.66, 68. **Material Culture**. *Animal Bone*: #130a, axial fragments fm med mammal. *Other*: Soil: #130A.
7618	**Description**. Debris layer of Brown (10YR 5/3) soil and mudbrick detritus with a few intact mudbricks. The matrix is very similar to that of Locus 7613 but had a higher concentration of mudbricks. Locus 7618 touches the north face of Wall 7612 from the third course down from the top to the eighth course and is considered to have been the northward collapse of Wall 7612. **Pottery Bags**. N.III.76.69, 73, 74, 75, 76. **Material Culture**. *Animal Bone*: #147, calcaneus (right) and 1st phalanx fm small mammal, cranial fragments fm fish, cranial fragments, distal and prox humerus, and three metacarpals or metatarsals fm sm mammal; #153, cranial fragment and spine fm med/lg fish, mandibular fragments fm med mammal, rib and distal epiphysis fm sm mammal, tooth fragments fm *sus*, lg (ud) fragment (possibly calcaneus, prox tibia and axial fragments fm med/lg mammal); #159, complete *Corbula*, cranial and spine fragments fm lg fish, tooth (premolar) of lophodont type (*equus?*), axial fragments, long bone shaft fragment and distal metapoidal epiphysis fm lg mammal, metatarsal bones fm small digitigrade, phalanges and tarsal bone fragments fm (fox-sized) animal. *Shell*: #132, fragments fm fresh-water gastropod (Belamaya?); #157, fragment similar to *Helicella*. *Terracotta*: #148, stamped amphora handle [**Ch. 3, #27**]. *Faience*: #154, ud fragments. *Metal*: #161, ud lump. *Stone/Mortar*: #155, fragment of pebble mosaic. White-gray lime or marble pebbles in gray, lime mortar; #156, fragment of pebble mosaic. White limestone or marble pebbles in a lime matrix. One honey-colored pebble may be alabaster. Mortar exhibits c. 0.1 cm terracotta (grog) temper. *Painted plaster*: #164, small fragment of white lime plaster with traces of red pigment on "exterior" surface [**Ch. 3, #80**], unillustrated. *Other*: Soil: #133.
7619	**Description**. Debris layer of Dark Grayish Brown (10YR 4/2) mudbrick detritus with loose (intact) mudbricks irregularly scattered throughout. The matrix of this locus is very similar to that of Locus 7618 except that there are more intact mudbricks in Locus 7619 than in Locus 7618. This locus has been interpreted as the collapse of Wall 7612 to the north. The bottom of Locus 7619 could not be reached since water filled the excavation area and excavation was brought to a halt. **Pottery Bags**. NIII.76.71, 72, 77. **Material Culture**. *Animal Bone*: #136, spine fragments fm lg fish, fragments of cranial, 1st phalanx, and prox epighysis for 1st phalanx fm sm mammal; #166, fragment of rib shaft fm sm/med mammal with cutmarks, and complete lumbar vertebra fm sm/med, immature mammal. *Stone*: #135 [**Ch. 3, #65a**] and #149 [**Ch. 3, #65b**], fragments of pavement. *Plaster*: #138, ud fragments. *Other*: Mortar: #150; Charcoal(?): #151; Kiln waste: #143.

Locus Summaries Lists Area 130

Locus	Description
13001	**Description**. Topsoil. **Pottery Bags**. N.III.130.01, 02. **Material Culture**. *Animal Bone*: #2, rib shaft fragment fm sm/med mammal, tooth fragment of herbivore type. *Stone*: #1, small (see photo 83:11:23,24) piece of white, coarse-grained marble veneer (*opus sectile?*).
13002	**Description**. Debris layer of compacted, Dark Brown (10YR 3/3) soil with pebble-sized kiln waste and fired brick inclusions. **Pottery Bags**. N.III.130.03, 04, 05. **Material Culture**. *Faience*: #7, ud fragments. *Metal*: #3, ud lump. *Stone*: #4, fragment of fluted column of soft white limestone [**Ch. 3, #63**]. *Other*: Mortar: #6.
13003	**Description**. Debris layer of compacted Dark Brown (10YR 3/3) soil, with pebble–cobble-sized kiln waste and fired brick inclusions. Matrix appears to be more "yellow" than the Locus 13002 material above it. Some of the fired bricks were concentrated along the west balk, stratigraphically above the Locus 13004 layer of limestone cobbles. **Pottery Bags**. N.III.130.06, 08. **Material Culture**. *Animal Bone*: #8, long bone shaft fragments fm sm-med mammal; and #14, long shaft fragment fm med mammal. *Plaster*: #13, fragments of decorated lime plaster [**Ch. 3, #71**].
13004	**Description**. Layer of limestone pebbles/cobbles, irregularly laid, below the concentration of cobble-sized fired bricks of Locus 13003. Building debris? **Pottery Bag**. N.III.130.15.
13005	**Description**. Layer of crushed (pebble-sized) fragments of fired brick, without any detectable soil matrix. Appears to represent building debris. **Pottery Bag**. N.III.130.09. **Material Culture**. *Plaster*: #15, ud fragments.
13006	**Description**. Artificial locus. Compact layer of Dark Brown (10YR 3/3) soil, relatively fine matrix, with pebble-sized kiln waste and fired brick inclusions. Material was similar in appearance to Locus 13003, but the locus number was changed to 13006 when the brick fragments of Locus 13005 were uncovered. **Pottery Bags**. N.III.130.07, 10, 17, 18, 19, 20. **Material Culture**. *Animal Bone*: #10, ud shaft fragments and highly fragmented (petrous bone pieces) alveolar(?); #22, axial and pelvic fragments fm med/lg mammal; #23, cranial fragment fm med fish, long bone shaft fragment, and fragments of patella fm med/lg mammal. *Shell*: #9, fresh-water gastropod (Bellamaya), fragments of *Donax trunculus*; #16, two complete *Donax trunculus*. *Terracotta*: #21, fragment of drapery from mold(?) [**Ch. 3, #15**]. *Faience*: #12 and #25, ud fragments.
13007	**Description**. Layer of compacted Very Dark Grayish Brown (10YR 3/2) detritus, with large fragments of Very Dark Grayish Brown (10YR 3/2) mudbricks and an occasional piece of fired brick. This material was interpreted as building material, but its origin was not clear. **Pottery Bags**. N.III.130.11, 14, 16, 20. **Material Culture**. *Plaster*: #20, fragment of decorated lime plaster [**Ch. 3, #72**].

Locus	*Description*
13008	**Description**. Lens(?) loose, Very Dark Grayish Brown (10YR 3/2) soil with frequent inclusions of pebble-sized kiln waste between Locus 13002 and Locus 13003. Locus extends from south balk to at least 1.50 north of south, from .35–.60 to 1.65–2.00 east of west balk, from 5.98 north and 6.11 south below 13002 down to 5.81 north and 6.00 south above 13003. After the balks were excavated, this locus appeared to have been a part of Locus 13003, sloping downward to the north.
13009	**Description**. Lens (possibly a pit) of extremely loose, Very Dark Grayish Brown (10YR 3/2) soil with pebble-sized inclusions of kiln waste and fired brick. **Pottery Bag**. N.III.130.12. **Material Culture**. *Plaster*: #17, fragments of decorated lime plaster **[Ch. 3, #70]**.
13010	**Description**. Loose, Very Dark Grayish Brown (10YR 3/2) soil matrix with some fired brick and mortar inclusions, and a layer of large fragments of relatively flat-lying pottery. This locus was stratigraphically below Locus 13009 and possibly acted as a lining for it, if Locus 13009 had actually been a pit. **Pottery Bag**. N.III.130.13. **Material Culture**. *Shell*: #18, fragments of *Cypraea (= Monetaria) annulus*, and *Bellamaya*. *Plaster*: #19, four small fragments of gray lime plaster decorated with darker gray "stripes" **[Ch. 3, #81]**, unillustrated.
13011	**Description**. Loose, Very Dark Grayish Brown (10YR 3/2) soil with some inclusions of pebble-sized kiln waste, located stratigraphically below Locus 13010. The bottom of the locus was not reached. Originally dug as part of 13006 and was differentiated only from the balks. No pottery or other material culture.

Locus Summaries Lists Area 144

Locus	Description
14401	**Description**. Topsoil. **Pottery Bags**. N.III.144.03, 14.
14402	**Description**. Probe, northeast quadrant, 10YR 4/4 layer. **Pottery Bags**. N.III.144.02, 05. **Material Culture**. *Other*: #1, Kiln waste.
14403	**Description**. Probe, northeast quadrant, 10YR 3/3 layer. **Pottery Bags**. N.III.144.08, 10. **Material Culture**. *Shell*: #4; #7. *Stone*: #6, fragment of white, coarse-grained marble. Nape of neck of a *kouros* statue(?) [**Ch. 3, #61**]. *Other*: #7, Soil; #9, Kiln waste.
14404	**Description**. Pit, northeast corner of northeast quadrant. **Pottery Bag**. Pottery not saved. **Material Culture**. *Shell*: #10, *Donax trunculus*. *Other*: Fired brick (no number).
14405	**Description**. Reddish layer with bricks along east balk probe, to c. 25 cm west of east balk. **Pottery Bag**. N.III.144.09. **Material Culture**. None.
14406	**Description**. Plaster/stone layer along east balk. **Pottery Bag**. No Pottery. **Material Culture**. None.
14407	**Description**. Soil layer below 14405 and 14406 along east balk. **Pottery Bag**. Pottery not saved. **Material Culture**. *Animal Bone*: #12, right mandible with molar fm *sus*, two incisors (root) fm canine.
14408	**Description**. Layer of mudbrick detritus. **Pottery Bag**. Pottery not saved. **Material Culture**. None.

Notes

[1] The field director at Kom Hadid was James Rehard.

[2] Work in Area 144 lasted less than two days. Since only open (top-soil, probe, or pit) loci were excavated, very little (if any) of the pottery and other elements of material culture was saved. See the Locus Summaries pp. 11–24.

[3] The top of Wall 7612 was fully exposed in Areas 62 and 48 (as Wall 6212 and Wall 4812 respectively).

[4] A few small fragments of cut and polished slabs of stone (c. 1.5 cm thick) were found in secondary archaeological contexts in both Areas 48 and 62 (see Ch. 3 #64a and b) and are considered here to be indication of a pavement of *opus sectile* somewhere on the site. However, if pieces of such stone had been used to decorate the northern face of Wall 7612, they may have been considered to be of sufficient value (in this stone-impoverished area) to justify the digging. Support for such an alternate hypothesis might be the slight indentation at the point that Trench 7617 meets Wall 7612 (fig. 1.6). This might have served as a base for the facing.

[5] The irregular top of this wall was subsequently shaved to a common level to protect it and associated loci from contamination.

[6] Note that although a part of Wall 6212 did cross the southern boundary of Area 62 and continued into Area 63 in the balk, we continued to record the wall as Wall 6212, or the already cumbersome Wall 7212/6212, rather than creating an even clumsier "Wall 7612/6212/6312."

[7] To ease some of the pressure on the recording system, shell and animal bone were usually collected in the same bag, so some MC#s may contain a mixture of the two types of material culture. These were later separated and studied by the appropriate specialist.

[8] Numbers in bold are inventory numbers used for this volume. Those in regular type are the original material culture numbers (MC#) assigned in each square at the time of excavation.

Chapter Two
Naukratis/Kom Hadid: A Ceramic Typology for Hellenistic Lower Egypt

Andrea M. Berlin

Introduction

Kom Hadid seems to have been a ceramic trash heap. Whereas the excavators could find no evidence of stratification on the small mound, they did recover tremendous quantities of pottery. This pottery consisted primarily of large fragments, many with a complete profile preserved. Close study reveals an unquestionable archaeological relationship between Kom Hadid and the nearby mound of Kom Ge'if, where settlement was continuous from the early fourth century to about the middle of the first century B.C. Not only is almost every ceramic shape and type variation found at Kom Hadid matched by stratified examples from Kom Ge'if, but in addition, both corpora lack certain widely available imported and/or decorated wares of the period (e.g. West Slope and/or Gnathia wares). Study of the two groups may thus be harmonized: the larger and more easily recognized forms from Kom Hadid are datable by their stratified appearance at Kom Ge'if, while some of the smaller fragments from Kom Ge'if can confidently be identified by comparison with the Kom Hadid assemblage. It appears that material from *both* mounds represents pottery available to, and used by, the Hellenistic settlers of Naukratis.[1]

While the fact of the relationship between Kom Ge'if and Kom Hadid is thus secure, its nature is ambiguous. Kom Hadid may have been an ancient depository, or even an ancient settlement whose architectural remains have disappeared. It may just as likely comprise the residue from activities in or around Kom Ge'if since antiquity, or even be related to the excavations of Sir Flinders Petrie at the end of the last century (it appears impossible to correlate precisely the areas in which he worked with the preserved sections of the present site). The location of the modern village immediately on and within the site's environs precluded large-scale topographic investigation or exploratory probes, so that the boundaries and full extent of the Hellenistic period settlement remain unknown. There may have been, for example, several areas of Hellenistic settlement, of which Kom Ge'if was the only one explored; if so, then the Kom Hadid pottery may derive from another contemporary area.

The Kom Hadid pottery corpus is almost certainly complete for its period: it includes types from every occupation phase found at Kom Ge'if, and so is chronologically comprehensive; and it contains as well every necessary type of household vessel, and so is functionally whole. The absence, noted above, of some common Hellenistic decorated wares and forms might seem to contradict this last statement, especially since examples of all of these are attested at nearby Alexandria. The Alexandria vessels, however, simply indicate that these wares were available in this general region. Their absence from the excavated assemblages of both Kom Ge'if and Kom Hadid suggests that the site's ancient inhabitants did not, or could not, acquire them. The more limited character of the Naukratis pottery is a direct reflection of the site's poverty, due to the recent foundation of Alexandria and its own vanished raison d'être as a Greek trading depot. The location—too close to Alexandria to grow in its own right (as, for example, Pelusium at the opposite end of the Delta), but too far from the coast or a main branch of the Nile to offer any significant geographic advantage—precluded prosperity. The Naukratis assemblages, then, belonged to a series of poor, rural Hellenistic settlements.

The pottery is grouped below by general shape and discussed by specific type, with correlations made to the Kom Ge'if stratigraphic sequence. Dating and distribution evidence from other sites—both in and outside of Egypt—is presented as well, though some wares and types have a different chronological history beyond their home region. The Naukratis assemblages are limited but typical—a circumstance that allows them to be presented as, in effect, a ceramic primer for rural Lower Egypt during the Hellenistic period. Finally, a chart summarizing the ceramic forms found at Naukratis and comparing the assemblage with that found at other sites in the eastern Mediterranean is offered in Table 2.6.

Table Vessels

The range of Hellenistic table wares found at Naukratis provides a telling reflection of the community's reduced status. Almost all of the vessels used for food and drink throughout the period were made of the local Delta silt, and only three shapes were common: thickened rim saucers, incurved rim bowls, and everted rim bowls (Table 2.1). These forms were new to the Egyptian ceramic corpus and were carefully modeled on recently acquired Greek originals. In fact, a few Attic and other imported black-glazed versions of these forms were found at Kom Hadid, all probably dating to the late fourth and early third centuries B.C.[2]

The Naukratis community was not alone in acquiring new, locally produced versions of Greek wares. Throughout the country, people adopted these shapes for their table vessels, but made them from the available Nile/Delta silt or desert marl clays (see parallels cited in shape discussions, below). As at Naukratis, these new table assemblages generally included few imported originals (Alexandria excepted). This combination of minimal imports and widespread, careful imitations is interesting on a number of counts. The quantity and fidelity of Egyptian production reflects knowledge of and admiration for the Greek originals. The relative paucity of these imported originals, however, reflects their general unavailability. This unavailability cannot be attributed to geography, since at large eastern Mediterranean sites outside the Ptolemaic realms, such as Antioch to the north and Sabratha to the west, Attic black glaze vessels were quite common (Waagé 1948: 7–15; Gill 1986). It is true, however, that the quantity of imported pottery in general found within Egypt is notably less than that found at sites beyond. At Maskhuta, in the Delta, no Hellenistic period imports occur (Holladay 1982: 57); at Coptos, in Upper Egypt, they comprise no more than five percent of the total in the Hellenistic-period corpus (personal study). In comparison, at Berenice, in Tunisia, imported vessels slightly outnumbered local products (Kenrick 1985: 86). It is possible that the Ptolemies levied taxes on pottery imported into Egypt proper, as they did with other foreign products. Those living in the countryside contented themselves with available and affordable imitations, which allowed the semblance of a Greek table service.

One table shape found at Naukratis is not Greek in origin (see p. 29, plain rim saucer). This is a dish of medium size (both in height and width), with an almost straight wall, sometimes very slightly incurving rim, and flat bottom. This form is traditionally Egyptian, being first attested in Middle Kingdom times; it apparently continued to be produced and used through the Hellenistic period.

Table 2.1. Hellenistic Table Vessels From Naukratis

Shape	Type	Fabric	Quantity	Kom Ge'if Phase	Naukratis Date
Saucer	Plain rim	Delta silt, plain & slipped	40	NW 2B	early 3rd cent. B.C.
	Thickened rim	Delta silt, plain & slipped	191	NW 3B	late 3rd cent. B.C.
		Terra Nigra	55	NW 7B	late 2nd cent. B.C.
	Drooping rim	Delta silt	1	NW 6C-8	late 2nd cent. B.C.
		Terra Nigra	6	NW 8A	late 2nd cent. B.C.
	Beveled rim	Terra Nigra	1	NW 8A	end 2nd cent. B.C.
		Delta silt, plain & slipped	6	NW 10	topsoil
Bowls/Cups	Incurved rim	Delta silt, plain & slipped	350	NW 2A	early 3rd cent. B.C.
		Marl	1	NW 2B	early 3rd cent. B.C.
		Terra Nigra	37	NW Hiatus A	end 2nd cent. B.C.
	Everted rim	Delta silt, slipped	48	NW 2B	3rd cent. B.C.
		Terra Nigra	36	NW 4B	2nd cent. B.C.
		Delta silt, plain	21	NW Hiatus C	1st cent. B.C.
	Koan-Knidian	Aegean import	1	none at KG	—
		Delta silt, slipped	4	NW 3B	late 3rd cent. B.C.
	Hemispherical	Delta silt, slipped	2	NW 4B	2nd cent. B.C.
		Black glazed import	1	NW 10	topsoil

Later Hellenistic residents of Naukratis continued to use the same forms, still locally produced, as earlier Hellenistic residents. In the second century, black-slipped versions (*terra nigra*) appear, along with a few new shapes. Four local silt versions of a *skyphos*, perhaps imitating the Koan-Knidian cup, were found, along with one imported example. A few local beveled rim saucers and hemispherical bowls occur, and one imported black-glazed hemispherical bowl was found in topsoil. Remaining table vessels include three Eastern Sigillata A vessels (one platter and two cups), imported from southern Phoenicia, and dating to the later second or early first centuries B.C. (figs. 2.5:8, 2.12:3).

Saucers

The earliest saucer type found at Naukratis, the plain rim saucer, is a simple, shallow form with a slightly rounded, plainly finished rim (fig. 2.4:1–7). This first occurs at Kom Ge'if in NW 1C/N 1, and dates to the site's initial Hellenistic phase. The form itself is older still; in various fabrics and finishes it was manufactured by Egyptian potters at least since Middle Kingdom times.[3] This type was certainly manufactured during the preceding period; examples made of Delta silt were found in the fifth century B.C. warehouse excavated at Tel Maskhuta (Holladay 1982: pl. 15.10). Plain rim saucers are not common at Naukratis: a total of sixteen fragments were found at Kom Hadid and twenty-four at Kom Ge'if. At Kom Ge'if they appeared primarily in the lower levels, and some examples may well be residual debris of earlier occupations. Potters probably stopped making the form in favor of the new, and soon very popular, thickened rim saucer (figs. 2.1, 2.2). This type first appears at Kom Ge'if in NW 3B/N 2C and dates to the mid or late third century B.C. A total of one hundred fifty-eight fragments were found at Kom Hadid, and eighty-eight at Kom Ge'if (82 percent of the total number of saucers). Most are made of the local Delta silt and of these, a little over half are slipped a smooth, semi-lustrous red-brown.

Beginning in the second century B.C., reduction-fired thickened rim saucers also appear at Naukratis, with gray-black paste and a slightly lustrous dull gray slip (fig. 2.3). The ware, an Egyptian version of Greek black glaze, is here called *terra nigra*. Regional production of *terra nigra* is attested at Tell el-Farâ'în, in the southwestern Delta, where kilns and workshops have been excavated (Seton-Williams 1967, 1969; Charlesworth 1969). Apparently potters there manufactured *terra nigra* table vessels exclusively. The widespread distribution of *terra nigra* throughout Egypt suggests that several production sites existed (Grataloup 1991: 23–26), though ethnographic studies show that a single specialized production site can supply a large area (Vossen 1984: 399–404). The Tell el-Farâ'în potters made the three most popular table shapes of the Hellenistic corpus: thickened rim saucers, incurved rim bowls, and everted rim bowls (Seton-Williams 1967: figs. 2.5–10, 3.1–3, 5–8, 10–12, 17–19). All of these *terra nigra* vessels are copies of early Hellenistic forms, but none seem to have been produced before the late third or early second century B.C. The Tell el-Farâ'în kilns themselves date to the second and first centuries B.C. The most securely dated *terra nigra* vessels from excavated domestic contexts come from Coptos, Tell Timai (ancient Thmuis), and the House of Dionysos at Paphos, on Cyprus. At Coptos thickened rim saucers appear in third century levels (personal study); at Tell Timai, an everted rim bowl comes from a floor level dated c. 200–150, and a thickened rim saucer from a subsequent floor dated c. 150–125 (Ochsenschlager 1967: figs. 12, 27); at Paphos thickened rim saucers appear only in the late second century B.C. (Hayes 1991: fig. 5.4–6, from quarry pit in room AL, dated late second century B.C.). *Terra nigra* ware is attested as far south as Qasr Ibrim, where it again is dated to the later Hellenistic period (Adams n.d.: 13, 26–27 [Ware RBB]). Other examples, from Karnak and Tell Fara'on-Imet, are simply dated as "Hellenistic" (Grataloup 1991: fig. 1.1; Mostafa 1988: fig. 1.7). The Naukratis data may now be added in support of these later dates; *terra nigra* thickened rim saucers do not appear at Kom Ge'if until NW 7B, dated to the later second century B.C.

The thickened rim saucer was a popular shape throughout the eastern Mediterranean.[4] Imported and locally made versions—slipped, painted, or left plain—have been found at almost every excavated site (see table 2.6). The form was probably inspired by the neatly made fourth century Attic rolled rim plate, which was always covered in that ware's lustrous blue-black glaze and often had rouletted circles or other impressed designs on the interior (Sparkes and Talcott 1970: nos. 1058–1060, pl. 36, fig. 10; Rotroff 1997: 142–45, figs. 46–50, pls. 60–62). In its latest and most elaborate version, produced in the mid or late second century B.C., probably in the southeastern Mediterranean (perhaps even Alexandria), the shape was slipped black and given an interior circlet of white painted laurel leaves (see examples from Tarsus in Jones 1950: figs. 127.137 [import], 179.34, 36–38, A, B [local]). The form's size and profile made it practical and handy; its open design allowed decoration to show. In its many variants, it was clearly the standard choice when setting a table. In this regard, the residents of Naukratis were in step with the fashion.

Only a few examples of two other saucer shapes were found at Kom Hadid. Both appear in second-century phases at Kom Ge'if. One is the drooping rim saucer, a vessel generally deeper than the thickened rim saucer, with a short, downturned rim (fig. 2.4:8–15). This type of rim usually occurs in conjunction with a specific body type in which an interior ridge encircles a small, central depression. The form is traditionally termed a "fish plate" on account of its similarity to larger late fourth century B.C. vessels that also have a downturned rim and central depression and have fish painted on them. The smaller, unpainted Hellenistic versions are unlikely to have been used for any fish larger than sardines and are here termed saucers. Evidence for this form in its entirety, in *terra nigra*, is provided by a complete example found among the debris of the Tell el-Farâ'în kilns (Seton-Williams 1967: fig. 3.4). The upper parts of only five such vessels came from Kom Hadid and two from Kom Ge'if. All but one are in *terra nigra*. The Kom Hadid examples, though not preserved below mid-wall, probably had the central depression as well.

The last type of saucer found at Naukratis is the beveled rim saucer, a broad, relatively deep vessel with a neatly trimmed rim (fig. 2.5:1–4). Only three examples were found at Kom Hadid, and four at Kom Ge'if. Most are made of silt, though one is of *terra nigra*. This type appears at Kom Ge'if in NW 8A/N 3A-B, which dates to the second century B.C. Similar vessels have been found at Paphos (Hayes 1991: figs. 15.8, 41.31), Berenice (Riley 1979, nos. 621–622, fig. 110), and Coptos (personal study), all in second century B.C. contexts as well. The type seems largely confined to Egyptian/Ptolemaic sites; it is notably absent from contemporary, non-Ptolemaic sites such as Ashdod, Samaria, and Tarsus.

Bowls/Cups

Bowls/cups are distinguished from saucers by narrower, deeper profiles. They could have held either food or drink. All those found at Naukratis are little, suitable for small portions only. Four types occur, but only two are common. The first is the incurved rim bowl (figs. 2.6–2.8), which appears at Kom Ge'if in NW 2A/N 1–2B, the earliest Hellenistic phase. Attic and other imported black glaze versions of this form were found at Kom Hadid, but the majority of the Naukratis vessels are of Delta silt, both plain and slipped. Some of these local versions faithfully replicate the niceties of the imports: a carefully formed, sturdy ring foot, often beveled on its outer face; a sharply inturned rim, sometimes thinned to a narrow rounded point; slim, even walls, smoothly finished; and a low, balanced profile. Many of the Naukratis vessels, however, made of the less refined local silt, have irregular walls and uneven profiles, with rims lazily upturned and simply thickened, and cursory, barely ring feet. The form, no matter how it was finished, was clearly a household necessity: one hundred forty-nine fragments were found at Kom Hadid and two hundred thirty-nine at Kom Ge'if. In both their ubiquity and varying quality, the Naukratis bowls match those from other Hellenistic table assemblages; the incurved rim form—imported, local, slipped, and plain—is the most popular bowl type of the early Hellenistic period.[5]

The everted rim bowl appears slightly later and soon matches the incurved rim form in popularity (fig. 2.10). At Naukratis seventy-five fragments were found at Kom Hadid and thirty at Kom Ge'if; the type first appears at Kom Ge'if in NW 2B, and so dates to the third century B.C. Like the incurved rim bowl, this form was modeled on Attic and other imported black glaze versions, and a range of profiles—from wide and shallow to deep and narrow—occurs.[6] Everted rim bowls are very common in Hellenistic table assemblages, sometimes outnumbering incurved rim bowls. This may be due to their more adaptable form: the open, out-turned rim renders this shape suitable for both food and drink, whereas incurved rim bowls could be used only for food.

Both forms continue in use through the second century B.C., during which time *terra nigra* versions also appear (figs. 2.9, 2.11). These latter vessels may have come from the *terra nigra* kilns at Tell el-Farâ'în; wasters of both shapes were found in the debris there (Seton-Williams 1967: figs. 2.7, 8, 10, 11, 3.1–3, 5–7, 10, 17–20). *Terra nigra* versions of incurved rim bowls first occur at Kom Ge'if in NW Hiatus A; everted rim vessels first occur in NW 4B. The second century date of these bowls, just as for the various saucer types, confirms a later Hellenistic date for *terra nigra* table vessels overall, at least in the Delta (they may occur earlier in Upper Egypt; at Coptos *terra nigra* appears already in strata of the third century B.C. [personal study]).

The third type of bowl found at Naukratis is the so-called Koan-Knidian bowl (or cup), a fairly deep vessel with a carinated profile, sharply everted lip, and opposed horizontal coil handles pressed on beneath the rim (fig. 2.5:9–11). One imported vessel was found at Kom Hadid, along with one in slipped silt; three more local versions come from Kom Ge'if. At Kom Ge'if one occurs in NW 3B, a phase dated to the late third century B.C. partially because of the appearance of this type. The form is elsewhere found in late third/early second century B.C. levels, and occurs almost everywhere that securely dated middle Hellenistic settlement is found.[7]

The last type of bowl found at Naukratis is the simple hemispherical bowl, an elegant form, narrow and deep, with a plain, slightly pointed lip (fig. 2.12:1, 2). Only one securely identified fragment was found at Kom Hadid, and two at Kom Ge'if. One appears at Kom Ge'if in NW 4B and so dates to the second century B.C. (Berlin in Leonard 1997: 6.1:8). Two of the vessels are of slipped silt, while one is an import—black glazed, with white painted bands on both the interior and exterior of the rim. The general form is probably copied from glass versions, such as the monochrome cast vessels of the Canosa Group, dating from the late third/early second century B.C. (Grose 1989: 186, fig. 92). These had no foot, and would have been used for drinking cups. Ceramic examples are not common, even including Eastern Sigillata A versions from the late second century B.C.[8] Their rarity is probably related to their function: such drinking vessels—capacious but unable to be set down—were suitable for prolonged and fancy parties, and those who could afford such entertainments probably owned these cups in glass or even plate.

Cooking Vessels

Cooking vessels are the heart of a household assemblage. At Naukratis, their importance is reflected in their numbers: the eleven different types found account for 26 percent of all vessels recovered (Table 2.2). The residents had at hand four distinct forms in which to prepare their meals: cooking pots, casseroles, stew pots, and baking dishes. The cooking pots have globular bodies, with short necks and relatively narrow mouths. The casseroles are just the opposite, having broad, fairly low bodies and wide mouths. The stew pots combine features of both: they have deep, round bodies and wide mouths. Finally, the baking dishes are low, broad, and flat-bottomed.

Any of these forms could have carried a lid, but at both Kom Hadid and Kom Ge'if almost no obvious lids were found. The most likely are a few small, plain dishes with a stubby disc "foot" that seems more like a handle. These dishes are too small for any shape but the cooking pots, which in any case are the most likely to require a lid. The reason for this is simply the nature of the food prepared in each sort of vessel. Cooking pots are designed for soups or legume-based dishes, which require longer cooking without significant water loss. To this end, a lid is desirable. Casseroles and stew pots, on the other hand, are more suited to braising large chunks of food—as their wide mouths indicate. It is commonplace in ceramic studies to describe the rim and/or lip design of a casserole as having a "lid device," implying that they were then so used (Lapp 1961: 188–90, types 71.2, 72.1; Edwards 1975: 122–24; Riley 1979: 243). It is far less common, however, to actually find many (or even any!) lids wide enough to have covered these vessels. Lots of things may have been put to such use (saucers, for example, or large sherds from broken amphorae), but few seem to have been produced deliberately.

All of the Naukratis cooking vessels are local productions, being made of plain or slipped Delta silt. But while their fabric is local, the ultimate origins of their various forms are largely Mediterranean. Though pots for cooking are naturally not a new item in the Egyptian ceramic corpus, cooking pots of the general shape found at Hellenistic Naukratis—with a globular body, a narrow mouth, and opposed short handles—do not appear in Egypt prior to the sixth century B.C.[9] Casseroles are an even newer form in the Egyptian ceramic corpus; the first examples appear only in the early third century. These vessels are close versions of fourth century B.C. Greek casseroles (e.g. Sparkes and Talcott 1970: no. 1965, fig. 18). In fact, at this time Greek-style casseroles begin to appear throughout the southeastern Mediterranean, a pronounced and widespread distribution that probably reflects the broad

Table 2.2. Hellenistic Cooking Vessels from Naukratis

Shape	Type	Fabric	#	Kom Ge'if Phase	Naukratis Date
Cooking pots	Angled rim	Delta silt, plain & slipped	31	NW 1C	early 3rd cent. B.C.
	Small ledge rim	Delta silt, plain & slipped	16	NW 3B	later 3rd cent. B.C.
	Tall ledge rim	Delta silt, plain & slipped	75	NW 3B	later 3rd cent. B.C.
	Plain rim	Delta silt, plain & slipped	19	NW 4B	2nd cent. B.C.
Stew pots	Ledge/folded lip	Delta silt, plain & slipped	98	NW 9A	2nd cent. B.C.
		Marl	1		
Casseroles	Angled rim	Delta silt, plain & slipped	13	NW 2B	3rd cent. B.C.
	Beveled lip	Delta silt, plain & slipped	31	none found KG	—
	Inset rim	Delta silt, plain & slipped	49	NW 6B	later 2nd cent. B.C.
	Squared lip	Delta silt, plain & slipped	14	NW 7B	later 2nd cent. B.C.
	Folded lip	Delta silt, plain & slipped	51	NW Hiatus C	1st cent. B.C.
Baking dishes	Plain rim	Delta silt, plain & slipped	23	NW 8B	end 2nd cent. B.C.
Lids	Dish-lids	Delta silt, plain & slipped	9	NW 2B	3rd cent. B.C.
		Marl	3		

settlement of Greeks in this region. Most of these casseroles are locally manufactured rather than imported. Price may have been a factor, but it is also likely that local clays made adequate cooking wares, so that imported fabrics provided no real advantage.

The residents of third century Naukratis had only cooking pots and casseroles in their kitchens. In the second century, however, residents also acquired locally made stew pots and baking dishes, along with four new casserole types. These second century forms are not similar to Greek types, and parallels occur in a restricted arc from Cyprus to Palestine to Upper Egypt. Stew pots are the most confined in distribution, appearing only in Egypt. The Naukratis cooking vessels reflect the pronounced regionalism of late Hellenistic ceramic production. It is interesting also to note that the second century residents enjoyed a greater variety of cooking vessels than did the third century residents, a situation opposite to that of the table vessels.

Cooking pots

The earliest type of Hellenistic-period cooking pot found at Naukratis is the angled rim cooking pot (fig. 2.16:1–8). This is a globular vessel with a short, outwardly angled rim, and a smoothly flattened or slightly rounded lip. There is usually a small flange or ledge at the interior juncture of rim and wall, which would provide support for a lid. Not many angled rim cooking pots were found at Naukratis: eight came from Kom Hadid and twenty-five from Kom Ge'if, beginning there in NW 1C. Other, similar vessels have been identified as variants (fig. 2.16:9–17). These have the outwardly angled rim, but differ in having wider mouths and ridged or folded lips. These oddities may have been intended as stew pots, though none share that form's elongated neck (for which reason they are not included there).

The angled rim cooking pot is specifically Hellenistic; the earliest parallels come from third century B.C. contexts at Coptos (personal study), Alexandria (Adriani 1940: fig. 53.59), Paphos (Hayes 1991: fig. 28.W11.61), and Samaria (Crowfoot, Crowfoot, and Kenyon 1957: fig. 41.10–18; Zayadin 1966, pl. 31.87).[10] Vessels were made either with two vertical strap handles, or one vertical strap and one horizontal coil; the latter arrangement may imitate mainland Greek types (e.g. Edwards 1975: 123, nos. 657–58, pls. 28, 61; Sparkes and Talcott 1970: pl. 94.1957, but this is probably not itself Attic). None of the Naukratis fragments are sufficiently preserved to identify the number and form of handles.

The second type of cooking pot found at Naukratis is the small ledge rim cooking pot (fig. 2.17:1–10). This type has a short vertical neck, sometimes thickened or slightly bulging, topped by a small ledge rim. Only sixteen such vessels were found at Naukratis: eleven from Kom Hadid and five from Kom Ge'if. They first appear at Kom Ge'if in NW 3B, which dates to the third century B.C. Small ledge rim cooking pots made of desert marl appear at Coptos in contexts of the late third century/early second century B.C. (personal study). A very similar form also appears in a third century domestic context at Samaria (Hennessy 1970: fig. 12.35). The small number recovered is surprising, since the form was apparently manufactured nearby at Kom Dahab (warped fragments of this type were recovered there; see Coulson and Wilkie 1986: fig. 18.E11.101.63).

The third form found at Naukratis, the tall ledge rim cooking pot, is distinguished by a high straight neck topped by a slim but pronounced ledge (fig. 2.18). Some wasters of this form were recovered from Kom Dahab, indicating local production (Coulson and Wilkie 1986: fig. 18.E11.12.9). The Naukratis vessels, all of which are in the local Delta silt, probably were made there. This is the most common cooking pot form found: fifty-two fragments were recovered from Kom Hadid, and twenty-three from Kom Ge'if. Examples first appear at Kom Ge'if in NW 3B. This early Hellenistic date is consistent with that of other Naukratis forms produced at Kom Dahab (see further, below). The tall flat rim cooking pot form occurs in both third and second century B.C. contexts in Egypt, at Coptos (personal study) and Maskhuta (Holladay 1982: pls. 29.2, 30.1, 2), and elsewhere in the southeastern Mediterranean, at Paphos (Hayes 1991: fig. 29.6), Samaria (Crowfoot, Crowfoot, and Kenyon 1957: figs. 41.6, 43.12), Tel Anafa (Berlin 1997: 90, PW 201–206, pls. 23, 78), and Tarsus (Jones 1950: fig. 187C). It is likely that local production and use continued at Naukratis into the second century as well.

The last type of cooking pot used at Naukratis is the plain rim cooking pot, so-called because the form's short, vertical neck was drawn up into a simple, rounded point (fig. 2.17:11–24). This type first appears at Kom Ge'if in NW 9A, but is never common: Fifteen fragments were found at Kom Hadid, and four at Kom Ge'if. Four of the Naukratis vessels are made of desert marl; the remainder are of Delta silt. All but two were partially slipped and/or painted on the exterior; some had slip dripped down the interior of the neck as well. The decoration might suggest that these vessels were intended as small jars instead of as cooking pots. However, similar vessels with decoration were found at Tel Anafa and were definitely used for cooking (Berlin 1997: 88, PW 184–86, pls. 21, 77). At Coptos, the same form, but without decoration, was so used as well (personal study). Both the Tel Anafa and Coptos cooking pots date to the late fourth/early third centuries B.C.

Stew pots

The many stew pots found at Naukratis all appear to be versions of a single type, the ledge/folded lip stew pot (figs. 2.19, 2.20) This is a deep-bodied, wide-mouthed vessel, with a high neck and variously thickened lip, finished as a roughly squared or triangular ledge. All vessels probably had opposed, wide, vertical strap handles. Stew pots were popular at Naukratis: a total of sixty-one fragments were found at Kom Hadid and thirty-eight at Kom Ge'if. One vessel is made of desert marl (fig. 2.20:16); all others are in the local Delta silt, and of these about half are slipped as well. The form first appears at Kom Ge'if in NW 4B, and so dates to the early/mid second century B.C. Similar stew pots were also found in second century B.C. contexts at Coptos; they include vessels made of a distinctive "bichrome" cooking ware as well as locally produced silt and marl versions (personal study). The limited distribution is at odds with the form's popularity at Naukratis and Coptos. Perhaps as more Hellenistic kitchen wares are published, additional examples will come to light.

Casseroles

The first type of casserole found at Naukratis, and the only one that dates to the early Hellenistic period, is the angled rim casserole (fig. 2.21). This has a vertical or slightly angled wall, and a plainly finished, wide, angled rim. A small flange juts out at the interior juncture of the rim and wall. The type first appears at Kom Ge'if in NW 2B, which dates to the third century B.C. A total of eleven fragments were found at Kom Hadid and two at Kom Ge'if; all are in the local silt and about half are slipped. The Naukratis casseroles have opposed horizontal coil handles—a feature common to other third century B.C. examples—and one derived directly from Greek models; similar vessels have been found at Alexandria (Adriani 1940: fig. 53.53) and Coptos (personal study). The second century versions more often have two small vertical strap handles; parallels occur at Berenice (Riley 1979: nos. 420, 423, fig. 98), Tell el-Herr (Gratien and Soulié 1988: fig. 3.9), Tell Timai (Ochsenschlager 1967: fig. 7), Ashdod (Dothan 1971: figs. 8.18, 99.11), Samaria (Crowfoot, Crowfoot, and Kenyon 1957: fig. 40.5; Hennessy 1970: fig. 7.34), Tel Anafa (Berlin 1997: 97–98, PW 234–40, pls. 28, 80), Paphos (Hayes 1991: figs. 32.1, 4, 33.1, 73.2), Knossos (Callaghan 1981: no. 51, fig. 8), and Athens (Thompson 1934: D72, E141, figs. 78, 121). The type appears at Sabratha as well (Dore 1989: 107, type 14, fig. 25), though not in dated Hellenistic contexts.

The second casserole type to appear at Naukratis is the beveled lip casserole, a form similar to the angled rim type but with the additional finishing touch of a thickened triangular-shaped lip (figs. 2.22, 2.23). Though none were found at Kom Ge'if, thirty-one were found at Kom Hadid. All of the Naukratis vessels are in the local Delta silt, and of these, three-quarters were slipped. Parallels for this form appear in third and second century B.C. levels at Coptos (personal study) and in a second-century B.C. context at Maskhuta (Holladay 1982, fig. 30.5). Outside of Egypt examples appear only from second-century B.C. deposits (Paphos: Hayes 1991, fig. 32.1; Samaria: Crowfoot, Crowfoot, and Kenyon 1957: fig. 41.20; Akko-Ptolemais: Dothan 1976: fig. 30.12; Tel Anafa: Berlin 1997: 98–99, PW 241–47, pls. 29, 80; Sabratha: Dore 1989: 106 [a single example of type 7, fig. 23 is similar, and comes from a possible second century B.C. context]).

The third casserole found at Naukratis, the inset rim casserole, has a vertical or slightly outwardly angled wall, sometimes offset midway (figs. 2.24–2.26). This terminates in a thickened, upright rim with an inset face. Handles, when present, are long horizontal coils, though parallels suggest that some vessels may have been handleless. A total of forty-three fragments were found at Kom Hadid and six at Kom Ge'if. All are in Delta silt and most are slipped. Local fabric notwithstanding, there are many small differences in profile and rim formation; these may reflect different manufacturers. Inset rim casseroles first appear at Kom Ge'if in NW 6B, and so date to the late second century B.C. An identical vessel, made of Delta silt, was found at Coptos in a late third-century B.C. deposit (personal study). Versions of this form occur at Sabratha (Dore 1989: type 21, fig. 25), Berenice (Riley 1979: nos. 424–37, fig. 98), Paphos (Hayes 1991: figs. 33.6, 73.6), Tel Anafa (Berlin 1997: 100–101, PW 254–58, pls. 30, 80), Corinth (Edwards 1975: nos. 670–671, pl. 29), and Athens (Thompson 1934: C74, E145, fig. 121)—all from second century contexts.[11]

The fourth type of casserole that appears at Naukratis is the squared lip casserole (fig. 2.27). It differs from the beveled lip form only in the rim terminus, here thickened into a squared lip rather than neatly tooled off. At Naukratis, this type appears at Kom Ge'if in NW 7B, late in the second century B.C.: Ten fragments have been identified from Kom Hadid and four from Kom Ge'if. All are in Delta silt and about half are slipped. Squared lip casseroles may be nothing more than sloppily made beveled lip forms. Identification as a separate type is suggested by very similar vessels, also found in late second century B.C. contexts, at Tell Maskhuta (Holladay 1982: pl. 30.4), Paphos (Hayes 1991: figs. 33.5: 73.1), and Tel Anafa (Berlin 1997: 99–100, PW 248–53, pls. 29, 80).

The final casserole type found at Naukratis is also one of the only first century B.C. forms at the site: folded lip casseroles (figs. 2.28–2.31). These are wide vessels with a broad ledge rim, thickened at the outer edge. This thickened lip looks as if it was folded over, although it was probably simply tooled off. Folded lip casseroles appear at Kom Ge'if beginning in NW Hiatus C; forty-seven fragments were found at Kom Hadid and four at Kom Ge'if. All examples are in Delta silt and half are slipped both inside and out. Parallels occur at Mendes (Wilson 1982, pl. XIII.4, dated "late Hellenistic"), Coptos (personal study) and Tel Anafa (Berlin 1997: 101, PW 259–65, pls. 30, 80)—the latter two in contexts dated to the early first century B.C. The Egyptian vessels are made of silt (Naukratis, Mendes, Coptos) and/or marl (Coptos) clays; the Tel Anafa examples are of a sandy cooking fabric perhaps imported from the coastal city of Akko-Ptolemais. The casserole's essentially simultaneous appearance over a fairly wide area is probably the result of a single, popular, broadly distributed prototype. The fact that three out of the four sites at which such casseroles occur are in Egypt suggests an Egyptian origin, but this is no more than a hypothesis.

Baking dishes

A single form of baking dish was found at Naukratis, here named the plain rim baking dish (figs. 2.32, 2.33). The shape is simple: broad and low, with thick, angled walls, and a plain rim. Some fragments preserve a thick horizontal coil handle, sometimes pulled up into a loop handle. Brian Sparkes (1962: 129, pl. V.5) discusses similar vessels found in the Athenian Agora; their high handles, which would facilitate lifting, might indicate use as a portable hearth. Not many such vessels were found at Naukratis: twenty-three fragments at Kom Hadid and only one at Kom Ge'if. The Kom Ge'if fragment appears in NW 8B, and so dates towards the end of the period. All of the Naukratis vessels were identified as being made of the local Delta silt, and almost all were slipped. Vessels identical in form to those from Naukratis, but in a gold-mica flecked fabric and with a heavily carbonized interior, appear at sites throughout the eastern Mediterranean, also all from later Hellenistic contexts.[12] They are not numerous at any individual site, however. A single origin for the micaceous baking dishes is probable, given the combination of their limited numbers and their wide distribution; the gold-colored mica within the fabric may indicate the region around Pergamon (Slane 1986: 312, n. 76).

Lids

While any saucer or bowl could have been used as a lid when necessary, included here are only vessels made of cooking ware, and so apparently designed to cover other cooking vessels. The single type found at Naukratis is the small dish-lid, a simple form that could have been used as a saucer as well; it has a plain rim and stubby disc foot-handle (fig. 2.50:15, 16). Dish-lids first appear at Kom Ge'if in NW 2B, but are uncommon: Three fragments were found at Kom Hadid and nine at Kom Ge'if. Their size makes them usable only with cooking pots (which also appear in the third century phases of the site). Comparable vessels appear at sites throughout the eastern Mediterranean in third and second century contexts, including Sabratha (Dore 1989: fig. 39.98.3295), Berenice (Riley 1979: nos. 759–65, 797–98, figs. 118–19), Alexandria (Adriani 1940: pl. 30.25, lower left), Coptos (personal study), Ashdod

(Dothan 1971: fig. 24.11), Samaria (Reisner, Fischer, and Lyon 1924: fig. 184.32a; Crowfoot, Crowfoot, and Kenyon 1957: fig. 41.22), Paphos (Hayes 1991: fig. 25.5, 30.3), Tarsus (Jones 1950: no. 223, figs. 135, 187, 191.D), and Athens (Thompson 1934: A58, fig. 8, D73, fig. 78). The form, which is the essence of simplicity, did not change, and vessels were probably produced locally in each case.

Utility Vessels

Utility vessels include large and small containers designed for mixing, pouring, and storing dry and wet goods (Table 2.3). Such vessels are generally undecorated, though often carefully fashioned and finished; their plain appearance reflects their everyday function. Most common at Naukratis are large forms: jugs, kraters, *dinoi*, and amphorae. The less common small vessels include juglets and unguentaria. Some fragments of low, heavy stands were found; their plain fabric and lack of burning indicate that they were used for water jars or amphorae. Lastly, there are vessels for storage: large and small jars, a *pithos*, and deep basins. A shape series here called shallow basins may have actually been used for any number of functions, from lids for deep basins to bread molds.

Most of the utility vessels from Naukratis are of the local Delta silt; in fact, wasters from the nearby kiln at Kom Dahab indicate that two jug and two amphora types were manufactured there (see Table 2.5). Local potters thus regularly supplied Naukratis residents with containers necessary for serving and storing the local vintage. This utility assemblage also includes some regional and Mediterranean imports: two imported black-glazed unguentaria, a few Upper Egyptian marl jugs and kraters, a couple of jugs from Aswan, six Aegean *lagynoi*, and six Koan amphorae. Other imported amphorae are attested by forty-three stamped handles—some found by Petrie and others in the course of this project's excavation. These include twenty-two Rhodian handles, three Thasian, six Knidian, two Samian, one Latin, one Chian, and one of the Egyptian Zenon group (Coulson, Wilkie and Rehard 1986; for a chronological breakdown, see Table 2.4).[13] Note that of the twenty-four dated handles, eighteen are early Hellenistic (through Grace's Period III, ending 175 B.C.), and only six are late Hellenistic. In the early Hellenistic period, at least, it seems that the Naukratis residents could afford some more expensive goods and were not cut off from the larger Mediterranean economy. This pattern is somewhat different from other Egyptian and southeastern Mediterranean sites, where Period IV–V handles (188–108 B.C.) are sometimes more, and sometimes almost as numerous (see discussions in Ariel 1990: 18–21 and table 2; Berlin 1997: 162). An especially notable and relevant example is Alexandria, where there are three times as many late Hellenistic (Period V) handles as middle Hellenistic (Period IV) ones (Grace 1985: 42). The decline in late Hellenistic imported amphorae at Naukratis further underscores the poverty and relative isolation of that period's settlement.

Unguentaria

A very small number of this normally ubiquitous Hellenistic form occurs at Naukratis: twelve fragments from Kom Hadid (fig. 2.34:1–12) and four from Kom Ge'if. Eight are made of Delta silt and six of these are slipped, three are *terra nigra*, one is desert marl, and two are black-glazed imports. The marl vessel is the first to appear at Kom Ge'if, in NW 2A; plain and slipped silt unguentaria do not occur there until NW Hiatus B and C respectively. The Naukratis vessels were probably supplied from Alexandria. Notably, there is no evidence for production at either of the kiln sites in the region (Kom Dahab and Tell el-Farâ'în).

No two of the Naukratis unguentaria are identical. Most, however, have a profile similar to a common eastern Mediterranean form, the banded fusiform unguentarium. These include two intact silt

Table 2.3. Hellenistic Utility Vessels from Kom Hadid

Shape	Type	Fabric	#	Kom Ge'if Phase	Naukratis Date
Unguent-aria	Banded fusiform	Delta silt plain, slipped	14	NW2A	3rd cent. B.C.
	Pared fusiform	Marl	1		
Juglets	Miscellaneous	Delta silt plain, slipped	24		
Jugs	Long necked delta rim	Delta silt plain, slipped	44	NW 1C	early 3rd cent. B.C.
		Marl	3	NW 1C	early 3rd cent. B.C.
	Folded rim jug	Marl	6	NW 2B	3rd cent. B.C.
	Narrow ledge rim	Delta silt plain, slipped	28	NW 2B	3rd cent. B.C.
		Marl	1	NW 2B	3rd cent. B.C.
		Aswan	2	NW 4B	2nd cent. B.C.
	Rolled rim jug	Delta silt plain, slipped	6	NW 6B	mid 2nd cent. B.C.
		Aswan	1		
	Long necked square rim	Delta silt plain	1	NW 2B	3rd cent. B.C.
		Marl	1	NW Hiatus A	later 2nd cent. B.C.
	Long necked flattened rim	Marl	1	N 1C	3rd cent. B.C.
	Black glaze	Silt 6, import	2		
	Lagynos	Aegean import	6	NW 3B	later 3rd cent. B.C.
		Delta silt slipped	6	NW 2B	3rd cent. B.C.
	Flanged rim	Delta silt plain, slipped	7	NW 10	topsoil
Hydriae/ Table Amphorae	Flanged rim	Delta silt plain, slipped	29	NW Hiatus A	later 2nd cent. B.C.
		Import	1		
Kraters	Short squared rim	Marl	10	NW 2B	3rd cent. B.C.
	Overhanging rim	Delta silt plain, slipped	45	NW 4B	2nd cent. B.C.
	"Nail head" rim	Delta silt plain, slipped	6	none found KG	—
	Necked	Delta silt slipped	5	none found KG	—
Dinoi	Ledge rim	Delta silt plain, slipped	25	NW 2B	3rd cent. B.C.
	Thickened rim	Delta silt plain, slipped	12	NW 7B	later 2nd cent. B.C.
		Marl	1		
Jars	Small holemouth	Delta silt plain, slipped	10	NW 4B	2nd cent. B.C.
	Large holemouth	Delta silt plain	12	NW Hiatus C	1st cent. B.C.
	Pithoi	Delta silt plain	1	NW Hiatus C	1st cent. B.C.
Stands	Low	Delta silt plain, slipped	13	none found KG	—
Basins	Shallow	Delta silt, handmade	13	NW 2B	3rd cent. B.C.
	Deep	Delta silt, handmade	12	none found KG	—
Amphorae	Beaded rim	Delta silt, wh. slipped	3	NW 2B	3rd cent. B.C.
		Calcareous	19	NW 2B	3rd cent. B.C.
	Squared rim	Delta silt plain	23	NW 3A	later 3rd cent. B.C.
	Koan	Koan	7	NW 7D	later 2nd cent. B.C.
	Inthickened rim	Delta silt plain	9	NW Hiatus C	1st cent. B.C.
	Concave rim	Delta silt plain	3	NW Hiatus C	1st cent. B.C.

Table 2.4. Chronology of Stamped Amphora Handles Found at Naukratis
(dates and identifications from Coulson, Wilkie and Rehard 1986)

Time Period	Origin	#	Period Total
Mid 4th/early 3rd century	Rhodian	2	4
	Thasian	2	
Mid/Late 3rd century	Rhodian	6	9
	Knidian	1	
	Chian	1	
	Zenon	1	
Late 3rd/early 2nd century	Rhodian	5	5
First half 2nd century	Rhodian	4	4
Second half 2nd century	Rhodian	1	2
	Knidian	1	

vessels from Kom Ge'if and all of the fragments from Kom Hadid (fig. 2.34:1–12). This form has a slim pear-shaped body atop a short, narrow peg-like toe, a short, narrow neck and a cupped rim. Painted bands encircle the lower neck and shoulder. The first versions come from Athens, in contexts of the early third century B.C.; the vessels are reduction-fired, with thin white bands around the neck and shoulder (Thompson 1934: A64, 65, fig. 9, B6, fig. 15; for the probable Athenian origin see Rotroff 1984: 258). Valuable contents, portable size, and well-established long-distance trade routes made the Attic vessels available throughout Greece, from Argos (Bruneau 1970b: 518, fig. 210:57.3, 57.4, 58.8, 185.23) and Corinth (Pemberton 1985: T2014, pl. 80) in the Peloponnesos to Amphipolis in Thrace (Samartzidou 1988: pl. 9); in the Aegean, on Delos (Bruneau 1970a: D154–158, pl. 46); in Asia Minor, at Labraunda (Hellström 1965: 25); on Cyprus, at Paphos (Hayes 1991: 68, pl. 14.7) and Vrysi (Dray, du Plat Taylor, and du Plat Taylor 1951: 109–110, fig. 58.2); and in Palestine, at Tel Anafa (Berlin 1997: 67, PW 110, pl. 15). The wide availability of these Attic models apparently inspired other eastern Mediterranean producers to imitation; by the later third century B.C., versions similar to the Naukratis vessels are far more common than Attic (or any) imports throughout this region (Berenice: Riley 1979: nos. 684–86, fig. 113; Alexandria: Adriani 1940: fig. 53.3, 18; Adriani 1952b: fig. 70.17; Coptos: personal study; Ashdod: Dothan 1971: fig. 9.5, 6; Samaria: Reisner, Fischer, and Lyon 1924: fig. 178.5, 9–12; Zayadin 1966: pl. 31.94; Hennessy 1970: fig. 9.23; Tarsus: Jones 1950: fig. 135.237, 239).

One unguentarium fragment found in Kom Ge'if NW 2A differs in form and fabric: it has a wide disc foot and is made of desert marl. It is similar to a late-second-century Phoenician type, the pared fusiform unguentarium. The Phoenician vessels are distinguished by their abbreviated spindles, flaring disc feet and careful horizontal paring around the lower body (Berlin 1997: 65, PW 94–98, pls. 13, 75). The Naukratis unguentarium shares the first two characteristics, though its fabric identifies it as Egyptian. No other examples have been published from Egyptian sites.

Jugs

At least eight distinct forms of jug were found at Naukratis.[14] Most are made of Delta silt and many are slipped. Besides these local productions, there are also ten fragments of desert marl and three of the smooth, pinkish white clay of Aswan. Six Aegean lagynoi were also found. These last are proba-bly the only vessels acquired for their contents, since none of the other jug forms are compatible with long-distance trade, all having a wide mouth that can not be stoppered easily.

The earliest and most common form found at Naukratis is the long-necked delta rim jug (figs. 2.36, 2.37:1–14), which first appears at Kom Ge'if in NW 1C and so dates to the early third century B.C. Thirty-three fragments were found at Kom Hadid and fourteen at Kom Ge'if. The form is quite sim-ple: a fairly wide mouth (between 10–15 cm), an elongated, cylindrical neck, and a long, sturdy vertical strap handle from mid neck to shoulder. The rim is thickened and slightly pulled out, resulting in a profile ranging from rounded to triangular (the latter resembling the Greek Δ, hence the name). Three of the Naukratis vessels are of Upper Egyptian desert marl and the remainder are of the local silt; about half of the silt jugs are slipped. This form was manufactured at the nearby kiln at Kom Dahab, as evidenced by numerous wasters recovered by the survey team (Coulson and Leonard 1983: 68 and fig. 4B). Similar-looking jugs occur elsewhere in Egypt and the southeastern Mediterranean (and far-ther afield as well), though it is difficult to assess the various stylistic and chronological relationships of such basic and simple vessels.[15]

A second type of jug found at Naukratis is the folded rim jug (fig. 2.38:1–4). Only four fragments appear at Kom Hadid, and two at Kom Ge'if; the type first appears at Kom Ge'if in NW 2B, dating to the third century B.C. All examples are in Upper Egyptian desert marl. This type is the standard early Hellenistic jug at Coptos (personal study), though it is unparalleled outside Egypt. Its appearance at Naukratis reflects some traffic between Upper and Lower Egypt during the third century.

The third form found is the narrow ledge rim jug (fig. 2.38:5–15). Examples occur in the local Delta silt, both plain and slipped (nineteen at Kom Hadid and nine at Kom Ge'if), in Upper Egyptian desert marl (one each at Kom Hadid and Kom Ge'if), and in the distinctive soft marl of Aswan (one each at Kom Hadid and Kom Ge'if). Delta silt and desert marl fragments appear at Kom Ge'if in NW 2B and in Aswan marl a century later, in NW 4B. Like the delta rim jug, the narrow ledge rim jug was also manufactured at Kom Dahab (Coulson and Leonard 1983: 68, figs. 4C, D). These jugs have a strongly everted, slightly curled rim whose outer face was neatly tooled off (sometimes creating a small flange) and a high arched handle (sometimes made from double coils, sometimes a flattened strap similar to a *lagynos*). A complete waster from the Kom Dahab kiln shows the handle curving up from the rim and back down to the shoulder, the body rather squat and globular, and the bottom pushed up into a high depression. This form is quite elaborate and is probably copied from metal examples. A popular and more costly original is also indicated by the variety of ceramic versions, from both Upper and Lower Egypt. Precise parallels for both the desert marl and Aswan productions occur at Coptos, both in third century levels (personal study).

A fourth form is the rolled rim jug (fig. 2.38:16–19). This is a rather fancy form: the rim curves around into a pronounced roll and a narrow ridge encircles the middle of the neck. Five fragments were found at Kom Hadid and two at Kom Ge'if, first appearing at the latter mound in NW 6B. Six of these rolled rim jugs are made of the local silt and one is of Aswan marl. It is interesting to note that all three Aswan vessels found at Naukratis occur in later Hellenistic levels. At Coptos, Aswan rolled rim jugs occur in stratified deposits of the late third century (personal study). Early Hellenistic trade between Upper and Lower Egypt is reflected by the appearance of Upper Egyptian marl folded rim jugs at Kom Ge'if in NW 2B; these later Hellenistic Aswan jugs indicate the continuation of this activity.

A couple jug fragments found at Naukratis may be long necked square rim jugs (fig. 2.39: 15, 16?). The form is difficult to distinguish in drawings from messy versions of delta rim or narrow ledge rim jugs. One probable example in silt appears at Kom Ge'if in NW 2B, while a marl version was found in NW Hiatus A. Both vessels are quite similar to a type of Upper Egyptian marl jug found in second-century B.C. levels at Coptos (personal study). A similar jug has also been found at Paphos (Hayes 1991: fig. 16.4).

A sixth jug form is the long neck flattened rim jug (fig. 2.39:1–5). A single marl example was found at Kom Ge'if in N1C; six similar fragments found at Kom Hadid are made of the local Delta silt. They have in common a wide, cylindrical neck topped by a flattened, slightly ledge-like rim. A very similar jug, also of Delta silt, with a wide strap handle from mid neck, was found in the early second century levels at Coptos (personal study). Other examples appear at Alexandria (Adriani 1940: fig. 53.14), Maskhuta (Holladay 1982: pl. 30.7), and at Paphos, on Cyprus (Hayes 1991: fig. 16.7).

Twelve *lagynoi* were found at Naukratis: seven at Kom Hadid and five at Kom Ge'if. The *lagynos* is the most distinctive Hellenistic jug form, having a squat, sometimes biconical body; long, narrow neck; small mouth; and single flat strap handle (fig. 2.39:13, 14). This is the single jug shape that could have been shipped full and without undue spillage, and in fact six of the *lagynoi* found at Naukratis were Aegean imports (on this fabric and its probable southwestern Aegean origins, see Hayes 1991: 19, Lagynos series 3). The other six *lagynoi* were of the local silt and might have been manufactured at Kom Dahab, where a single intact but fire-cracked *lagynos* was recovered from the kiln debris (Coulson and Leonard 1983: 68–9, fig. 4A). At Naukratis, both the local and the imported *lagynoi* occur in early Hellenistic contexts (Kom Ge'if NW 2B and 3B, respectively). Their absence from the later Hellenistic phases is odd; at this time the shape became increasingly popular throughout the southeastern Mediterranean (Berlin 1997: 47–49). But this should probably be taken as a further reflection of the rural, and reduced, status of the Naukratis community.

The final form identified here is the flanged rim jug (fig. 2.39:6–12). This vessel has a wide neck and mouth, and a rim with a rather thick ridge, or flange, jutting out beneath the lip. Seven fragments were found (seven at Kom Hadid, two at Kom Ge'if), though none in a stratified Hellenistic deposit. All are in the local silt; four are slipped as well. No Egyptian parallels are known to me; the form is very close to a Phoenician table amphora variation made in the early first century B.C. (Berlin 1997: 39, PW 6–7, pl. 1). The Naukratis fragments may derive from small table amphorae as well; both they and the better-preserved Phoenician vessels have rim diameters between 10 and 12 cm.

Hydriae/Table Amphorae

The fragments included here share the characteristics of a very wide, flanged rim (15–18 cm) and broad, cylindrical neck (fig. 2.40). None have preserved handles. They are similar in form to both the narrow ledge rim jugs (see above) and the overhanging rim kraters (see below), but are midway between these shapes in size. They are consistent in both form and size with *hydriae* and table amphorae. Both shapes are reasonably common in Egypt and elsewhere in the southeastern Mediterranean, though for quite different purposes.[16] *Hydriae*, such as the famous ones found in Alexandrian cemeteries, were used for cinerary urns, while table amphorae were used during meals for mixed wine. All of these vessels were generally highly decorated with slip, additional paint, incision, and sometimes pieces of clay, coiled or molded (Adriani 1940: fig. 48.1, 2, pls. 47, 48.5, 7; Adriani 1952: figs. 13, 16).[17] At Kom Ge'if these fragments first appear in NW Hiatus A, which dates to the late second century B.C. A total of thirty were found: twenty-two at Kom Hadid and eight at Kom Ge'if. One of the Kom Hadid rims is an import (fig. 2.40:1); the rest are made of the local Delta silt. The imported rim, and most of the silt rims, have a thin slip smoothed over the rim and interior mouth. The shape of the

Naukratis fragments is especially close to a second century B.C. West Slope table amphora from Paphos, identified as a product of Pergamon (Hayes 1991: fig. 4.1).

Kraters and Dinoi

Kraters and *dinoi* are both broad, deep vessels, with two or more handles. Though none of the Naukratis examples are well enough preserved, comparanda indicates that both forms were footed, and so could stand. Both shapes were clearly designed as large mixing bowls, for either wet or dry goods. They are distinguished from one another, however, by a specific formal characteristic: on kraters, the body wall curves in below the rim, while on *dinoi*, the body wall angles out. This formal distinction may have had practical consequences. The more open profile of the krater is well-suited for pouring or ladling. The rim of a *dinos*, on the other hand, has an inturned ledge that would make pouring an especially messy operation. It may be, therefore, that kraters were used as part of a table service, while *dinoi* were kept in the kitchen.

There are few kraters found in the early Hellenistic phases at Naukratis; the ones that do appear are made of desert marl and so are of Upper Egyptian manufacture. These are short squared rim kraters—simple, broad vessels with a short, thick, squared-off ledge rim (fig. 2.432–4, 6–8). Six were found at Kom Hadid and four at Kom Ge'if, beginning in NW 2B. Identical kraters, also of desert marl, appear at Coptos in the earliest Hellenistic levels (personal study), and very similar vessels were found at Berenice as well (Riley 1979: 279, nos. 594, 596, fig. 109).

The overhanging rim krater first appears at Kom Ge'if in NW 4B. This form's distinguishing feature is a wide, arcing rim, whose lip is either tooled off with a small flange or worked into a pinched pie-crust design (figs. 2.44, 2.45). Two (or more?) horizontal coil handles sit on the shoulder. This is by far the most common krater form found at Naukratis: thirty-nine fragments come from Kom Hadid and six from Kom Ge'if. Examples first appear at Kom Ge'if in NW 4B. This second century date is consistent with finds elsewhere in Egypt, as seen by dated parallels from Maskhuta (Holladay 1982: pl. 28.18), Tell el-Herr (Gratien and Soulié 1988: fig. 3.d), and Coptos (personal study). In the second and first centuries B.C. the form appears throughout the eastern Mediterranean in various fabrics, most presumably local: Sabratha (Dore 1989: type 213, fig. 52), Berenice (Riley 1979: nos. 801–809, fig. 120; at these north African sites the form appears only in the late first century B.C. and is most abundant in the following century), Samaria (Reisner, Fischer, and Lyon 1924: fig. 184.31a), Tel Anafa (Berlin 1997: 135–36, PW 393–99, pls. 42, 83), Paphos (Hayes 1991: fig. 56.20), Tarsus (Jones 1950: fig. 190.H), Corinth (Williams 1978: no. 8, pl. 23), and Athens (Thompson 1934: D33, fig. 62; D67, figs. 76, 122). The Naukratis vessels, too, are local; all are in Delta silt and two-thirds of these are slipped as well. Like the other second century silt forms found at Naukratis, no examples were found from Kom Dahab, so the precise origin is unknown.

Two other krater forms were found only at Kom Hadid. The first is, as far as I know, unique to Naukratis; the excavators named it a "nailhead" rim krater (fig. 2.46). This vessel has a wide mouth, angled rim, and thickened, half-rounded lip, which provides its unusual profile. Only six such vessels were found, all made of Delta silt. All are slipped as well.

The final krater form is here called a necked krater; this has a short straight neck, topped by a thick ledge rim (fig. 2.47). Horizontal coil handles are attached to the upper shoulder. In some cases these are short and flattened against the wall; in others they are long, and pulled up and over the rim. Five necked kraters were found, all made of Delta silt and covered with a fugitive white slip. Very similar forms were found at Saqqarah (Giddy, Smith, and French 1992: pl. 61.6, 7, found in topsoil) and

Paphos (Hayes 1991, fig. 60.20.7, from a first century B.C. deposit that also contained early Ptolemaic coins, and perhaps earlier pottery as well). A single example of this krater form was found at Coptos in a mid/late third century B.C. deposit (personal study).

Two forms of *dinoi* were found at Naukratis. The earlier, and more common, is the ledge rim *dinos* (fig. 2.48). On this form the upper body wall curves inward, so that the mouth is somewhat constricted, then turns out into a wide, slightly thickened ledge rim. Fragments of twenty-two ledge rim *dinoi* were found at Kom Hadid, and three at Kom Ge'if, beginning in NW 2B. All are in Delta silt; eleven are slipped as well. The identical form appears at Coptos in the early Hellenistic period; all examples at that site are in desert marl (personal study). Similar vessels, but glazed, are known from Samaria (Crowfoot, Crowfoot, and Kenyon 1957: fig. 57:5–8) and Knossos (Callaghan 1981: no. 45, fig. 8).

The second *dinos* form found at Naukratis is the thickened rim dinos (fig. 2.49). Most examples are wider than ledge rim *dinoi*, from which they are distinguished by a thick, almost triangular, rim that juts over both the mouth and the body wall. Thirteen fragments were found: one at Kom Ge'if in NW 7B and the remainder at Kom Hadid. One is desert marl, the rest Nile silt; half are slipped. Thickened rim *dinoi* are more confined in distribution than ledge rim *dinoi*; similar vessels have been found only in Egypt, at Tell el-Herr (Gratien and Soulié 1988: fig. 2b, in silt) and Coptos (beginning in late third century B.C. levels, all examples made of desert marl [personal study]).

Jars

"Jar" is an unwieldly category. Since the name does not encompass a single closely defined form or function, it is a catchall for a wide variety of shapes, both large and small. The one characteristic that all jars have in common is that they are closed vessels, which makes them appropriate as containers, for wet or dry goods. Some jars have more specific designations. The most obvious examples are amphorae, which are generally thought of as long-distance transport vessels, mostly for wine and oil (these are treated separately, below). But many other vessels may be considered jars, and in fact many of the vessels found at Kom Ge'if are so identified. Few of these so-called jars appear at Kom Hadid, so these identifications are a kind of default: without more complete examples or parallels, I do not know exactly what vessel the fragment represents. Examples of three recognizable jar forms were found at Kom Hadid and Kom Ge'if, small and large holemouth jars, and a pithos.

Small holemouth jars have a thin rounded rim, a narrow mouth (8–12 cm in diameter), and a piriform body (fig. 2.50: 9–14). Six fragments were found at Kom Hadid and four at Kom Ge'if, beginning in NW 4B. All are made of the local silt, and all are slipped as well. I do know of no parallels for this form from Hellenistic contexts. Large holemouth jars have an elongated piriform body with the upper wall constricting towards the mouth; the rim is simply the slightly thickened terminus of the wall (fig. 2.50:1–8). Two wide vertical strap handles drop from the rim, or immediately below, to the shoulder. Fragments of eight were found at Kom Hadid, and four at Kom Ge'if. They do not appear at the latter mound until NW Hiatus C, which dates to the early first century B.C. One of these large holemouth jars is handmade, the others turned on the wheel; all are in the local silt. This form is similar to early Hellenistic Punic amphorae, but the correspondence is probably accidental; the amphorae' handles are different in form and placement, and of course, Punic amphorae are not made of Delta silt.[18] I can find no similar vessels from other Hellenistic sites.

A single *pithos* rim was found at Kom Ge'if in NW Hiatus C (Berlin in Leonard 1997: fig. 6.36: 4). The vessel was handmade of the local silt. The wide, thick, ledge rim is recognizable because most *pithoi* have similar rims, which are designed to provide a solid resting place for a lid—an important aspect on a vessel used for long-term dry storage (e.g. *pithoi* from Athens [Thompson 1934: 69, fig. 54]) and Tel Anafa [Berlin 1997: 156, PW 484–87, pls. 58, 89, 90]). This is the only such vessel found at Naukratis, and I can find no parallels from other Hellenistic Egyptian sites.[19]

Stands

Stands are a standard item in the Egyptian ceramic corpus. Both small and large examples are found in Dynastic contexts (Hope 1987: figs. 38, 41, 46, 55) and the form continued to be produced in Hellenistic (and Roman) times (Mond and Meyers 1934: shapes 57, 58, 63; figs. 140, 141). At Naukratis, the bottom portions of thirteen stands were found, all at Kom Hadid. They are low stands with thick walls and a plainly finished foot (fig. 2.51:1–13). All are in Delta silt; most are slipped. Similar stands appear in Hellenistic deposits at Coptos (made of desert marl [personal study]), at the Bucheum (Mond and Meyers 1934: type 58R), and at Maskhuta (Holladay 1982: pl. 29.10). The Naukratis stands, as well as the other Hellenistic Egyptian examples, were probably used to support amphorae or round-bottom jars (such as fig. 2.51:16); the absence of burning on any of the fragments argues against kitchen use. Despite their apparent utility, however, there is quite a discrepancy between the quantities of amphorae and stands found at Naukratis: one hundred seven amphorae (fifty-seven local rim fragments, seven imported rims, and forty-three imported stamped handles) vs. thirteen stands (but see "deep basins" below). This is probably because, in most cases, amphorae were simply leaned up against a wall, with their toes worked into the dirt floor. Stands were necessary only when an amphora was placed on a paved, or overly hard-packed surface. In the rooms excavated at Kom Ge'if, dirt floors were the norm; no paved surfaces were encountered *in situ* (cf. chapter 3).

Basins

Two forms of handmade silt vessels were found at Naukratis. The first are here defined as shallow basins (figs. 2.52:1–6, 2.53:1–8). These vessels are very wide, with a short, thick, vertical upper wall and a slightly thickened ledge or triangular-shaped rim. The lower wall (or vessel floor?) turns inward sharply, but none are preserved below this point. A single fragment was found at Kom Ge'if in NW 2B; fourteen were found at Kom Hadid. Similar low, wide, handmade vessels, also with a short, vertical wall/rim were found at Coptos, beginning in the early Hellenistic period (personal study). The Coptos vessels have been identified provisionally as bread discs or molds, based on their correspondence—in size as well as form—to the bread discs still used in Upper Egypt today. This shape is traditional to Upper Egypt only; the bread that is baked there is called "sun bread" because it rises outdoors, resting on these discs in the full sun. The Naukratis vessels may have been bread discs as well, or even lids for storage vessels (such as the deep basins, pithos, or holemouth jars).

The vessels here defined as deep basins are all handmade of Delta silt (figs. 2.54, 2.55). Most have a simple vertical wall and or slightly thickened rim; on some the rim is pulled out into a rounded or triangular lip, and on others the wall constricts inward below the rim. Twelve such rim fragments were found at Kom Hadid, along with four fairly narrow, thick, flat bottoms; no such vessels were found at Kom Ge'if. These deep-bodied fragments may have functioned as some kind of receptacle. The upper body fragments, especially those whose walls constrict, are very similar to the basins of late Hellenistic braziers (such as those found at Paphos [Hayes 1991: 77, no. 24, pl. 18.11, 12]), though the absence of burning argues against such a use. A very suggestive modern parallel is provided by vessels used in the Delta as water jar supports; they are identical to both the upper and lower Naukratis fragments in scale and form (Heinein 1992: 18, no. 18B). Such a use for these "deep basins" could account for some of the numerical discrepancy between jars and stands noted above.

Amphorae

In the Hellenistic period, amphorae were the vessel of choice for transporting and storing liquids—primarily wine and oil. This heavy-duty function required careful manufacture: transport amphorae typically have neat, evenly formed rims for holding a stopper in place; well-attached, easy-to-grasp handles; and fairly thick, consistently fired walls. These characteristics made amphorae among the most durable of ancient containers, which in turn allowed for many cycles of reuse.[20] In Egypt, especially, finds of imported amphorae may be suspected of representing not the initial, happy acquisition of finer vintages, but the secondary, mundane function of potable water storage.

Fragments of one hundred seven Hellenistic amphorae were found at Naukratis, a figure that includes forty-three stamped handles published previously (see above). The amphorae are a diverse group, comprising four types made in Egypt, along with vessels from Rhodes, Kos, Knidos, Samos, Chios, Thasos, and the Italian peninsula. Here I do discuss only the non-stamped fragments that are of Egyptian manufacture.[21]

Beaded rim amphorae (fig. 2.56:1, 2) are characterized by an evenly cylindrical neck topped by a narrow rounded rim providing a beaded profile. At Naukratis, two fabrics occur: the local Delta silt and a gritty, lime-tempered, dirty-white calcareous fabric.[22] The calcareous type is much more common: nineteen fragments were found, fourteen at Kom Hadid and five at Kom Ge'if. The type first appears at Kom Ge'if in NW 2B. Only three silt vessels occur, two at Kom Hadid and one in NW 2B at Kom Ge'if. The silt vessels are all covered with a thin, pale slip, which may have been intended to mimic the white surface of the calcareous type. Silt beaded rim amphorae were made at Kom Dahab, whence the Naukratis vessels surely derive (wasters there also are white-slipped). The calcareous vessels may be from the region of Aswan (J. Hayes, personal communication). Certainly the form is very common in Upper Egypt, appearing at Coptos beginning in the late third century B.C. (personal study), the Bucheum (Mond and Meyers 1934: pls. 147, 148, types 88d, 88g), Karnak (Jacquet-Gordon n.d.: nos. 35, 57, 267, 620), Elephantine (Gempeler 1992: pl. 127, nos. 9–10, fig. K754), and in and around the Red Sea port of Berenice (J. Hayes, personal communication). This beaded rim form is a popular one for locally made amphorae of the Hellenistic period, not only in Egypt, but at Berenice in North Africa (Riley 1979: Hellenistic amphora 1, fig. 68) and at Paphos (Hayes 1991: 86, fig. 37.1–9, nos. 16–20). All of these versions are essentially similar to, and probably based on, the widely distributed Rhodian and/or Koan amphorae.[23]

The second amphora form found at Naukratis, the squared rim amphora (figs. 2.56:3–8, 2.57:4,5), occurs only in Delta silt. On this form the rim is slightly wider than the neck, and has a square or rectangular profile, usually demarcated by a narrow groove. This is the single most common type: thirteen fragments were found at Kom Hadid and thirteen at Kom Ge'if, beginning at the latter mound in NW 3A. Examples of this form, all in silt, occur in early and mid second century B.C. contexts in the Delta at Maskhuta (Holladay 1982, pl. 33.13) and Tell Timai (Ochsenschlager 1967, fig. 9), as well as in a late third century B.C. context in Upper Egypt, at Coptos (personal study) and in a late second century B.C. context at Paphos (Hayes 1991: 87, Amphora list no. 27, pl. 22.2, fig. 47, Amphora list no. 28, fig. 73.4). All of the squared rim amphorae found at Naukratis were probably made at Kom Dahab; this is the likely source for those from Paphos and other Delta sites as well.[24] Unlike the widely copied beaded rim form, squared rim amphorae are confined in distribution. The form is likely original with Hellenistic Egyptian potters.

Beaded and squared rim amphorae were used at Naukratis throughout the third and second centuries B.C. Two new silt forms appear in first century B.C. deposits. The more common are inthickened

Table 2.5. Kom Dahab Kiln Products Found at Naukratis

Shape/Type	First occur at Kom Ge'if	Naukratis Date	Kom Dahab Reference: Coulson & Wilkie 1986
Saucer, thickened rim	NW 3B	later 3rd cent. B.C.	Fig. 18.E11.101.29
Bowl, incurved rim	NW 2A	early 3rd cent. B.C.	Fig. 18.E11.101.24
Cooking pot, small ledge rim	NW 3B	later 3rd cent. B.C.	Fig. 18.E11.101.63
Cooking pot, tall ledge rim	NW 3B	later 3rd cent. B.C.	Fig. 18.E11.12.9
Jug, delta rim	NW 1C	early 3rd cent. B.C.	Fig. 15.E11.101.27
Jug, narrow ledge rim	NW 2B	3rd cent. B.C.	Fig. 15.E11.122.1
Amphora, beaded rim	NW 2B	3rd cent. B.C.	Figs. 15.E11.101.23, 19.E11.130, 20
Amphora, squared rim	NW 3A	later 3rd cent. B.C.	Figs. 19. E11.124.10, E11.69

rim amphorae (fig. 2.57:1–3). Nine were found: three at Kom Hadid, the rest at Kom Ge'if, beginning in NW Hiatus C. This form is similar to, and probably a development of, the squared rim type; it is distinguished by an inset, or groove, on the top of the rim, creating a small inward thickened flange. The Naukratis inthickened rim amphorae are similar to the second (later) form made at Tell el-Haraby, on the coast west of Alexandria, production of which may have begun in the later Ptolemaic period (Majcherek and Shennawi 1991: fig. 1B. Dating is hampered by the lack of recorded examples at other Egyptian sites; I do speculate a beginning in the first century B.C., possibly continuing into the first or second century A.D.). The form also appears in first century B.C. contexts at Coptos (personal study) and at Quseir al-Qadim on the Red Sea coast (Whitcomb and Johnson 1979: 23p; Whitcomb and Johnson 1982: 14g). Outside of Egypt, similar vessels occur only in North Africa, at Berenice, in late first century A.D. deposits (Riley 1979: 169–70, Early Roman amphora 13, no. 172, fig. 78). These are questioned as local, and they may have been imports from Egypt.

The final silt amphora form found at Naukratis is the concave rim amphora (fig. 2.57: 6–8). Three fragments come from Kom Ge'if, all in a NW Hiatus C deposit. Examples of this form have been found in Alexandria (Majcherek 1992: fig. 1.4, considered a local variant of the Dressel Ic), Quseir al-Qadim (Whitcomb and Johnson 1979: pls. 21.z, 22.e), Abu Rihal, on the Red Sea coast near Berenice (J. Hayes, personal communication), and Coptos (personal study), all from contexts dated to the late first century B.C. and first century A.D. A possible single example was found at Paphos (Hayes 1991, fig. 38.14). No production sites have been found.

A Note on the Kom Dahab Kiln

Many of the forms found at Kom Hadid and Kom Ge'if have parallels in kiln wasters found in and around the kiln at nearby Kom Dahab (see Table 2.5; Coulson and Leonard 1983: 66–70 and figs. 4–5; Coulson and Wilkie 1986: 65–73). All of these comparable fragments, from both Kom Dahab and the two Naukratis mounds, were manufactured of the local Delta silt. The proximity of the sites, along with the consistency of vessel form and fabric, support the hypothesis that the Kom Dahab potters supplied the settlement at Naukratis. When the Kom Dahab kiln was discovered, the excavators could adduce no firm date for its use, since none of the forms were known from stratified and datable contexts. A single coin of Ptolemy X (beginning of the first century B.C.) from the accumulated debris within the collapsed main chamber provided only a *terminus ante quem.* Using this as a guide, along with an intact, small *lagynos*—a ceramic form invented sometime during the third century B.C. and quite popular throughout the second and first centuries as well—the excavators surmised that the kiln operated during the latter part of the Ptolemaic period (Coulson and Leonard 1983: 69). In a later article (Coulson and Wilkie 1986: 70) the excavators noted again that the debris represented the time when the kiln was already being used as a dump and that its original use dates could well be earlier. Now, with the identification of Kom Dahab vessels in the stratified deposits of Kom Ge'if, the kiln's periods of production can be identified.

The Naukratis data help to pinpoint both the beginning and the possible end of production at Kom Dahab. Every single Kom Dahab form found at Kom Ge'if occurs there in early Hellenistic deposits (see table 2.5). Therefore, the Kom Dahab kiln must have begun in, and continued to operate through, the third century B.C. In the second century many new silt shapes appear at Kom Ge'if, but not a single fragment of any of these was recovered from Kom Dahab. This does not prove that production there ceased; the Kom Dahab potters may have continued to make only the same eight forms as before. It does, however, indicate that in the second century at least one other pottery manufactory began production, and that this as-yet-unidentified center also supplied the Naukratis community. This new center must be in addition to the second century workshops at Tell el-Farâ'în, since none of the Naukratis silt forms of that period were found there either.

No large serving or mixing vessels seem to have been made at any of the production centers yet isolated. Among the shapes in Delta silt that are found at Naukratis, but are unattested at either Kom Dahab or Tell el-Farâ'în are hydriae/table amphorae, kraters (all types), and *dinoi* (all types). While narrow specialization among rural pottery producers is rare (either in antiquity or in more recent times), some degree of compartmentalization is not. So, for example, the Tell el-Farâ'în workshops made a variety of table vessels, but no cooking vessels. A similar situation is attested from northern Israel during early and middle Roman times, where two major pottery production centers have been isolated: Kfar Hananiah and Shikhin. The former primarily made cooking vessels of various shapes along with some jugs; the latter made large storage jars, kraters, and lamps (Adan-Bayewitz 1993; Adan-Bayewitz and Perlman 1990). Similar patterns have been noted for early/mid twentieth century Morocco (Vossen 1984: 366–67), for southern Arabia in the 1950s (Tufnell 1961), and for modern Egypt (Nicholson and Patterson 1985).

Between the third century workshops at Kom Dahab, the second century workshops at Tell el-Farâ'în, and other second century workshops, Delta potters made vessels for most basic needs: for table use, including both serving and eating, for cooking, and for storage. It was the Kom Dahab potters, however, who seem to have supplied the bulk of the pottery used at Naukratis. Within each general shape category found at the site, the Kom Dahab versions are the most common ones. The Naukratis residents' dependence on this close local supply further underscores the rural and largely isolated nature of their settlement.

Table 2.6. Summary Chart Comparing Ceramic Forms Found at Naukratis with Other Sites in the Eastern Mediterranean

Period	TYPES	BERENICE	COPTOS	ALEXANDRIA	NAUKRATIS	MASKHUTA	ASHDOD	SAMARIA	ANAFA	PAPHOS	TARSUS	ATHENS
5th/4th cent. B.C.	mortarium		×		×	×	×	×	×			
	plain rim saucer				×	×						
	rounded rim jar				×	×						
Early Hellenistic 3rd-early 2nd cent. B.C.	thickened rim saucer	×	×	×	×	×	×	×		×	×	×
	everted rim bowl	×	×	×	×		×	×	×	×	×	×
	Koan-Knidian cup	×	×	×	×		×	×	×	×	×	
	incurved rim bowl	×	×	×	×	×	×	×	×	×	×	×
	short unguentarium	×	×	×	×		×	×	×	×	×	×
	short sq. rim krater	×	×		×	×		×				
	ledge rim dinos		×		×							
	narrow ledge rim jug		×		×	×		×				
	long necked sq. rim jug	×	×		×		×					
	long necked delta rim jug	×	×		×	×	×					
	long necked flat rim jug	×	×	×	×	×						
	lagynos	×	×		×		×	×	×	×		
	angled rim cook pot		×		×			×		×		
	flattened rim cook pot		×		×			×	×	×		
	angled rim casserole	×	×	×	×	×		×	×	×	×	
	small dish-lid	×	×	×	×		×	×	×	×	×	×
	stand		×		×		×					
	beaded rim amphora	×	×		×	×		×		×		
	squared rim amphora	×	×		×	×		×		×		
Late Hellenistic mid 2nd-1st cent. B.C.	beveled rim saucer	×	×		×				×	×		×
	hemispherical bowl	×	×		×			×	×	×	×	×
	Aswan ledge rim jug		×		×							
	hydria		×	×	×	×				×		
	krater, overhanging rim	(×)	×		×	×		×	×	×	×	
	ledge/folded rim stew pot		×	×	×					×		×
	inset rim casserole	×	×	×	×	×			×	×		
	squared rim casserole		×		×				×	×		×
	folded rim casserole		×		×				×			
	E. Med. baking dish	(×)	×		×		×		×	×	×	×
	inthickened rim amphora		×		×	×		×	×	×	×	×

■ Indicates sites/areas under Ptolemaic control for most or all of the period
(×) Indicates type appears in later levels and could be residual Hellenistic material

Notes

[1] The present volume concentrates on the finds from Kom Hadid, but there are a few exceptions: Some of the *terra nigra* vessels and imported amphorae were actually found at Kom Ge'if. It was originally planned that because the two types were the exception at Kom Ge'if, but the norm at Kom Hadid, they should be illustrated as a unit and this is how the plates were assembled.

Fabric descriptions of the individual pieces are given in the captions for the illustrations. Fabric types, consisting mainly of "local" Delta silts and (Upper Egyptian?) desert marls, are presented in Appendix 1.

[2] In the field, lamps, imported amphorae, faience and metal objects were registered as separate objects of material culture. A discussion of these items is included in Chapter 3.

[3] See, for example, this shape in Nile silt (Bourriau 1981: no. 129) dated to early Dynasty XI. Several examples in coarse red marl appear in the Middle Kingdom levels at Coptos (personal study).

[4] Via variants produced in Italy, such as Lamboglia form 55 in Campana A, it was also widely distributed through the west in the second century B.C. (Kenrick 1985: 16).

[5] An extremely abbreviated sampling of parallels from the larger region includes (moving from west to east): Sabratha (Dore 1989: 172–73, type 147, fig. 45), Berenice (Riley 1979: nos. 609–614, fig. 110), Alexandria (Adriani 1940: figs. 40.1, 4, 6, 53.55, 63, 64), Maskhuta (Holladay 1982: pl. 28.9–13), Ashdod (Dothan 1971: fig. 15.20), Samaria (Crowfoot, Crowfoot, and Kenyon 1957, fig. 49), Paphos (Hayes 1991: fig. 13.1–9), and Tarsus (Jones 1950: figs. 121.51, 64, 122.57, 70, 71, 80, 180.51–80, A–N).

[6] A short list of parallels includes Berenice (Riley 1979: nos. 607, 608, fig. 110), Alexandria (Adriani 1940: fig. 40.3; Adriani 1952b: fig. 70.25), Paphos (Hayes 1991: figs. 5.9–10), and Tarsus (Jones 1950: figs. 121.42, 179.41, 42, H).

[7] Hayes 1991: 23–24 gives a roundup of find-spots and discussion of dating (Ware A). To his long list add Berenice (Riley 1979: nos. 602–5, fig. 109; these are local versions), Alexandria (Adriani 1940: figs. 53.57, 58; Adriani 1952b, fig. 70.24), Coptos (personal study), and Ashdod (Dothan 1971: figs. 9.15, 10.15).

[8] Black-glazed versions have been found at Samaria (Crowfoot, Crowfoot, and Kenyon 1957: fig. 53.2), Tarsus (Jones 1950: fig. 181D), and Athens (Rotroff 1997: 109–10, nos. 328–30, fig. 20). The Athenian vessels are the most closely dated, having been found in a workshop dump of the first quarter of the second century B.C. (Rotroff 1997: 110). A single example was found at Berenice (Riley 1979: no. 649, fig. 111, identified as local production). For ESA versions see Hayes 1986: 22, form 18, pl. 3.5.

[9] The earliest examples I can find come from the foundation deposit of Amosis II (569–527 B.C.) at Nebesheh

(Kelley 1976: pl. 86.2.25). Nothing of this sort is pictured in the standard references to Dynastic period pottery, such as Hope 1987.

[10] A single example of a "deep casserole/pan" from Sabratha was found in a context that may date as early as the fourth century B.C. (Dore 1989: 113, fig. 27.30.30, type 27).

[11] The Berenice vessels are called "predominately early Hellenistic" (Riley 1979: 243), but on no apparent evidence; the only parallels cited are the Corinthian vessels, which themselves date from the mid-second century B.C.

[12] The form is classified by Hayes as a frying pan of form Knossos I = Miletos 30 (1983: 105–8, figs. 5–7, 9). Though this Hellenistic form is similar to early/mid-Roman period frying pans in shape, it lacks that vessel's distinctive (and useful) horizontal coiled handle. Examples are infrequently burned on the bottom, and they are more likely to have been used inside an oven rather than over one. Other Hellenistic micaceous baking dishes have been found at Athens (Thompson 1934: E139, fig. 105), Corinth (Wright 1980: pl. 31.77; Slane 1986: fig. 15.91), Tarsus (Jones 1950: figs. 191.F, 201.E), Paphos (Hayes 1991: figs. 28.1 bottom, 32.7, 34.99), Tel Anafa (Berlin 1997: 110–11, PW 298–301, pls. 34, 81), Akko-Ptolemais (Dothan 1976: fig. 45.9), Tel Michal (Fischer 1989: fig. 13.3.27), Samaria (Crowfoot, Crowfoot, and Kenyon 1957: fig. 41.23), and Ashdod (Dothan 1971: fig. 24.6).

[13] Seven handles are of unknown origin and nineteen undated; these are not included in Table 2.3.

[14] Jugs are among the most difficult forms to identify confidently, even when one is handling the actual fragments. Because jugs tend to be relatively thin walled, they break into small pieces. This makes it difficult to estimate rim diameter, a crucial measurement for distinguishing jugs from forms with similar rims, such as jars and cooking pots. Moreover, it is rare to have enough preserved to count handles, so even when the diameter is knowable, it is hard to distinguish between jugs and jars. Finally, there are no standard, widely published forms as there are, for example, for table and cooking vessels. This last feature especially compounds the identification difficulties of the present project, in which I do work solely with field drawings and fabric descriptions. Since jugs are particularly problematic, I have been cautious in identifying this shape, and here discuss only fragments with both shape *and* fabric parallels. Many more jugs were probably found at Naukratis than are included in this section.

[15] See examples from Paphos (Hayes 1991: fig. 16.5), Ashdod (Dothan 1971: fig. 11.1, pl. XIV.11), Maskhuta (Holladay 1982: pl. 30.11), Coptos (personal study), Berenice (Riley 1979: no. 1100, fig. 135; this is called a "coarse hydria" and has the requisite horizontal handle, which some of the Naukratis examples may have had as well), and Sabratha (Dore 1989: type 395, fig. 69, beginning of third century B.C.). The form is startlingly similar to the common water pitcher found

in Hellenistic Athens (Thompson 1934: 464–65, A53–55, B39, figs. 8, 23).

[16] At Coptos, a single imported flanged rim *hydria*, possibly of Rhodian manufacture, was found in an early second century deposit, and a number of very similar vessels made from Upper Egyptian desert marl were found in deposits dating from the mid second through the early first centuries B.C. (personal study). Other similar vessels were found at Paphos (Hayes 1991: fig. 41.31) and Sabratha (Dore 1989: type 219, fig. 52). For Alexandrian *hydriae*, see following note.

[17] Several fabrics and production sites have been defined for the *hydriae* found in the necropoli of Alexandria. On the Cretan white ground series, see Callaghan and Jones 1985: 1–2 and Enklaar 1985: figs. 1a-e. On the Rhodian variant, see Callaghan and Jones 1985: 2. On the Alexandrian clay ground type, see Callaghan and Jones 1985: 1–2 and references there.

[18] This is Cintas type 315/Carthage Early Amphora I/ Berenice Hellenistic amphora 10. It is common at Carthage in the fourth and third centuries B.C. (Hayes 1976a: E1, 112), and in Hellenistic deposits at Berenice (Riley 1979: 136) and Sabratha (Fulford 1986: no. 77, fig 86; Keay 1989, type 3e, fig. 4.35–37).

[19] This rim is similar to a locally made *dolium* found at Berenice (Riley 1979: no. 751, fig. 118); the vessel is there dated Late Roman, though Riley admits that the form is common in other periods, and that "no satisfactory typological sequence could be established" (p. 317).

[20] The *locus classicus* for this is the observation by Herodotus (*Hist.* 3.6) that amphorae imported to Egypt were frequently saved and reused as water jars. Other citations, contemporary with this period, occur in the Zenon papyri, which mention various reuses of Milesian, Samian, Lesbian, and Chian jars (Tcherikower 1937: 76–77, n. 23). The vast quantities of imported Hellenistic amphora handles from Alexandria have been taken as material evidence for the jars' reuse there (Fraser 1972: I, 161, 165–68). Grace (1962: 107–8) interpreted the nine Hellenistic Rhodian and Knidian handles found at the desert site of Nessana (on the border between the Sinai peninsula and the Negev of Israel) as jars reused for water (as suggested by Herodotus).

[21] Not having seen the material firsthand, I will confine my discussion only to forms that are obviously Egyptian. Amphorae are most reliably identified via stamped handles, and sec-

ondarily by visual inspection of vessel fabric and form. It is now apparent that many locales produced their own versions of some widely distributed types, making positive identifications of unstamped, fragmentary pieces difficult (see, for example, probable and possible local versions of Knidian, Rhodian, Chian, and Koan amphorae from Paphos [Hayes 1991: 85–86, Amphora list nos. 1–7, 8–13, 14–15, 16–20, respectively]).

[22] I identify these vessels as calcareous beaded rim amphorae with some hesitation. The fabric is not dissimilar to that of some Aegean island productions, and the form is close as well. Some of the Naukratis vessels may in fact be Rhodian imports. However, during the excavations at Naukratis, the excavators were unaware that a gritty, light-colored amphora fabric of *Egyptian* origin existed, with the result that they classified all such vessels as imports. I do think it is likely that many of these "imports" were in fact this common Egyptian type. However, since it is impossible on the basis of drawings and fabric identifications made in the field to separate the Egyptian products from the imported ones, I have chosen to regard them as a local group.

[23] The form continues to be popular into early Roman times, notably in the manufacture of Dressel 2–4, a Koan imitation made at several western Mediterranean sites (see recent discussion and bibliography in Keay 1989: 38–39, type 13).

[24] Two types of silt amphorae were also produced at Tell el-Haraby, on the Mediterranean coast 173 km west of Alexandria (Majcherek and Shennawi 1991, figs. 1A, B), beginning in the late Ptolemaic period. The earlier Tell el-Haraby amphora (Type A, fig. 1A) has a somewhat squared-off rim, as the Kom Dahab form, but is distinguished by a slight groove or bevel in the upper surface of the rim. Two of the Kom Hadid silt squared rim amphorae appear similar (figs. 2.57:1, 2.56:8), but it is impossible to assign them to this source without visual inspection. A third squared rim amphora production site might be postulated based on the finds from Coptos. M. Lawall, who is studying and will publish these amphorae, says that "the fabrics [of] the Naukratis examples do not lend themselves to a close comparison with the fabrics found at Coptos" (personal communication). However, the absence of squared rim amphorae from other Hellenistic deposits in Upper Egypt might suggest that the Coptos amphorae came to that site via Nile traffic from Lower Egypt.

Fig. 2.1.   Pieces of Table Vessels from Kom Hadid

No.	Locus	Pottery bag no.	Field no.	Description
Thickened Rim Saucers:				
1	13006	N.III.130.20	3023	Delta silt (Fabric I)
2	4810	N.III.48.05	3947	Delta silt (Fabric I)
3	7610	N.III.76.51	1703	Delta silt (Fabric I)
4	4803	N.III.48.09	4206	Delta silt (Fabric I)
5	14402	N.III.144.05	981	Delta silt (Fabric I)
6	7610	N.III.76.51	1707	Delta silt (Fabric I)
7	7613	N.III.76.41	1569	Delta silt (Fabric I)
8	7601	N.III.76.17	860	Delta silt (Fabric I)
9	7601	N.III.76.02	289	Delta silt (Fabric I)
10	4807	N.III.48.10	4093	Delta silt (Fabric I)
11	7608	N.III.76.33	1304	Delta silt (Fabric I)
12	7605	N.III.76.54	1670	Delta silt (Fabric I)
13	6207	N.III.62.16	3196	Delta silt (Fabric I)
14	7601	N.III.76.02	285	Delta silt (Fabric I)
15	7602	N.III.76.03	240	Delta silt (Fabric I)
16	4808	N.III.48.11	4124	Delta silt (Fabric I)
17	7606	N.III.76.19	2025	Delta silt (Fabric I)
18	7610	N.III.76.35	1373	Delta silt (Fabric I)
19	7606	N.III.76.23	949	Delta silt (Fabric I)
20	7613	N.III.76.41	1576	Delta silt, slipped (Fabric IA)
21	13006	N.III.130.17	1969	Delta silt, slipped (Fabric IA)
22	6215	N.III.62.38	3972	Delta silt, slipped (Fabric IA)
23	6305	N.III.63.18	4352	Delta silt, slipped (Fabric IA)

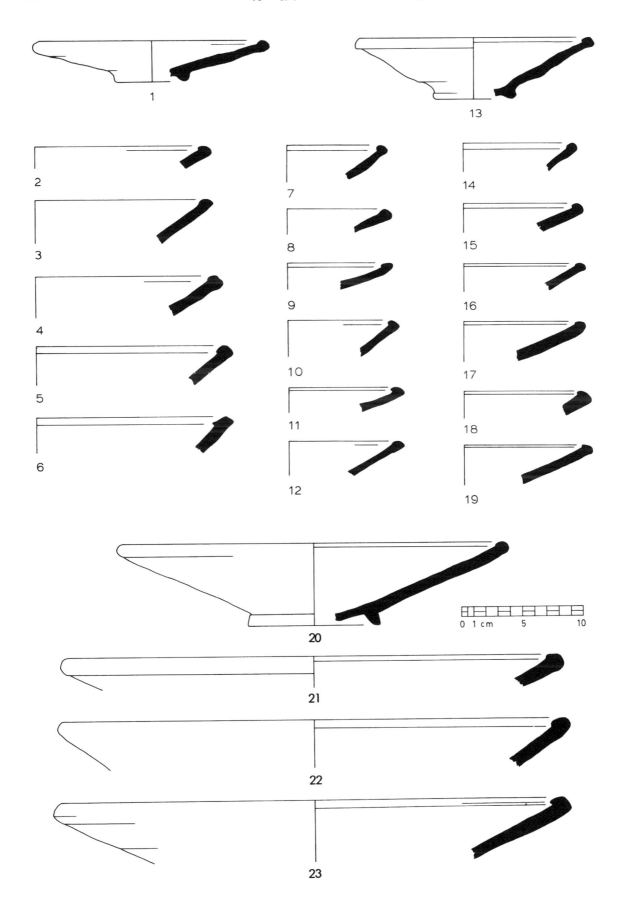

FIG. 2.1

Fig. 2.2.   Pieces of Table Vessels from Kom Hadid

No.	Locus	Pottery bag no.	Field no.	Description
Thickened Rim Saucers:				
1	6304	N.III.63.05	3673	Delta silt, slipped (Fabric IB)
2	6209	N.III.62.26	3769	Delta silt, slipped (Fabric IB)
3	7613	N.III.76.64	2096	Delta silt, slipped (Fabric IB)
4	6205	N.III.62.46	4173	Delta silt (Fabric I)
5	6302	N.III.63.03	3498	Delta silt (Fabric I)
6	6305	N.III.63.12	4290	Delta silt (Fabric I)
7	6209	N.III.62.33	3393	Delta silt (Fabric I)
8	6209	N.III.62.30	3959	Delta silt, slipped (Fabric IB)
9	6305	N.III.63.12	4257	Delta silt, slipped (Fabric IB)
10	6305	N.III.63.18	4311	Delta silt, slipped (Fabric IB)
11	6207	N.III.62.24	3826	Delta silt, slipped (Fabric IB)
12	7601	N.III.76.17	847	Delta silt, slipped (Fabric IB)
13	6215	N.III.62.38	3972	Delta silt, slipped (Fabric IB)
14	6205	N.III.62.46	4169	Delta silt, slipped (Fabric IB)
15	7605	N.III.76.09	447	Delta silt, slipped (Fabric IIA)
16	7605	N.III.76.29	1080	Delta silt, slipped (Fabric IIA)
17	7613	N.III.76.41	1572	Delta silt, slipped (Fabric IIA)
18	6304	N.III.63.05	3682	Delta silt, slipped (Fabric IIA)

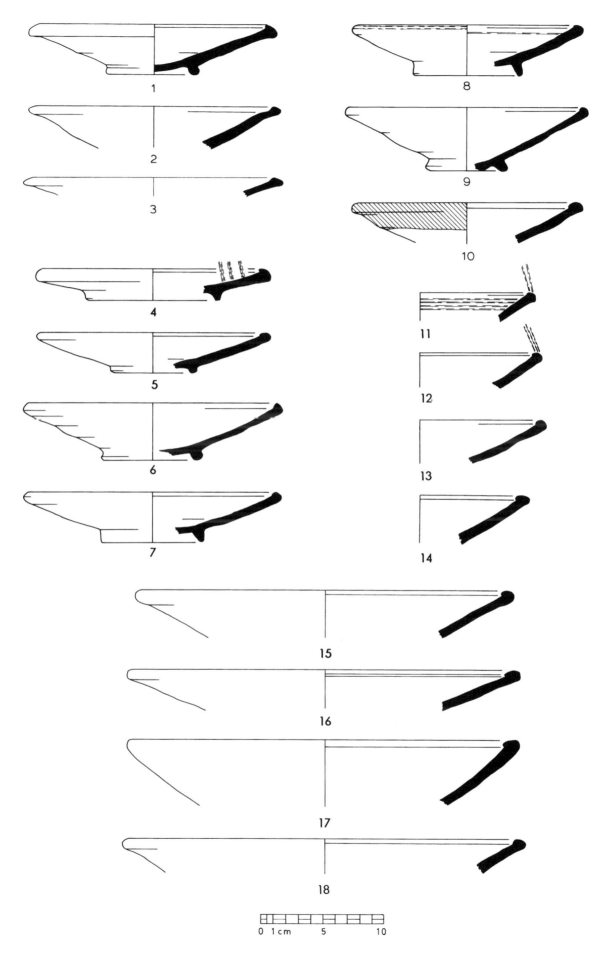

FIG. 2.2

Fig. 2.3.   Pieces of Table Vessels from Kom Hadid

No.	Locus	Pottery bag no.	Field no.	Description
Thickened Rim Saucers, Terra Nigra:				
1	6201	N.III.62.06	3124	Shiny black in/out, with areas mottled Brown. Well-levigated clay. White sand-sized grit occasionally to 1 mm, very few micaceous inclusions. Fabric/core c. 10YR 5/3 (Brown).
2	4802	N.III.48.02	3432	Dull black in/out. Fabric between 7.5YR 5/2-5/4 (Brown) with core (c. 1 mm) of 10R 3/6 (Dark Red); occasional red and gray-brown sand-sized inclusions.
3	6207	N.III.62.19	3293	Dull black in/out. sand-sized micaceous inclusions and very rare "orange" grit to 1 mm Fabric/core: 2.5YR N6/–N5/ (Gray).
4	7606	N.III.76.14	843	Shiny black in/out. Well-levigated clay. White sand-sized grit occasionally to 1 mm, very few micaceous inclusions. Gray-brown fabric without a distinct core c. 10YR 3/2 (Very Dark Grayish Brown)
5	7606	N.III.76.19	739	Shiny black in/out. Very well-levigated clay. Sand-sized micaceous inclusions. Fabric c. 10YR 3/2 (Very Dark Grayish Brown).
6	6304	N.III.63.05	3714	Shiny black in/out. Very well-levigated clay. Gray-brown fabric with 10YR 4/3 Dark Brown) core.
7	6203	N.III.62.13	2047	Dull black in/out but slightly lustrous in places. Well-levigated clay. White sand-sized grit occasionally to 1 mm, very few micaceous inclusions. Fabric/core between 10YR 5/3 (Brown) and 4/3 (Dark Brown).
8	7605	N.III.76.09	433	Dull black in/shiny out. Some mottling to brown. Very well-levigated clay with occasional white grit to 1 mm and sand-sized micaceous inclusions. Fabric between 7.5YR 5/4 (Brown) and 10YR 4/3 (Dark Brown).
9	6305	N.III.63.12	4270	Shiny black in/out. Well-levigated clay with occasional white grit to 1 mm and sand-sized micaceous inclusions. Fabric/core 10YR 6/3 (Pale Brown).
10	6305	N.III.63.12	—	Shiny to lustrous black in/out. Well-levigated clay. Sand-sized white grit and micaceous inclusions. Core 5YR 5/2 (Reddish Gray) c. 4mm thick, beneath gray sandwich. (Fabric TN-4C).
11	6304	N.III.63.05	1130	Shiny black in/out. Very well-levigated clay. Occasional sand size mica and very fine straw casts. Rare gray grit to c. 2 mm in core. Fabric between 7.5YR 5/2–5/4 (Brown), with core between 10R 4/6 (Red) and 3/6 (Dark Red).
12	6302	N.III.63.06	4307	Sherd missing.
13	7606	N.III.76.13	461	Well-levigated clay. No visible tempering agent(s). Fabric 2.5YR 4/6 (Red) with thin (less than 1 mm) gray core where sherd is thickest.
14	6207	N.III.62.19	3817	Dull black in/out. Well-levigated clay. Sand-sized micaceous inclusions (only). Thin (c. 2 mm) core c. 10YR 6/1 (Gray) sandwiched by 10YR 5/2 (Grayish Brown).
15	49214	N.I.492.40	100	Dull black in/out. Well-levigated clay. Sand-sized white grit and micaceous inclusions. Thin gray core sandwiched by 10YR 5/2 (Grayish Brown).
16	49150	N.I.491.172	4348	Dull black in/out. Well-levigated clay. Sand-sized white grit and micaceous inclusions. Thin 5YR 5/1 (Gray) core sandwiched by 10YR 5/2 (Grayish Brown).
17	7608	N.I.76.33	1315	Dull black in/out. Well-levigated clay. Sand-sized white grit and micaceous inclusions. Thin gray core sandwiched by 10YR 5/2 (Grayish Brown).
18	7604	N.III.76.08	431	Shiny black where not abraded. Well-levigated clay. Sand-sized white grit and micaceous inclusions. Thin gray core sandwiched by 10YR 3/2 (Very Dark Grayish Brown).
19	13007	N.III.130.20	3026	Shiny in/out. Gray fabric. Well-levigated clay. Occasional sand-sized white grit with few to c. 1 mm. Interior surface mottled towards gray. (Fabric TN-3).
20	49004	N.I.490.98	4043	Dull in/out. Very well-levigated clay. Occasional white grit and micaceous inclusions often to 1 mm. Medium gray fabric throughout. (Fabric TN-3).
21	6304	N.III.63.07	3736	Dull in/out, slightly silvery in places. Well-levigated clay. Occasional sand-sized white grit with few to c. 1 mm (some grit breaks surfaces), and fine straw casts. Fabric black throughout. (Fabric TN-3).
22	6305	N.III.63.12	4268	Shiny in/out. Well-levigated clay. Occasional sand-sized white grit with few to c. 1 mm. Interior surface mottled towards gray. Gray fabric. (Fabric TN-3).
23	13006	N.III.130.17	1973	Shiny brown in/out. Well-levigated clay. Sand-sized white grit and micaceous inclusions. Fabric/core 5YR 4/3–4/4 (Reddish Brown) "Slip" of c. 7.5YR 4/4 (Weak Red) shiny (closely burnished ?) in/out.
24	4807	N.III.48.12	4191	Shiny to lustrous black in/out. Exterior mottled through 5YR 3/3–3/4 Dark Reddish Brown) and 10YR 6/2 (Light Reddish Gray) to 10YR 6/1 (Gray). Very well-levigated clay. Occasional sand-sized white grit and micaceous inclusions. Fabric between 10YR 4/3 (Dark Brown) and 4/6 (Dark Yellowish Brown).
25	6304	N.III.63.05	3714	Shiny brown in/out. Interior slightly mottled to c. 10YR 4/3-2/3 (Dark Brown). Very well-levigated clay. No trace of tempering agents. Fabric 10YR 4/2 (Dark Grayish Brown)–4/3 (Dark Brown).

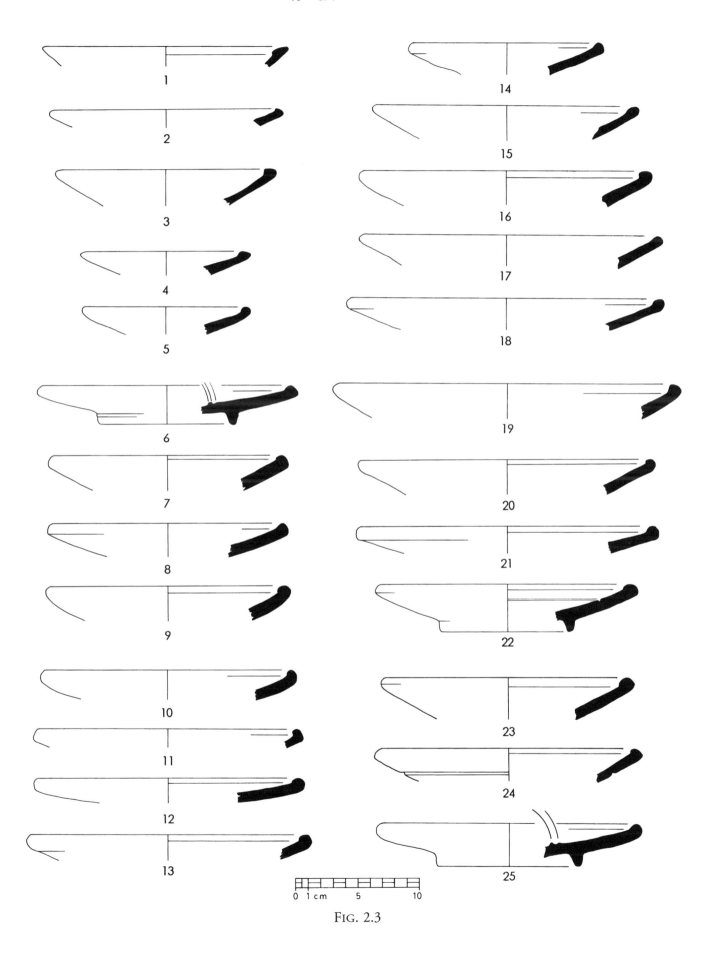

FIG. 2.3

Fig. 2.4.   Pieces of Table Vessels from Kom Hadid

No.	Locus	Pottery bag no.	Field no.	Description
Plain Rim Saucers:				
1	7605	N.III.76.30	1017	Delta silt (Fabric II)
2	6203	N.III.62.13	2026	Delta silt (Fabric II)
3	7603	N.III.76.03	915	Delta silt (Fabric II)
4	6203	N.III.62.42	4079	Delta silt, slipped (Fabric IIA)
5	7618	N.III.76.69	3166	Delta silt, slipped (Fabric IIA)
6	7605	N.III.76.53	1584	Delta silt, slipped (Fabric IIA)
7	6209	N.III.62.35	3654	Delta silt, slipped (Fabric IIA)
Drooping Rim Saucers, Terra Nigra:				
8	7605	N.III.76.09	435	Lustrous gray in/out. Very well-levigated clay. Occasional sand-sized micaceous inclusions and fine straw casts. Dark gray fabric. (Fabric TN-3).
9	4805	N.III.48.06	—	Shiny in/out. Interior surface mottled towards gray. Well-levigated clay. Occasional sand-sized white grit with few to c. 1 mm. Gray fabric.
10	7603	N.III.76.06	3099	Mottled black to c. 5YR 3/4 (Dark Reddish Brown) in/out. Very well-levigated clay. Frequent sand-sized micaceous inclusions. Fabric 5YR 4/4 (Reddish Brown) to 4/6 (Yellowish Red).
11	4808	N.III.48.11	464	Shiny black in/out. Well-levigated clay with occasional white grit to 1 mm and sand-sized micaceous inclusions. Fabric/core 10YR 6/3 (Pale Brown).
12	49131	N.I.491.133	3028	Shiny black in/out. Core (over 5 mm): light gray. Sandwich: dark gray.
13	7606	N.III.76.14	842	Shiny black in/out. Well-levigated clay. Occasional sand-sized white grit and frequent sand-sized micaceous inclusions. Fabric c. 10YR 4/3 (Dark Brown).
14	6202	N.III.62.41	4238	Shiny black in/out. Core: 5YR 5/4 (Reddish Brown). Import.
15	7613	N.III.76.34	832	Shiny gray in/out. Very well-levigated clay. Occasional sand-sized micaceous inclusions and fine straw casts. Dark gray fabric. (Fabric TN-3).

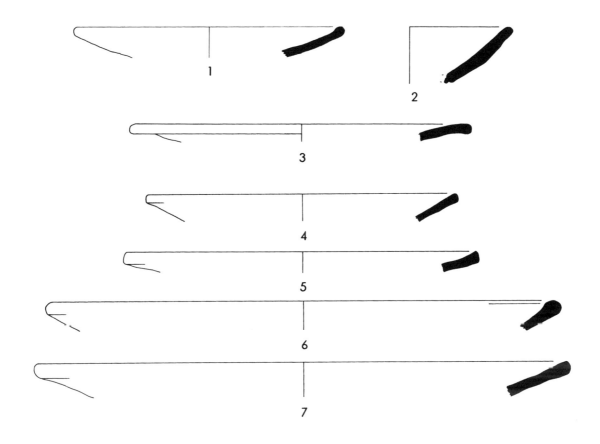

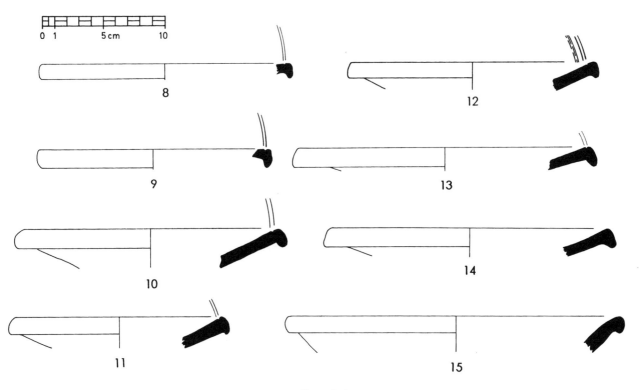

FIG. 2.4

Fig. 2.5. Pieces of Table Vessels from Kom Hadid

No.	Locus	Pottery bag no.	Field no.	Description
Beveled Rim Saucers:				
1	7604	N.III.76.07	1426	Delta silt, slipped (Fabric IIC)
2	7618	N.III.76.74	3220	Delta silt (Fabric II)
3	7610	N.III.76.51	1708	Delta silt (Fabric II)
4	6207	N.III.62.16	3197	Delta silt (Fabric II)
Miscellaneous Terra Nigra:				
5	49131	N.I.491.146	1635	Shiny black in/dull black out. Well-levigated clay. Occasional sand-sized white grit and frequent sand-sized micaceous inclusions. Fabric 10YR 4/2 (Dark Grayish Brown).
6	7607	N.III.76.19	1119a	Dull black in, shiny black out. Very well-levigated clay with occasional white grit to 1 mm and sand-sized micaceous inclusions. Fabric 10YR 4/3 (Dark Brown).
7	49002	N.I.490.27	1483	Shiny black in/out. well-levigated clay. Occasional sand-sized white grit and frequent sand-sized micaceous inclusions. Fabric 10YR 3/2 (Very Dark Grayish Brown)–10YR 4/3-3/3 (Dark Brown). No distinct core. (Fabric TN-4A).
Eastern Sigillata A Platter:				
8	7604	N.III.76.25	1289	Extremely well-levigated clay with no trace of tempering agent. Fabric: near but lighter than 7.5YR 7/6 (Reddish Yellow) (no exact Munsell). Dull slip in/out: c. 2.5YR 4/6 (Red).
Koan-Knidian Bowls/Cups:				
9	7618	N.III.76.76	3602	Well-levigated clay with frequent sand-sized white grit. Fabric: between 5YR 7/4 (Pink)–7/6 (Reddish Yellow). Slip in/out: dull 2.5YR 4/6–4/8 (Red).
10				
11	6205	N.III.62.46	4184	Delta silt, slipped (Fabric IA)

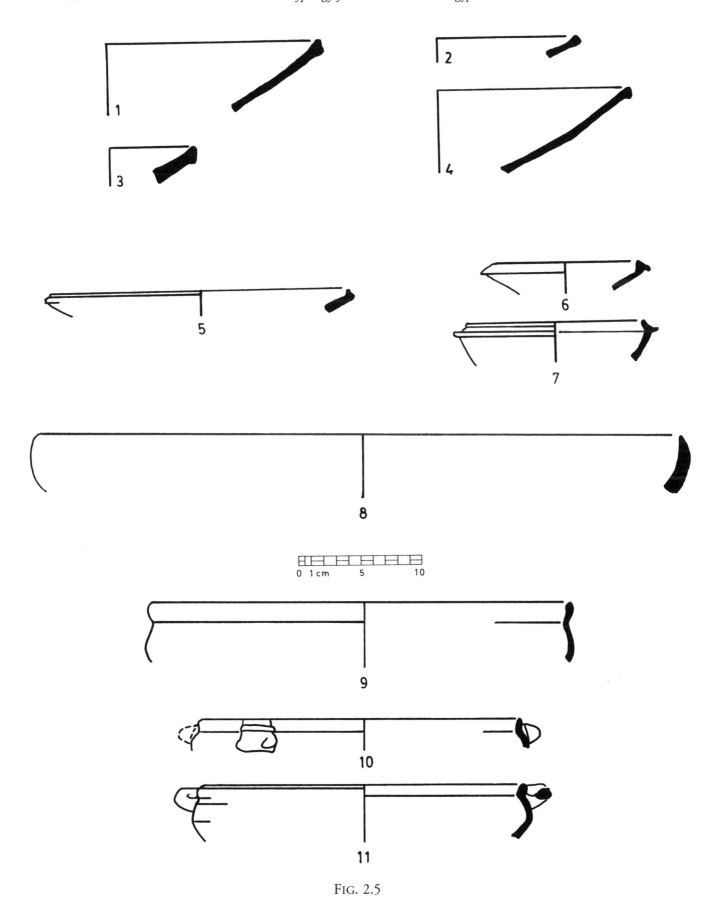

FIG. 2.5

Fig. 2.6.   Pieces of Table Vessels from Kom Hadid

No.	Locus	Pottery bag no.	Field no.	Description
Incurved Rim Bowls:				
1	6209	N.III.62.33	3397	Delta silt (Fabric I)
2	6217	N.III.62.25	3036	Delta silt (Fabric I)
3	7602	N.III.76.03	244	Delta silt (Fabric I)
4	6209	N.III.62.33	3402	Delta silt (Fabric I)
5	14401	N.III.144.03	816	Delta silt (Fabric I)
6	6202	N.III.62.03	1680	Delta silt (Fabric I)
7	7604	N.III.76.07	334	Delta silt (Fabric I)
8	7601	N.III.76.02	287	Delta silt (Fabric I)
9	7613	N.III.76.59	1967	Delta silt (Fabric I)
10	7605	N.III.76.29	1086	Delta silt (Fabric I)
11	6207	N.III.62.19	3803	Delta silt (Fabric I)
12	7610	N.III.76.51	—	Delta silt (Fabric I)
13	4803	N.III.48.09	4209	Delta silt (Fabric I)
14	4803	N.III.48.09	4202	Delta silt (Fabric I)
15	7601	N.III.76.02	259	Delta silt (Fabric I)
16	7603	N.III.76.20	907	Delta silt (Fabric I)
17	7605	N.III.76.30	1027	Delta silt (Fabric I)
18	6304	N.III.63.07	3716	Delta silt (Fabric I)
19	7616	N.III.76.57	1095	Delta silt (Fabric I)
20	7605	N.III.76.30	1009	Delta silt (Fabric I)
21	6217	N.III.62.37	3559	Delta silt (Fabric I)
22	6203	N.III.62.13	2021	Delta silt (Fabric I)
23	7605	N.III.76.54	1673	Delta silt (Fabric I)
24	14403	N.III.144.08	1255	Delta silt (Fabric I)
25	7617	N.III.76.68	3005	Delta silt (Fabric I)
26	7605	N.III.76.30	1029	Delta silt (Fabric I). Overfired.
27	7610	N.III.76.52	1724	Delta silt (Fabric I)
28	7608	N.III.76.42	1604	Delta silt (Fabric I)
29	13006	N.III.130.17	1968	Delta silt (Fabric I)
30	7605	N.III.76.54	1668	Delta silt (Fabric I)

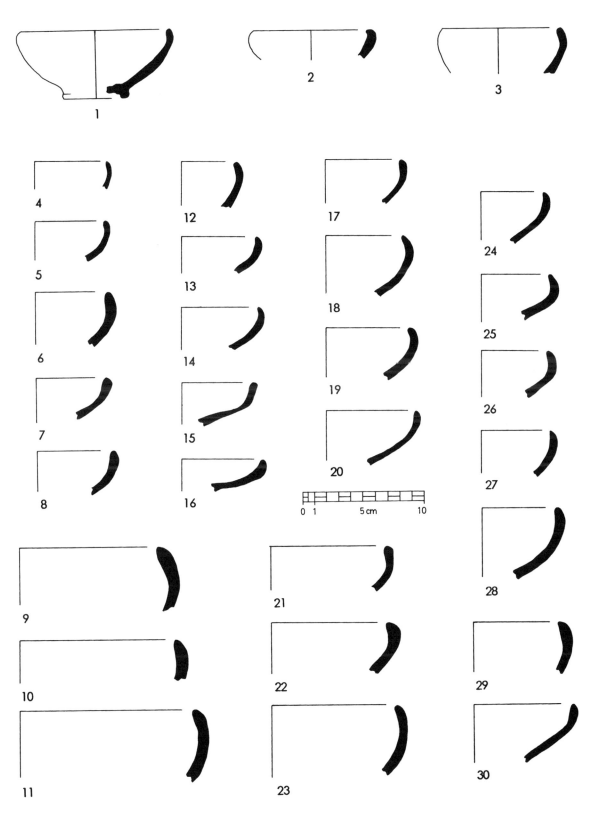

FIG. 2.6

Fig. 2.7.   Pieces of Table Vessels from Kom Hadid

No.	Locus	Pottery bag no.	Field no.	Description
Incurved Rim Bowls:				
1	6217	N.III.62.37	3551	Delta silt, slipped (Fabric IA)
2	7603	N.III.76.16	627	Delta silt, slipped (Fabric IA)
3	7603	N.III.76.05	349	Delta silt, slipped (Fabric IA)
4	7610	N.III.76.35	1369	Delta silt, slipped (Fabric IA)
5	6305	N.III.63.18	4275	Delta silt, slipped (Fabric IA)
6	7606	N.III.76.23	947	Delta silt, slipped (Fabric IA)
7	6209	N.III.62.35	3656	Delta silt, slipped (Fabric IA)
8	6305	N.III.63.18	4353	Delta silt, slipped (Fabric IA)
9	7606	N.III.76.13	468	Delta silt, slipped (Fabric IA)
10	6203	N.III.62.12	3047	Delta silt, slipped (Fabric IA)
11	7610	N.III.76.51	1710	Delta silt, slipped (Fabric IA)
12	7608	N.III.76.43	1656	Delta silt, slipped (Fabric IA)
13	7608	N.III.76.28	1113	Delta silt, slipped (Fabric IA)
14	7618	N.III.76.76	3599	Delta silt, slipped (Fabric IA)
15	7609	N.III.76.58	3354	Delta silt, slipped (Fabric IA)
16	6304	N.III.63.05	3690	Delta silt, slipped (Fabric IA)
17	7609	N.III.76.58	3356	Delta silt, slipped (Fabric IA)
18	7606	N.III.76.37	1520	Delta silt, slipped (Fabric IA)
19	7613	N.III.76.44	1552	Delta silt, slipped (Fabric IA)
20	7608	N.III.76.26	1268	Delta silt, slipped (Fabric IA)
21	7613	N.III.76.64	2083	Delta silt, slipped (Fabric IA)
22	7608	N.III.76.28	1115	Delta silt, slipped (Fabric IA)
23	7603	N.III.76.05	396	Delta silt, slipped (Fabric IA)
24	7618	N.III.76.76	3598	Delta silt, slipped (Fabric IA)
25	14402	N.III.144.05	976	Delta silt, slipped (Fabric IA)
26	6202	N.III.62.06	3110	Delta silt, slipped (Fabric IA)
27	6217	N.III.62.37	3634	Delta silt, slipped (Fabric IA)
28	7603	N.III.76.05	415	Delta silt, slipped (Fabric IA)
29	6207	N.III.62.19	3288	Delta silt, slipped (Fabric IA)

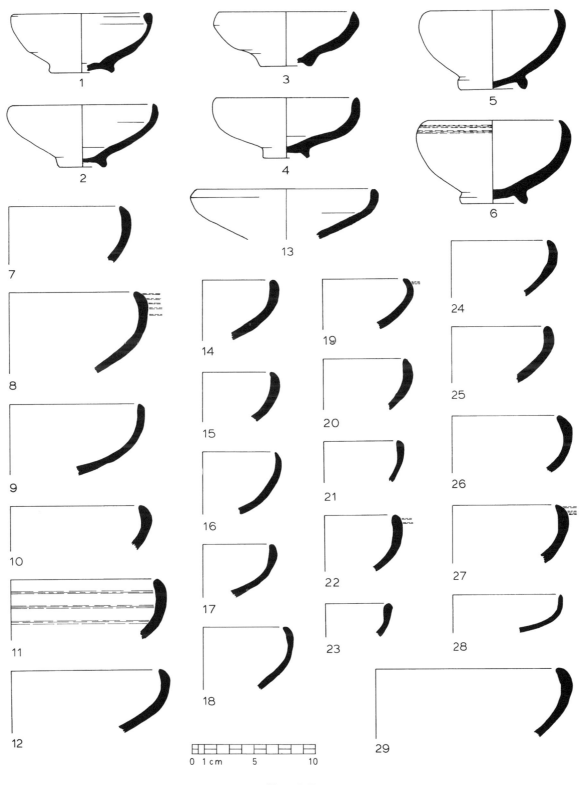

FIG. 2.7

Fig. 2.8.   Pieces of Table Vessels from Kom Hadid

No.	Locus	Pottery bag no.	Field no.	Description
Incurved Rim Bowls:				
1	7610	N.III.76.51	1700	Delta silt, slipped (Fabric IIC)
2	7615	N.III.76.45	1732	Delta silt, slipped (Fabric IIC)
3	7603	N.III.76.05	359	Delta silt, slipped (Fabric IIC)
4	7606	N.III.76.37	1509	Delta silt, slipped (Fabric IIC)
5	7603	N.III.76.50	1755	Delta silt, slipped (Fabric IIC)
6	7605	N.III.76.55	1813	Delta silt, slipped (Fabric IIC)
7	6305	N.III.63.18	4360	Delta silt (Fabric II)
8	6203	N.III.62.05	1939	Delta silt (Fabric II)
9	7617	N.III.76.68	3017	Delta silt, slipped (Fabric IIA)
10	6217	N.III.62.37	3552	Delta silt, slipped (Fabric IIA)
11	6203	N.III.62.13	2031	Delta silt, slipped (Fabric IIB)
12	6201	N.III.62.01	1848	Delta silt, slipped (Fabric IB)
13	6305	N.III.63.18	4358	Delta silt, slipped (Fabric IB)
14	6207	N.III.62.22	3244	Delta silt, slipped (Fabric IB)
15	6305	N.III.63.12	4289	Delta silt, slipped (Fabric IB)
16	6215	N.III.62.38	3974	Delta silt, slipped (Fabric IB)
17	7605	N.III.76.10	675	Delta silt, slipped (Fabric IB)
18	7603	N.III.76.05	369	Delta silt, slipped (Fabric IB)
19	4807	N.III.48.10	4098	Delta silt, slipped (Fabric IB)
20	6304	N.III.63.10	4726	Delta silt, slipped (Fabric IB)
21	7613	N.III.76.44	1544	Delta silt, slipped (Fabric IB)
22	7608	N.III.76.33	1311	Delta silt, slipped (Fabric IB)
23	7606	N.III.76.13	490	Delta silt, slipped (Fabric IB)
24	7613	N.III.76.41	1579	Delta silt, slipped (Fabric IB)
25	7608	N.III.76.33	1326	Delta silt, slipped? [Fabric I variant with traces of slip in/out: 10YR 8/3 (Very Pale Brown)]

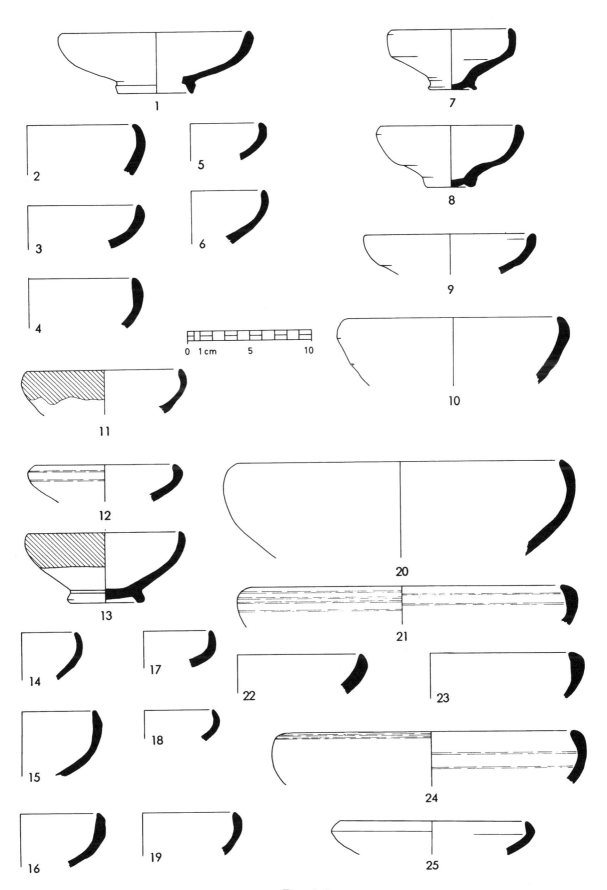

FIG. 2.8

Fig. 2.9.   Pieces of Table Vessels from Kom Hadid

No.	Locus	Pottery bag no.	Field no.	Description
Incurved Rim Bowls, Terra Nigra:				
1	7605	N.III.76.55	1837	Dull black in/out. Traces of horizontal burnishing (lustrous) bands on exterior Very well-levigated clay. Sand-sized white grit and micaceous inclusions. Gray core with sandwich of 7.5YR 5/2–5/4 (Brown).
2	7613	N.III.76.44	2044	Dull black in/out but slightly lustrous in places. Well-levigated clay. White sand-sized grit occasionally to 1 mm, very few micaceous inclusions. Fabric between 10YR 5/3 (Brown) and 4/3 (Dark Brown) with c. 1 mm gray core. Traces of "burnishing" on exterior of rim.
3	—	—	—	Sherd missing.
4	7613	N.III.76.44	1552	Shiny black in/out; interior mottled to brown. Very well-levigated clay, no visible trace of tempering agents. Core 10YR 3/2 (Very Dark Grayish Brown).
5	6302	N.III.63.03	3546	Shiny to lustrous black in/out. Very well-levigated clay. Sand-sized micaceous inclusions. Core (amorphous) c. 10YR 4/2 (Dark Grayish Brown) merging to black below surface(s).
6	4802	N.III.48.02	3431	Mottled from shiny to dull brown in/out. Exceptionally well-levigated . Occasional white grit and sand-sized micaceous inclusions. Core (3 mm) c. 7.5YR 7/4 (Pink) sandwiched with 5YR 7/4 (Pink)–7/6 (Reddish Yellow). "Glaze" in/out varies from 5YR 3/3 (Dark Reddish Brown) where thickest to c. 3/4 (Dark Reddish Brown) where thinner.
7	7606	N.III.76.13	462	Shiny in/out. Well-levigated clay. Sand-sized micaceous inclusions and fine straw casts. Dark gray fabric. (Fabric TN-3).
8	7613	N.III.76.41	1580	Shiny in/out. Very well-levigated clay. Occasional sand-sized micaceous inclusions and fine straw casts. Dark gray fabric. (Fabric TN-3).
9	6305	N.III.63.18	4309	Shiny in/out. Very well-levigated clay. Occasional sand-sized micaceous inclusions and fine straw casts. Dark gray fabric.
10	7613	N.III.76.44	1547	Shiny in/out. Very well-levigated clay. Occasional sand-sized micaceous inclusions and fine straw casts. Dark gray fabric. (Fabric TN-3).
11	49004	N.I.490.94	3888	Shiny in/dull out Very well-levigated clay. Occasional sand-sized micaceous inclusions and fine straw casts. Dark gray fabric. (Fabric TN-3).
12	—	—	4285	Shiny in/out. Well-levigated clay. Sand-sized micaceous inclusions. Fabric c. 10YR 3/2 (Very Dark Grayish Brown) with a thin c. 7.5YR 3/6 (Red) core.
13	7606	N.III.76.37	1510	Dull black in/out. Very well-levigated clay. sand-sized white grit and micaceous inclusions. Core (c. 2 mm) from light gray (no Munsell) to 2.5YR N6/ (Gray). Fabric (as sandwich) c. 7.5YR 4/2 (Dark Brown).
14	7613	N.III.76.41	1580	Shiny black in/out. Very well-levigated clay. Infrequent sand-sized white grit and micaceous inclusions. Fabric 10YR 4/2 (Dark Grayish Brown).
15	7613	N.III.76.34	1408	Shiny black in/out. Occasional white grit to 1 mm. Fabric gray with thin 10YR 4/2 (Dark Grayish Brown).
16	6207	N.III.62.19	3295	Lustrous black in/out. Very well-levigated clay. Infrequent sand-sized white grit and micaceous inclusions. Fabric 10YR 4/2 (Dark Grayish Brown).
17	6305	N.III.63.18	4309	Lustrous black in/out. Very well-levigated clay. Infrequent sand-sized white grit and micaceous inclusions. Fabric 10YR 4/3-3/3 (Dark Brown).
18	7606	N.III.76.19	745	Shiny to lustrous black in/out. Sand-sized micaceous inclusions only. Black core to 3 mm. Thin sandwich c. 5YR 4/3 (Reddish Brown) outside of which is c. 5YR 4/2 (Dark Reddish Gray).
19	7613	N.III.76.38	1459a	Shiny black in/out. Well-levigated clay. Infrequent sand-sized white grit and micaceous inclusions. Fabric 10YR 4/3 (Dark Brown)–4/4 (Dark Yellowish Brown).
20	49001	N.I.490.05	752	Shiny black in/out. Well-levigated clay. Infrequent sand-sized white grit and micaceous inclusions. Fabric 7.5 YR 5/4 (Brown) to 5/6 (Strong Brown).
21	49203	NI.492.03	210	Mottled dull black to shiny black in/out. Very well-levigated clay. Infrequent sand-sized white grit and micaceous inclusions. Fabric c. 2.5Y 4/2 (Dark Grayish Brown).
22	6203	N.III.62.12	727a	Lustrous black in/out. Well-levigated clay. White sand-sized grit to 1 mm, very few micaceous inclusions. Fabric between 7.5YR 5/4 (Brown) and 4/3 (Dark Brown).

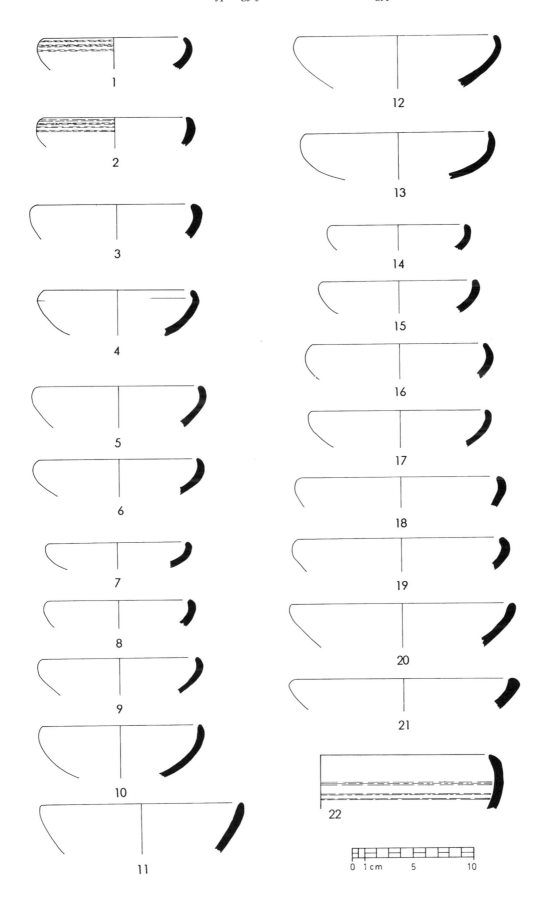

Fig. 2.9

Fig. 2.10.   Pieces of Table Vessels from Kom Hadid

No.	Locus	Pottery bag no.	Field no.	Description
Everted Rim Bowls:				
1	14402	N.III.144.05	982	Delta silt, slipped (Fabric IA)
2	6305	N.III.63.18	4286	Delta silt, slipped (Fabric IIC)
3	7606	N.III.76.19	728	Delta silt, slipped (Fabric IIC)
4	6305	N.III.63.11	4143	Delta silt (Fabric I)
5	7613	N.III.76.44	1542	Delta silt, slipped (Fabric IA)
6	6305	N.III.63.12	4283	Delta silt, slipped (Fabric IA)
7	4803	N.III.48.09	4200	Delta silt, slipped (Fabric IA)
8	7605	N.III.76.10	672	Delta silt, slipped (Fabric IA)
9	4808	N.III.48.11	4125	Delta silt, slipped (Fabric IA)
10	6217	N.III.62.37	3558	Delta silt, slipped (Fabric IA)
11	6305	N.III.63.12	4283	Delta silt, slipped (Fabric IA)
12	7606	N.III.76.19	727	Delta silt, slipped (Fabric IA)
13	7608	N.III.76.28	1112	Delta silt, slipped (Fabric IA)
14	7606	N.III.76.37	1512	Delta silt, slipped (Fabric IA)
15	6203	N.III.62.13	2034	Delta silt, slipped (Fabric IA)
16	7606	N.III.76.23	962	Delta silt, slipped (Fabric IA)
17	6207	N.III.62.22	3246	Delta silt, slipped (Fabric IB)
18	7613	N.III.76.65	3746	Delta silt, slipped (Fabric IB)
19	6209	N.III.62.26	3774	Delta silt, slipped (Fabric IB)
20	7613	N.III.76.70	3277	Delta silt, slipped (Fabric IB)
21	6207	N.III.62.24	4234	Delta silt, slipped (Fabric IB)
22	7613	N.III.76.61	1981	Delta silt, slipped (Fabric IB)
23	6215	N.III.62.38	3975	Delta silt, slipped (Fabric IB)
24	6207	N.III.62.19	3821	Delta silt, slipped (Fabric IB)
25	6203	N.III.62.12	3930	Delta silt, slipped (Fabric IB)

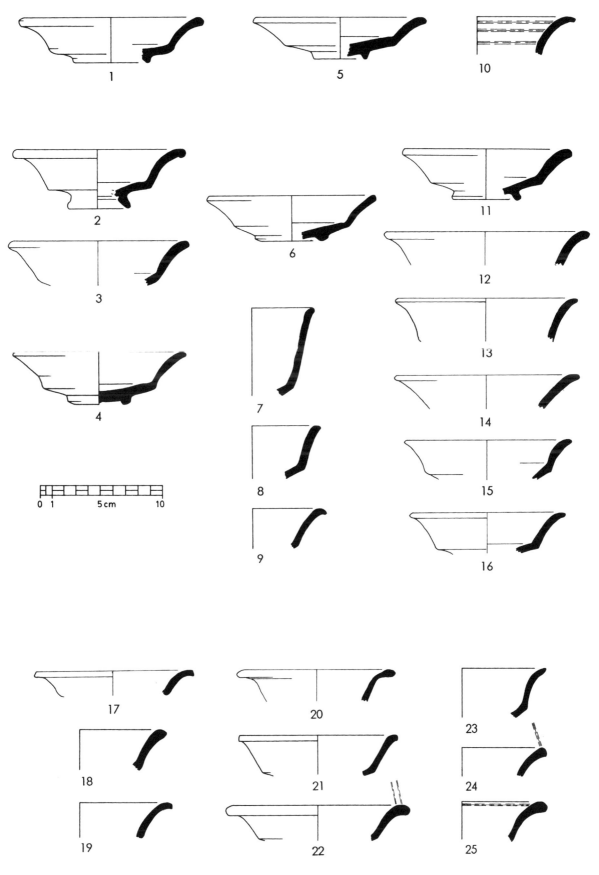

FIG. 2.10

Fig. 2.11.   Pieces of Table Vessels from Kom Hadid

No.	Locus	Pottery bag no.	Field no.	Description
Everted Rim Bowls, Terra Nigra:				
1	6203	N.III.62.42	4082	Dull black in, burnishing strokes on exterior. Well-levigated clay with infrequent sand-sized white grit and micaceous inclusions. Core (thick c. 3 mm) 7.5YR 6/2 (Pinkish Gray). Sandwich (as fabric?) color of exterior unslipped 10YR 5/2 (Grayish Brown)–4/2 (Dark Grayish Brown).
2	62005	N.III.62.46	2017	Lustrous black in/out. Very well-levigated clay. Infrequent sand-sized white grit and micaceous inclusions. Fabric 10YR 4/3–3/3 (Dark Brown).
3	6202	N.III.62.41	4068	Dull black in/ shiny black out. Some mottling to brown. Very well-levigated clay with occasional white grit to 1 mm and sand-sized micaceous inclusions. Fabric between 7.5YR 5/4 (Brown) and 10YR 4/3 (Dark Brown).
4	7606	N.III.76.13	460	Dull black in/shiny black out. Interior mottled to light brown. Red core c. 1 mm.
5	6207	N.III.62.24	3827	Shiny black in/dull black out. Mottled toward 7.5YR 3/2 (Dark Brown) on interior. Very well-levigated clay. Occasional sand-sized white grit and micaceous inclusions. Some fine straw casts. Core 10R 4/4 (Weak Red) almost throughout sandwiched by layer of c. 10YR 4/3 (Dark Brown) 1mm thick.
6	7617	N.III.76.66	3184	Mottled black to gray exterior and from 2.5Y 5/2 (Grayish Brown) to 10YR 5/3 (Brown) on interior. Core 10R 5/3 (Weak Red) with double sandwich: 10YR 4/2 (Dark Grayish Brown) outside 5YR 4/6 (Yellowish Red).
7	6305	N.III.63.18	4308	Shiny black in/out, exterior mottled to 10YR 3/3 (Brown).
8	7617	N.III.76.66	3014	Interior mottled black to 10YR 5/2 (Grayish Brown). Core 7.5 YR 5/4 (Brown).
9	1010	N.I.1.11	72	Shiny to lustrous black in/out. Very well-levigated clay, occasional sand size white grit and micaceous inclusions. Fabric c. 10YR–3/3 (Dark Brown), with 5YR 4/8 (Red) sandwich around gray core. (Fabric TN-4C).
10	7606	N.III.76.19	3812	Dull black in/out. Very well-levigated clay. Fabric 10YR 4/2 (Dark Grayish Brown) to 4/3 (Dark Brown), with 2 mm core c. 5YR 6/2 (Pinkish Gray).
11	6203	N.III.62.12	4328	Dull black in/out. Well-levigated clay. Sand-sized (rarely to 1 mm) white grit, and sand-sized mica. Fabric (below surfaces) 10YR 4/2 (Dark Grayish Brown) with sandwich of 2.5YR 4/6 (Red) on either side of thin (1 mm) light gray core.
12	13007	N.III.130.11	3918	Black mottled to brown in places; shiny in/out. Red sandwich around gray core.
13	6207	N.III.62.19	3815	Very dull black in/out. Light gray core c. 2 mm sandwiched by 7.5YR 4/2 (Dark Brown) fabric.
14	6209	N.III.62.14	2067	Shiny to lustrous black in/out. Very well-levigated clay, occasional sand size white grit and micaceous inclusions. Fabric 10YR 4/3–3/3 (Dark Brown) to black below exterior surface.
15	6205	N.III.62.46	4166	Lustrous black in/out. Very well-levigated clay. Infrequent sand-sized white grit and fine straw casts, occasional sand-sized micaceous inclusions. Core 10YR 4/2 (Dark Grayish Brown). Horizontal burnishing or paddling marks out.
16	7613	N.III.76.46	1882	Black in/out. Core c. 5YR 4/3 (Reddish Brown). Import.
17	6305	N.III.63.18	4308	Shiny black in/out. Very well-levigated clay. Infrequent sand-sized white grit and micaceous inclusions. Fabric 10YR 4/3–3/3 (Dark Brown).
18	6207	N.III.62.19	3812	Shiny black in/out. Well-levigated clay. Infrequent sand-sized white grit and micaceous inclusions. Fabric 10YR 4/3-3/3 (Dark Brown).
19	6305	N.III.63.11	4136	Shiny black in/out. Very well-levigated clay. Occasional sand-sized white grit and frequent sand-sized micaceous inclusions. Fabric/core 10YR 4/3 (Dark Brown) in center gradually darkening to 4/2 (Dark Grayish Brown) beneath slip.
20	6209	N.III.62.35	3659	Shiny black in/shiny to lustrous black out. Well-levigated clay. Infrequent sand-sized white grit and micaceous inclusions. Fabric 10YR 4/3 (Dark Brown)–4/4 (Dark Yellowish Brown).
21	6201	N.III.62.01	1852	Fabric 3. Shiny in/out. Very well-levigated clay. Occasional sand-sized micaceous inclusions and fine straw casts. Dark gray fabric.
22	6201	N.III.62.06	3137	Fabric 3. Shiny in/out. Very well-levigated clay. Occasional sand-sized micaceous inclusions and fine straw casts. Dark gray fabric.
23	6302	N.III.63.03	3549	Fabric 3. Shiny to lustrous in/out. Very well-levigated clay. Occasional sand-sized micaceous inclusions. Dark gray core
24	6302	N.III.63.03	3548	Dull to shiny black in/out. Thick core and fabric as #4136. Thin gray sandwich below both surfaces.
25	6304	N.III.63.05	3711	Dull black exterior. Most of interior fired(?) to 10YR 4/2 (Dark Grayish Brown). Very well-levigated clay. Occasional sand-sized grit and micaceous inclusions. A few very fine straw casts. Fabric/core between 10YR 4/3 and 3/3 (Dark Brown).

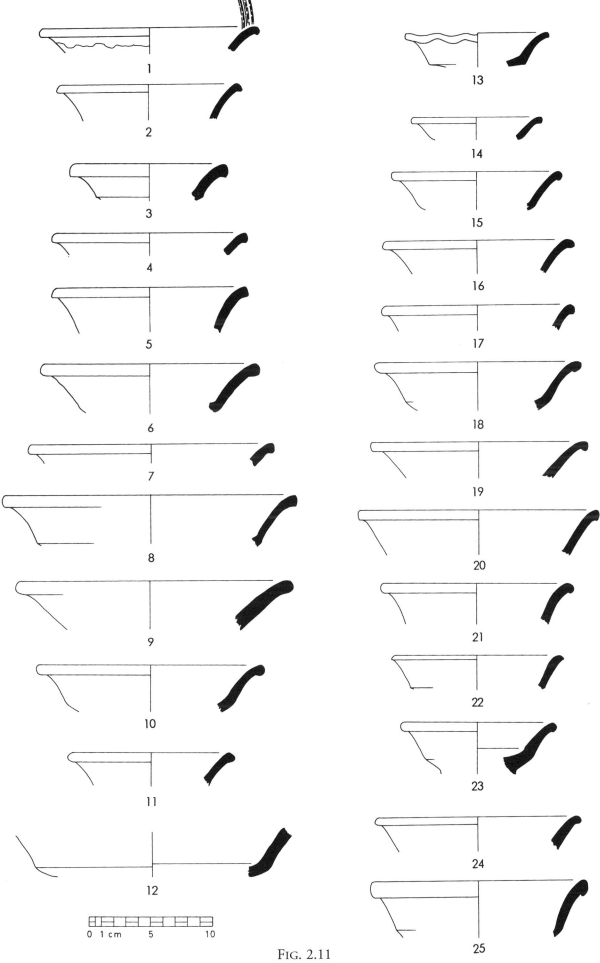

F<small>IG</small>. 2.11

0 1 cm 5 10

Fig. 2.12. Pieces of Table Vessels from Kom Hadid

No.	Locus	Pottery bag no.	Field no.	Description
Hemispherical Bowls:				
1	6205	N.III.62.15	3839	Shiny to lustrous black in/out. Very well-levigated clay. Occasional sand-sized grit. Fabric 10YR 4/3–3/3 (Dark Brown) to black below exterior surface.
2	7613	N.III.76.61	1982	Fabric: Mineral-tempered Red Ware with exterior slip and interior: 5YR 8/4 (Pink). Out: 7.5YR 4/2–4/4 (Weak Red). (Fabric X variant).
Carinated Cups:				
3	—		3141	Shiny black out, dull black in. Well-levigated clay with occasional white grit to 1mm and sand-sized micaceous inclusions. Fabric c. 10YR 3/2 (Very Dark Grayish Brown) with 3 mm core of 2.5YR 6/2 (Pale Red). Fabric TN-4C.
4	13006	N.III.130.17	1974	Lustrous black in/out. Very well-levigated clay. Occasional sand-sized white grit and micaceous inclusions. Core 10YR 4/2 (Dark Grayish Brown) to gray.
5	7606	N.III.76.13	463	Fabric 3. Shiny in/out. Very well-levigated clay. Occasional sand-sized micaceous inclusions and fine straw casts. Dark gray throughout.
6	6203	N.III.62.07	3841	Delta silt, slipped (Fabric IA).
7	7606	N.III.76.13	486	Well-levigated clay with infrequent white and red grit c. 1 mm and fine straw casts. Fabric: 5YR 6/8–8/8 (Reddish Yellow). Interior surface as fabric. Exterior surface slipped 10YR 8/3–8/4 (Very Pale Brown).
8	7603	N.III.76.05	335	Very well-levigated clay with occasional white and gray grit to 1 mm and sand-sized micaceous inclusions. Fabric 7.5YR 7/6 (Reddish Yellow). Sherd abraded but looks as if unslipped.

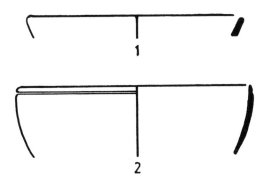

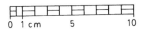

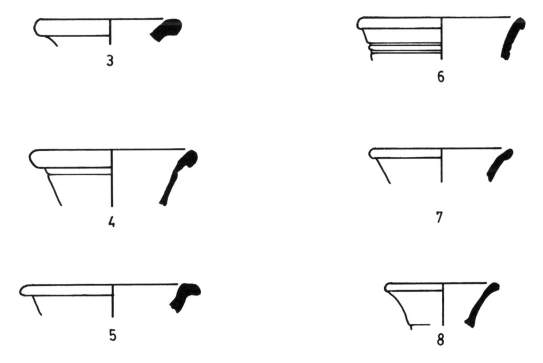

FIG. 2.12

Fig. 2.13.   Pieces of Table Vessels from Kom Hadid

No.	Locus	Pottery bag no.	Field no.	Description
Bowls/Cups Feet:				
1	7605	N.III.76.10	685	Delta silt, slipped (Fabric IA)
2	7613	N.III.76.61	1984	Delta silt, slipped (Fabric IA)
3	6209	N.III.62.33	3396	Delta silt, slipped (Fabric IA)
4	6302	N.III.63.03	3522	Delta silt, slipped (Fabric IA)
5	—	N.III.62.44	4243	Delta silt, slipped (Fabric IA)
6	6203	N.III.62.13	2023	Delta silt, slipped (Fabric IA)
7	7608	N.III.76.43	1652	Delta silt, slipped (Fabric IA)
8	6202	N.III.62.04	1843	Delta silt, slipped (Fabric IA)
9	7603	N.III.76.05	354	Delta silt, slipped (Fabric IA)
10	6304	N.III.63.05	3675	Delta silt, slipped (Fabric IA)
11	7602	N.III.76.03	236	Delta silt, slipped (Fabric IA)
12	7604	N.III.76.08	424	Delta silt, slipped (Fabric IA)
13	—	N.III.76.58	3353	Delta silt, slipped (Fabric IA)
14	7603	N.III.76.05	358	Delta silt, slipped (Fabric IA)
15	7605	N.III.76.55	1796	Delta silt, slipped (Fabric IA)
16	7605	N.III.76.55	1797	Delta silt, slipped (Fabric IA)
17	7608	N.III.76.33	1309	Delta silt, slipped (Fabric IA)
18	7610	N.III.76.51	2033	Delta silt (Fabric II)
19	6303	N.III.63.07	3954	Delta silt (Fabric II)
20	6304	N.III.63.05	255	Delta silt (Fabric II)
21	4808	N.III.48.11	397	Delta silt (Fabric II)
22	7608	N.III.76.28	1119	Delta silt, slipped (Fabric IB)
23	7603	N.III.76.16	797	Delta silt, slipped (Fabric IB)
24	7603	N.III.76.22	888	Delta silt, slipped (Fabric IB)
25	6202	N.III.62.06	3111	Delta silt, slipped (Fabric IB)
26	7602	N.III.76.03	237	Delta silt, slipped (Fabric IX variant)
27	6304	N.III.63.09	3455	Delta silt, slipped. Bottom only slipped c. 10YR 8/3–8/4 (Very Pale Brown). (Fabric IX variant).
28	7603	N.III.76.05	394	Delta silt, slipped. 10YR 8/2 (White)–8/3 (Very Pale Brown) slip in/out. (Fabric IX variant).
29	7603	N.III.76.50	1759	Delta silt, slipped. Very Pale Brown slip in/out. (Fabric IX variant).
30	7605	N.III.76.55	1830	Delta silt, slipped. Very Pale Brown/ Pink slip out and bottom. (Fabric IX variant).
31	7603	N.III.76.05	347	Delta silt, slipped. Interior plain and exterior covered with white slip (no Munsell). (Fabric IX variant).
32	7603	N.III.76.20	924	Delta silt, slipped. Lustrous slip on exterior: 10YR 8.3 (Very Pale Brown). (Fabric IX variant).
33	7605	N.III.76.29	736	Delta silt, slipped. White slip out and bottom only: 10YR 8/3–8/4 (Very Pale Brown). (Fabric IX variant).
34	6215	N.III.62.38	3966	Delta silt, slipped). Slip out only, where thin: 10YR 8/2 (White)–8/3 (Very Pale Brown); where thicker: 5YR 8/3–8/4 (Pink). (Fabric IX variant).
35	7609	N.III.76.27	1172	Delta silt, slipped. White slip out only: 10YR 8/3–8/4 (Very Pale Brown). (Fabric IX variant).
36	6203	N.III.62.12	3939	Delta silt, slipped. White slip out only: 10YR 8/3–8/4 (Very Pale Brown). (Fabric IX variant).
37	13006	N.III.130.17	1970	Delta silt, slipped. Slip out only: c. 10YR 8/3–8/4 (Very Pale Brown). (Fabric IX variant).

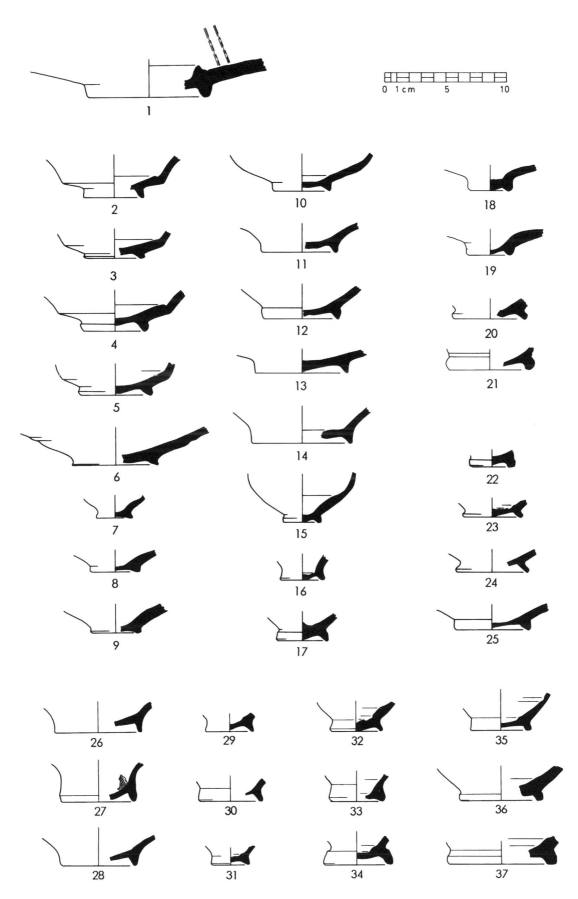

FIG. 2.13

FIG. 2.13

Fig. 2.14.   *Pieces of Table Vessels from Kom Hadid*

No.	Locus	Pottery bag no.	Field no.	Description
Terra Nigra Bowls/Cups Feet:				
1	—	N.III.76.11	3793	Shiny to lustrous black in/out. Very well-levigated clay, occasional sand-sized white and micaceous inclusions. Fabric 2.5YR 6/6 (Light Red) fired to 5YR 7/4 (Pink) just below surfaces.
2	6304	N.III.63.07	3739	Dull black in/out. Frequent sand-sized white and micaceous inclusions. Fabric 10YR 4/3 (Dark Brown). Joins with 2730.
3	6207	N.III.62.22	3233	Shiny black in/out. Very well-levigated clay. Occasional sand-sized white, and infrequent micaceous inclusions. A few fine straw casts. Core 2.5YR 5/4 (Reddish Brown). Fabric 5YR 4/6 (Yellowish Red).
4	6215	N.III.62.38	3996	Shiny black in/out; interior mottled to brown. Very well-levigated clay. Infrequent white grit and fine straw casts. Thin core (1–2 mm) c. 10YR 6/4 (Light Yellow Brown). Fabric c. 10R 4/6 (Red). Thin (less than 1 mm) layer of "brown" 5YR 4/6 (Yellow Red) below surfaces.
5	6304	N.III.63.09	3482	Shiny black in/out; interior mottled c. 5YR 3/2–3/3 (Dark Reddish Brown). Very well-levigated clay, occasional sand-sized white grit and micaceous inclusions. Medium gray fabric.
6	4805	N.III.48.06	4060	Exterior mottled black to brown. Core (to 3 mm wide in foot and 5 mm in vessel wall) from 5YR 5/2 (Reddish Gray) to 5YR 5/3 (Reddish Brown).
7	6304	N.III.63.07	3735	Shiny black interior, dull black exterior. Very well-levigated clay. White sand-sized grit and fine straw casts. Fabric 10YR 3/2 (Very Dark Grayish Brown).
8	6209	N.III.62.39	3565	Shiny black in/out. Very well-levigated clay. Infrequent sand-sized white grit and micaceous inclusions. Fabric 10R 4/2 (Dark Grayish Brown)–4/3 (Dark Brown).
9	7606	N.III.76.19	743	Shiny black in, lustrous black out. Very well-levigated clay. Sand-sized white grit and a few fine straw casts. Fabric 10YR 4/3 (Dark Brown). Joins with 746.
10	6209	N.III.62.32	2049	Dull black in/out. Very well-levigated clay. Infrequent sand-sized white grit and micaceous inclusions. Fabric 10YR 4/3 (Dark Brown) with 2–3 mm core of 2.5YR 5/2–5/3 (Weak Red).
11	7609	N.III.76.19	742	Dull black out; shiny black in. Fabric 5YR 3/4 (Dark Reddish Brown)–3/6 (Dark Red). Import.
12	6305	N.III.63.18	4275	Shiny black in, shiny to lustrous black out. Very well-levigated clay. Sand-sized white grit and micaceous inclusions, infrequent red grit to c. 1 mm. Fabric 10YR 4/2 (Dark Grayish Brown).
13	7608	N.III.76.28	1177	Lustrous black in/out. Very well-levigated clay. Sand-sized white grit and some fine straw casts. Fabric 10YR 4/3 (Dark Brown).
14	6217	N.III.62.40	3427	Shiny black in/out. Slightly mottled to brown on exterior. Very well-levigated clay. Occasional sand-sized white grit and frequent micaceous inclusions. Fabric 10YR 4/2 (Dark Grayish Brown)–4/3 (Dark Brown).
15	6305	N.III.63.12	4269	Shiny to lustrous black in/out. Very well-levigated clay. Occasional white grit and some fine straw casts. Fabric 10YR 4/2 (Dark Grayish Brown).
16	6207	N.III.62.19	3813	Shiny black in, lustrous black out. Very well-levigated clay. Sand-sized white grit and a few fine straw casts. Fabric 10YR 5/3 (Brown)–4/3 (Dark Brown).

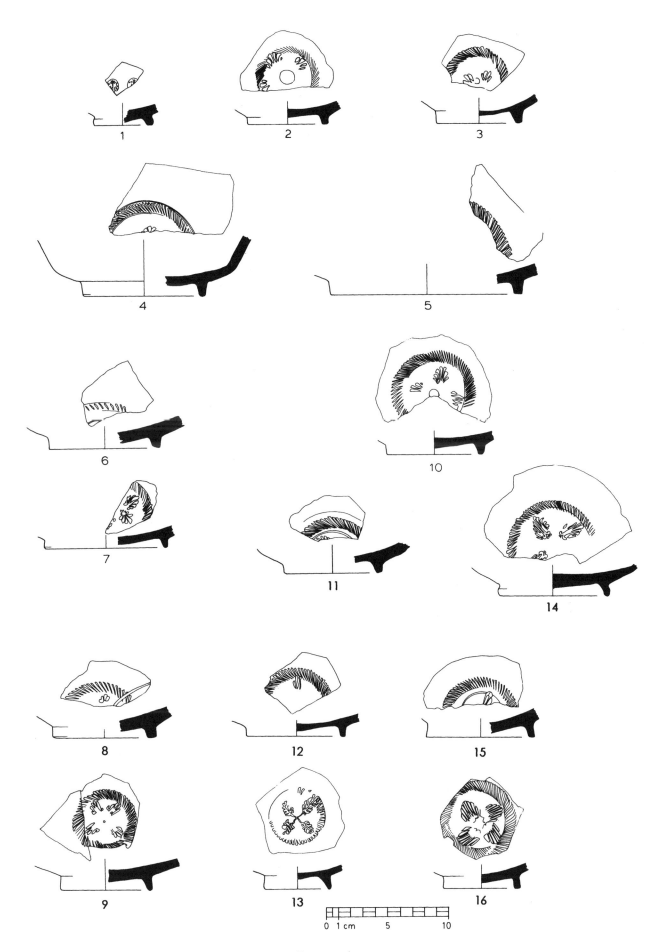

FIG. 2.14

Fig. 2.15. Pieces of Table Vessels from Kom Hadid

No.	Locus	Pottery bag no.	Field no.	Description
Terra Nigra and Imported Bowls/Cups Feet:				
1	6209	N.III.62.33	3417	Shiny in/out. Very well-levigated clay. Occasional sand-sized micaceous inclusions and fine straw casts. Dark gray fabric. (Fabric TN-3).
2	31514	N.I.315.50	684	Dull in/out. Interior unslipped(?). Well-levigated clay. Occasional sand-sized micaceous inclusions and fine straw casts. Dark gray throughout. (Fabric TN-3).
3	6206	N.III.62.06	3140	Shiny in/out. Very well-levigated clay. Occasional sand-sized micaceous inclusions and fine straw casts. Dark gray fabric. (Fabric TN-3).
4	6302	N.III.63.03	3547	Shiny in/out. Very well-levigated clay. Occasional sand-sized micaceous inclusions and fine straw casts. Dark gray fabric. (Fabric TN-3).
5	6207	N.III.62.19	3294	Dull black in/out. Well-levigated clay. Sand-sized white grit and micaceous inclusions. Thin gray core sandwiched by 10YR 5/2 (Grayish Brown).
6	6207	N.III.62.19	3814	Lustrous black in/out. Very well-levigated clay. Sand-sized white grit and micaceous inclusions. Light gray core to 3 mm sandwiched with 7.5YR 4/2 (Dark Brown) fabric.
7	6305	N.III.63.12	4267	Dull black in/out. Well-levigated clay. Sand-sized micaceous inclusions (only). Thin (c. 2 mm) core c. 10YR 6/1 (Gray) sandwiched by 10YR 5/2 13.
8	7606	N.III.76.14	841	Very well-levigated clay with occasional fine straw casts. Fabric 7.5YR 7/2 (Pinkish Gray)–7/4 (Pink). Core (2 mm) c. 2.5YR 6/6 (Light Red). Slip out and bottom between 2.5Y 8/2 (White)–8/4 (Pale Yellow). Interior surface as core. Import.
9	6202	N.III.62.06	3126	Well-levigated clay with white grit sand-sized to 1 mm. Fabric c. 2.5YR 6/6 (Light Red). Slip in/out 7.5YR 8/2 (Pinkish White)– 8/4 (Pink). Import?
10	7604	N.III.76.24	938	Very well-levigated clay with occasional sand-sized white grit and micaceous inclusions. Fabric 7.5YR 7/6–6/6 (Reddish Yellow). Surfaces (slipped?) 5YR 7/6–6/6 (Reddish Yellow). Painted band 10R 5/8–4/8 (Red). Import?
11	7606	N.III.76.37	1526	Well-levigated clay with frequent white grit sand-sized to 1 mm and occasional sand-sized micaceous inclusions. Core/fabric 5YR 6/6–6/8 (Reddish Yellow). Slip in/out c. 2.5Y 8/2 (White). Import?
12	7601	N.III.76.02	268	Well-levigated clay with sand-sized micaceous inclusions, sand-sized red and gray grit, and infrequent fine straw casts. Core/fabric/ interior surface: 5YR 7/6 (Reddish Yellow). Exterior surface streaky slip 7.5YR 8/2 (Pinkish White)–8/4 (Pink). Import?
13	6207	N.III.62.19	3292	Very well-levigated clay with occasional sand-sized micaceous inclusions. Core (thin) 2.5YR 4/6 (Red). Fabric gray. Lustrous black out, dark in. Import.
14	7601	N.III.76.15	768	Extremely well-levigated clay with occasional sand-sized micaceous inclusions. Core (thin) 2.5YR N4/ (Dark Gray). Fabric/ sandwich 5YR 4/2 (Dark Reddish Gray). Lustrous black in/out. Import.
15	7605	N.III.76.55	1801	Very well-levigated clay with occasional sand-sized micaceous inclusions only. Core/fabric 5YR 6/6 (Reddish Yellow) on unburnt side; c. 2.5YR 6/6 (Light Red) on burnt side. Slip out c. 2.5Y 8/2 (White). Interior fired (secondarily) black. Very hard (primary) fired traces of secondary burning int. Import?
16	13006	N.III.130.10	1887	Well-levigated clay with sand-sized to 1 mm red and white grit. Core (slight) c. 5YR 7/4 (Pink). Interior/exterior surfaces and outer parts of fabric between 2.5YR 8/2 (White)–8/4 (Pale Yellow). Import?
17	7619	N.III.76.72	3198	Well-levigated clay with white and red grit sand-sized to occasionally 1 mm and sand-sized micaceous inclusions. Core/fabric 10YR 7/4 (Very Pale Brown). Slip in/out 10YR 8/4 (Very Pale Brown). Import?
18	7606	N.III.76.36	1475	Extremely well-levigated clay with occasional sand-sized white grit, rare sand-sized red grit, and a few fine straw casts. Fabric 5YR 7/6 (Reddish Yellow). Interior surface unslipped as fabric. Exterior surface thin 10YR 8/3–8/4 (Very Pale Brown). Import.
19	6304	N.III.63.09	3461	Exceptionally well-levigated clay with occasional sand-sized micaceous inclusions only. Fabric between 5YR 7/6 (Reddish Yellow)–7.5YR 7/6 (Reddish Yellow). Interior surface as fabric. Slip out (thin) 10YR 8/2 (White)–8/3 (Very Pale Brown). Import.
20	7605	N.III.76.55	1837	Dull black in/out. Traces of horizontal burnishing (lustrous) bands on exterior. Very well-levigated clay. Sand-sized white grit and micaceous inclusions. Gray core with sandwich of 7.5YR 5/2–5/4 (Brown).
21	—	N.I.76.33	1315	Dull black in/out. Well-levigated clay. Sand-sized white grit and micaceous inclusions. Thin gray core sandwiched by 10YR 5/2 (Grayish Brown).
22	7608	N.III.76.31	1045	Very well-levigated clay with infrequent white grit to 1 mm Core/fabric c. 5YR 6/6 (Reddish Yellow). Slipped? Import.
23	7609	N.III.76.27	1158	Well-levigated clay with sand-sized to 1 mm white grit and some fine straw casts. Core c. 5YR 6/6 (Reddish Yellow). Surfaces (not slipped?) between 7.5YR 7/4 (Pink)–7/6 (Reddish Yellow). Import?
24	7617	N.III.76.66	3178	Very well-levigated clay with white grit and micaceous inclusions sand-sized to occasionally 1 mm Fabric/core/surfaces between 5YR 7/6 (Reddish Yellow).
25	13007	N.III.130.14	3102	Very well-levigated clay with no trace of temper except sand-sized micaceous inclusions. Fabric/interior surface 7.5YR 7/6–6/6 (Reddish Yellow). Slip out c. 5YR 6/6 (Reddish Yellow). Greek.
26	6202	N.III.62.11	1994	Shiny black interior and exterior. Mottled from black through 5YR 3/4 (Dark Reddish Brown) to 5YR 5/4 (Reddish Brown). Moderately well-levigated clay. Core 7.5YR 5/4 (Brown) to gray sandwiched by layer of 5YR 5/1 (Light Gray) and a layer of 5YR 3/3 (Dark Reddish Brown).
27	7608	N.III.76.33	1321	Very well-levigated clay with no trace of temper. Fabric between 5YR 7/4 (Pink)–7/6 (Reddish Yellow). Slip in/out 2.5Y 8/2 (White)–8/4 (Pale Yellow). Import?
28	7613	N.III.76.65	3748	Fabric/core 7.5YR 8/4 (Pink). Slip in/out 5Y 8/1–8/2 (White). Import.
29	6304	N.III.63.09	3475	Very well-levigated clay with sand-sized micaceous inclusions and occasional white grit sand-sized to 1 mm. Fabric/interior surface c. 7.5YR 8/4 (Pink). Exterior traces of slip 5YR 5/4 (Reddish Brown) mottled to 5YR 3/2 (Dark Reddish Brown). Import.
30	7605	N.III.76.55	1821	Very well-levigated clay with frequent sand-sized white grit. Fabric/surfaces 5YR 7/6–6/6 (Reddish Yellow). Import.
31	49101	N.I.491.47	4349	Shiny black in/out. 10YR 4/3.
32	6303	N.III.63.04	3457	Very well-levigated clay with sand-sized mica, occasional white grit (c. 1 mm), and some fine straw casts. Fabric 7.5YR 6/6 (Reddish Yellow). Interior surface 5YR 7/4 (Pink)–7/6 (Reddish Yellow). Exterior surface 7.5YR 8/4 (Pink)–8/6 (Reddish Yellow). Slipped with 5YR 5/3 (Reddish Brown)–3/3 (Dark Reddish Brown). Finger splotches on exterior of base where held when pot was dipped.

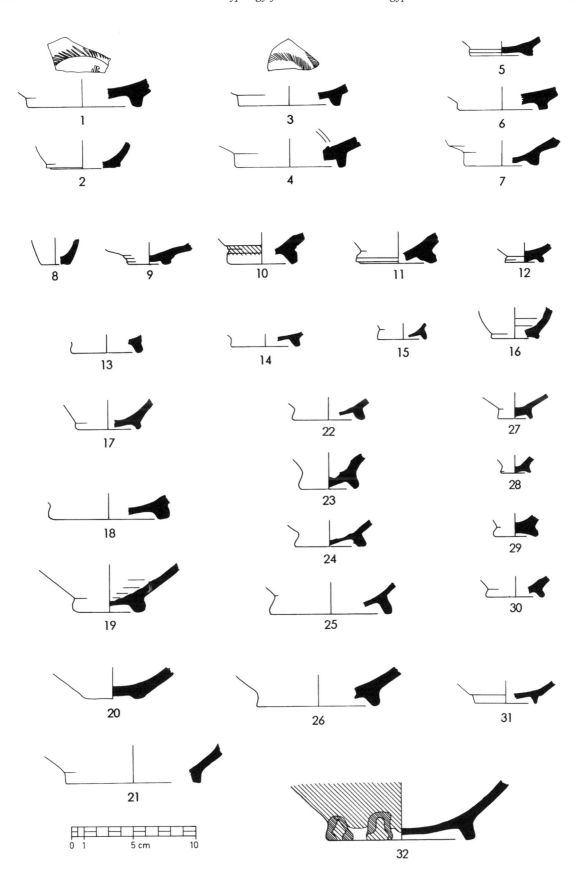

FIG. 2.15

Fig. 2.16.   Pieces of Cooking Vessels from Kom Hadid

No.	Locus	Pottery bag no.	Field no.	Description
Angled Rim Cooking Pots:				
1	7608	N.III.76.42	1610	Delta silt, slipped (Fabric IB)
2	—	N.III.62.44	4230	Delta silt, slipped (Fabric IB)
3	13002	N.III.130.04	1427	Delta silt, slipped (Fabric IIC)
4	6207	N.III.62.19	3306	Delta silt, slipped (Fabric IA)
5	7613	N.III.76.64	2095	Delta silt, slipped (Fabric IB)
6	13002	N.III.130.04	1328	Delta silt, slipped (Fabric IB)
7	7613	N.III.76.70	3282	Delta silt (Fabric I)
8	6304	N.III.63.09	3454	Delta silt (Fabric I)
Angled Rim Cooking Pots, Variants:				
9	6305	N.III.63.12	3218	Delta silt, slipped (Fabric IA)
10	6203	N.III.62.05	178	Delta silt, slipped (Fabric IA)
11	6304	N.III.63.07	1809	Delta silt, slipped (Fabric IA)
12	7617	N.III.76.68	496	Delta silt, slipped (Fabric IA)
13	7613	N.III.76.46	1881	Delta silt, slipped (Fabric IIC)
14	7603	N.III.76.05	368	Delta silt, slipped (Fabric IA)
15	7603	N.III.76.50	1754	Delta silt, slipped (Fabric IA)
16	7604	N.III.76.25	1297	Delta silt, slipped (Fabric IA)
17	13006	N.III.130.20	3024	Delta silt (Fabric I), Traces of a handle attached below rim

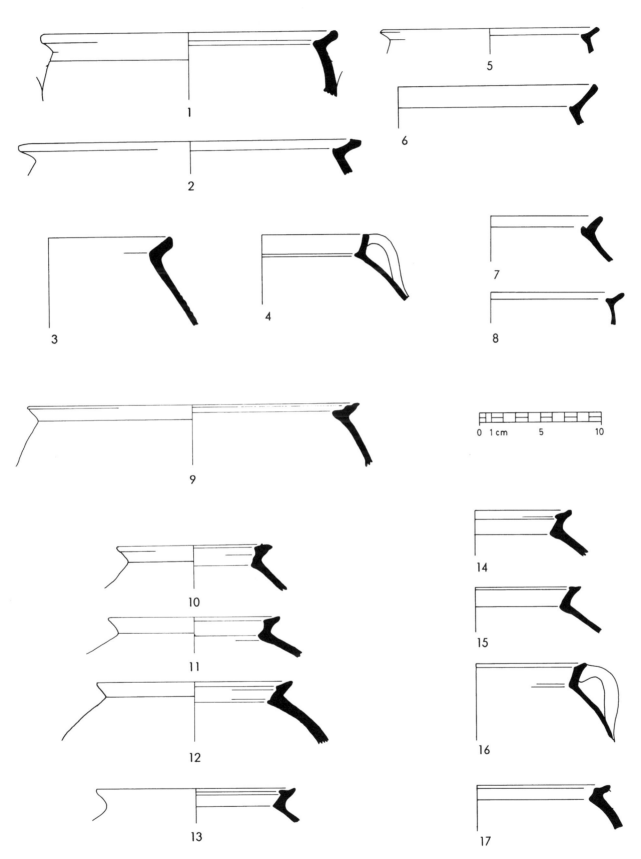

FIG. 2.16

Fig. 2.17. Pieces of Cooking Vessels from Kom Hadid

No.	Locus	Pottery bag no.	Field no.	Description
Small Ledge Rim Cooking Pots:				
1	7608	N.III.76.28	1118	Delta silt, slipped (Fabric IA)
2	6203	N.III.62.05	1944	Delta silt, slipped (Fabric IA)
3	6304	N.III.63.09	3440	Delta silt, slipped (Fabric IA)
4	6305	N.III.63.18	4317	Delta silt, slipped (Fabric IB)
5	6201	N.III.62.01	1851	Delta silt, slipped (Fabric IA)
6	6202	N.III.62.06	3138	Delta silt, slipped (Fabric IA)
7	6304	N.III.63.05	3684	Delta silt, slipped (Fabric IA)
8	6304	N.III.63.07	3734	Delta silt, slipped (Fabric IA)
9	6215	N.III.62.38	873	Delta silt, slipped (Fabric IIB)
10	6203	N.III.62.12	3927	Delta silt, slipped (Fabric IB)
Plain Rim Cooking Pots:				
11	6304	N.III.63.08	3849	Delta silt, slipped. (Fabric IX variant). Exterior abraded white slip. Interior slipped white at top (no good Munsell) and 5YR 7/4 (Pink)–7/6 (Reddish Yellow).
12	7605	N.III.76.09	450	Delta silt, slipped (Fabric IE, variant). Int/ext slipped c. 10YR 8/3 (Very Pale Brown) "mottled" (or fired ?) to 5YR 7/3 (Pink), carried over rim and allowed to drip down side. Very fugitive band of c. 5YR 7/6 (Reddish Yellow) paint at neck.
13	7613	N.III.76.59	1963	Delta silt, slipped (Fabric IB).
14	7610	N.III.76.56	3162	Delta silt, slipped (Fabric IE, variant). 5YR 8/4–7/4 (Pink) slip on exterior and over rim on interior. Stripe of 10R 4/4 (Weak Red) on exterior.
15	6209	N.III.62.32	3640	Very well-levigated clay with no trace of temper. Fabric/surfaces c. 5Y 8/3–8/4 (Pale Yellow). Stripe out c. 5YR 4/2 (Dark Reddish Gray)–5YR 4/3 (Reddish Brown). Import.
16	7610	N.III.76.51	1719	Very well-levigated clay with no trace of temper. Fabric 7.5YR 8/4 (Pink). Slip in/out 10YR 8/2 (White). 3 bands. Band 1 & 2 5YR 6/6 (Reddish Yellow) (possibly thinner version of band 3). Band 3 5YR 4/2 (Dark Reddish Gray)–4/3 (Reddish Brown). Import.
17	6209	N.III.62.33	3404	Fabric not described. Painted bands. Band 1: between 10YR 8/2 (White)–5YR 8/4 (Pink). Band 2: c. 7.5R 5/4–4/4 (Weak Red).
18	6209	N.III.62.33	3405	Delta silt, slipped, (Fabric ID). Traces of band of c. 10R 5/2–4/2 (Weak Red) painted on exterior.
19	7613	N.III.76.64	2090	Delta silt, slipped (Fabric ID). Stripe of c. 10R 5/2–4/2 (Weak Red) painted on exterior.
20	6307	N.III.63.07	3721	Delta silt, slipped (Fabric ID). Red slip and band of 7.5R 5/2–4/2 (Weak Red) painted at neck.
21	7606	N.III.76.23	952	Delta silt, slipped (Fabric ID). Painted band of 7.5R 4/2 (Weak Red) at neck.
22	7608	N.III.76.28	1123	Delta silt, slipped (Fabric ID). Band c. 7.5R 5/2–4/2 (Weak Red) painted at neck.
23	6215	N.III.62.38	3963	Delta silt, slipped (Fabric ID variant). Painted 7.5R 5/2–4/2 (Weak Red) stripe at neck and over rim.
24	6205	N.III.62.46	4177	Delta silt, slipped (Fabric IA variant). Exterior band of 10R 4/1–3/1 (Dark Reddish Gray).

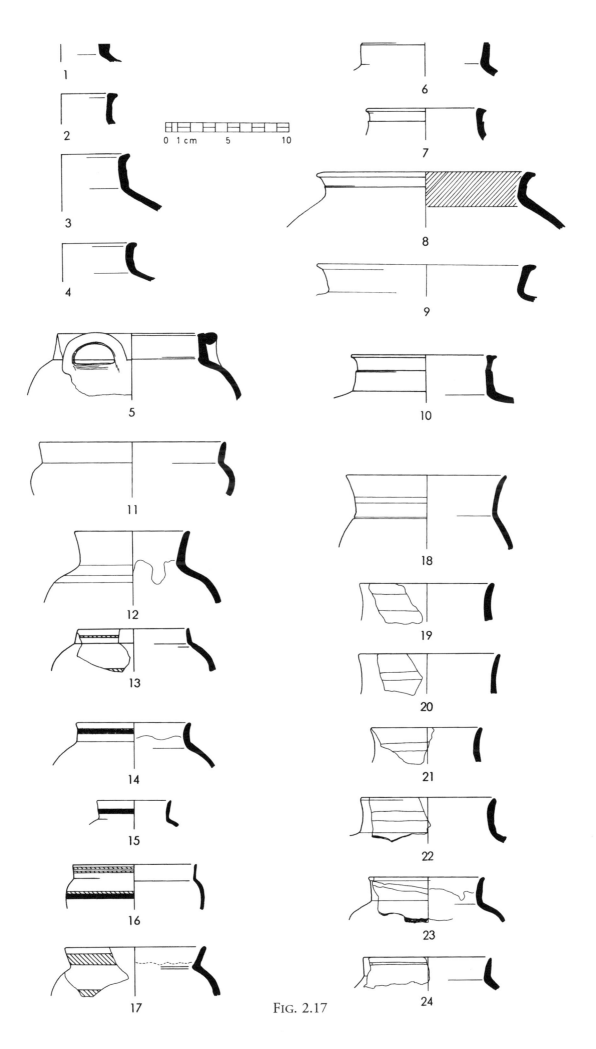

FIG. 2.17

Andrea M. Berlin

Fig. 2.18.   Pieces of Cooking Vessels from Kom Hadid

No.	Locus	Pottery bag no.	Field no.	Description
Tall Ledge Rim Cooking Pots:				
1	6215	N.III.62.38	3960	Delta silt, slipped (Fabric IA)
2	6202	N.III.62.06	3125	Delta silt, slipped (Fabric IA)
3	6203	N.III.62.13	2014	Delta silt, slipped (Fabric IA)
4	6210	N.III.62.43	4051	Delta silt, slipped (Fabric IA)
5	7606	N.III.76.23	957	Delta silt, slipped (Fabric IIC)
6	7613	N.III.76.41	1556	Delta silt, slipped (Fabric IIC)
7	13001	N.III.130.01	1140	Delta silt, slipped (Fabric IIC)
8	4803	N.III.48.09	4216	Delta silt, slipped (Fabric IIC)
9	7617	N.III.76.68	3021	Delta silt, slipped (Fabric IIC)
10	6304	N.III.63.07	3732	Delta silt, slipped (Fabric IA)
11	7605	N.III.76.10	667	Delta silt, slipped (Fabric IA)
12	6202	N.III.62.06	3114	Delta silt, slipped (Fabric IA)
13	7605	N.III.76.09	438	Delta silt, slipped (Fabric IA)
14	14401	N.III.144.14	1097	Delta silt, slipped (Fabric IA)
15	6203	N.III.62.05	1937	Delta silt, slipped (Fabric IA)
16	7608	N.III.76.33	1305	Delta silt, slipped (Fabric IA)
17	6209	N.III.62.33	3398	Delta silt, slipped (Fabric IA)
18	7606	N.III.76.19	725	Delta silt, slipped (Fabric IA)
19	6215	N.III.62.47	4228	Delta silt, slipped (Fabric IA)
20	7605	N.III.76.30	1026	Delta silt, slipped (Fabric IA)
21	6203	N.III.62.13	2038	Delta silt, slipped (Fabric IA)
22	7606	N.III.76.19	718	Delta silt, slipped (Fabric IA)

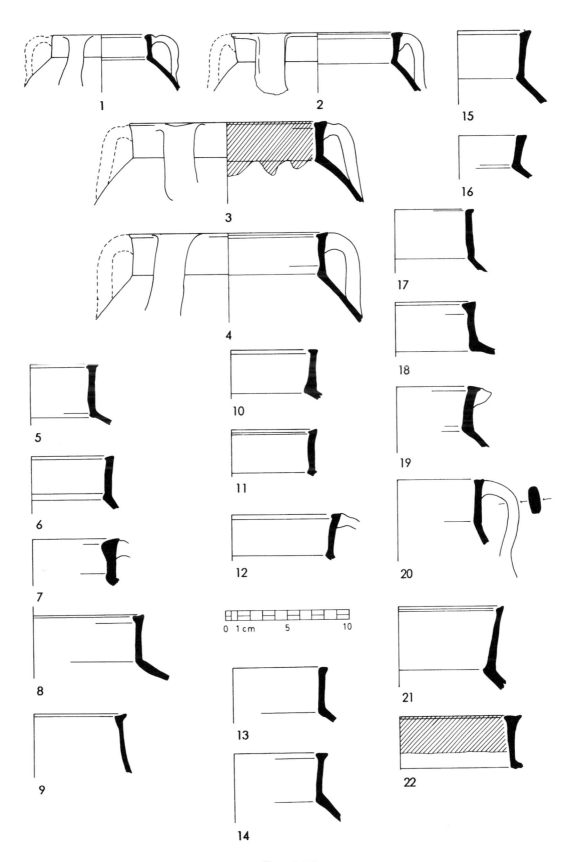

FIG. 2.18

Fig. 2.19.   Pieces of Cooking Vessels from Kom Hadid

No.	Locus	Pottery bag no.	Field no.	Description
Ledge/Folded Lip Stew Pots:				
1	6203	N.III.62.07	3088	Delta silt, slipped (Fabric IB)
2	6215	N.III.62.47	4227	Delta silt, slipped (Fabric IB)
3	6203	N.III.62.12	3932	Delta silt, slipped (Fabric IB)
4	6203	N.III.62.42	3823	Delta silt (Fabric I)
5	4803	N.III.48.09	4211	Delta silt (Fabric I)
6	6202	N.III.62.18	4035	Delta silt (Fabric I)
7	7610	N.III.76.51	1709	Delta silt (Fabric I)
8	6303	N.III.62.07	3094	Delta silt (Fabric I)
9	7617	N.III.76.68	3012	Delta silt (Fabric I)
10	7603	N.III.76.50	1760	Delta silt (Fabric I)
11	6304	N.III.63.05	3702	Delta silt (Fabric I)
12	7601	N.III.76.17	857	Delta silt (Fabric I)
13	4808	N.III.48.11	4127	Delta silt (Fabric I)
14	7613	N.III.76.70	868	Delta silt, slipped (Fabric IIB)
15	6203	N.III.62.12	865	Delta silt, slipped (Fabric IIB)
16	7613	N.III.76.61	1979	Delta silt, slipped (Fabric IA)
17	6301	N.III.63.02	3591	Delta silt, slipped (Fabric IA)

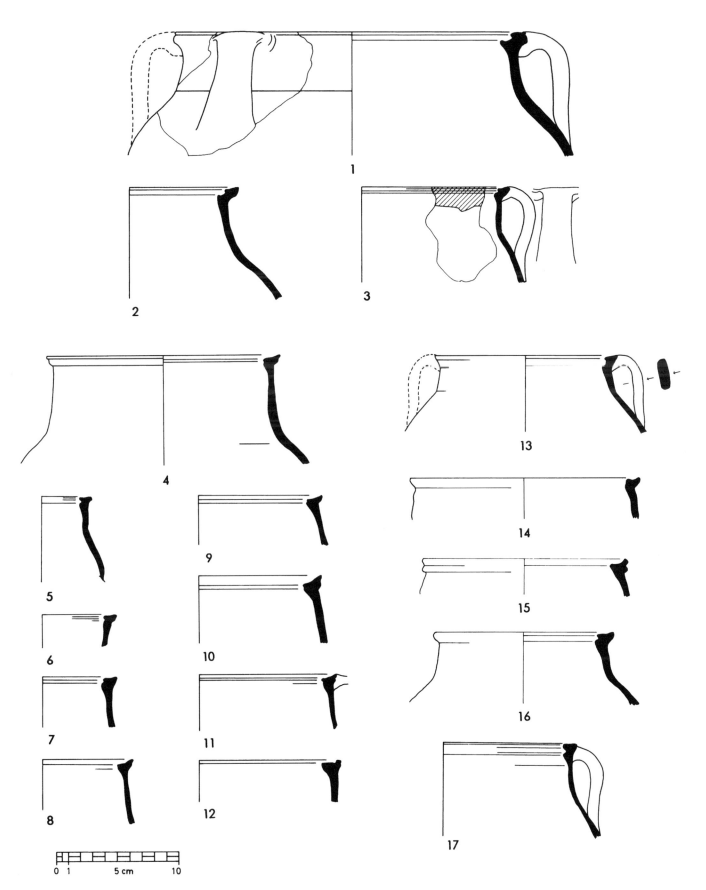

FIG. 2.19

Fig. 2.20.   Pieces of Cooking Vessels from Kom Hadid

No.	Locus	Pottery bag no.	Field no.	Description
Ledge/Folded Lip Stew Pots:				
1	7616	N.III.76.57	1904	Delta silt, slipped (Fabric IA)
2	7617	N.III.76.66	3186	Delta silt, slipped (Fabric IA)
3	7605	N.III.76.55	1833	Delta silt, slipped (Fabric IA)
4	7606	N.III.76.13	480	Delta silt, slipped (Fabric IA)
5	7605	N.III.76.09	442	Delta silt, slipped (Fabric IA)
6	6210	N.III.62.43	4049	Delta silt, slipped (Fabric IA)
7	7605	N.III.76.55	1815	Delta silt, slipped (Fabric IA)
8	6304	N.III.63.05	3674	Delta silt, slipped (Fabric IA)
9	6203	N.III.62.42	4074	Delta silt, slipped (Fabric IA)
10	6305	N.III.63.18	4300	Delta silt, slipped (Fabric IA)
11	7605	N.III.76.29	1091	Delta silt, slipped (Fabric IA)
12	13002	N.III.130.05	1492	Delta silt, slipped (Fabric IA)
13	7608	N.III.76.28	1121	Delta silt, slipped (Fabric IA)
14	6203	N.III.62.05	1947	Delta silt, slipped (Fabric IA)
15	7609	N.III.76.58	3367	Delta silt, slipped (Fabric IID)
16	7605	N.III.76.29	1072	Coarse marl (Fabric IV)
17	7613	N.III.76.34	1423	Delta silt, slipped (Fabric IID)
18	7605	N.III.76.09	434	Delta silt, slipped (Fabric IID)
19	7609	N.III.76.27	1181	Delta silt, slipped (Fabric IID)

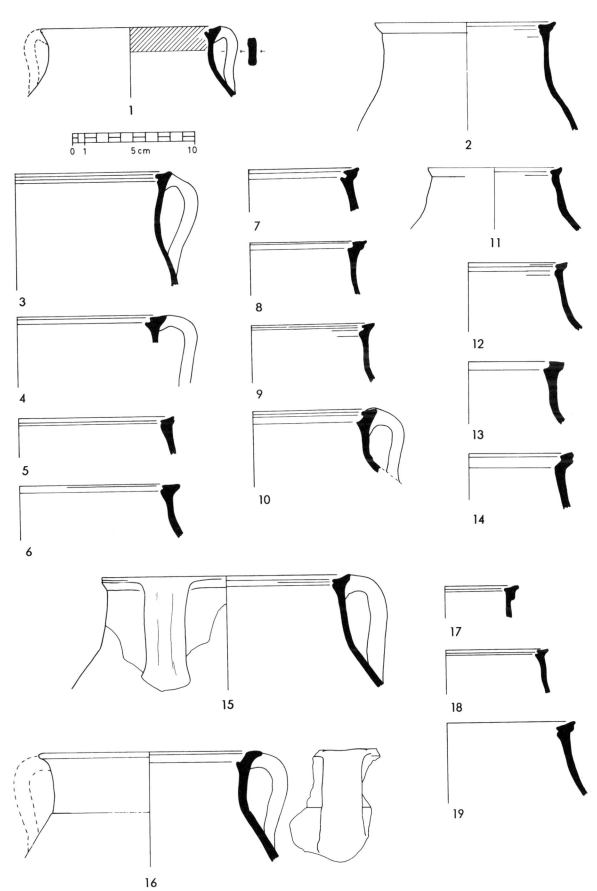

FIG. 2.20

Fig. 2.21.   Pieces of Cooking Vessels from Kom Hadid

No.	Locus	Pottery bag no.	Field no.	Description
Angled Rim Casseroles:				
1	13003	N.III.130.08	1785	Delta silt (Fabric II)
2	13010	N.III.130.13	3067	Delta silt, slipped (Fabric IA)
3	13007	N.III.130.11	1925	Delta silt, slipped (Fabric IA)
4	6203	N.III.62.05	1933	Delta silt, slipped (Fabric IA)
5	7605	N.III.76.30	1002	Delta silt (Fabric I)
6	7608	N.III.76.28	1111	Delta silt, slipped (Fabric IIC)
7	6304	N.III.63.09	3433	Delta silt, slipped (Fabric IA)
8	6305	N.III.63.18	4306	Delta silt, slipped (Fabric IA)

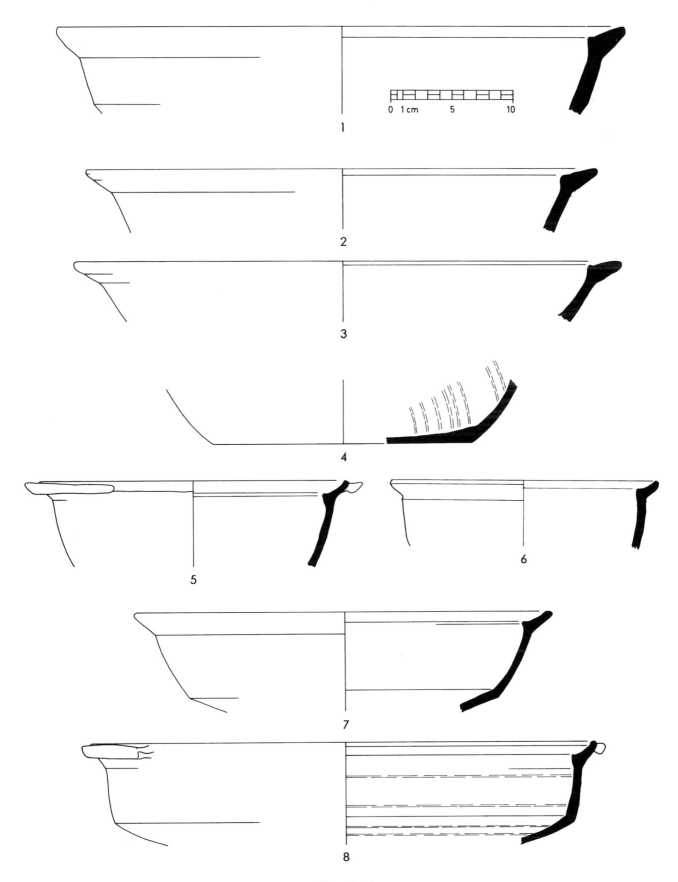

FIG. 2.21

Fig. 2.22.   Pieces of Cooking Vessels from Kom Hadid

No.	Locus	Pottery bag no.	Field no.	Description
Beveled Lip Casseroles:				
1	7609	N.III.76.58	3372	Delta silt, slipped (Fabric IA)
2	—	N.III.144.04	1333	Delta silt, slipped (Fabric IA)
3	6305	N.III.63.12	4262	Delta silt, slipped (Fabric IA)
4	6304	N.III.63.05	3693	Delta silt, slipped (Fabric IA)
5	6305	N.III.63.12	4255	Delta silt, slipped (Fabric IA)
6	6304	N.III.63.05	3696	Delta silt, slipped (Fabric IA)
7	6305	N.III.63.11	4147	Delta silt, slipped (Fabric IA)
8	6203	N.III.62.05	1936	Delta silt, slipped (Fabric IA)
9	7613	N.III.76.34	1421	Delta silt, slipped (Fabric IA)
10	6304	N.III.63.07	3723	Delta silt, slipped (Fabric IA)
11	7617	N.III.76.68	3006	Delta silt, slipped (Fabric IA)
12	6304	N.III.63.05	3668	Delta silt, slipped (Fabric IA)

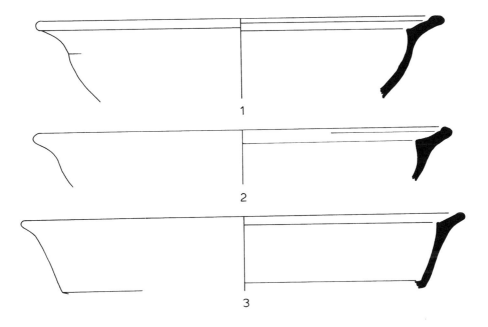

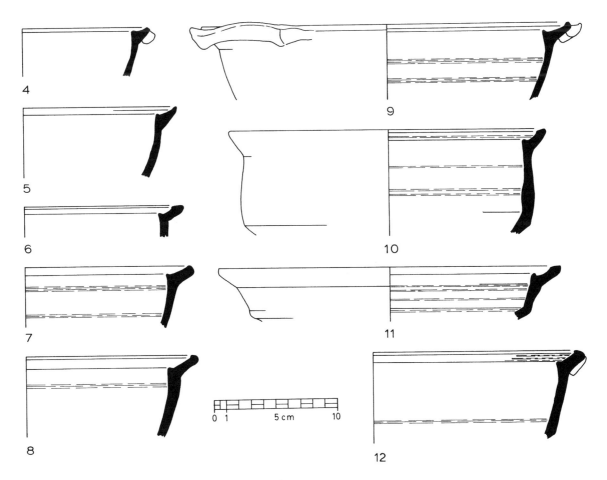

FIG. 2.22

Fig. 2.23   Pieces of Cooking Vessels from Kom Hadid

No.	Locus	Pottery bag no.	Field no.	Description
Beveled Lip Casseroles:				
1	6305	N.III.62.12	3938	Delta silt, slipped (Fabric IA)
2	6305	N.III.63.12	4253	Delta silt, slipped (Fabric IA)
3	6209	N.III.62.35	4357	Delta silt, slipped (Fabric IA)
4	6304	N.III.63.05	3672	Delta silt, slipped (Fabric IA)
5	7609	N.III.76.58	3335	Delta silt, slipped (Fabric IA)
6	7610	N.III.76.56	3155	Delta silt, slipped (Fabric IA)
7	6202	N.III.62.06	3118	Delta silt, slipped (Fabric IA)
8	7613	N.III.76.41	1575	Delta silt, slipped (Fabric IA)
9	6305	N.III.63.18	4357	Delta silt, slipped (Fabric IA)
10	7603	N.III.76.50	1758	Delta silt, slipped (Fabric IA)
11	6305	N.III.63.18	4359	Delta silt, slipped (Fabric IIC)

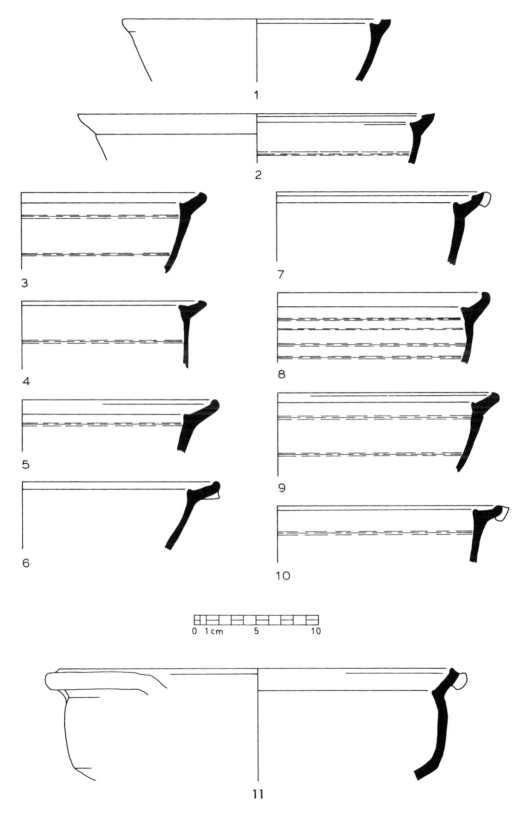

FIG. 2.23

Fig. 2.24.   Pieces of Cooking Vessels from Kom Hadid

No.	Locus	Pottery bag no.	Field no.	Description
Inset Rim Casseroles:				
1	7618	N.III.76.75	3890	Delta silt, slipped (Fabric IIA)
2	6215	N.III.62.38	3963	Delta silt, slipped (Fabric IIA)
3	7605	N.III.76.09	447	Delta silt, slipped (Fabric IIA)
4	7605	N.III.76.29	1080	Delta silt, slipped (Fabric IIA)
5	7613	N.III.76.41	1572	Delta silt, slipped (Fabric IIA)
6	6304	N.III.63.05	3682	Delta silt, slipped (Fabric IIA)
7	7606	N.III.76.23	972	Delta silt, slipped (Fabric IIA)
8	7605	N.III.76.55	1818	Delta silt, slipped (Fabric IIA)
9	7609	N.III.76.58	3352	Delta silt, slipped (Fabric IIA)
10–13		Information Lost		

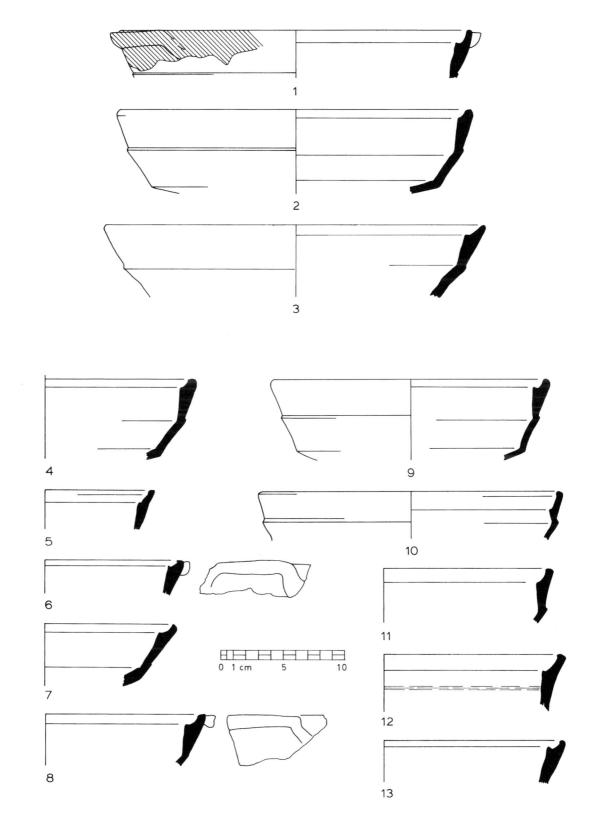

FIG. 2.24

Fig. 2.25.   Pieces of Cooking Vessels from Kom Hadid

No.	Locus	Pottery bag no.	Field no.	Description
Inset Rim Casseroles:				
1	6203	N.III.62.12	3038	Delta silt, slipped (Fabric IB)
2	7610	N.III.76.51	1713	Delta silt (Fabric I)
3	7608	N.III.76.28	1132	Delta silt, slipped (Fabric IIC)
4	7608	N.III.76.33	1323	Delta silt, slipped (Fabric IIC)
5	7613	N.III.76.44	1540	Delta silt, slipped (Fabric IB)
6	6202	N.III.62.04	1841	Delta silt, slipped (Fabric IB)
7	7613	N.III.76.59	1961	Delta silt, slipped (Fabric IIC)
8	6203	N.III.62.05	1938	Delta silt (Fabric I). Traces of wheel burnishing on interior of rim.
9	7606	N.III.76.19	724	Delta silt, slipped (Fabric IA)
10	7608	N.III.76.28	1124	Delta silt, slipped (Fabric IA)
11	7605	N.III.76.30	1013	Delta silt, slipped (Fabric IA)
12	7605	N.III.76.09	440	Delta silt, slipped (Fabric IA)
13	7608	N.III.76.31	1040	Delta silt, slipped (Fabric IA)
14	6207	N.III.62.19	3303	Delta silt, slipped (Fabric IA)
15	6209	N.III.62.32	3624	Delta silt, slipped (Fabric IA)
16	6201	N.III.62.01	1849	Delta silt, slipped (Fabric IA)
17	6217	N.III.62.37	3562	Delta silt, slipped (Fabric IA)
18	7606	N.III.76.19	726	Delta silt, slipped (Fabric IA)
19	7605	N.III.76.10	697	Delta silt, slipped (Fabric IA)

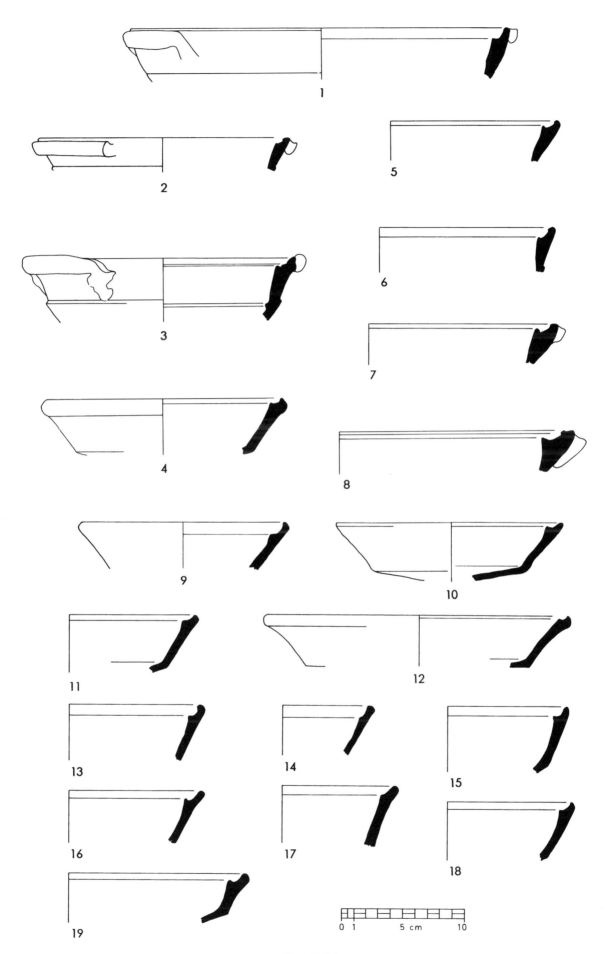

FIG. 2.25

Fig. 2.26.   Pieces of Cooking Vessels from Kom Hadid

No.	Locus	Pottery bag no.	Field no.	Description
Inset Rim Casseroles:				
1	7605	N.III.76.53	1583	Delta silt (Fabric I)
2	6203	N.III.62.07	3083	Delta silt (Fabric I)
3	7602	N.III.76.03	248	Delta silt (Fabric I)
4	7603	N.III.76.05	389	Delta silt (Fabric I)
5	7617	N.III.76.18	3018	Delta silt (Fabric I)
6	6203	N.III.62.13	2012	Delta silt (Fabric I)
7	7617	N.III.76.68	3010	Delta silt (Fabric I)
8	6217	N.III.62.37	3565	Delta silt (Fabric I)
9	7613	N.III.76.59	1966	Delta silt, slipped (Fabric IB)
10	4803	N.III.48.09	4210	Delta silt (Fabric II)
11	7609	N.III.76.58	3357	Delta silt, slipped (Fabric IA)

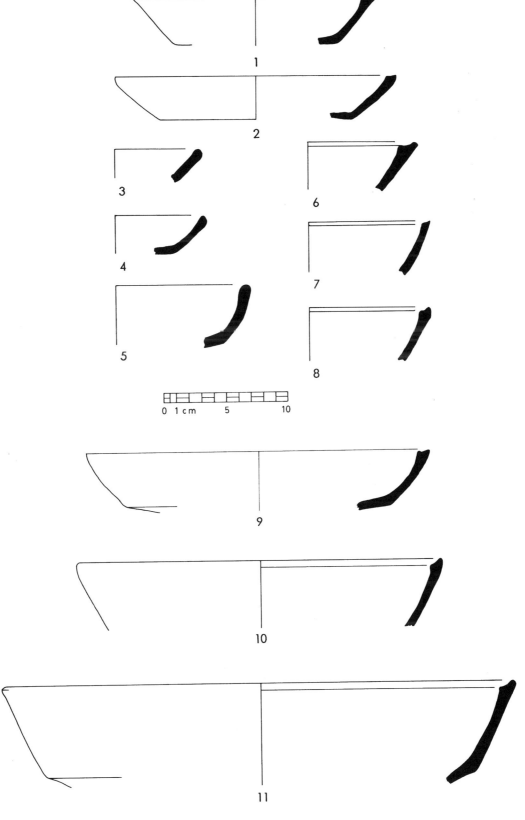

Fig. 2.26

Fig. 2.27. Pieces of Cooking Vessels from Kom Hadid

No.	Locus	Pottery bag no.	Field no.	Description
Squared Lip Casseroles:				
1	6207	N.III.62.19	3798	Delta silt, slipped (Fabric IB)
2	4808	N.III.48.11	4131	Delta silt (Fabric I)
3	7605	N.III.76.54	1674	Delta silt (Fabric I)
4	7606	N.III.76.37	1511	Delta silt (Fabric I)
5	7603	N.III.76.20	913	Delta silt (Fabric I)
6	6207	N.III.62.19	3298	Delta silt (Fabric I)
7	4803	N.III.48.09	4198	Delta silt (Fabric I)
8	6207	N.III.62.16	3194	Delta silt, slipped (Fabric IB)
9	6203	N.III.62.42	4072	Delta silt, slipped (Fabric IB)
10	7601	N.III.76.17	862	Delta silt, slipped (Fabric IIC)
11	7608	N.III.76.42	3148	Delta silt, slipped (Fabric IIC)
12	7606	N.III.76.23	969	Delta silt, slipped (Fabric IIC)
13	7606	N.III.76.23	956	Delta silt, slipped (Fabric IIC)
14	7608	N.III.76.42	1611	Delta silt, slipped (Fabric IIC)
15	14403	N.III.144.08	1260	Delta silt (II)

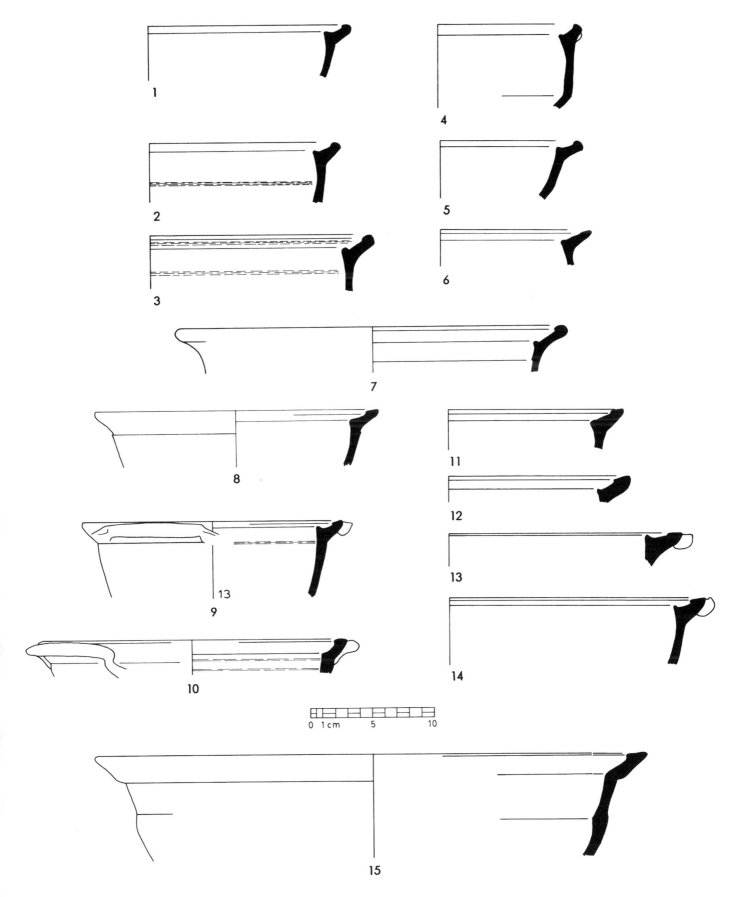

FIG. 2.27

Fig. 2.28.   Pieces of Cooking Vessels from Kom Hadid

No.	Locus	Pottery bag no.	Field no.	Description
Folded Lip Casseroles:				
1	7609	N.III.76.58	3360	Delta silt, slipped (Fabric IA)
2	4807	N.III.48.10	4100	Delta silt (Fabric I)
3	7617	N.III.76.68	3008	Delta silt (Fabric I)
4	7605	N.III.76.09	1110	Delta silt, slipped (Fabric IIB)
5	7609	N.III.76.27	1191	Delta silt, slipped (Fabric IA)
6	6203	N.III.62.05	1942	Delta silt, slipped (Fabric IA)

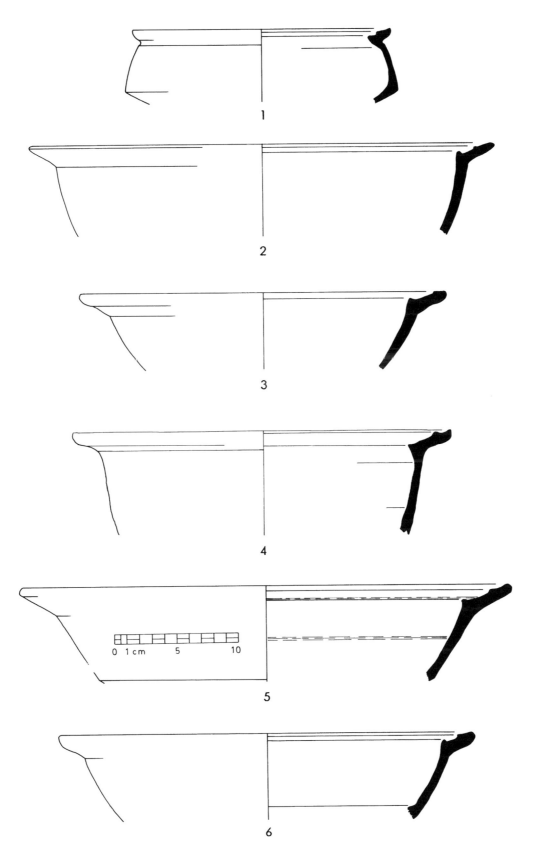

0 1 cm 5 10

Fig. 2.28

Fig. 2.29.   Pieces of Cooking Vessels from Kom Hadid

No.	Locus	Pottery bag no.	Field no.	Description
Folded Lip Casseroles:				
1	7609	N.III.76.27	1147	Delta silt, slipped (Fabric IIA)
2	7606	N.III.76.19	714	Delta silt, slipped (Fabric IIA)
3	13002	N.III.130.04	1431	Delta silt (Fabric II)
4	7602	N.III.76.03	234	Delta silt (Fabric II)
5	7603	N.III.76.22	897	Delta silt (Fabric II)
6	7602	N.III.76.03	227	Delta silt (Fabric II)
7	7603	N.III.76.05	373	Delta silt, slipped (Fabric IIA)
8	7602	N.III.76.03	229	Delta silt (Fabric II)
9	6203	N.III.62.05	1945	Delta silt (Fabric II)
10	7609	N.III.76.58	3337	Delta silt (Fabric II)
11	7609	N.III.76.27	1195	Delta silt (Fabric II)
12	7602	N.III.76.03	242	Delta silt (Fabric II)
13	4803	N.III.48.09	4203	Delta silt (Fabric II)

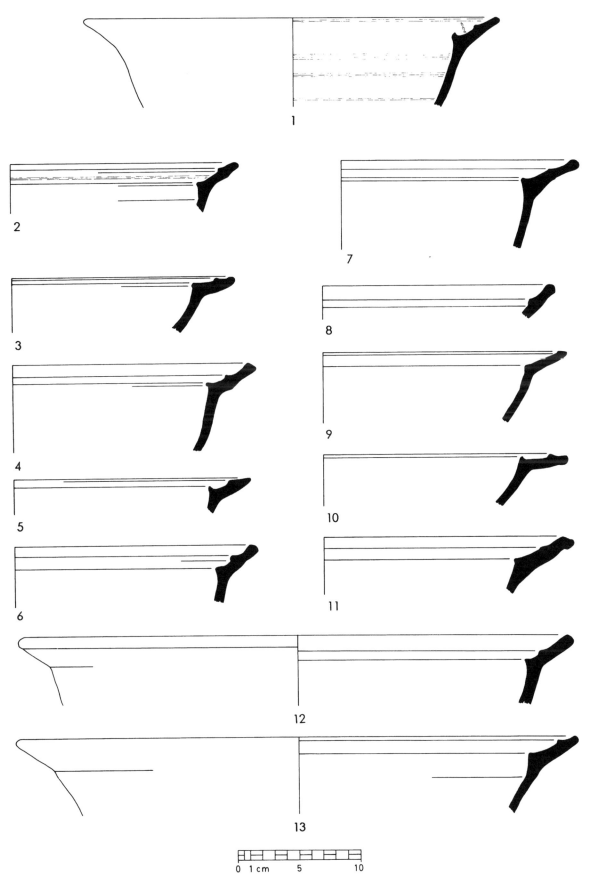

FIG. 2.29

Fig. 2.30.   Pieces of Cooking Vessels from Kom Hadid

No.	Locus	Pottery bag no.	Field no.	Description
Folded Lip Casseroles:				
1	7609	N.III.76.58	3345	Delta silt, slipped (Fabric IA)
2	Balk Trim	N.III.76.21	995	Delta silt, slipped (Fabric IA)
3	7609	N.III.76.27	1176	Delta silt, slipped (Fabric IA)
4	7610	N.III.76.10	1716	Delta silt, slipped (Fabric IA)
5	6203	N.III.76.05	387	Delta silt, slipped (Fabric IA)
6	6203	N.III.76.05	386	Delta silt, slipped (Fabric IA)
7	7609	N.III.76.27	1189	Delta silt, slipped (Fabric IIC)
8	7603	N.III.76.50	1752	Delta silt, slipped (Fabric IA)
9	7603	N.III.76.05	390	Delta silt, slipped (Fabric IA)
10	7604	N.III.76.25	1302	Delta silt, slipped (Fabric IIA)
11	7609	N.III.76.27	1178	Delta silt, slipped (Fabric IIC)

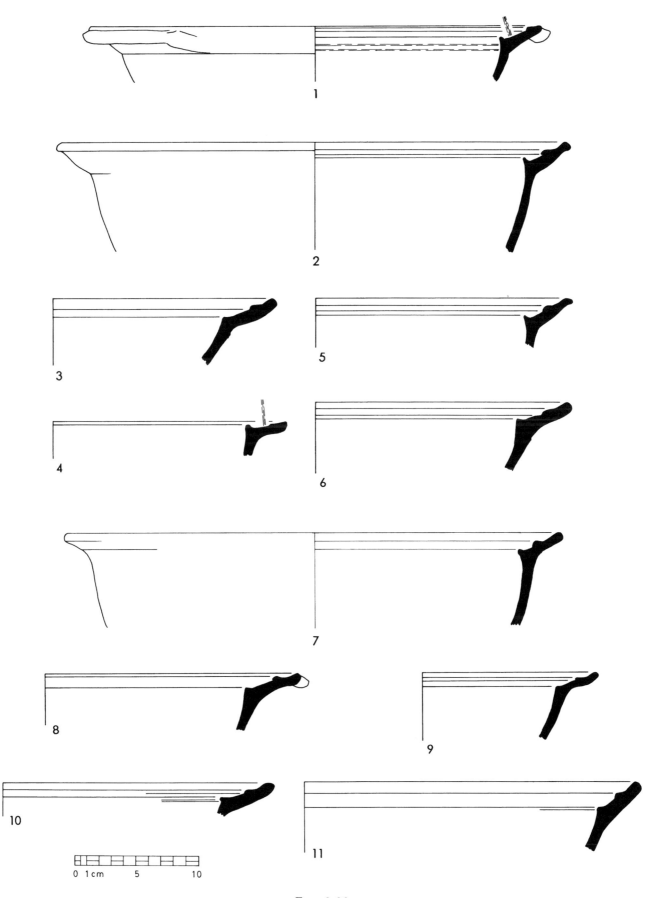

FIG. 2.30

Fig. 2.31.   Pieces of Cooking Vessels from Kom Hadid

No.	Locus	Pottery bag no.	Field no.	Description
Folded Lip Casseroles:				
1	6202	N.III.62.11	2005	Delta silt, slipped (Fabric IA)
2	7603	N.III.76.50	1753	Delta silt, slipped (Fabric IA)
3	7609	N.III.76.27	3187	Delta silt, slipped (Fabric IA)
4	4803	N.III.48.09	1201	Delta silt (Fabric II)
5	7609	N.III.76.27	1171	Delta silt (Fabric II)
6	6203	N.III.62.05	174	Delta silt, slipped (Fabric IA)
7	7606	N.III.76.19	737	Delta silt, slipped (Fabric IIC)
8	7603	N.III.76.20	912	Delta silt (Fabric I)

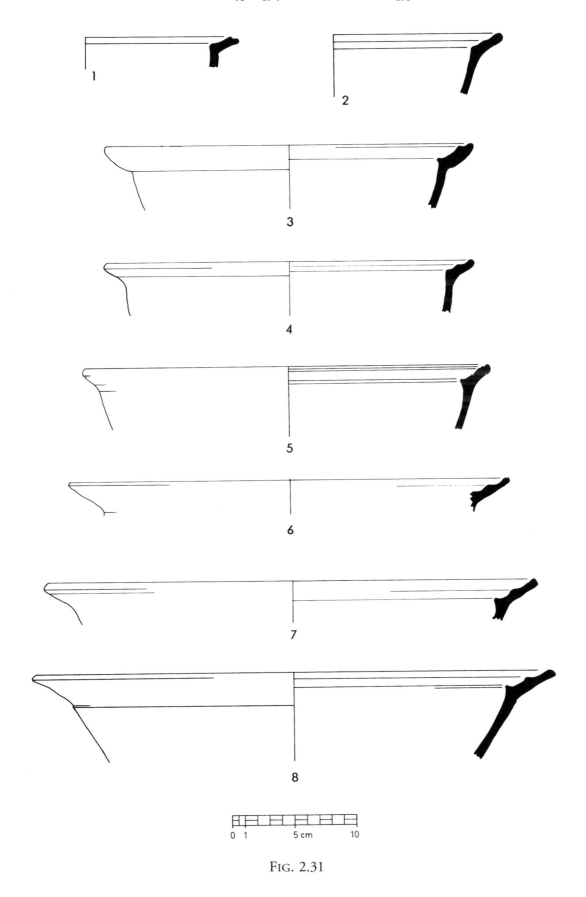

FIG. 2.31

Fig. 2.32.   Pieces of Cooking Vessels from Kom Hadid

No.	Locus	Pottery bag no.	Field no.	Description
Baking Dishes:				
1	7610	N.III.76.51	1715	Delta silt (Fabric I)
2	7605	N.III.76.30	1012	Delta silt (Fabric I)
3	7601	N.III.76.02	261	Delta silt, slipped (Fabric IB)
4	6215	N.III.62.38	3967	Delta silt, slipped (Fabric IB)
5	6207	N.III.62.24	3831	Delta silt, slipped (Fabric IB)
6	6208	N.III.62.12	3933	Delta silt, slipped (Fabric IA)
7	7613	N.III.76.41	1564	Delta silt, slipped (Fabric IA)
8	6215	N.III.62.38	3988	Delta silt, slipped (Fabric IA)
9	6207	N.III.62.19	3804	Delta silt, slipped (Fabric IA)
10	7605	N.III.76.30	1004	Delta silt, slipped (Fabric IA)
11	7606	N.III.76.13	471	Delta silt, slipped (Fabric IA)
12	4803	N.III.48.09	4201	Delta silt, slipped (Fabric IA)
13	6202	N.III.62.11	1992	Delta silt, slipped (Fabric IA)

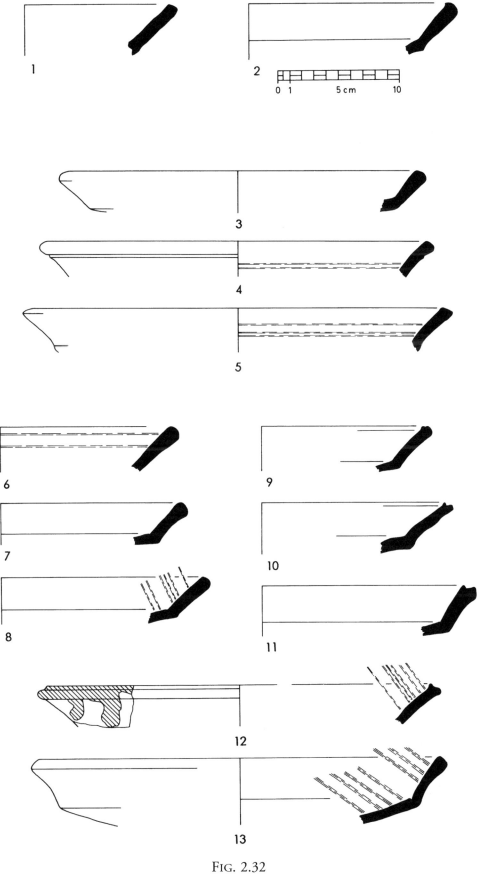

FIG. 2.32

Fig. 2.33.　Pieces of Cooking Vessels from Kom Hadid

No.	Locus	Pottery bag no.	Field no.	Description
Baking Dishes:				
1	7605	N.III.76.55	1818	Delta silt, slipped (Fabric IIA)
2	7609	N.III.76.58	3352	Delta silt, slipped (Fabric IIA)
3	7617	N.III.76.66	3179	Delta silt (Fabric II)
4	7603	N.III.76.16	632	Delta silt (Fabric II)
5	4803	N.III.48.09	362	Delta silt (Fabric I)
6	7605	N.III.76.29	1074	Delta silt, slipped (Fabric IA)
7	7601	N.III.76.17	878	Delta silt, slipped (Fabric IA)
8	6203	N.III.62.12	3935	Delta silt, slipped (Fabric IA)
9	6305	N.III.63.18	4274	Delta silt, slipped (Fabric IIC)
10	7601	N.III.76.48	1730	Delta silt, slipped (Fabric IA)

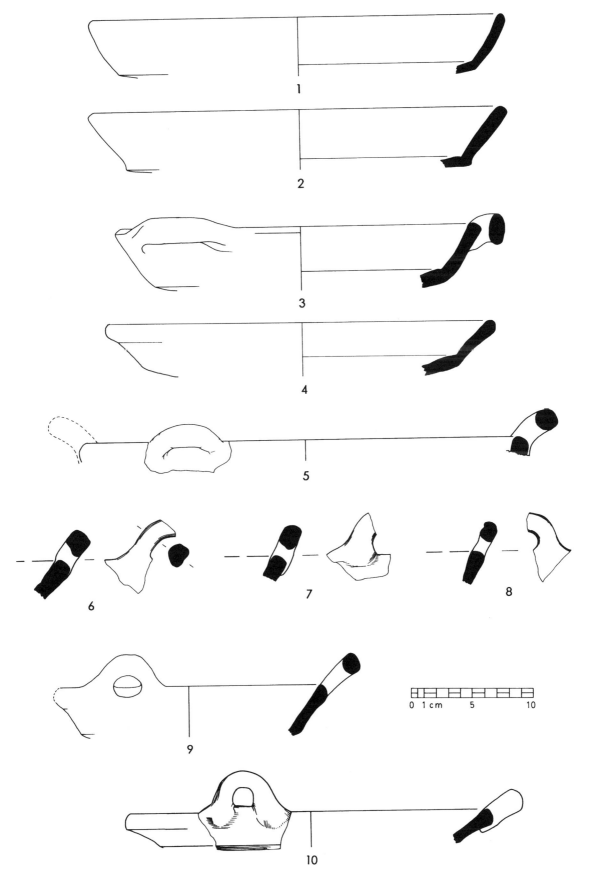

FIG. 2.33

Fig. 2.34.   Pieces of Utility Vessels from Kom Hadid

No.	Locus	Pottery bag no.	Field no.	Description
Unguentaria:				
1	6203	N.III.62.12	3973	Delta silt, slipped (Fabric IA)
2	7603	N.III.76.16	641	Delta silt, slipped (Fabric IA)
3	7610	N.III.76.52	1726	Delta silt, slipped (Fabric IA)
4	7613	N.III.76.41	4178	Extremely well-levigated clay with occasional sand-sized white and mica inclusions. Core gray. Over- or misfired in places to 5YR 5/2 (Reddish Gray)–5/3 (Reddish Brown). Rest of surface gray as core.
5	6203	N.III.62.05	3368	Delta silt, slipped (Fabric IC ?). Faint traces of band of fugitive white "paint" (no Munsell) at neck.
6	7605	N.III.76.10	702	Shiny black out. Well-levigated clay. Sand-sized white grit and micaceous inclusions. Interior 2/3 of section light gray, exterior 1/3 of section 10YR 4/2 (Dark Grayish Brown).
7	—	N.I.492.03	209	Dull black in/out. Exceptionally well-levigated clay with occasional sand-sized micaceous inclusions only. Fabric (inner) 7.5YR 5/4 (Brown); (outer) 2.5YR 4/4 (Reddish Brown). Related to Fabric IVC?
8	7608	N.III.76.43	1661a	Gray core and interior, black exterior. Very well-levigated clay. Occasional sand-sized micaceous inclusions and fine straw casts. Dark gray fabric. (Fabric TN-3).
9	—	N.III.76.43	1661b	Shiny black out/dull in. Well-levigated clay with occasional white grit to 1 mm and sand-sized micaceous inclusions. Fabric 10YR 4/3 (Dark Brown).
10	7603	N.III.76.06	514	Delta silt (Fabric II)
11	6305	N.III.63.18	4310	Delta silt, slipped (Fabric IA)
12	6202	N.III.62.04	1843	Delta silt, slipped (Fabric IA)
Juglets:				
13	7609	N.III.76.27	1175	Moderately well-levigated clay with sand-sized micaceous inclusions and white and gray grit c. 1 mm. Core c. 2.5YR 6/4 (Light Reddish Brown). Slip out mottled 2.5YR 6/6–6/8 (Light Red). Slip in 5YR 8/4 (Pink)–10YR 6/6 (Light Red). Import?
14	7606	N.III.76.19	716	Delta silt, slipped (Fabric IA)
15	7603	N.III.76.05	398	Delta silt (Fabric I)
16	7605	N.III.76.54	1672	Delta silt, slipped (Fabric IA)
17	7605	N.III.76.10	694	Delta silt, slipped (Fabric IA)
18	—	—	3132	
19	7601	N.III.76.02	262	Delta silt, slipped (Fabric IID)
20	7610	N.III.76.35	1372	Delta silt, slipped (Fabric IID)
21	7603	N.III.76.05	350	Delta silt, slipped (Fabric IA)
22	6207	N.III.62.22	3228	Delta silt, slipped (Fabric IB)
23	6305	N.III.63.18	4324	Delta silt (Fabric II)
24	7608	N.III.76.43	1644	Delta silt, slipped (Fabric IA)
25	49148	N.I.491.120	1750	Shiny black out/dull in. Well-levigated clay with occasional white grit to 1 mm and sand-sized micaceous inclusions. Fabric/core turns to black immediately below surfaces.
26	7603	N.III.76.06	508	Delta silt, slipped (Fabric IA).

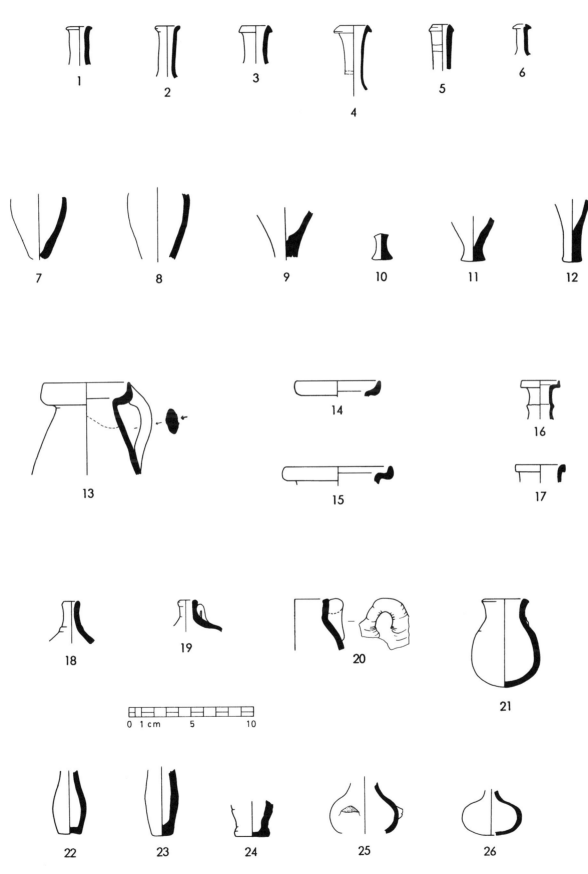

FIG. 2.34

Fig. 2.35.   Pieces of Utility Vessels from Kom Hadid

No.	Locus	Pottery bag no.	Field no.	Description
Juglets:				
1	—	N.III.76.18	793	Well-levigated clay with sand-sized micaceous inclusions. Fabric c. 2.5YR 6/8 (Light Red) but lighter (no good Munsell). Interior fired(?) to light gray.
2	6203	N.III.62.05	1934	Delta silt, slipped (Fabric IA)
3	6205	N.III.62.15	3838	Delta silt, slipped (Fabric IA)
4	6302	N.III.63.03	3530	Delta silt, slipped (Fabric IA)
5	6302	N.III.63.03	3534	Delta silt, slipped (Fabric IA)
6	7606	N.III.76.13	472	Delta silt (Fabric I)
7	7609	N.III.76.27	1194	Well-levigated clay with sand-sized micaceous inclusions and white grit to 1 mm. Fabric/core 5YR 5/4 (Reddish Brown)–6/4 (Light Reddish Brown). Slip out and over rim on interior 5YR 7/3–7/4 (Pink). Import?
8	6203	N.III.62.12	3926	Delta silt, slipped (Fabric IA)
9	7606	N.III.76.37	1508	Delta silt, slipped (Fabric IA)
10	6305	N.III.63.18	4299	Delta silt, slipped (Fabric IA)
Juglet/Jug Handles:				
11	7606	N.III.76.13	478	Delta silt, slipped (Fabric IA)
12	6209	N.III.62.26	3770	Delta silt, slipped (Fabric IB)
13	7005	N.III.76.10	686	Delta silt (Fabric I)
14	7606	N.III.76.13	479	Delta silt (Fabric I)
15	14405	N.III.144.09	1367	Delta silt (Fabric I)
16	6304	N.III.63.09	8478	Delta silt (Fabric I)
17	7602	N.III.76.03	246	Delta silt (Fabric I)
18	6305	N.III.63.11	4144	Delta silt, slipped (Fabric IB)
19	7603	N.III.76.06	500	Mineral-tempered Red Ware with white slip near 2.5Y 8/2 (White)–8/4 (Pale Yellow).
20	6304	N.III.63.09	3455	Mineral-tempered Red Ware fired weak red in/out and bottom only slipped c. 10YR 8/3–8/4 (Very Pale Brown).
21	7603	N.III.76.05	394	Mineral-tempered Red Ware with Red slip but with 10YR 8/2 (White)–8/3 (Very Pale Brown) slip in/out.
22	7604	N.III.76.25	1295	Delta silt, slipped (Fabric IA)
23	6201	N.III.62.01	1857	Delta silt, slipped (Fabric IA)
24	6203	N.III.62.12	3035	Delta silt (Fabric I)

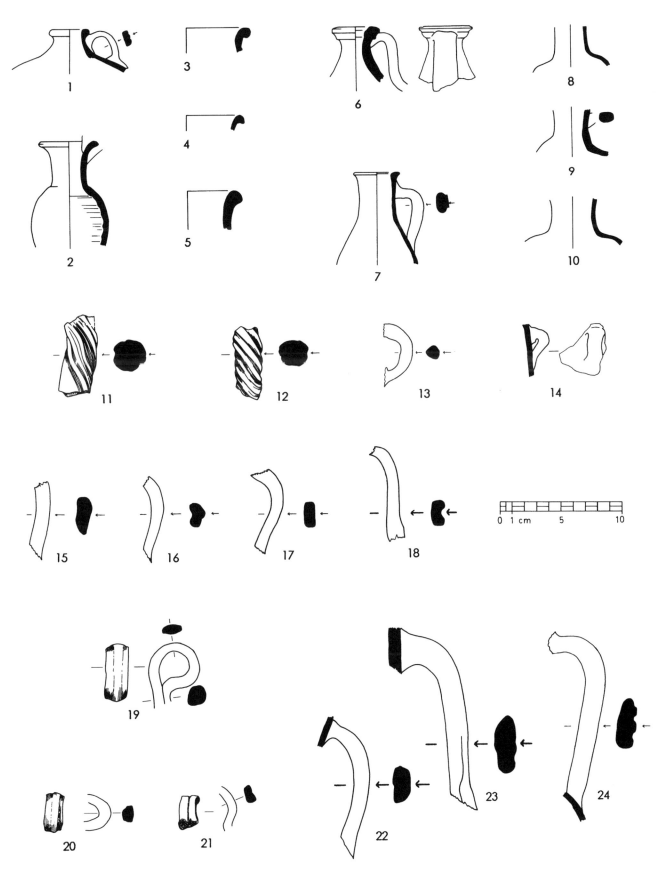

FIG. 2.35

Fig. 2.36.   Pieces of Utility Vessels from Kom Hadid

No.	Locus	Pottery bag no.	Field no.	Description
Long Necked Plain Rim Jugs:				
1	7613	N.III.76.70	463	Shiny black in/out. Very well-levigated clay. Occasional sand-sized white grit and frequent sand-sized micaceous inclusions. Fabric/core 10YR 4/3 (Dark Brown) in center gradually darkening to 4/2 (Dark Grayish Brown) beneath slip.
2	6215	N.III.62.38	3994	Shiny black in/out. Very well-levigated clay. Occasional white sand-sized white grit and infrequent sand-sized micaceous inclusions. Fabric/core between 10YR 4/1 (Dark Gray) and 4/2 (Dark Grayish Brown).
3	6302	N.III.63.03	3521	Delta silt, slipped (Fabric IA)
4	6302	N.III.63.03	3496	Delta silt, slipped (Fabric IA)
5	6217	N.III.62.37	3554	Delta silt, slipped (Fabric IA)
6	6207	N.III.62.22	3236	Delta silt, slipped (Fabric IB)
7	7618	N.III.76.73	3763	Delta silt, slipped (Fabric IB)
8	7608	N.III.76.43	1652	Delta silt, slipped (Fabric IB)
9	7605	N.III.76.09	454	Delta silt, slipped: Traces of 10YR 8/2 (White)–8/3 (Very Pale Brown) slip in/out. (Fabric X variant).
10	4807	N.III.48.10	3633	Delta silt, slipped (Fabric IA)
11	6302	N.III.63.03	3527	Delta silt, slipped (Fabric IA)
12	7613	N.III.76.38	1456	Delta silt, slipped (Fabric IA)
13	7605	N.III.76.55	1803	Delta silt, slipped (Fabric IA)
14			1803A	Delta silt, slipped (Fabric IA)
15	6305	N.III.63.18	4316	Delta silt, slipped. Painted area (stripe?) 5R 5/3–4/3 (Weak Red) on exterior. (Fabric ID variant).
16	6304	N.III.63.07	3739	Delta silt, slipped. Painted stripe below rim 5R 5/3–4/3 (Weak Red) on exterior. (Fabric ID variant).
17	7609	N.III.76.58	3369	Delta silt (Fabric I)
18	—	N.III.144.14	1098	Delta silt (Fabric I)
19	6202	N.III.62.03	1688	Delta silt (Fabric I)
20	13007	N.III.130.11	1929	Delta silt (Fabric I)
21	7605	N.III.76.54	1669	Delta silt (Fabric I)
22	7613	N.III.76.41	1565	Delta silt (Fabric I)
23	6203	N.III.62.07	3093	Delta silt, slipped (Fabric IA)
24	6203	N.III.62.07	3095	Delta silt, slipped (Fabric IA)
25	6207	N.III.62.19	3308	Delta silt, slipped (Fabric IA)

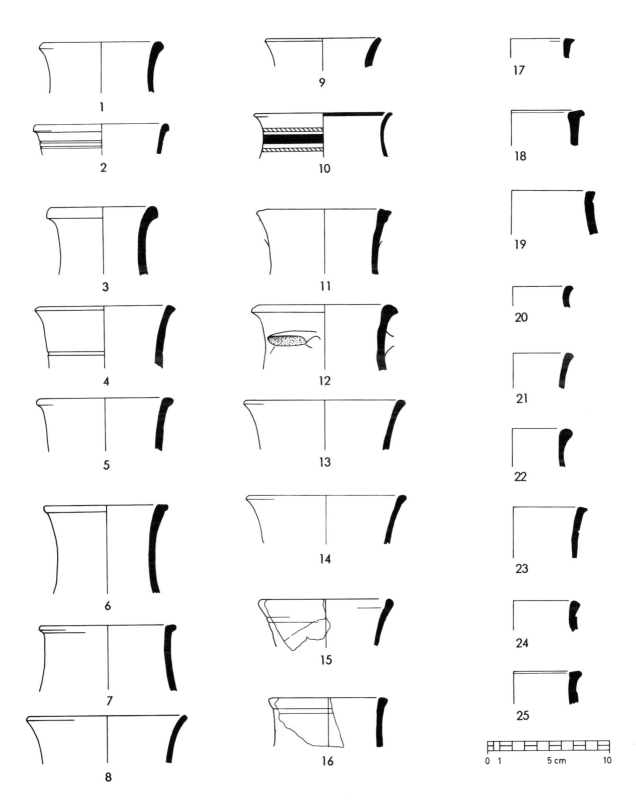

FIG. 2.36

Fig. 2.37.   Pieces of Utility Vessels from Kom Hadid

No.	Locus	Pottery bag no.	Field no.	Description
Long Necked Delta Rim Jugs:				
1	6302	N.III.63.03	3529	Coarse marl (Fabric IV)
2	7618	N.III.76.74	3219	Coarse marl (Fabric IV)
3	6302	N.III.63.06	3860	Delta silt (Fabric I)
4	7606	N.III.76.23	965	Delta silt (Fabric I)
5	7606	N.III.76.13	473	Delta silt (Fabric I)
6	7605	N.III.76.55	177	Delta silt (Fabric I)
7	6302	N.III.63.06	3857	Delta silt (Fabric I)
8	6203	N.III.62.12	3937	Coarse marl (Fabric IV)
9	13006	N.III.130.07	1890	Coarse marl (Fabric IV)
10	7608	N.III.76.42	1617	Delta silt (Fabric I)
11	6304	N.III.63.07	3717	Traces of white "paint" band at rim between 7.5YR 8/2 (Pinkish White) and 8/4 (Pink).
12	14402	N.III.144.02	645	Delta silt (Fabric I)
13	6305	N.III.63.12	4243	Delta silt (Fabric I)
14	13006	N.III.130.07	1891	Coarse marl, slipped (Fabric IVA)
Miscellaneous Jugs:				
15	—	N.III.62.92	4077	Delta silt, slipped (Fabric IA)
16	7613	N.III.76.34	265	Delta silt, slipped (Fabric IA)
17	6305	N.III.63.18	4350	Delta silt, slipped (Fabric IA)
18	7603	N.III.76.16	799	Delta silt, slipped (Fabric IA)
19	13001	N.III.130.02	1212	Delta silt, slipped (Fabric IA)
20	6207	N.III.62.24	3828	Delta silt (Fabric IE) with a thin band of c. 10YR 8/2 (White)–8/3 (Very Pale Brown) and a band of c. 7.5R 4/4 (Weak Red).

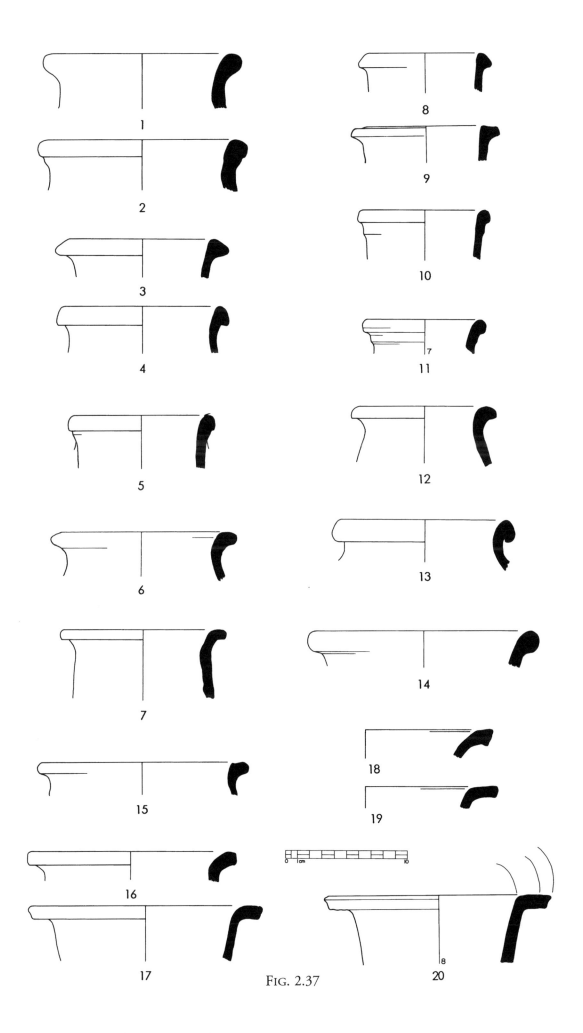

FIG. 2.37

Fig. 2.38.   Pieces of Utility Vessels from Kom Hadid

No.	Locus	Pottery bag no.	Field no.	Description
Folded Rim Jugs:				
1	7613	N.III.76.64	2082	Coarse marl, slipped (Fabric IVC)
2	7608	N.III.76.42	1613	Coarse marl, slipped (Fabric IVC)
3	7613	N.III.76.34	1406	Coarse marl, slipped (Fabric IVC)
4	7613	N.III.76.70	3274	Coarse marl, slipped (Fabric IVC)
Narrow Ledge Rim Jugs (Aswan and Local):				
5	7606	N.III.76.37	1517	Very well-levigated clay with little trace of temper. Core 7.5YR 8/6–7/6 (Reddish Yellow). Slip in/out 2.5Y 8/2 (White)–8/4 (Pale Yellow). Stripe 10R 5/8 (Red). Import?
6	6215	N.III.62.38	3973	Delta silt, slipped (Fabric IA)
7	6304	N.III.63.05	3670	Delta silt, slipped (Fabric IA)
8	7606	N.III.76.37	1518	Delta silt, slipped (Fabric IA)
9	6304	N.III.63.08	3845	Delta silt, slipped (Fabric IA)
10	6304	N.III.63.07	3722	Delta silt, slipped (Fabric IA)
11	6207	N.III.62.22	3243	Delta silt, slipped (Fabric IB)
12	7613	N.III.76.70	3280	Delta silt, slipped (Fabric IB)
13	7602	N.III.76.05	247	Delta silt, slipped (Fabric IB)
14	7616	N.III.76.57	1960	Delta silt, slipped (Fabric IIA)
15	7606	N.III.76.13	481	Delta silt, slipped (Fabric IA)
Rolled Rim Jugs:				
16	6209	N.III.62.33	3407	Delta silt, slipped (Fabric IA)
17	6202	N.III.62.18	3789	Delta silt, slipped (Fabric IB)
18	7610	N.III.76.35	1377	Delta silt (Fabric I)
19	6202	N.III.62.03	1689	Delta silt (Fabric I)
Lagynos?:				
20	6202	N.III.62.03	1683	Very well-levigated clay with very fine straw casts to 1 mm Core/slip 7.5YR 8/4 (Pink). Import?
Miscellaneous Jugs:				
21	7603	N.III.76.05	395	Delta silt, slipped. 10YR 8/3 (Very Pale Brown) slip in. (Fabric IXA variant?)
22	—	N.III.62.34	4016	Delta silt, slipped (Fabric IXA variant)

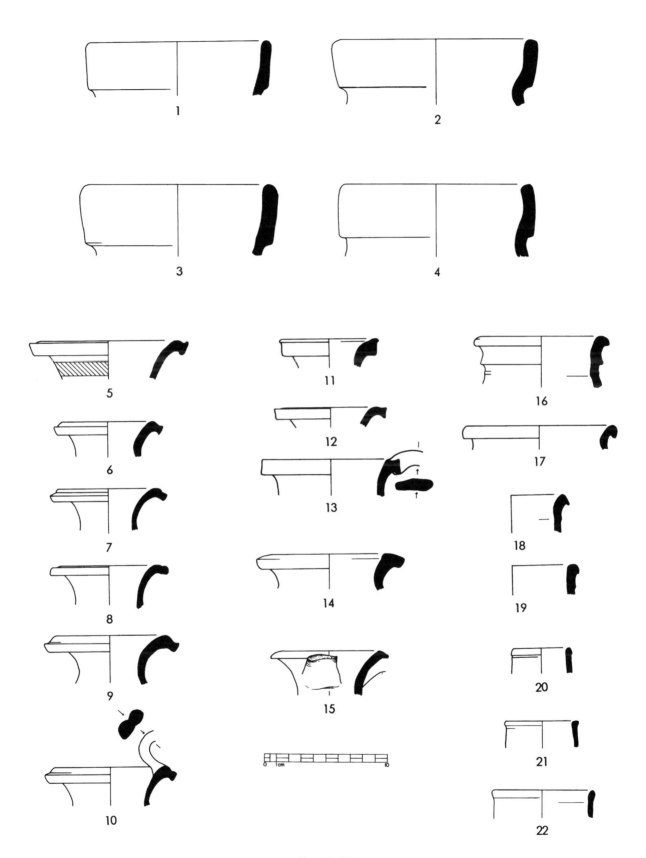

FIG. 2.38

Fig. 2.39.   Pieces of Utility Vessels from Kom Hadid

No.	Locus	Pottery bag no.	Field no.	Description
Long Necked Flattened Rim Jugs:				
1	7617	N.III.76.68	3016	Delta silt (Fabric I)
2	13003	N.III.130.08	1784	Delta silt, slipped (Fabric IA)
3	6304	N.III.63.05	3689	Delta silt, slipped (Fabric IIA)
4	6202	N.III.62.03	1685	Delta silt, slipped (Fabric IA)
5	6304	N.III.63.05	3705	Delta silt (Fabric I)
Flanged Rim Jugs:				
6	7605	N.III.76.55	1812	Delta silt, slipped (Fabric IA)
7	6209	N.III.62.14	2065	Delta silt (Fabric I)
8	7603	N.III.76.05	353	Delta silt, slipped (Fabric IA)
9	6202	N.III.62.04	1845	Delta silt (Fabric I)
10	7617	N.III.76.68	1272	Delta silt (Fabric I)
11	6202	N.III.62.03	1677	Delta silt (Fabric I)
12	7617	N.III.76.66	3182	Delta silt (Fabric II)
Lagynoi:				
13	6207	N.III.62.19	3800	Exceptionally well-levigated clay with occasional sand-sized micaceous inclusions and rare white grit to 1 mm. Fabric 7.5YR 7/6 (Reddish Yellow). Surface 10YR 8/4 (Very Pale Brown).
14	7603	N.III.76.22	883	Delta silt, slipped (Fabric IA)
Miscellaneous Jugs:				
15	7603	N.III.76.05	378	Delta silt, slipped. Exterior plain. Interior bands of 5R 5/2–4/2 (Weak Red) and 10YR 8/2 (White). (Fabric IE variant).
16	surface	N.III.85.01	172	Delta silt (Fabric II)
17	7613	N.III.76.70	3264	Coarse marl (Fabric IV)
18	6202	N.III.62.06	3122	Delta silt, slipped (Fabric IA)
19	6304	N.III.63.09	3449	Very well-levigated clay with occasional white and pink grit to 1 mm. Core (thick) 10YR 6/4 (Light Yellowish Brown). Sandwich (thin) c. 5YR 7/4 (Pink). Slip in/out mottled 2.5Y 8/2 (White)–7/2 (Light Gray)–6/2 (Light Grayish Brown). Import.
20	7609	N.III.76.27	1159	Delta silt (Fabric I)
21	14402	N.III.144.03	814	Delta silt (Fabric I)

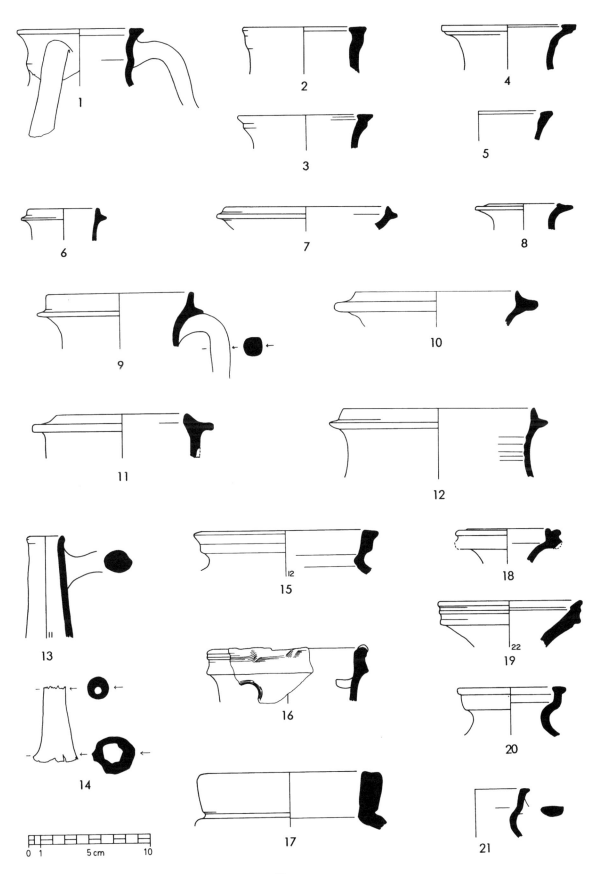

FIG. 2.39

Fig. 2.40.   Pieces of Utility Vessels from Kom Hadid

No.	Locus	Pottery bag no.	Field no.	Description
Hydriae/Table Amphorae:				
1	7605	N.III.76.32	1208	Well-levigated clay with white, gray, and red grit to 1 mm. Core/ fabric (variegated) 7.5YR 7/4 (Pink)–7/6 (Reddish Yellow). Slip in/out (misfired?) c. 10YR 7/1 (Light Gray). Import? Misfired?
2	7609	N.III.76.58	3349	Delta silt, slipped. Band of 7.5R 4/2–4/4 (Weak Red). (Fabric ID variant).
3	7618	N.III.76.73	792	Delta silt, slipped. Interior drippy slip c. 5YR 8/4 (Pink). Exterior white slip (no Munsell) with three bands. Bands 1&3 c. 10R 6/6–6/8 (Light Red). Band 2 2.5YR 4/4 (Reddish Brown)–3/4 (Dark Reddish Brown). (Fabric IE)
4	7603	N.III.76.20	918	Delta silt, slipped. Exterior plain. Interior "slip/paint" bands of 10R 4/2–4/3 (Weak Red) and 5YR 8/3–8/4 (Pink). (Fabric IE).
5	7603	N.III.76.05	378	Delta silt, slipped. Exterior plain. Interior bands of 5R 5/2–4/2 (Weak Red) and 10YR 8/2 (White). (Fabric IE).
6	6305	N.III.63.18	4323	Delta silt, slipped (Fabric IIA)
7	7608	N.III.76.33	1310	Delta silt (Fabric I)
8	6305	N.III.63.18	4355	Delta silt, slipped (Fabric IIA)
9	7601	N.III.76.17	879	Delta silt (Fabric I)
10	7606	N.III.76.19	733	Delta silt, slipped (Fabric IIC)
11	7613	N.III.76.38	1459b	Delta silt, slipped (Fabric IID)
12	7613	N.III.76.44	1550	Delta silt, slipped (Fabric IA)
13	7613	N.III.76.61	1978	Delta silt, slipped (Fabric IB)
14	6305	N.III.63.18	4327	Coarse marl (Fabric IV)
15	6201	N.III.62.06	661	Delta silt, slipped (Fabric IIC variant?)

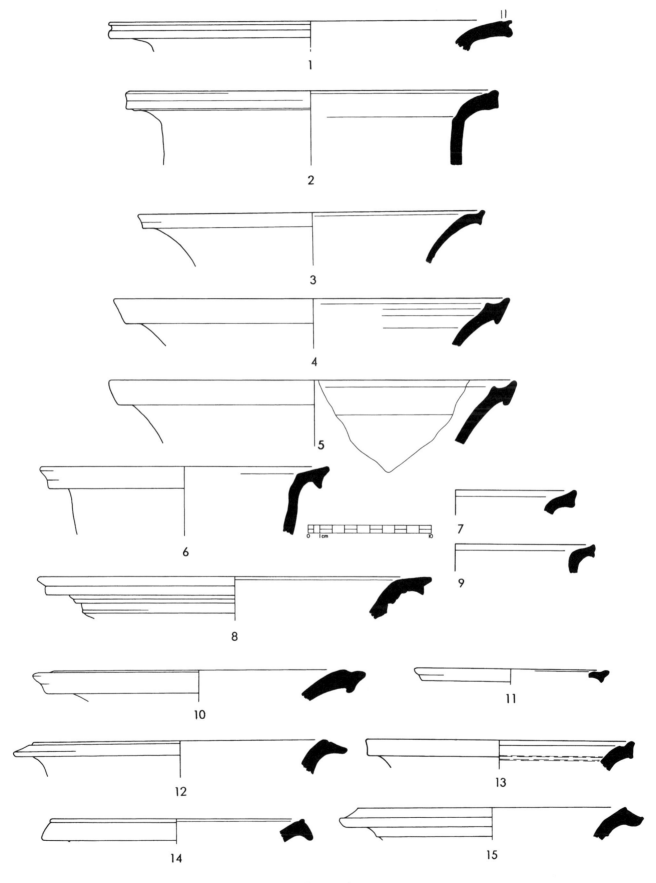

FIG. 2.40

Fig. 2.41.   Pieces of Utility Vessels from Kom Hadid

No.	Locus	Pottery bag no.	Field no.	Description
Jugs/Hydriae Ring Feet:				
1	6209	N.III.62.26	3775	Delta silt, slipped. Fired 7.5R 5/2–4/2 (Weak Red) just under exterior slip, but interior approaches Fabric IB in color. Fugitive slip exterior and bottom 10YR 8/2 (White)–2.5Y 8/2 (White). (Fabric IE variant?)
2	7601	N.III.76.17	852	Delta silt (Fabric I)
3	7601	N.III.76.17	858	Delta silt (Fabric I)
4	14402	N.III.144.03	818	Delta silt (Fabric I)
5	7601	N.III.76.17	855	Delta silt (Fabric I)
6	7601	N.III.76.02	294	Delta silt (Fabric I)
7	7605	N.III.76.05	407	Delta silt (Fabric I)
8	7609	N.III.76.58	3595	Delta silt, slipped (Fabric IB)
9	6207	N.III.62.19	1663	Delta silt, slipped (Fabric IB)
10	6202	N.III.62.03	3951	Delta silt, slipped (Fabric IB)
11	6305	N.III.63.18	277	Delta silt, slipped (Fabric IB)
12	6217	N.III.62.37	4233	Delta silt, slipped (Fabric IA)
13	6209	N.III.62.32	3630	Delta silt, slipped (Fabric IA)
14	7608	N.III.76.42	1603	Delta silt, slipped (Fabric IA)
15	6202	N.III.62.04	1844	Delta silt (Fabric I)
16	7608	N.III.76.42	1612	Delta silt (Fabric I)
17	7613	N.III.76.65	3750	Delta silt (Fabric I)
18	6215	N.III.62.38	633	Delta silt (Fabric I)
19	7601	N.III.76.48	856	Delta silt (Fabric I)
20	4803	N.III.48.09	1828	Delta silt, slipped (Fabric IIA)

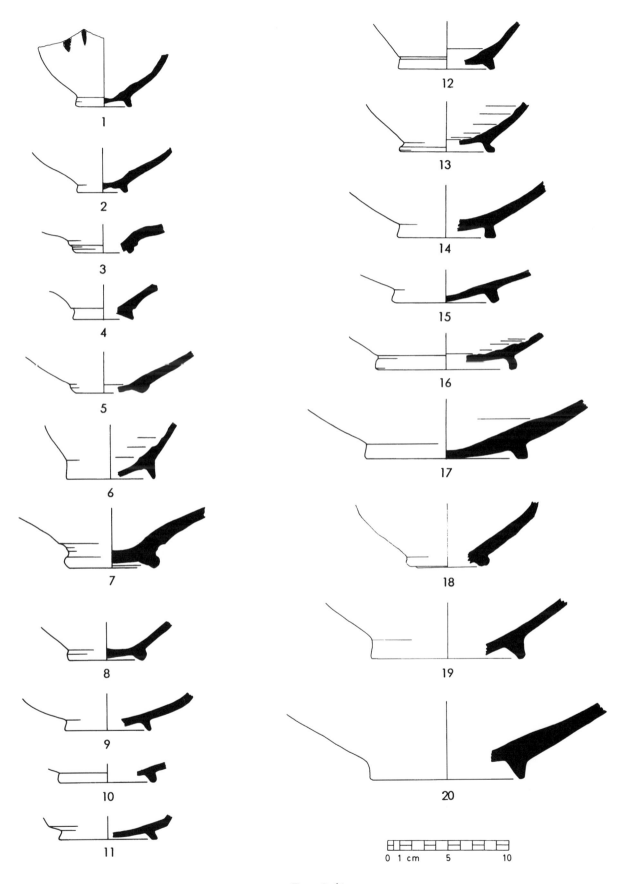

FIG. 2.41

Fig. 2.42.   Pieces of Utility Vessels from Kom Hadid

No.	Locus	Pottery bag no.	Field no.	Description
Jugs/Hydriae Ring Feet:				
1	7606	N.III.76.23	961	Delta silt, slipped (Fabric IA)
2	13002	N.III.130.05	1491	Delta silt, slipped (Fabric IA)
3	13006	N.III.130.20	3025	Delta silt, slipped (Fabric IA)
4	7608	N.III.76.33	1306	Delta silt, slipped (Fabric IA)
5	7603	N.III.76.05	400	Delta silt, slipped (Fabric IA)
6			3962	Delta silt, slipped (Fabric IB)
7	7601	N.III.76.02	286	Delta silt (Fabric I)
8	6215	N.III.62.38	3782	Delta silt, slipped. Exterior slip 7.5R 4/4 (Weak Red) but covered with slip c. 2.5Y 8/2 (White). (Fabric IX).
9	7613	N.III.76.38	1454	Delta silt, slipped. Fabric traces of 10YR 8/2 (White) slip out. (Fabric IX).
10	7603	N.III.76.05	346	Delta silt, slipped (Fabric IA)
11	7604	N.III.76.08	422	Delta silt, slipped (Fabric IA)
12	7601	N.III.76.15	763	Delta silt, slipped (Fabric IA)
13	7601	N.III.76.17	871	Delta silt, slipped (Fabric IA)
14	7613	N.III.76.59	1964	Delta silt, slipped (Fabric IIA)
15	7609	N.III.76.58	3338	Delta silt, slipped (Fabric IIA)
16	7613	N.III.76.64	2080	Delta silt, slipped (Fabric IIA)
17	14402	N.III.144.02	824	Delta silt, slipped (Fabric IA)
18	6203	N.III.63.12	4258	Delta silt, slipped (Fabric IA)
19	6201	N.III.62.01	1853	Delta silt, slipped. Red slip with weak red exterior and c. 10YR 8/2 (White) interior. (Fabric IE or IX variant?)

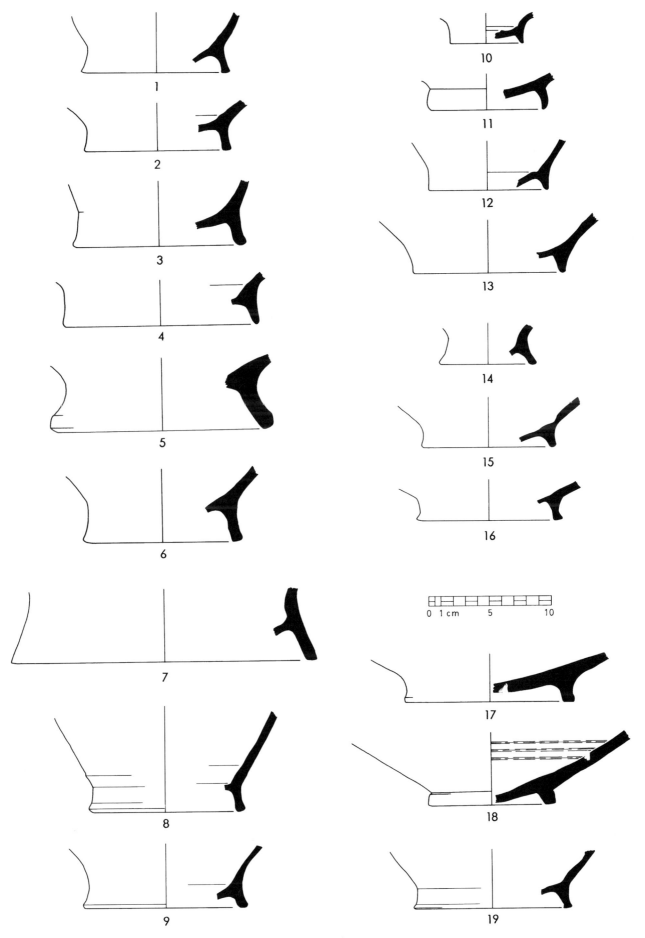

FIG. 2.42

Fig. 2.43.   Pieces of Utility Vessels from Kom Hadid

No.	Locus	Pottery bag no.	Field no.	Description
Short Squared Rim Kraters (2–4, 6–8):				
1	7609	N.III.76.27	1157	Coarse marl (Fabric IV)
2	6305	N.III.63.18	4351	Coarse marl (Fabric IV)
3	7613	N.III.76.41	1560	Coarse marl (Fabric IV)
4	6305	N.III.63.11	4133	Coarse marl, slipped (Fabric IVA)
5	7608	N.III.76.43	1658	Delta silt, slipped (Fabric IIA)
6	6203	N.III.62.12	3928	Coarse marl (Fabric IV)
7	7613	N.III.76.59	1957	Coarse marl (Fabric IV)
8	7613	N.III.76.70	3263	Coarse marl, slipped (Fabric IVC)
9	13006	N.III.130.07	1892	Coarse marl, slipped (Fabric IVC)

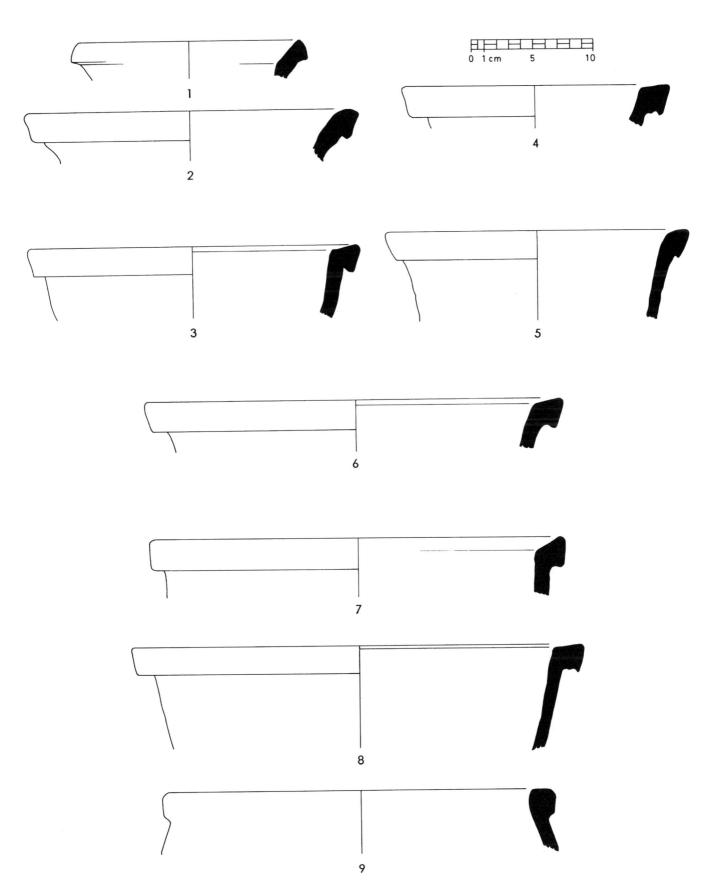

FIG. 2.43

Fig. 2.44.   Pieces of Utility Vessels from Kom Hadid

No.	Locus	Pottery bag no.	Field no.	Description
Overhanging Rim Kraters:				
1	6202	N.III.62.02	3109	Delta silt, slipped (Fabric IA)
2	7603	N.III.76.05	4315	Delta silt, slipped (Fabric IA)
3	7608	N.III.76.42	1602	Delta silt, slipped (Fabric IA)
4	6305	N.III.63.18	4272	Delta silt, slipped (Fabric IA)
5	6305	N.III.63.12	4287	Delta silt, slipped (Fabric IA)
6	6202	N.III.62.04	1842	Delta silt, slipped (Fabric IA)
7	6209	N.III.62.35	3657	Delta silt, slipped (Fabric IA)
8	7606	N.III.76.36	1480	Delta silt, slipped (Fabric IA)

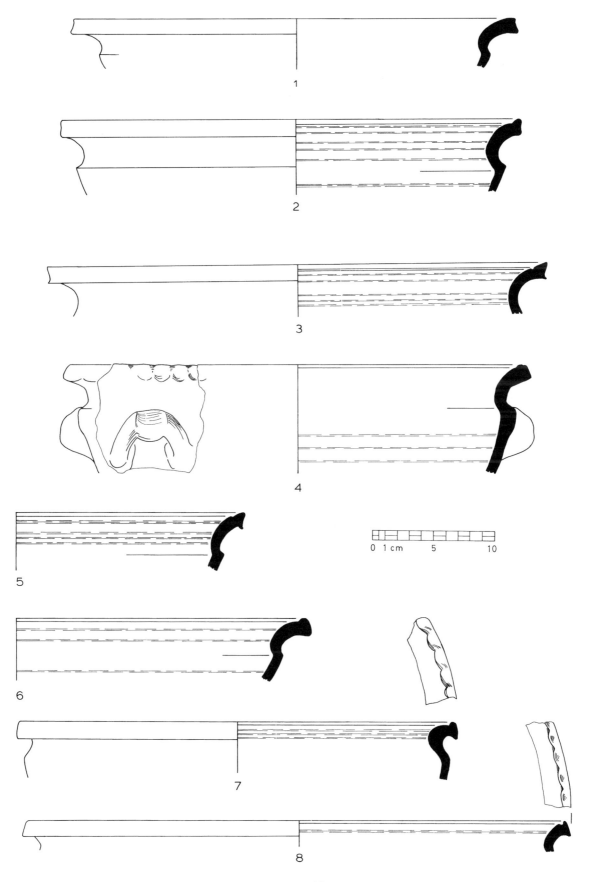

FIG. 2.44

Fig. 2.45.   Pieces of Utility Vessels from Kom Hadid

No.	Locus	Pottery bag no.	Field no.	Description
Overhanging Rim Kraters:				
1	6304	N.III.63.05	3664	Delta silt, slipped (Fabric IA)
2	7603	N.III.76.50	1765	Delta silt (Fabric I)
3	6201	N.III.62.01	758	Delta silt, slipped (Fabric IIB)
4	6302	N.III.63.03	3500	Delta silt, slipped (Fabric IIC)
5	4803	N.III.48.09	4219	Delta silt, slipped (Fabric IIC)
6	7604	N.III.76.24	945	Delta silt, slipped (Fabric IIC)
7	7608	N.III.76.42	1605	Delta silt, slipped (Fabric IB)
8	7605	N.III.76.55	1825	Delta silt, slipped (Fabric IA)

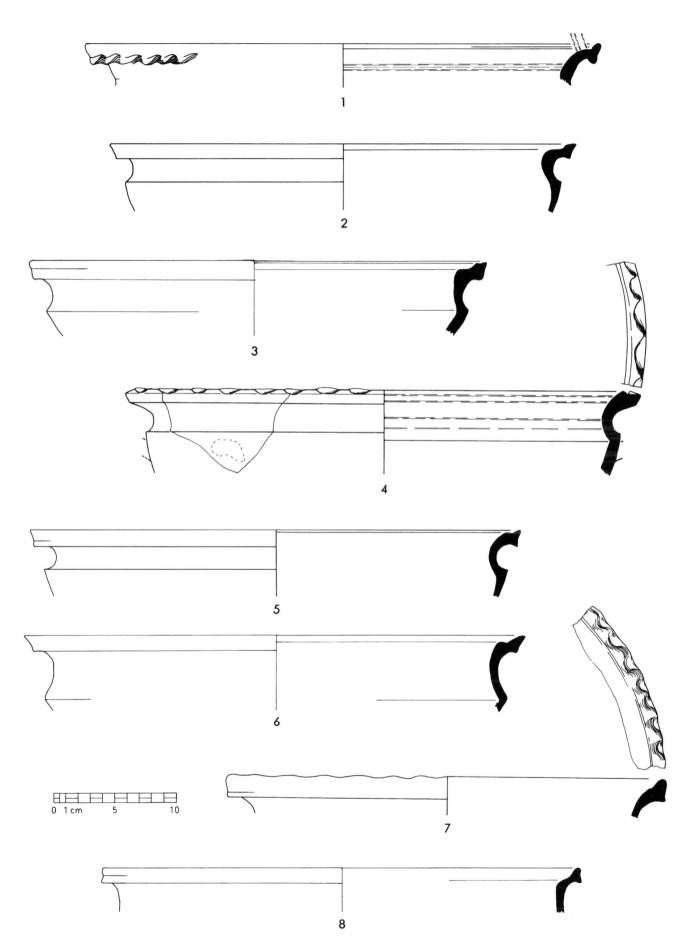

FIG. 2.45

Fig. 2.46. Pieces of Utility Vessels from Kom Hadid

No.	Locus	Pottery bag no.	Field no.	Description
"Nailhead" Kraters:				
1	6207	N.III.62.19	3799	Delta silt, slipped (Fabric IA)
2	6304	N.III.63.09	3434	Delta silt, slipped (Fabric IA)
3	13002	N.III.130.05	272	Delta silt, slipped (Fabric IA)
4	7608	N.III.76.33	3797	Delta silt, slipped (Fabric IA)
5	7605	N.III.76.55	1826	Delta silt, slipped (Fabric IIA)
6	7605	N.III.76.55	1823	Delta silt, slipped (Fabric IIA)

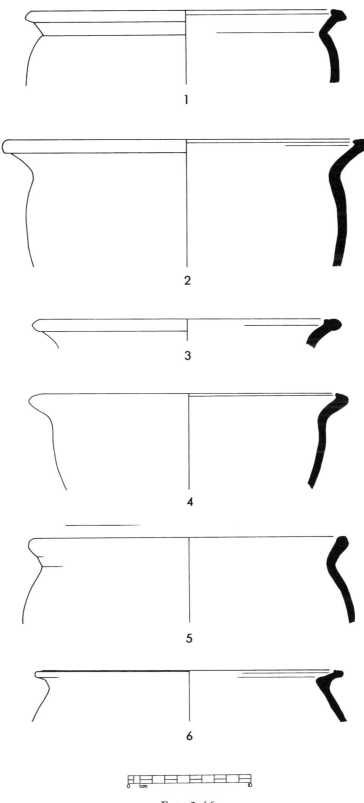

FIG. 2.46

Fig. 2.47.   Pieces of Utility Vessels from Kom Hadid

No.	Locus	Pottery bag no.	Field no.	Description
Necked Kraters:				
1	7605	N.III.76.29	1040	Delta silt, slipped. Stripe of c. 5R 4/3 (Weak Red) on exterior. (Fabric ID).
2		N.III.36.30	1007	Delta silt, slipped. Painted band c. 7.5R 4/2 (Weak Red) on exterior. (Fabric ID).
3	7618	N.III.76.73	3767	Delta silt, slipped. 10YR 8/2 (White) and 5R 4/2–4/3 (Weak Red) decoration on exterior. (Fabric IE).
4	6304	N.III.63.07	3733	Delta silt, slipped. Traces of fugitive paint 10R 5/3–4/3 (Weak Red) on exterior. Areas of 10YR 8/3 (Very Pale Brown); where very thick 5YR 8/3 (Pink). (Fabric IE).
5	7619	N.III.76.77	3661	Delta silt, slipped. (Fabric IB).

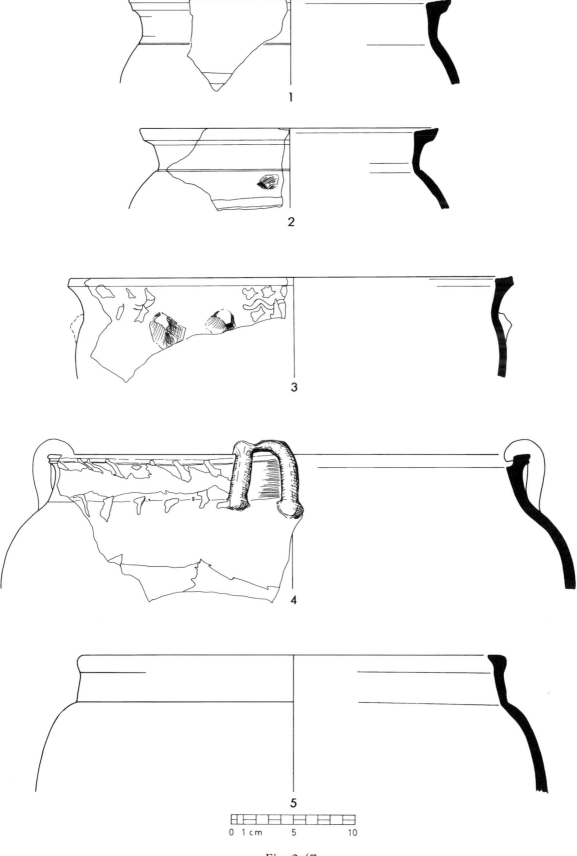

Fig. 2.47

Fig. 2.48.   Pieces of Utility Vessels from Kom Hadid

No.	Locus	Pottery bag no.	Field no.	Description
Ledge Rim Dinoi:				
1	6305	N.III.63.18	4320	Delta silt, slipped (Fabric IA)
2	6305	N.III.63.18	4302	Delta silt, slipped (Fabric IA)
3	7610	N.III.76.35	1378	Delta silt (Fabric II)
4	7605	N.III.76.10	681	Delta silt (Fabric I)
5	6305	N.III.63.11	4142	Delta silt (Fabric I)
6	7605	N.III.76.54	1675	Delta silt (Fabric I)
7	7606	N.III.76.23	963	Delta silt (Fabric I)
8	7605	N.III.76.30	1008	Delta silt (Fabric I)
9	4802	N.III.48.08	4087	Delta silt (Fabric I)
10	4807	N.III.48.10	4101	Delta silt (Fabric I)
11	7613	N.III.76.64	2072	Delta silt, slipped (Fabric IIA)
12	7605	N.III.76.10	698	Delta silt, slipped (Fabric IID)
13	7603	N.III.76.05	403	Delta silt, slipped (Fabric IA)
14	6305	N.III.63.18	4303	Delta silt, slipped (Fabric IA)
15	7606	N.III.76.23	953	Delta silt, slipped (Fabric IA)
16	7604	N.III.76.25	1291	Delta silt, slipped (Fabric IA)
17	6205	N.III.62.46	4162	Delta silt (Fabric I)
18	6304	N.III.63.07	1126	Delta silt (Fabric I)
19	7606	N.III.76.13	3299	Delta silt (Fabric I)
20	6202	N.III.62.03	720	Delta silt (Fabric I)
21	7603	N.III.76.05	2024	Delta silt (Fabric I)
22	13007	N.III.130.11	—	Delta silt, slipped (Fabric IA)

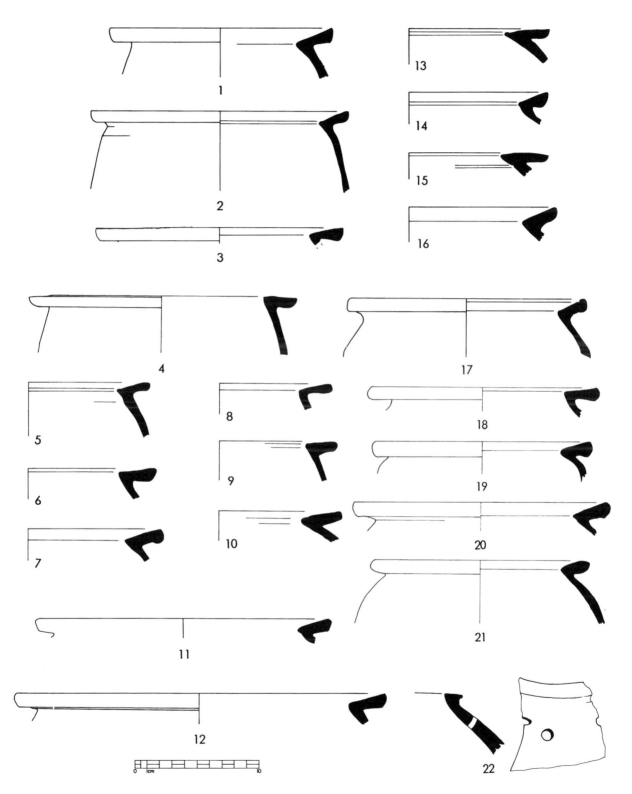

FIG. 2.48

Fig. 2.49.   Pieces of Utility Vessels from Kom Hadid

No.	Locus	Pottery bag no.	Field no.	Description
Thickened Rim Dinoi:				
1	surface	N.III.85.01	179	Delta silt, slipped (Fabric IIC)
2	7603	N.III.76.22	901	Delta silt, slipped (Fabric IA)
3	7604	N.III.76.25	1298	Delta silt, slipped (Fabric IIC)
4	14403	N.III.144.10	1235	Delta silt (Fabric I)
5	7603	N.III.76.06	493	Delta silt (Fabric I). Strap handle applied diagonally.
6	7603	N.III.76.20	909	Delta silt, slipped (Fabric IA)
7	7603	N.III.76.22	889	Delta silt, slipped (Fabric IA)
8	7063	N.III.76.05	413	Delta silt, slipped (Fabric IA)

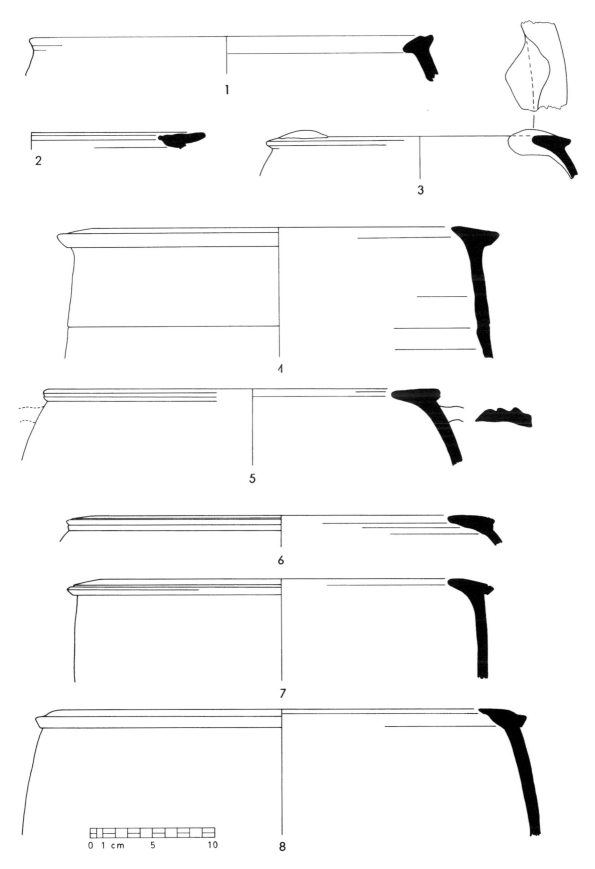

FIG. 2.49

Fig. 2.50.   *Pieces of Utility Vessels from Kom Hadid*

No.	Locus	Pottery bag no.	Field no.	Description
Large Holemouth Jars:				
1	—		3190	
2	7603	N.III.76.16	638	Delta silt, slipped (Fabric IID)
3	7613	N.III.76.34	1414	Delta silt, slipped (Fabric IIA)
4	7603	N.III.76.20	919	Delta silt, slipped. (Fabric X variant ?) Traces of 5YR 8/4 (Pink) slip exterior and interior, lighter where thinner.
5	7608	N.III.76.33	1317	Delta silt, slipped (Fabric IA)
6	7605	N.III.76.30	1016	Delta silt, slipped (Fabric IA)
7	7605	N.III.76.30	1010	Delta silt, slipped (Fabric IA)
8	14402	N.III.144.03	821	Delta silt, slipped (Fabric IA)
Small Holemouth Jars:				
9	7606	N.III.76.19	717	Delta silt, slipped (Fabric IA)
10	7606	N.III.76.13	469	Delta silt, slipped (Fabric IA)
11	6202	N.III.63.03	3540	Delta silt, slipped (Fabric IA)
12	6207	N.III.62.19	3316	Delta silt, slipped (Fabric IB)
13	6205	N.III.62.42	4080	Delta silt, slipped (Fabric X ?)
14	6209	N.III.62.32	3636	Delta silt, slipped (Fabric X ?)
Dish-Lids:				
15	6209	N.III.62.33	3394	Coarse marl (Fabric IV)
16	7618	N.III.76.74	3215	Delta silt (Fabric II)

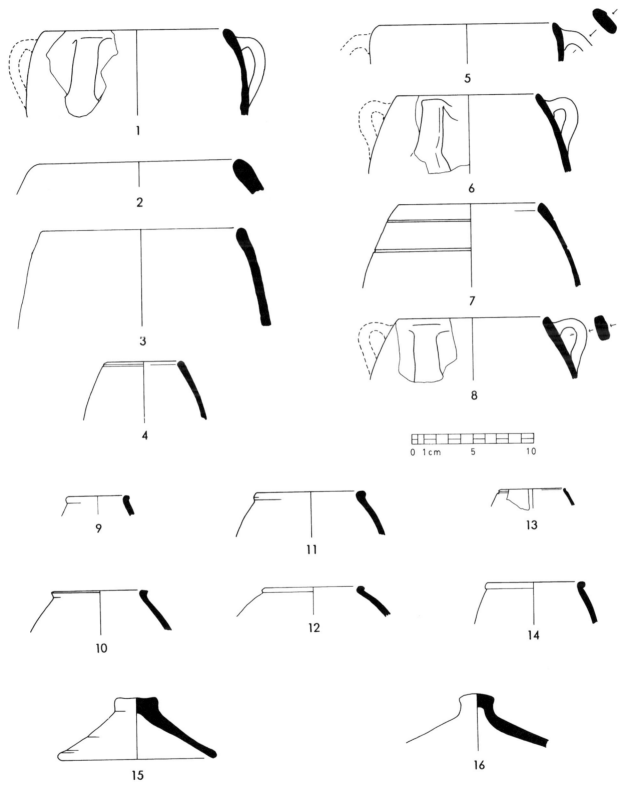

Fig. 2.50

Fig. 2.51.   Pieces of Utility Vessels from Kom Hadid

No.	Locus	Pottery bag no.	Field no.	Description
Low Stands:				
1	7604	N.III.76.24	930	Delta silt, slipped (Fabric IA)
2	7609	N.III.76.47	1664	Delta silt, slipped (Fabric IA)
3	6301	N.III.76.80	1030	Delta silt, slipped (Fabric IA)
4	6304	N.III.63.02	3590	Delta silt, slipped (Fabric IA)
5	6207	N.III.63.05	3678	Delta silt, slipped (Fabric IA)
6	6302	N.III.62.16	3193	Delta silt, slipped (Fabric IA)
7	7605	N.III.63.03	3510	Delta silt, slipped (Fabric IA)
8	7605	N.III.76.30	1005	Delta silt, slipped (Fabric IA)
9	7601	N.III.76.02	262	Delta silt, slipped (Fabric IA)
10	6302	N.III.63.06	3494	Delta silt, slipped (Fabric IA)
11	6203	N.III.62.13	2028	Delta silt (Fabric II)
12	7617	N.III.76.68	3009	Delta silt, slipped (Fabric IIC)
13	6303	N.III.63.04	4006	Delta silt, slipped (Fabric IIC)
Jar Bottoms:				
14	7610	N.III.76.52	1721	Delta silt, slipped (Fabric IIC)
15	6301	N.III.63.01	3900	Delta silt, slipped (Fabric IA)
16	6202	N.III.62.20	3175	Delta silt (Fabric I)
Pan Handles:				
17	6209	N.III.62.39	3616	Delta silt, slipped (Fabric IB)
18	7605	N.III.76.32	1205	Delta silt, slipped (Fabric IIC)

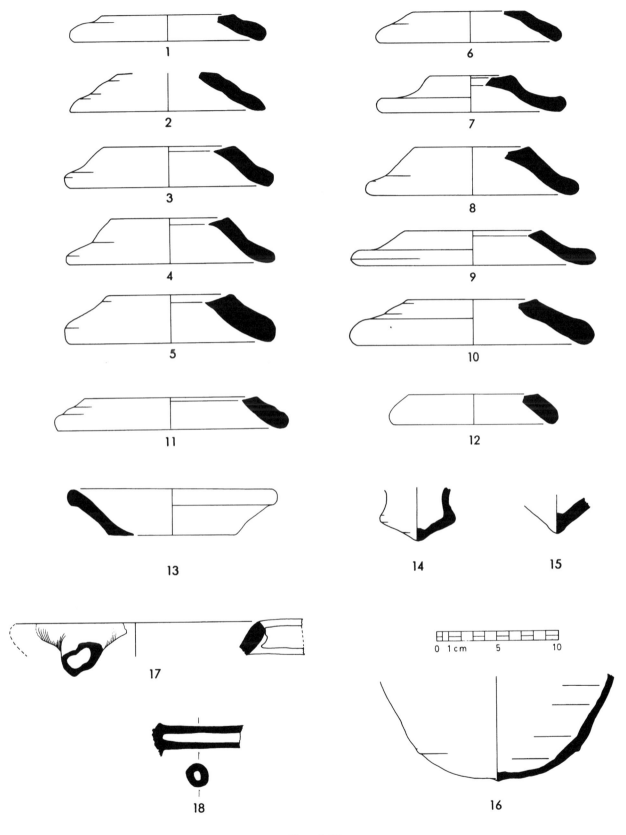

FIG. 2.51

Fig. 2.52.   Pieces of Utility Vessels from Kom Hadid

No.	Locus	Pottery bag no.	Field no.	Description
Shallow Basins/Bread Discs:				
1	7618	N.III.76.76	3606	Coarse marl (Fabric IV)
2	7604	N.III.76.24	942	Delta silt, slipped (Fabric IIC)
3	4808	N.III.48.11	4129	Delta silt, slipped (Fabric IIC)
4	7613	N.III.76.41	1573	Delta silt, slipped (Fabric IIC)
5	6203	N.III.62.07	3089	Coarse marl, slipped (Fabric IVB)
6	7609	N.III.76.27	1174	Coarse marl, slipped (Fabric VA)
Deep Basin:				
7	6301	N.III.63.01	3903	Delta silt, slipped (Fabric IA)

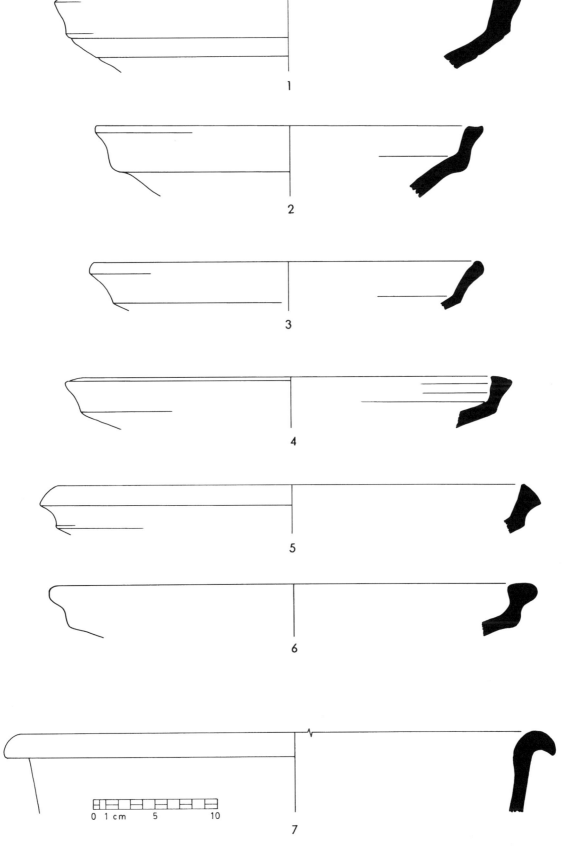

FIG. 2.52

Fig. 2.53.   Pieces of Utility Vessels from Kom Hadid

No.	Locus	Pottery bag no.	Field no.	Description
Shallow Basins/Bread Discs:				
1	6304	N.III.63.07	3724	Coarse marl, slipped (Fabric VB)
2	7613	N.III.76.70	3279	Coarse marl, slipped) YR 7/6–6/6 (Reddish Yellow) slip in/out. (Fabric VB)
3	7613	N.III.76.64	2073	Coarse marl, slipped. 5YR 7/6–6/6 (Reddish Yellow) slip in/out. (Fabric VB)
4	6215	N.III.62.38	3973	Coarse marl, slipped (Fabric VB)
5	7613	N.III.76.45	1739	Coarse marl, slipped (Fabric VB)
6	7609	N.III.76.58	3328	Coarse marl, slipped. Very thin 5YR 7/4 (Pink)–7/6 (Reddish Yellow) slip/ wash wiped on interior and exterior. (Fabric VB)
7	6302	N.III.63.03	3490	Coarse marl, slipped. Traces of 10YR 8/2 (White) "slip" on exterior. (Fabric VB)
8	6304	N.III.63.09	3451	Coarse marl, slipped (Fabric VB)
Miscellaneous:				
9	7605	N.III.76.29	1082	Delta silt, slipped (Fabric IIC). String cut base.
10	14402	N.III.144.03	823	Delta silt, slipped (Fabric IIC)

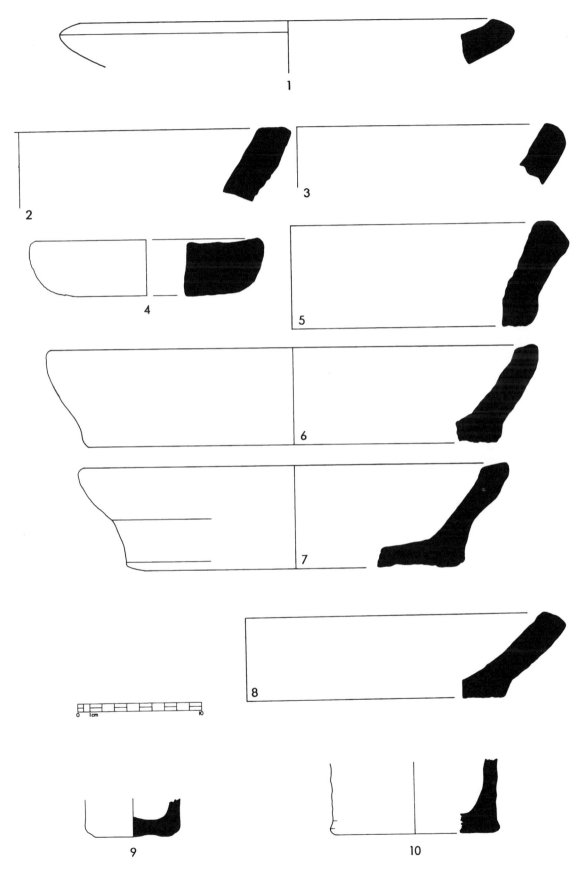

FIG. 2.53

Fig. 2.54.   Pieces of Utility Vessels from Kom Hadid

No.	Locus	Pottery bag no.	Field no.	Description
Deep Basins:				
1	7606	N.III.76.36	1468	Coarse marl, slipped (Fabric VB)
2	7601	N.III.76.01	173	Coarse marl, slipped (Fabric VA). Traces of smooth 10YR 8/2 (White) slip on exterior, fired (secondarily) to black on interior.
3	7613	N.III.76.64	2071	Coarse marl, slipped (Fabric VB) with thin 10YR 8/2 (White) "slip" on exterior.
4	7605	N.III.76.30	1031	Coarse marl, slipped (Fabric VB)
5	7608	N.III.62.42	4081	Coarse marl, slipped (Fabric VB) with smearing of 10YR 8/2 (White) slip/wash on exterior. Fired gray on interior.
6	7615	N.III.76.45	1738	Coarse marl, slipped (Fabric VB)
7	6215	N.III.62.38	3780	Coarse marl (Fabric IV)
8	7605	N.III.76.10	663	Coarse marl (Fabric IV)
9	6209	N.III.62.26	3779	Coarse marl, slipped (Fabric VB) with 5YR 6/6 (Reddish Yellow) "slip" secondarily fired to black in places.
10	6304	N.III.63.05	3665	Coarse marl, slipped (Fabric VB)

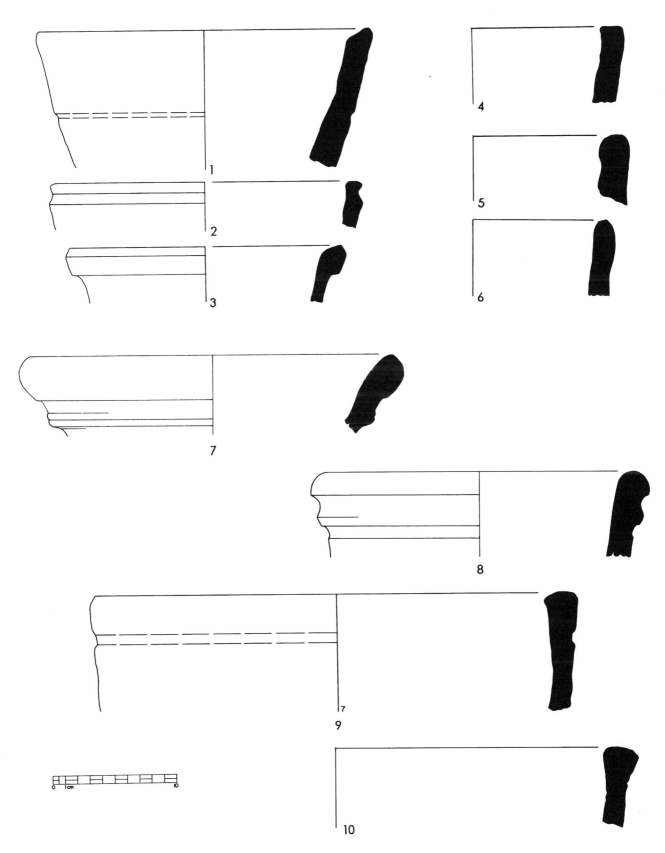

FIG. 2.54

Fig. 2.55.   Pieces of Utility Vessels from Kom Hadid

No.	Locus	Pottery bag no.	Field no.	Description
Deep Basins:				
1	6207	N.III.62.24	3820	Coarse marl, slipped. 7.5YR 7/6 (Reddish Yellow) slip on exterior. (Fabric VB)
2	7601	N.III.76.02	299	Coarse marl, slipped (Fabric VB)
3	7603	N.III.76.20	926	Coarse marl, slipped (Fabric VB)
4	7613	N.III.76.41	1581	Coarse marl, slipped (Fabric VB)

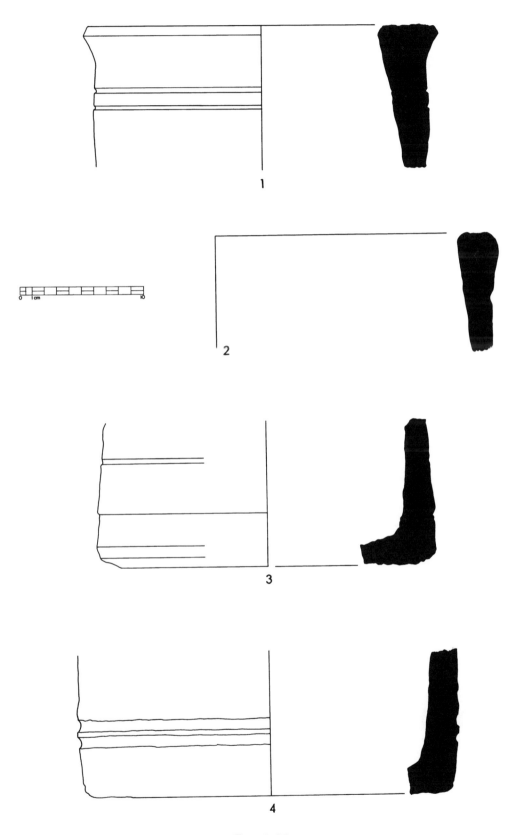

FIG. 2.55

Fig. 2.56. Pieces of Utility Vessels from Kom Hadid

No.	Locus	Pottery bag no.	Field no.	Description
Beaded Rim Amphorae:				
1	7618	N.III.76.76	3609	Poorly levigated clay with white grit 1–2 mm and straw/chaff casts to 4 mm. Core/fabric c. 5YR 5/6 (Yellowish Red). Traces of slip in/out where thick 10YR 8/4 (Very Pale Brown), where thin 10YR 8/3 (Very Pale Brown).
2	7602	N.III.76.03	230	Moderately well-levigated clay with white grit c. 1 mm and some fine straw casts. Fabric 2.5YR 6/6–6/8 (Light Red). Slip in/out c. 2.5Y 8/2 (White). Local imitation.
Squared Rim Amphorae:				
3	6305	N.III.63.11	4151	Moderately well-levigated clay with sand-sized white grit, sand-sized micaceous inclusions, and straw casts 2–3 mm. Fabric/core blends to surface colors. Interior surface 5YR 5/3–4/3 (Reddish Brown). Exterior surface 7.5YR 5/4 (Brown). Traces of slip on exterior c. 7.5YR 7/2 (Pinkish Gray).
4	6201	N.III.62.01	1856	Moderately well-levigated clay with white grit to 1 mm and straw casts. Gray core. Sandwich 2.5YR 6/6 (Light Red). In/out 5YR 5/4–4/4 (Reddish Brown).
5	6305	N.III.63.18	4278	Moderately well-levigated clay with sand-sized white grit, sand-sized micaceous inclusions, and straw casts 2–3 mm. Fabric/core completely dark gray. Interior surface 10R 5/4 (Weak Red)–5/6 (Red). Exterior surface where unslipped 2.5YR 5/6 (Red); smeary slip where thick near handle 10YR 8/2 (White) gives exterior surface c. 5YR 6/4 (Light Reddish Brown).
6	4810	N.III.48.05	3950	Moderately well-levigated clay with sand-sized to 1 mm white and gray grit and some straw casts to 1 mm. Core 7.5YR 6/4 (Light Brown)–6/8 (Reddish Yellow)–c. 2.5YR 5/6 (Red) below exterior surface. Exterior mottled as core colors and to light gray. Local amphora rim.
7	6305	N.III.63.18	4305	Moderately well-levigated clay. Fabric/core as 4304. Slip in/out 10R 6/6 (Light Red)–5/6 (Red). Local amphora rim.
8	—	N.III.62.44	4229	Moderately well-levigated clay with frequent 1 mm white grit and fine straw casts. Fabric/core 10R 4/4 (Weak Red)–4/6 (Red). Slip in/out (overfired to?) 5Y 8/2 (White)–7/2 (Light Gray). Local amphora rim.
Amphora Handle:				
9	7603	N.III.76.05	411	Moderately well-levigated clay with white and gray grit to 1 mm and fine straw casts. Fabric 5YR 5/3–5/4 (Reddish Brown). Slip (thin wash) 10R 5/3 Weak Red).

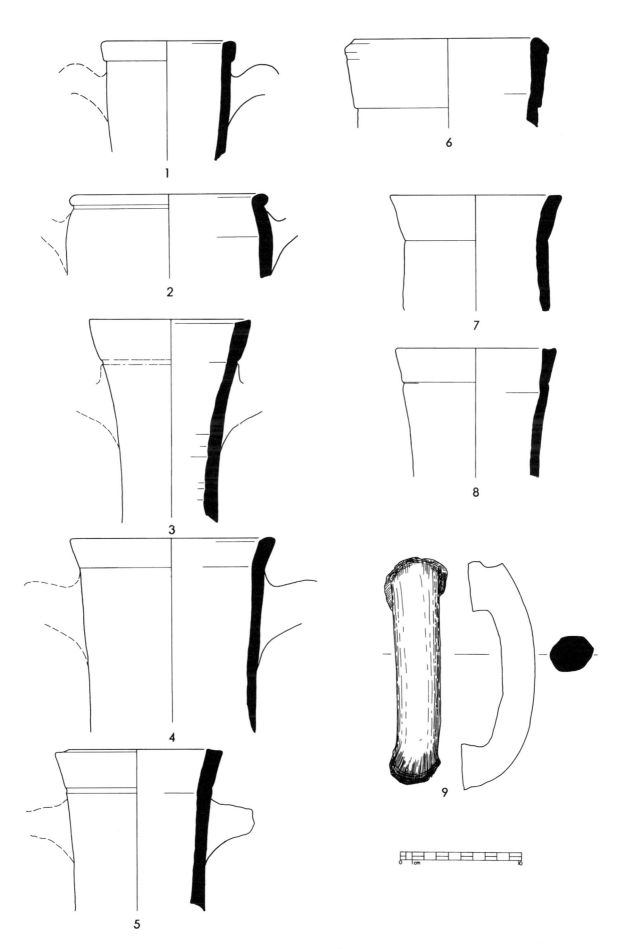

FIG. 2.56

Fig. 2.57.   *Pieces of Utility Vessels from Kom Hadid*

No.	Locus	Pottery bag no.	Field no.	Description
Inthickened Rim Amphorae:				
1	6305	N.III.63.18	4281	Moderately well-levigated clay with sand-sized micaceous inclusions, white grit c. 1 mm and fine straw casts. Core/fabric/inner surface c. 10R 5/8–4/8 (Red). Outer surface thin, splotchy 10YR 8/2 (White) slip gives most of surface 5YR 7/3–7/4 (Pink) look.
2	7609	N.III.76.27	1187	Fabric/core as Mineral-tempered Red Ware. Sandwich c. 2 mm each side as Mineral-tempered Brown Ware except white grit more commonly 1 mm. Slip in/out 5YR 7/4 (Pink)–7/6 (Reddish Yellow) in many places.
3	7605	N.III.76.29	1089	Poorly-levigated clay with dense black grit 1–2 mm and sand-sized to 1 mm white grit. Core light gray. Sandwich (thin) c. 10R 6/6–6/8 (Light Red). Surfaces 10R 5/4–4/4 (Weak Red). Slip (very thin and splotchy on exterior) c. 2.5Y 8/2 (White).
Squared Rim Amphorae:				
4	7603	N.III.76.05	351	Moderately well-levigated clay with white and gray grit 1–2 mm, sand-sized micaceous inclusions, and straw casts to 3 mm. Fabric/core c. 10R 5/8 (Red). exterior surface slipped (?) 10R 5/4 (Weak Red); interior 10R 5/6 (Red).
5	7601	N.III.76.17	844	Moderately-levigated clay with white and gray grit to 2 mm, sand-sized micaceous inclusions, and straw casts to 4 mm. Core variegated gray, and 7.5R 4/4 (Weak Red). Sandwich c. 10R 5/8 (Red) below surfaces. Surface (slipped?) exterior 10R 5/4 (Weak Red); interior 10R 5/6 (Red).
Concave Rim Amphorae:				
6	7605	N.III.76.55	1829	Moderately-well-levigated clay with sand-sized white grit, sand-sized micaceous inclusions, and straw casts 2-3 mm. Core 10R 4/6–5/8 (Red). Fabric/sandwich 5YR 5/6 (Yellowish Red). Slip in/out 5YR 7/4 (Pink)–7/6 (Reddish Yellow).
7	7603	N.III.76.05	375	Moderately well-levigated clay with white grit 1–2 mm and fine straw casts. Core black. Slip(?) in/out c. 2.5YR 6/4 (Light Reddish Brown).
8	13006	N.III.130.17	1971	Well-levigated clay with sand-sized white grit and micaceous inclusions. Core (thin) 10R 4/8 (Red). Fabric 5YR 5/6–4/6 (Yellowish Red). Slip in/out 10R 4/2–4/3 (Weak Red).
Amphorae Handles:				
9	7603	N.III.76.05	409	Moderately well-levigated clay with white and gray grit c. 1 mm and fine straw casts. Core completely gray. Slip exterior 5YR 7/3–7/4 (Pink).
10	7603	N.III.76.05	340	Moderately well-levigated clay with sand-sized micaceous inclusions and white grit c. 1 mm. Fabric 7.5R 6/6 (Light Red)–5/6 (Red). Slip 5Y 8/2 (White)–8/3 (Pale Yellow).

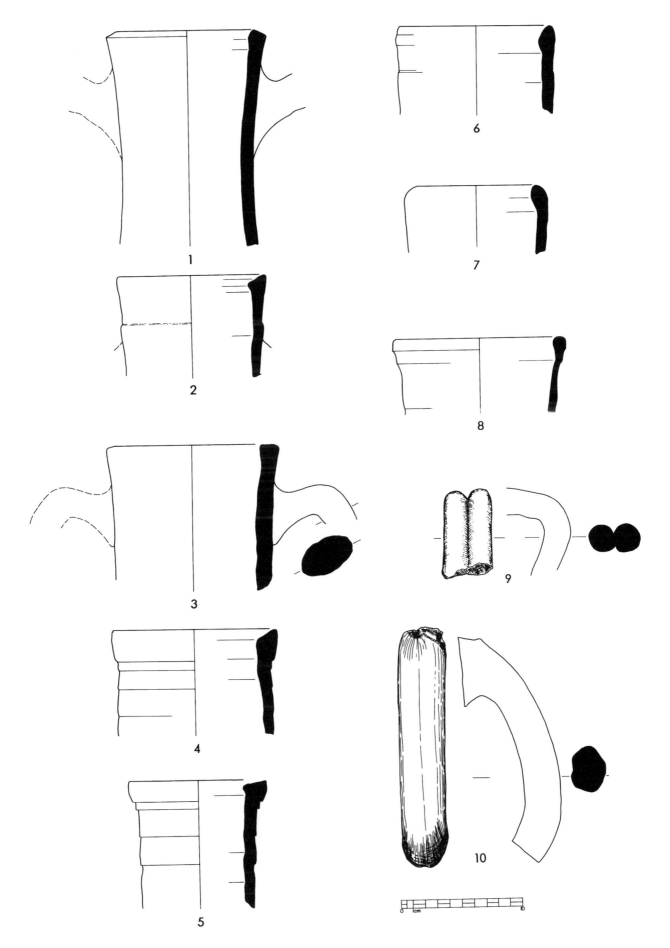

FIG. 2.57

Chapter Three
Miscellaneous Material Culture

Albert Leonard, Jr.

Terracotta Masks, Figurines, and Plaques

Introduction[1]

It appears that the Greeks at Naukratis began to utilize the local Nile clays for the production of terracotta figurines and masks soon after they founded their settlement toward the end of the seventh century B.C. (Higgins 1967: 56; 1969: 404). The earliest archaeological evidence for this practice is the series of Daedalic plaques executed in a hybrid style that mixed Rhodian and local Egyptian elements (Higgins 1969: 404, with references). Local production of figurines is considered to have continued at Naukratis during the fifth and fourth centuries B.C., but in the absence of a sizable corpus of well-dated examples, very little can be said about the development of the genre during that period (Higgins 1967: 93). It was after the cosmopolitan city of Alexandria was founded in 331 B.C., however, that the coroplasts' art can be seen to flourish in Egypt (Higgins 1967: 129–33). At first, the immigrant artisans in the new capital were forced to compete for sales with their counterparts at Naukratis. Soon, however, a true Alexandrian school of terracotta figurines developed, one that can be clearly defined by the large number of well-preserved examples from the many cemeteries (Chatby, Hadra) of the ancient city. By 200 B.C., these two cities had lost whatever exclusivity they may have shared, and figurine production became widespread throughout the Ptolemaic Kingdom of Egypt, especially at sites around the Fayoum Oasis. These new workshops produced figurines and plaques characterized by an eclecticism in which an array of complex and distinctive Graeco-Egyptian religious motives appeared side-by-side with a range of themes and characters drawn from the Greek comic stage.[2] Indeed, many of these manufacturing centers continued to be prolific well into the Roman Period.

Terracotta masks and figurines were some of the earliest finds at the site of Naukratis, over 400 of them being reported by Gutch (1898/99: 67) from the spring campaign of 1899. Our work at the site, however, was less productive in this regard with less than two dozen fragments being recorded.[3]

1. Mask fragment. Miniature (pl. 3.1)
Locus 6207   N.III.62.19   MC#37
Technique: Moldmade, some handtool finishing. Open back.
Fabric: Well-levigated Delta silt.[4]
Thick gray core with 7.5YR 4/2 (Weak Red) to 10R 5/8 (Red) sandwich. Surfaces mottled from 10R 5/4 (Weak Red) to gray. Finely ground (sand-sized to 1 mm) white, gray, and red grit temper, as well as micaceous inclusions of similar size, are frequent. Traces of fugitive white paint(?) on exterior.
Description: Fragment of mask. Only a portion of the forehead and the upper part of the eyes/brows remain. Maximum preserved H. 4.9 cm, W. 3.6 cm.
Date: 3rd–2nd century B.C.

Discussion: Of the masks that Webster sketches to illustrate the various types that were utilized in ancient Greek Comedy (1969b: 13–26), the Naukratis mask comes closest to his Type C (Old Man) and Type GA (Old Man),[5] but neither of these faces is as extremely contorted (note the severe angle of the eyes) nor exudes such a demonic feeling as does the Naukratis fragment.[6]

Possible Comparanda: Theatrical masks: Petrie 1905: 2, pl. XLIX: 79, from Ehnasya; Goldman 1950: 347, no. 276, fig. 234, from Tarsus; Bell 1981: 221, no. 809, pl. 125, from Morgantina; Breccia 1930: 65, Tav. XXXVII (from Alexandria).

2. Mask fragment. Hair and side of face (pl. 3.2)
Locus 6304   N.III.63.09   MC#20

Technique: Moldmade. Open back. After firing, the mask had been pierced through at right (of the now-broken edge) for suspension/use.

Fabric: Well-levigated Delta silt. Fabric ranges from 7.5R 5/6 (Red) to 10R 5/4 (Weak Red), with 7.5R 4/2 (Weak Red) core. Finely ground (sand-sized to 1 mm) white, gray, and red grit temper with frequent micaceous inclusions of similar size.

Description: Theatrical mask showing hair combed away from the face. White paint or lime encrustation on exterior. Maximum preserved H. c. 7.6 cm. W. c. 3.4 cm.

Date: 2nd century B.C.(?).

Discussion and Possible Comparanda: Two very good parallels, with equally straight hairline and suspension hole at the transition of the hair to the face, can be cited for this piece. One was found at Morgantina, where it was thought to represent one of the youths of New Comedy (Bell 1981: 69, 218–19, nos. 782 and 783, pl. 122); the other is said to have been found in Alexandria (Birmingham Museum 1968: 43, no. 190, pl. 14). A mask, with an equally vertical hairline, appears on a fragment from Tarsus, along with bits of a small pointed ear that led Goldman to suggest that the (unpierced) Tarsus example had been a votive mask dedicated to Dionysos (1950: 347, no. 290, fig. 235). Another fragment from Troy, also similar to the Naukratis fragment, is published as a slave from Greek comedy (Goldman 1950: 347, no. 275, fig. 235).

3. Figurine fragment. Harpocrates (pl. 3.3)
Locus 7605   N.III.76.30   MC#62

Technique: Moldmade in three (?) pieces: front, back, and (solid) head. Joined by seams at sides of body. Closed back with traces of very small (c. 1.5 cm) vent at midback.

Fabric: Well-levigated Delta silt. 7.5R 5/6 (Red) to 10R 5/4 (Weak Red) fabric, with a 7.5YR 4/2 (Weak Red) core that is mottled to 10R 5/8 (Red). Tempered with finely ground (sand-sized to 1 mm) white, gray, and red grit with frequent micaceous inclusions of similar size. Traces of white paint on face, arm and hair; pink on garment and headdress; and light blue near right ear and left shoulder.

Description: Harpocrates, wearing headdress culminating in the Double Crown. Right finger in/at mouth and cornucopia (?) in left arm against shoulder. Only the head and upper torso are preserved which is not sufficient to determine whether the god was standing or seated. Both types are common. Maximum preserved H. 8.0 cm, W. 4.8 cm.

Date: 3rd–1st century B.C.(?)

Discussion and Possible Comparanda: Harpocrates was the son of Osiris and Isis (with some assistance from the magic of Thoth). He is usually shown as a young boy with his hair pulled to the right and worn as a sidelock behind, or covering, the right ear (see **#4** below). His youth is further emphasized by his gesture of placing a finger(s) to or into his mouth. He can be depicted also wearing a variety of headdresses, the most popular being the Double Crown of Upper and Lower Egypt (as shown here) symbolizing his dominion over the entire land, and the triple *Atef* Crown with feathers and discs representing his role as successor to Osiris and emphasizing his solar nature. He was an extremely popular deity among the general population and is shown in combination with a wide range of other gods and iconographic paraphernalia, some of which are identifiable and others of which are not (Lurker 1988: 66).

Very good parallels for this figurine can be found, *inter alia*, in: Philipp 1972: 19, Cat. no. 5, Taf. IV (standing); Kaufmann 1915: Taf. 18; Bayer-Niemeyer 1988: 84, no. 68, Taf. 13 (seated), and 118–20, nos. 118–20, Tafs. 22–23 (standing); and possibly Petrie 1905: 2, pl. XLVII: 38, 40 (standing); Laumonier 1956: 379, no. 1435, pl. 41 (head only); Dunand 1990: 80, no. 160 (standing); and Breccia 1978: 20, pl. V:19 (without crown, from the Hadra cemetery).

4. Figurine head. Harpocrates (pl. 3.4)
Locus 7613   N.III.76.70   MC#146a
Technique: Moldmade in bipartite mold: front and back pieces joined at seams behind the ears and sidelock.
Fabric: Well-levigated Delta silt. Fabric ranges from 7.5R 5/6 (Red) to 10R 5/4 (Weak Red), over a 7.5YR 4/2 (Weak Red) to 10R 5/8 (Red) core. Temper consists of finely ground (sand-sized to 1 mm) white, gray, and red grit, and frequent micaceous inclusions of similar size.
Description: Head of the young god Harpocrates wearing sidelock on the right side of his head. Maximum preserved H. 4.1 cm, W. 4.0 cm.
Date: 2nd–1st century B.C.
Discussion and Possible Comparanda: At first inspection, this figure might appear to represent a comic actor or one of the grotesques that abound in Late Hellenistic terracottas and that are especially popular in Egypt and the eastern Mediterranean world (such as the grotesque with greatly exaggerated right ear from first century B.C. Smyrna [Bol and Kotera 1986: 182, no. 94]). The presence of the sidelock, however, readily identifies the figure as Harpocrates despite the fact that he does not hold his finger(s) to his mouth. Furthermore, he is shown smooth-headed and does not appear to wear one of the distinctive headdresses or crowns with which he is usually depicted. The bits of clay that still adhere to the top of the god's head are considered to indicate the lesser quality of the piece rather than the remains of a (broken) lotusbud crown.[7]

Of the figurine fragments published from the earlier Naukratis excavations, three (Gutch 1898/99: 90, 93–94 , 136, 142, 210, pls. XII–XIII) are similar to the present piece.

For the smoothheaded Harpocrates with pronounced sidelock, cf. Dunand 1990: 117, no. 294; Schürmann 1989: 284, no. 1072, Taf. 158, (with hand to mouth); Bayer-Niemeyer 1988: 77–78, 234: no. 53–54, 56, 57, Taf. 10:3,4, 11:2; 96:7. Cf. also Harpocrates with sidelock, Petrie 1905:2, pl. XLVIII:56; and the dwarfish Harpocrates, Petrie 1905: 2, and pl. LI:124.

5. Figurine fragment. Head of Aphrodite(?) wearing a wreath (pl. 3.5)
Locus 6203   N.III.62.12   MC#20
Technique: Moldmade. Solid head with hollow, bipartite body.
Fabric: Well-levigated Delta silt. Surfaces range from 10YR 6/3 (Pale Red) to 10R 6/2 (Pale Red) with a core mottled between 10R 4/2 (Weak Red) and 5YR 4/6 (Yellowish Red). Tempered with fine (sand-sized to 1 mm) white, gray, and red grit, with frequent micaceous inclusions of similar size.

Description: Head and back of neck preserved. Top of head abraded. Maximum preserved H. c. 5.6 cm, W. c. 4.5 cm.

Date: 2nd century B.C.

Discussion and Possible Comparanda: With only the head preserved, it is impossible to be certain as to the sex of the individual portrayed or even her/his status as human or divine. Three heads, similar in appearance to the Naukratis head, from Morgantina (Bell 1981: 89–90 nos. 523, 546, and 563) are interpreted as representing the young god Hades on the day of his wedding to Persephone; a youthful (and beardless) Herakles wearing a bound crown with fillet is known from Troy (Thompson 1963: 72, no. 2, with additional notes under no. 3). Thompson published a very similar head from the Kosmos Cistern on the slopes of the Aereopagos (Thompson et al. 1987: 355, no. 7[a], pl. 72), which she identified as a young male, whose rather Ptolemaic visage she paralleled with examples from the Chatby cemetery in Alexandria (1987: 355, no. 17, reference to Breccia 1912: 229, 231, pl. LXXIV, nos. 494ff. See also Breccia 1930: 60 [no. 302], Tav. XIX:3).

However, on the basis of the comparanda offered below,[8] interpretation as a goddess (preferably Aphrodite or Isis-Aphrodite) wearing a thick, floral wreath (itself an Egyptian custom)[9] is preferred here. Identification as a human, however, is equally possible since, during the Late Hellenistic period, both the wreath and the Knidian coiffure (Thompson 1963: 37–38, 45–48) appeared throughout the Greek world on a wide variety of figure types including men, women, children, and even slaves (Thompson 1963: 46).

Chronologically, the popularity of these figurines extends from the fourth through the first centuries B.C. (Bell 1981: 66, 76), but this form of the wreath is most popular during the second century B.C. (Thompson 1963: 49–50; Bell 1981: 166), a date to which the Naukratis piece should most probably be assigned.

An alternate identification would call attention to the small bits of clay that adhere to the area around the mouth. These could be interpreted as either surplus pieces of clay from the mold that carelessly had been left on the figurine when it was fired, or as the remains of some attribute of the figure that had disappeared when the figurine was broken. If the latter were to have been the case, the only suitable attribute would be the finger(s) of the young Harpocrates. Not only is this hybrid Egyptian divinity frequently shown making such a gesture, but he can also be depicted wearing a crown that is quite similar to the wreath on the present piece.[10]

Arguing against such an interpretation would be the fact that there are many examples of otherwise very carefully crafted figurines that have not been completely cleaned after being removed from the mold, with the resultant bits of surplus clay giving strange or unusual features to the personage represented. Such features, however, appear to have been either unimportant or unnoticed in the ancient marketplace.[11]

6. Figurine. Head of young male (pl. 3.6)
Locus 6207   N.III.62.24   MC#48a

Technique: Moldmade in bipartite mold. Front and back pieces joined at sides of head.

Fabric: Well-levigated Delta silt. Fabric ranges between 5YR 6/3 (Light Reddish Brown) and 5/3 (Reddish Brown) with a gray to 10R 5/8 (Red) core. Tempered with fine (sand-sized to 1 mm) white, gray, and red grit, with frequent micaceous inclusions of similar size. Traces of white and pink paint.

Description: Head of young male slightly upturned (and to the right). Broken at neck, only head remains. Chips from top of head missing. Maximum preserved H. 5.9 cm, W. 3.5 cm.

Date: 3rd–2nd century B.C.(?).

Discussion and Possible Comparanda: The length of the hair, as well as the upward gaze, are shared by some representations of the young Harpocrates wearing a lotusbud crown. It is not impossible that such a crown once existed where parts of the present head are now broken and missing. Cf. Dunand 1990: 80, nos. 180–81, and also 123, no. 317 (with Double Crown, which is similar to depictions of Isis wearing the same crown, Dunand 1990: 156, no. 419.)

7. Figurine fragment. Young male(?) with pointed hat(?) (pl. 3.7)
Locus 6209   N.III.62.14   MC#28

Technique: Moldmade. Hand-tooled details(?).

Fabric: Well-levigated Delta silt. Fabric ranges from 5YR 6/3 (Light Reddish Brown) to 5/3 (Reddish Brown) with 5YR 4/6 (Yellowish Red) core. Tempered with fine (sand-sized to 1 mm) white, gray, and red grit, and frequent micaceous inclusions of similar size. Surfaces as fabric (no slip?).

Description: Fragment of a figurine of indeterminate gender (a child?). Only the head and pointed hat(?) preserved. Horizontal band of hair(?) indicated on forehead. Facial features very faintly indicated. Maximum preserved H. c. 2.5 cm, W. 2.3 cm.

Date: 3rd–2nd century B.C.

Discussion and Possible Comparanda: This piece is open to many different interpretations. The hat or hood worn by the figure may be a separate article of clothing such as can be worn by Harpocrates (Petrie 1905:1, pl. XLVIII:54; Graindor 1939: 136, pl. XIX: 55; Perdrizet 1921: 30 [no. 87], 31 [no. 88], and pl. XXIII [from the Fayoum]); and others (Breccia 1930: 73 [nos. 471–72], Tav. XXIII: 4, 5 [from Alexandria]). Or it could have been intended to depict a himation tightly drawn over the head. Very often, when worn in this manner, the garment forms a point at the top of the head above the face (cf. Morgantina Types VI–VIII, Bell 1981: 52, fig. C; and specifically 200: nos. 621 and 742 [Type VIII]; Breccia 1978: 20, pl. IV:15, V:18, from Hadra cemetery). Such an interpretation, however, would not explain what is happening to the hood above the face at either side of the figurine. Was this part of a group figure?

Also worth considering are an infant (Dunand 1990: 265, no. 781), the head of a warrior or hunter (Thompson, et al 1987: 159, no. 13, Athenian Agora), a small child being carried by a black male (Adriani 1940: 170 [inv. no. 25091], pl. LXVIII:3, purchased in Alexandria), Attys with "cedar cone" cap (Petrie 1905: 2, pl. XLVIII:53,54, from Ehnasya), Telesphoros (difficult to determine if the hood circles under the chin [Bell 1981: #356–58, Morgantina]), or Athena wearing a Thracian helmet (Bell 1981: #220, 223, p. 158, pl. 56, Morgantina). Also possible is the "flowing" hood, cf. a "circus rider" (Schürmann 1989: 311, no. 1169, Taf. 194), a gladiator (Schürmann 1989: 311–12, no. 171, Taf. 194) or a comic actor (Bell 1981: 68, 213–14, no. 742, pl. 117).

It is not impossible to reconstruct this figure as a woman wearing a kerchief, and that the piece has fractured along the lines where the kerchief would have been tied under the chin as in Laumonier 1956: 249, nos. 1141–42, pl. 86. Also relevant are Dunand 1990: 239, no. 671; and Breccia 1930: 32, Tav. D1; and 42, Tav. XIII:7.

8. Figurine fragment. Isis-Aphrodite(?) (pl. 3.8a)
Locus 7608   N.III.76.26   MC#52

Technique: Moldmade in bipartite mold. Front and back pieces joined by seams at sides. Handtooling to emphasize the legs and to delineate the toes.

Fabric: Well-levigated Delta silt. Fabric c. 7.5R 4/2 (Weak Red) mottled through 10R 5/2–4/2 (Weak Red) to gray and black. Temper consists of finely ground (sand-sized to 1 mm) white, gray, and red grit, and frequent micaceous inclusions of similar size. Exterior surfaces frequently mottled to black (secondary burning?).

Description: Female(?) standing frontally (nude or wearing a very tight garment), with legs pressed together tightly. Only the feet (and sandals?) below the ankles remain. Maximum preserved H. 4.1 cm, W. 3.6 cm.

Date: 3rd–2nd century B.C.

Discussion and Possible Comparanda: The best parallel in terms of similarity and provenance for this figurine is the well-preserved combination of Aphrodite and Isis from Naukratis in the British Museum (Higgins 1967: XXXVIII, 132 [BM Cat. C574], pl. 63E), which is so similar that they could have been made from the same mold. Similar statuettes of Isis-Aphrodite displaying the same stance are known from Bubastis (Schürmann 1989: 271–72, nos. 1031–34, Taf. 171–72), and elsewhere in Egypt (Graindor 1939: 107–9, no. 36, pl. XIV, and references page 108 note 1; Birmingham Museum 1968: 40, no. 164, pl. 28; Philipp 1972: 23 and 32, cat. nos. 18 and 47, Abb. 17 and 43–44; Breccia 1930: 44 no. 172, Tav. LIII:21 [Hadra Cemetery, Alexandria]; and Dunand 1990: 125, no. 327 and 130, no. 338). Several similar pieces, without the legs preserved, are in the collections of the Louvre (Dunand 1990, especially nos. 328–39).[12]

In spite of the probability that these feet represent Isis-Aphrodite, the identification cannot be considered to be absolutely certain since both the frontality and the tightly pressed legs can be found on other figurine types: Silenus-Hermes (Köster 1926: 202, no. 744, Taf. 123); and *Fruchtbarkeitsgöttin* (Bayer-Niemeyer 1988: 141–42, no. 244 [with anklets], 245–47; and the *göttin mit Kalathos* (Weber 1914: 132–35, nos. 200–206, and Taf. 20). Similar pieces are published by Perdrizet 1921: 1–4 and pl. III (left and right), pl. IV (with elaborately painted decoration preserved); Breccia 1930: 72, Tav. LIII:21 (from Alexandria) or even Harpocrates (Kaufmann 1915: pl. 18, top middle and pl. 36 top).

9. Figurine fragment. Isis-Aphrodite(?) (pl. 3.8b)
Locus 6210   N.III.62.27   MC#52a

Technique: Moldmade in bipartite mold. Front and back pieces joined by seams at sides. Handtooling to emphasize the legs and to delineate the toes.

Fabric: Well-levigated Delta silt. Fabric c. 7.5R 4/2 (Weak Red) mottled through 10R 5/2–4/2 (Weak Red) to gray and black. Temper consists of finely ground (sand-sized to 1 mm) white, gray, and red grit, and frequent micaceous inclusions of similar size. Exterior surfaces frequently mottled to black (secondary burning?).

Description: Female(?) standing frontally (nude or with very tight garment), with legs pressed together tightly. Only the feet (and sandals?) below the shins remain. Preserved H. 5.8 cm, W. 3.6 cm.

Date: 3rd–2nd century B.C.

Discussion and Possible Comparanda: See #8, above.

10. Figurine fragment. Isis-Aphrodite(?) (pl. 3.8c)
Locus 6207   N.III.62.16   MC#26

Technique: Moldmade in bipartite mold. Front and back pieces joined by seams at sides. Handtooling to emphasize the legs and to delineate the toes.

Fabric: Well-levigated Delta silt. Fabric c. 7.5R 4/2 (Weak Red) mottled through 10R 5/2–4/2 (Weak Red) to gray and black. Temper consists of finely ground (sand-sized to 1 mm) white, gray, and red grit, and frequent micaceous inclusions of similar size. Exterior surfaces frequently mottled to black (secondary burning?).

Description: Female(?) standing frontally (nude or with very tight garment), with legs pressed together tightly. Only the feet (and sandals?) below the knees remain. Maximum preserved H. 9.7 cm, W. 3.6 cm.

Date: 3rd–2nd century B.C.

Discussion and Possible Comparanda: See #8, above.

11. Figurine fragment. Male youth wearing himation (pl. 3.9)

Locus 7605   N.III.76.10   MC#158

Technique: Moldmade in bipartite mold: front and back joined at sides. Back plain with circular vent, c. 2.7 cm in diameter at midback.

Fabric: Well-levigated Delta silt. Fabric from 5YR 6/3 (Light Reddish Brown) to 5/3 (Reddish Brown), with gray to 10R 5/8 (Red) core. Tempered with fine (sand-sized to 1 mm) white, gray, and red grit, and frequent micaceous inclusions of similar size. Surfaces as fabric (no visible slip). White (lime?) accretions and black spots (secondary burning) on exterior surfaces.

Description: Standing/advancing male in chiton and himation. Right hand bent at elbow, left hand to side. Head and neck as well as legs below the knees are missing. Maximum preserved H. c. 8.1 cm, W. c. 4.0 cm.

Date: 3rd century B.C.

Discussion and Possible Comparanda: In the field, this piece was identified and catalogued as an advancing male with long phallus, a theme that would be quite at home at Naukratis, but one for which it is difficult to find close parallels. Without the phallic attribute, however, the figurine resembles a series of comic actors from Morgantina (Bell 1981: 214–15, nos. 745, 751, pl. 118; based on his no. 743), which Bell has interpreted as *pseudokore* figures from the *phlyax* of Middle Comedy of the third century B.C., where male actors in women's roles were especially common (1981: 68, 214–15).

For the mirror image (or reverse) of the pose of the Naukratis figure, in which the right arm hangs to the side (holding the garment?) and the left is bent at elbow with hand held in front of the chest, see Higgins 1967: 116–17, pl. 56E (youth with himation). Evidently, figurines of young men wearing the himation (and often carrying a quiver behind the neck parallel to the ground) were popular during the first few centuries before and after Christ. The example in the British Museum published by Higgins (1967: xxxix) was signed by the coroplast Diphilos and dated to the first century A.D. A similar piece (Knaben in Mantel) is published in Bayer-Niemeyer (1988: 60. no. 2, Taf.1:3).

12. Terracotta vessel fragment. Grapes(?) or stylized hair curls(?) (pl. 3.10)

Locus 7606   N.III.76.14   MC#29

H. c. 5.8 cm, P.W. c. 4.2 cm.

Technique: Moldmade in bipartite mold.

Fabric: Well-levigated Delta silt. Core from 7.5YR 4/2 (Weak Red) to 10R 5/8 (Red) below an exterior surface c. 10R 5/3 (Weak Red) fading to c. 10R 6/1 (Reddish Gray). Tempered with fine (sand-sized to 1 mm) white, gray, and red grit; with frequent micaceous inclusions of similar size.

Description: Fragment of terracotta vessel depicting about one dozen semispherical pellets arranged in three rows. Broken, in part, along a seam at which point the back of the vessel would have been attached. Maximum preserved H. 5.8 cm, W. 4.2 cm.

Date: 2nd century B.C.

Discussion and Possible Comparanda: Although this fragment could be interpreted as the tightly curled hairs of a herm (Thompson et al. 1987: 434, pl. 58 [T1566] from Athens), it is more likely that it originally formed a part of a bunch of grapes or, as will be noted, hair in the form of grapes. Moldmade, terracotta representations of bunches of grapes, or the molds themselves, range from isolated bunches for suspension as an ornament (Laumonier 1956: 268, nos. 1257, 1258, pl. 96), as part of the overflowing bounty of a cornucopia (Laumonier 1956: 280, nos. 1353, 1354, pl. 100; Thompson et al. 1987: 12–13, no. 12, pl. 5), or as part of a feast for a lion (Laumonier 1956: 284, no. 1372, pl. 103). Also relevant is the series of moldmade terracotta (and later blown glass) cluster-of-grapes vessels that were common in the Egyptian Fayoum.[13] This type could represent a bunch of grapes by itself (Bayer-Niemeyer 1988: 282–83, nos. 757–59, Taf. 129, 3rd century B.C., Dunand 1990: 331, nos. 1002–3, Roman; and Kaufmann 1915: [nos. 808–10] Taf. 74 a variety of types), or the form could be modified to serve, *inter alia*, as the beard of Dionysos/Bacchus (Bayer-Niemeyer 1988: 283, no. 760, Taf. 130:2; Dunand 1990: 330–31, nos. 1000–1001) or Serapis (Kaufmann 1915: Taf. 14:74). Similar in concept, but on a larger scale, are the masks of Dionysos Botrys, pierced to be worn or suspended, that probably served in part as the inspiration for the smaller containers (Laumonier 1956: 124, no. 315, pl. 34 with references).

Morphologically, however, it is not impossible that what are interpreted as grapes on the Naukratis piece may have been the spherical projections (flames?) that are represented above the doorways on some moldmade terracotta "lanterns" in the form of a lighthouse, perhaps representing the *pharos* at Alexandria (Bayer-Niemeyer 1988: 261–62, nos. 665–70, Taf. 116–17).[14]

13. Figurine/plaque fragment. Drapery (pl. 3.11)
Locus 7603   N.III.76.22   MC#85

Technique: Closed back. Moldmade in two pieces: front and back. Joined at the sides. Trace of seam remains, but rest of back is missing.

Fabric: Well-levigated Delta silt. Fabric from 5YR 6/3 (Light Reddish Brown) to 5/3 (Reddish Brown) with 5YR 5/1 (Gray) through 5YR 4/1 (Dark Gray) core. Tempered with finely ground (sand-sized to 1 mm) white, gray, and red grit, with frequent micaceous inclusions of similar size. Interior-fired black in spots; traces of pink (no Munsell equivalent) paint on front of drapery.

Description: Small fragment of vertically hanging drapery with moderately deep folds. Preserved H. c. 5.5 cm, W. c. 2.3 cm.

Date: 3rd–2nd century B.C.

Discussion and Possible Comparanda: Pendant drapery is an integral part of many of the themes of Tanagra and other Hellenistic figurines. Although fragmentary, this segment of drapery most probably hung from the outstretched left hand/arm of a standing female figurine (Kleiner 1984: 251, 261, Taf. 12a, b; 116–118, Taf. 19a–f; Bol and Kotera 1986: 146–148, nos. 74–75, and possibly no. 150; cf. also Köster 1926: no. 44–49; and Breccia 1930: 27, Tav. A2, D1 and D2 from Alexandria).

14. Fragment of a mold(?) for plaque or figurine. Drapery (pl. 3.12)
Locus 6305   N.III.63.18   MC#43

Technique: Handmade or moldmade with heavy handtooling.

Fabric: Well-levigated Delta silt. Fabric ranges from c. 7.5R 5/6 (Red) to c. 10R 5/4 (Weak Red) with a thin 7.5YR 4/2 (Weak Red) to 10R 5/8 (Red) core. Tempered with finely ground (sand-sized to 1 mm) white, gray, and red grit; with frequent micaceous inclusions of similar size. The front (exterior) surface was slipped c. 7.5YR 3/6 (Dark Red); and the unslipped back (interior) surface had been fired between 10R 6/8 (Light Red) and 10R 5/8 (Red).

Description: Representation of a piece of drapery, hanging in six folds. Maximum preserved H. 3.9 cm, W. 4.1 cm.

Date: Uncertain.

Discussion and Possible Comparanda: This fragment of drapery appears to be in the negative, and it may have served as an archetype or patrix from which other molds (for sculpture in terracotta or another medium) would have been fashioned.[15] The original sculpture, of which this is but a small fragment, would have been fairly large. The representation of the drapery, itself, is too general for meaningful comparanda, but the fact that the folds do not hang vertically, but show some evidence of an S-curve (curls?), might indicate that the garment clothed someone engaged in (a lateral?) movement (cf. the chiton on a young girl playing *ephedrismos* [Birmingham Museum 1968: 32, no. 120, pl. 34]).

15. Fragment of a mold(?). Drapery (pl. 3.13)
Locus 13006   N.III.130.17   MC#21
Technique: Moldmade.

Fabric: Well-levigated Delta silt. Surfaces mottled 10R 5/4 (Weak Red) through gray, with 7.5YR 4/2 (Weak Red) core. Temper consists of sand-sized to 1 mm white, gray, and red grit, with micaceous inclusions of similar size.

Description: Vertical folds of a heavy garment. Possibly from a mold(?). Maximum preserved H. 4.1 cm, W. 2.4 cm.

Date: Indeterminate.

Discussion: The small piece of drapery is too generic for a specific attribution.

Possible Comparanda: None offered.

16. Plaque fragments (two non-joining) (pl. 3.14a, b)
Locus 7613   N.III.76.70   MC# 146b
Technique: Moldmade. Open back.

Fabric: Well-levigated Delta silt. Core ranges from 7.5YR 4/2 (Weak Red) to 10R 5/8 (Red) shading to gray on the interior. Finely ground (sand-sized to 1 mm) white, gray, and red grit temper, with frequent micaceous inclusions of similar size. A thick 7.5YR 4/6 (Red) to 3/6 (Dark Red) slip covers the exterior.

Description:
    a. Hoof(?). Maximum preserved H. 4.4 cm, W. 3.4 cm.
    b. Unidentifiable object. Maximum preserved H. 1.8 cm, W. 2.4 cm.

Date: Indeterminate.

Discussion: These two pieces were found together in the same debris locus and, therefore, they most probably come from the same plaque. The thick slip that covers the exterior surface of these pieces makes them superior to most of the other pieces in the assemblage and among most of the comparanda.[16] The individual pieces, however, do not give any clue to the original subject matter.

Possible Comparanda: For the tentative identification of the one image as a hoof, cf. Dunand 1990: 87, no. 184, which depicts a young Harpocrates (carrying an ovoid pot) riding on a camel.

17. Plaque fragment with architectural element(?) (pl. 3.15)
Locus 7603   N.III.76.04   MC#23
Technique: Moldmade. Hollow with closed back.
Fabric: Well-levigated Delta silt. Fabric from 5YR 6/3 (Light Reddish Brown) to 5/3 (Reddish Brown), with 10R 5/8 (Red) to 5YR 4/6 (Yellowish Red) core. Tempered with fine (sand-sized to 1 mm) white, gray, and red grit, and frequent micaceous inclusions of similar size. Surfaces as fabric (no visible slip). Traces of 10YR 7/6 (Yellow) paint on lower left (as viewed) of base.
Description: Small fragment of terracotta figurine. Seam present, back missing. Subject matter indeterminable. Maximum preserved H. c. 6.5 cm, W. c. 3.4 cm.
Date: Indeterminate.
Discussion and Possible Comparanda: This fragment is really too small to allow identification of the subject matter with any certainty.[17] Two possible interpretations are: the front of a chair or throne (Petrie 1905: 2, pl. XLVI:16 [seated Serapis from Ehnasya]; Rohde 1968: 46, fig. 30; Bayer-Niemeyer 1988: 132–33, no. 220, Taf. 42:5, also nos. 273–74?; Philipp 1972: 26, cat. no. 27, Abb. 24 [Isis and Harpocrates]; Köster 1926: pl. 80); Dunand 1990: 98–99, nos. 219–20 (invert the Naukratis piece); or some element in an architectural setting (Bayer-Niemeyer 1988: 270–71, nos. 700–702, Taf. 121:5–7 [lanterns of unknown provenance]). Most of these examples, however, have been assigned dates that are later than those offered for the Naukratite pieces.

Terracotta Lamps

Ten complete or fragmentary lamps were found during our four seasons of excavations at Naukratis, a surprisingly small number when one considers the amount of other ceramic material that the work had produced and the fact that Petrie had found 280 lamps during the first season of his work at the site (1886: 45). The lamps are presented below according to the method of their manufacture. The dates offered can only be considered approximate as the study of Ptolemaic lamps has been hampered by the fact that most are known primarily from multiple-burial funerary contexts and museum collections, and they are rarely from stratigraphically secure domestic deposits.[18]

Wheelmade Lamps[19]

18. Lamp (pl. 3.16 a, b and fig. 3.1:1)
Locus 7613   N.III.76.45   MC#104
Preservation: Intact. H. c. 7.5 cm; W. c. 7.1 cm
Technique: Wheelmade saucer, pinched at sides to form a lip or channel for the wick. String-cut base.
Fabric: Well-levigated Delta silt. Fine (sand-sized to 1 mm) white, gray, and red grit temper with frequent micaceous inclusions of similar size. Fabric c. 7.5R 5/6 (Red) to 10R 5/4 (Weak Red), with a core ranging from 7.5YR 4/2 (Weak Red) to 10R 5/8 (Red), and a slip between 10YR 6/8 (Light Red) and 5/8 (Red). Burnt black at tip of the pinched lip.
Date: Third Intermediate–Ptolemaic Periods.
Discussion: Among the lamps found by Petrie during his first season of work at Naukratis were 32 examples of "little flat dishes pinched in to form a spout" (Petrie 1886: 45). Only a single example of this type, however, was found during our excavations.

The origins of the saucer lamp can be traced back at least to the beginnings of the Middle Bronze Age in Palestine when the old, four-spouted lamp of the Early Bronze IV (Early–Middle Bronze) period gave way to the single-spouted variant (Amiran 1969: 82, pl. 22:11 vs 22:16; and pl. 24:13 vs 24:14). This lamp type continued to develop in the Levant throughout the Iron Age and was still common in the Iron IIC/Persian period (Amiran 1969: 291–93 and pl. 100), which was contemporary with the earlier part of the Third Intermediate Period in Egypt. In the Athenian Agora, Thompson viewed the Cocked Hat type as a local Egyptian product and also noted that it was one of the two most popular lamp types in the Chatby Cemetery at Alexandria (Howland 1958: 7–8 [Type 1], 12 [Type 3], 12–13 [Type 4]).

Daszewski 1987 included similar Egyptian pieces in his group of *lampes tournées ouvertes*, which he divided into three subtypes (1–3), primarily on the distinctiveness of the spout/lip. The Naukratis lamp would fall somewhere between his types 2 and 3.

Noting the lack of attention paid to this form of lamp in Egyptian contexts, Hayes suggested a date in the third century B.C. for their demise in Egypt, at a time when wheelmade Greek types first began to be common there (1980a: 4–5). Daszewski, however, would see their popularity continue into the second century B.C. (1987: 51–52).

Saucer lamps from Naukratis are in the Royal Ontario Museum (Hayes 1980a: 5, nos. 7–9) and in the British Museum (Bailey 1975, I: 240 and 244, no. Q515).[20]

19. Lamp. (pl. 3.17 and fig.3.1:2)
Balk Trim (locus uncertain)   N.III.76.60   MC#121
Preservation: Almost complete, section of nozzle missing. Double convex body with flattened top above the carination. Body separated from the rim of the filling hole by a relatively deep groove. Raised base, slightly concave. Trace of a (vestigial?) lug/wing on left hand side. Nozzle splayed outward ending in slight flukes. Top of nozzle flattened with ridges parallel to the sides.
L. 8.0 cm; W. 5.2 cm; H. 2.9 cm.
Technique: Wheelmade.
Fabric: Well-levigated Delta silt. Fine (sand-sized to 1 mm) white, gray, and red grit temper with frequent micaceous inclusions of similar size. Fabric c. 7.5R 5/6 (Red) to 10R 5/4 (Weak Red), with a core ranging from 7.5YR 4/2 (Weak Red) to 10R 5/8 (Red) to which has been added a 7.5YR 4/6 (Red) to 3/6 (Dark Red) slip. Exterior surfaces mottled to black in places.
Date: Last quarter of 4th and first half of the 3rd century B.C.
Discussion: Morphologically this lamp is closely related to examples of Daszewski's Egyptian *lampes tournées fermées* Types 4 and 5 (1987: 52 and fig. 1), that he describes as most closely following Howland's Type 25 series from the Athenian Agora (Howland 1958: 67–82). The form is included within Broneer's Type VII at Corinth (1930: 45–46 and nos. 114–36) and shares some elements of Shier's Type A1.1 and A2.1 lamps at Karanis (1978: 13–15).[21] Thompson considered the angular variant of these lamps (his Type IX) to have been among the most popular lamps in use in Athens during the third century B.C. (Thompson et al. 1987: 423, 447, 461).[22] That this Athenian fashion was as popular as it was in Egypt should not be surprising since it was also the Athenian lamp type that had the most influence on the local lampmakers even further west at Sidi Khrebish (Berenice) in Libya (Bailey 1985: 191).

Moldmade Lamps[23]

The moldmade lamp now appears to have made its appearance in Egyptian contexts sometime early in the third century B.C. (Daszewski 1987: 550; Shier 1978: 4–5, 17), about the same time that

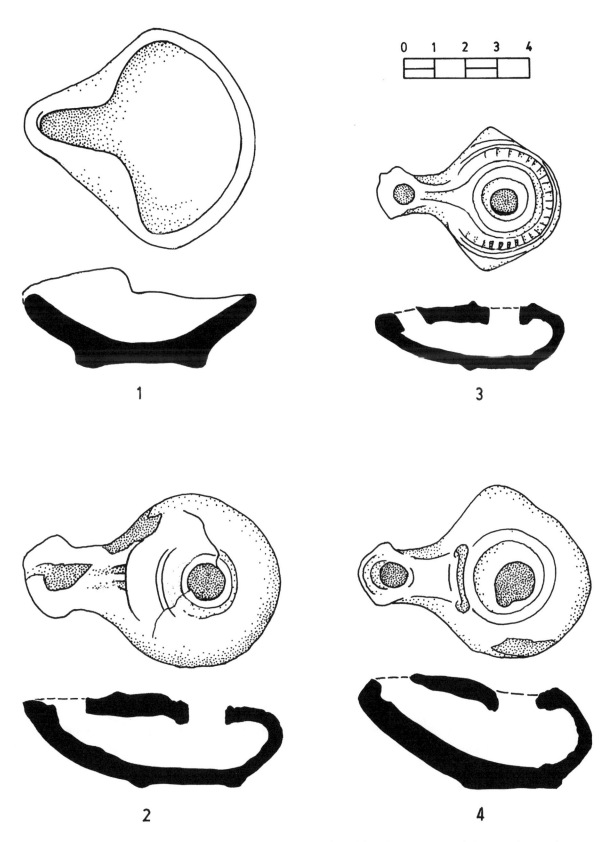

Fig. 3.1. Terracotta wheelmade (1, #18 and 2, #19) and moldmade (3, #20 and 4, #21) lamps from Kom Hadid.

the type arrived in Greece (Howland 1958: 179; Broneer 1930: 54; Thompson et al. 1987: 161), and not in the mid-second century B.C. as had previously been thought (Walters 1914: xxii).

20. Lamp. (pl. 3.18 a, b and fig. 3.1:3)
Locus 7605   N.III.76.09   MC#33
Preservation: Double-convex body with rounded carination at the join. Ridge and shallow channel around the filling hole. Solid (unturned) disc base. Sloping nozzle of medium length, flattened on top, and flaring toward embryonic flukes at the sides of the wick hole. Two opposing, solid lugs form angular projections (wings) at the sides.
Complete. L. 6.5 cm; W. 5.1 cm; H. 2.1 cm.
Technique: Moldmade in two pieces.
Fabric: Well-levigated Delta silt. Frequent (sand-sized to 1 mm) white, gray, and red grit temper with occasional micaceous inclusions of similar size. Fabric c. 7.5R 5/6 (Red) to 10R 5/4 (Weak Red), with a core ranging from 7.5YR 4/2 (Weak Red) to 10R 5/8 (Red). Top of upper surface mottled from fabric color through gray to black.
Date: End of 3rd and into the 2nd century B.C.
Discussion: In Athenian terms, this lamp most closely resembles Howland's Type 45A, a lamp with molded, relief decoration that was imported to Athens during the middle years of the third century B.C. (Howland 1958: 143–45),[24] and was copied enthusiastically for several centuries by the Athenian lampmakers using local Attic clays. Howland suggested an Alexandrian origin for these moldmade lamps on the basis of the grayish fabric of the examples from the Agora (1958: 145), but the Naukratis lamp is crafted from the reddish Delta silt that is so common at the site and is only mottled gray (in places) through secondary burning.[25]

   In Egyptian terms this lamp would fall morphologically somewhere between Daszewski's molded Hellenistic lamps of Type 12 and Type 13 (1987: 55, and fig. 2), in that it contains some attributes of both. At Karanis in the Fayoum, this is Shier's Type A.4.1 (1978: 9, 18 [with comparanda], especially no. 10 [p. 55] and pls. 1, 10). Similar lamps from Egypt, but without specific provenance, in the British Museum are dated by Bailey to the second century B.C. (1975: 255–56, especially nos. Q546 [Luxor?] and Q549 [Thebes?]), and/or into the early part of the first century B.C. (1975: 271–73, especially nos. Q589, Q590, Q592 [Dakeh, Nubia?], and Q593 [Buto/Tell el-Fara'in]). A related, but much more carefully crafted lamp was excavated by Petrie at Naukratis during his first season of work at the site (Bailey 1975: 273–74, Q594, with comparanda). Several similar lamps, also from the Fayoum but now in the Royal Ontario Museum, were published by Hayes and dated primarily in the second century B.C. (1980a: 21–23, 34–35, especially nos. 78–79, 84–85, and 161).

21. Lamp. (pl. 3.19 and fig. 3.1:4)
Locus 6304   N.III.63.09   MC#19
Preservation: Practically complete, small portion of right shoulder missing. Bi-conical body with small filling hole and groove around edge of shallow, concave discus. Solid, triangular lug/wing on left side possibly matched by opposing lug on right side (now missing). Flat base. Nozzle flattened on top, outsplayed to small flukes. Shallow parallel grooves on both sides of nozzle with volutes at the junction with the body of the lamp, between the nozzle and the discus.
L. 7.7 cm; W. 5.8 cm; H. 3.6 cm.
Technique: Moldmade.

Fabric: Well-levigated Delta silt. Fine (sand-sized to 1 mm) white, gray, and red grit temper with frequent micaceous inclusions of similar size. Fabric c. 7.5R 5/6 (Red) to 10R 5/4 (Weak Red), with a core ranging from 7.5YR 4/2 (Weak Red) to 10R 5/8 (Red) and traces of an abraded 7.5YR 4/6 (Red) to 3/6 (Dark Red) slip. Black charring at nozzle.

Date: Last quarter of 3rd through first half of 2nd century B.C.

Discussion: It is difficult to assign this lamp precisely, but it seems to be related (at least morphologically) to Howland's Athenian Agora Type 43A or to some of the poor relations included in his Type 43D, both of which, however, have raised bases (1958: 133–38). His unglazed Type 43D prime that exhibits the flat base of the Kom Hadid lamp is thought to date to the first half of the second century B.C. (1958: 138).

Imported Amphorae[26]

Simple Rims

The majority of the amphorae from Kom Hadid display rather simple rims (fig. 3.2) and were crafted from a fabric that suggests a Rhodian origin.[27]

In presenting this material we use as a base-point a fragment of the upper portion of an amphora from our excavations in the South Mound at Kom Ge'if. It was executed in a c. 5YR 7/6–6/6 (Reddish Yellow) fabric, with a c. 10YR 8/3 (Very Pale Brown) slip, and a band of fugitive c. 10YR 5/8–4/8 (Red) paint below the rim. It also bore the impression of a stamp on its handle that Rehard attributed to a Rhodian fabricant and to which he assigned a date in the second century B.C. (Rehard in Coulson 1996: 152, no. 17, fig. 59:17, pl. XX:7). This association of shape, fabric, and provenance is strengthened by the presence of a similar amphora fragment in the Kom Hadid corpus: see #26 below, whose handle also had been stamped with a Rhodian eponym thought to date to the second century B.C. and, perhaps more specifically, between the destruction of Carthage in 146 B.C. and the demise of Samaria in 108 B.C. (Rehard in Coulson 1996: 150, no. 7, fig. 57:7, and pl. XIX:7). Because the fabric/slip, and especially the internally beveled rim, of these two pieces can be paralleled very closely by fig. 3.2:9 (complete with red band) and figs. 3.2:14–15,18–19 (without the painted band),[28] it would seem safe to assume that these five pieces should also be considered to be of Rhodian manufacture and to date within the third–second centuries B.C.[29]

Morphologically related forms executed in the same or similar fabric that exhibit a rounder but still beveled rim (fig. 3.2:4) as well as a flatter form in the same fabric (fig. 3.2:21) are considered to have been of Rhodian manufacture. This is also true for examples of the apparently associated rims (in the same fabric) with a slight groove or channel around the top, either with (fig. 3.2:11) or without (fig. 3.2:12) the painted red band.[30]

The rims of several other imported amphorae, however, are less easy to identify and/or to analyze. For instance, the concavity of the inner profile of fig. 3.2:2 (visually similar to the "Rhodian" fabric discussed above), is also present on fig. 3.2:10, which has been crafted from a visibly different fabric. Morphologically, the closest parallels from the Naukratis survey that display such a profile are pieces that were included by Coulson in his Type X amphora rim, all of which were of local clay and thought to be of Roman inspiration.[31] At a later date, a distinctively concave inner-profile will appear on the widely-traded Dressel 20 amphorae whose necks were shorter than those of the Kom Hadid pieces.[32] The Dressel 20, however, is believed to have evolved from the more elongated Oberaden 83 shape, the rims of which often display a very subtle concavity to their interior profiles, and whose floruit began in

Figure 3.2. Naukratis (Kom Hadid) Pottery Corpus: Imported Amphora Neck/Rims

No.	Pottery Bag	Locus	Field no.	Description
1	N.III.130.04	13002	1428	Very well-levigated clay. 7.5YR 8/4 (Pink) fabric with sand-sized micaceous inclusions and infrequent white grit to 1 mm. Surfaces as fabric. Hole in side of vessel is the result of spalling.
2	N.I.490.40	—	1879	Well-levigated clay. Fabric between 2.5YR 6/8 (Light Red) and 5/8 (Red) with white and gray mineral inclusions from sand-sized to c. 1 mm (white grits very infrequently to 2 mm) and occasional fine straw casts. Interior slipped c. 5YR 8/4 (Pink) near rim to 7/6 (Reddish Yellow) lower down; exterior slipped (thicker) with 10YR 8/2 (White).
3	N.III.62.38	6215	3990	5YR 6/6–6/8 (Reddish Yellow) with infrequent sand-sized white grit. Very thin slip in/out 7.5YR 8/2 (Pinkish White) to 8/4 (Pink).
4	N.III.63.05	6304	3701	Very well-levigated clay. Fabric between 7.5YR 8/6 and 7/6 (Reddish Yellow) with occasional sand-sized red grit and micaceous inclusions; very fine straw casts. Core (c. 5 mm) between 5YR 7/4 (Pink) and 7/6 (Reddish Yellow). Slip in/out 10YR 8/3–8/4 (Very Pale Brown).
5	N.III.85.01	—	171	Moderately well-levigated clay. Fabric/core 5YR 7/6–6/6 (Reddish Yellow) with frequent sand-sized white grit and micaceous inclusions; occasional fine straw casts. Slip in/out 10YR 8/4 (Very Pale Brown).
6	N.III.62.22	6207	3232	Well-levigated clay. Fabric between 2.5YR 6/8 (Light Red) and 5/8 (Red) with white and gray mineral inclusions from sand-sized to c. 1 mm; occasional fine straw casts. Interior slipped(?) as fabric; exterior covered with thin white slip that leaves the surface c. 5YR 8/3 (Pink).
7	N.III.76.43	7608	1638	Well-levigated clay. Fabric/core 5YR 7/4 (Pink) with infrequent white grit sand-sized to (occasionally) 1 mm. Slipped in/out 10YR 8/3–8/4 (Very Pale Brown).
8	N.III.63.03	6302	3519	Very well-levigated clay. Fabric/core between 2.5YR 6/6 (Light Red) and 5YR 6/6 (Reddish Yellow) with sand-sized white grit and micaceous inclusions. Slipped exterior and over rim, 10YR 8/3–8/4 (Very Pale Brown).
9	N.III.62.19	6207	—	Very well-levigated clay. No trace of tempering agents. Core and interior surface 7.5YR 8/4 (Pink)–8/6 (Reddish Yellow). Exterior slipped c. 7.5YR 8/2 (Pinkish White). Faint traces of band painted in c. 10R 6/8 (Light Red) on neck.
10	N.III.76.27	7609	1166	Extremely well-levigated clay. Rare sand-sized white grit. Core (thick) of c. 7.5YR 7/6 (Reddish Yellow) sandwiched by thin layer of 2.5YR 5/8 (Red). Slipped exterior and over rim, 10YR 8/3 (Very Pale Brown); interior slipped 5YR 8/4 (Pink) ranging to 7/6 (Reddish Yellow) in places.
11	N.III.76.31	7608	1043	Extremely well-levigated clay. No trace of tempering agents. Fabric/core between 7.5YR 7/6–6/6 (Reddish Yellow). Slipped in/out between 10YR 8/2 (White) and 8/3 (Very Pale Brown). Traces of painted band, c. 10R 5/6–5/8 (Red), on neck.
12	N.III.62.33	6209	3395	Extremely well-levigated clay. Fabric/core c. 5YR 7/6 (Reddish Yellow) changing gradually to c. 7.5YR 7/6 (Reddish Yellow) below surfaces, with occasional white mineral grit temper. Exterior slipped 10YR 8/3 (Very Pale Brown); interior nearer 10YR 8/4 (Very pale Brown).
13	N.III.76.33	7608	1307	Very well-levigated clay. Fabric/core 5YR 8/4–7/4 (Pink) with infrequent sand-sized white grit temper. Slipped in/out whiter than 10YR 8/3 (Very Pale Brown).
14	N.III.76.27	7609	1183	Very well-levigated clay. Fabric/core 7.5YR 7/6 (Reddish Yellow) with occasional sand-sized white grit and micaceous inclusions. Thin 7.5YR 8/4 (Pink) slip out and over rim; interior (unslipped?) 7.5YR 7/4 (Pink).
15	N.III.130.05	13002	1489	Well-levigated clay. Fabric/core 7.5YR 7/6 (Reddish Yellow) with sand-sized white and (occasional) red grit; fine straw casts. Slip out/in 10YR 8/4 Very Pale Brown.
16	N.III.76.58	7609	3366	Well-levigated clay. Fabric/core 7.5YR 7/6–6/6 (Reddish Yellow) approaching c. 10YR 7/4 (Very Pale brown) towards the exterior with frequent sand to 1 mm white grit and sand-sized micaceous inclusions; infrequent red grit to 1 mm. Slip out/in 10YR 8/4 Very Pale Brown. Traces of band of paint(?) below rim on exterior 2.5YR 6/6 (Light red)–5YR 6/6 (Reddish Yellow).
17	N.III.63.18	6305	4278	Well-levigated clay. Fabric between 2.5YR 6/8 (Light Red) and 5/8 (Red). Infrequent white and gray mineral inclusions from sand-sized to c. 1 mm; occasional fine straw casts. Interior slipped(?) as fabric; exterior covered with thin white slip approximating 5YR 8/3 (Pink).
18	N.III.76.55	7605	1806	Extremely well-levigated clay. Fabric c. 7.5YR 7/6 Reddish Yellow) with occasional sand-sized white grit. Slip out and over rim c. 2.5Y 8/2 (White), interior as fabric.
19	N.III.63.04	6303	4004	Extremely well-levigated clay. Fabric/core c. 5YR 7/6 (Reddish Yellow) changing gradually to c. 7.5YR 7/6 (Reddish Yellow) below surfaces, with occasional white mineral grit temper. Exterior slipped 10YR 8/3 (Very Pale Brown), interior nearer 10YR 8/4 (Very Pale Brown).
20	N.III.48.09	4803	4284	Extremely well-levigated clay. Fabric/core between 2.5YR 6/4 (Light Reddish Brown) to 6/8 (Light Red) with relatively frequent white sand-sized to 1 mm grit, and infrequent sand-sized micaceous inclusions. Slip c. 7.5YR 8/2 (Pinkish White) to 8/4 (Pink) on upper exterior, rest "fired" toward color of fabric.
21	N.II.144.03	—	820	Moderately well-levigated, but very gritty, clay with frequent sand-sized to 1 mm white grit (occasionally to 2 mm). Slip in/out c. 2.5Y 8/2 (White).

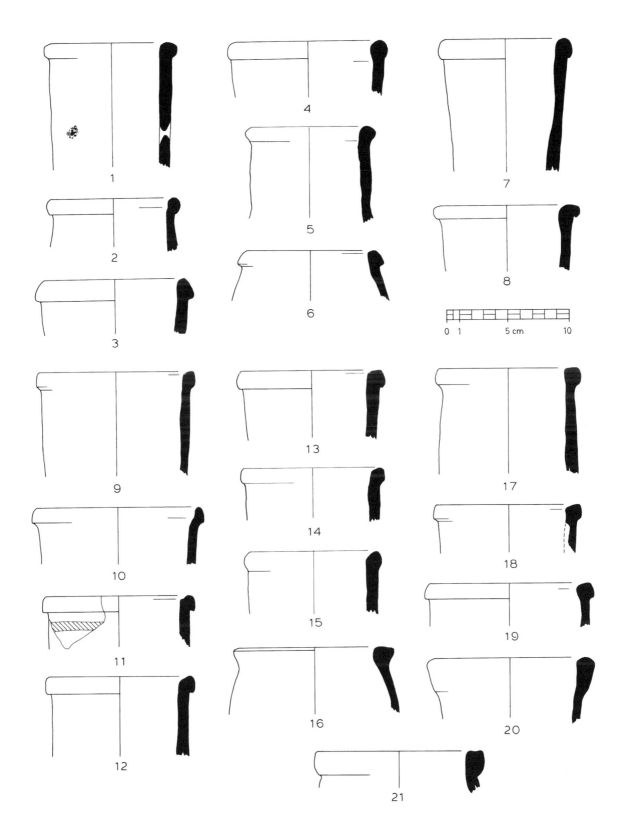

Fig. 3.2. Naukratis (Kom Hadid) Pottery Corpus: Imported Amphora Neck/Rims.

the Augustan Age.[33] Such concavity does appear on the rims of some of the Dressel 2–4 published by Laubenheimer from French contexts, some of which were executed in eastern fabrics (1989: 18–23, and fig. 6:5, especially nos. 3–5).[34] The chronological interface between the Oberaden 83 and the more conservative forms of the Dressel 20 is thought to have been close to the millennial change, and such a date would fit more closely with other aspects of the material culture at Naukratis.[35]

Likewise, the profile of fig. 3.2:3, executed in the fabric here associated with Rhodes, is similar to (albeit slightly more open than) that of fig. 3.2:6, though this was made from a very different (Knidian?) fabric. The closest parallels to the shape of these rims that were encountered during the Naukratis survey, were considered by Coulson to be "local imitations of amphorae from the island of Cos" (1996: 48, and fig. 23; his Types I [especially no. 1560] and J [no. 27]). The rim of the rather closed-mouth vessel illustrated on fig. 3.3:3 is very difficult to parallel as it has been drawn and, in retrospect, should probably be visualized as coming from a more open form and included here with fig. 3.2:3 and 6.

A second, smaller group of sherds in the Kom Hadid corpus also appears to form a distinctive fabric type. These pieces are characterized by a c. 5YR [or 7.5YR] 8/4 (Pink) core/fabric that had been covered with a 10YR 8/3–8/4 (Very Pale Brown) slip. This combination of fabric and slip, as well as slight variations of it, is the hallmark of most of the bifed (double rolled or double barrelled) handles found at Kom Hadid (see fig. 3.3:6–7, 11–12). This is a distinctive type of handle that is usually associated with the island of Cos. Thus a Koan origin or prototype is assumed for vessels made from this fabric.[36] Koan amphorae and their derivatives were said by Coulson to have been the second largest group of amphorae recovered during his survey of the environs of Naukratis (1996: 47).[37]

Three relatively simple rims appear in this fabric at Kom Hadid. Fig. 3.2:1 and 7 may be considered to be variants of a rolled or rounded bead rim not unlike those included among the widely distributed Class 9 amphorae of Peacock and Williams (1986: 102–3).[38] They appear in at least seven different fabrics only two of which were believed to have come from the island of Rhodes whose forms they seem to imitate (1986: 15; Peacock 1977). Similarities in profile, however, can also be found with examples of Peacock and Williams' Class 10 amphorae[39] that were also produced in several workshops (and hence they are made of different fabrics), which they describe as "the most important western Mediterranean wine amphora of the early Empire" (1986: 106). Although the bifed handles of the latter group definitely indicate a high degree of Koan inspiration for the class, it is perhaps best to recall the caveat of Peacock and Williams that "it is impossible to distinguish production centers on the basis of shape" (1986: 106). That certainly seems to be the case with fig. 3.2:5 and 8, although the pulled out rim of the latter piece can be paralleled on pseudo-Koan amphorae found at Paphos (Hayes 1991: 86, no. 18, fig. 37:5).

The slightly more angular profile of fig. 3.2:13 seems to be morphologically midway between the squarer variants of the Koan, or Koan-inspired, forms and some of the internally beveled rims that are assigned above to the island of Rhodes.[40]

The rim shown on fig. 3.2:20 could possibly be related to the Haltern 70 amphora whose "collar rim is distinctive and always everted" (Sealey 1985: 59, and fig. 8:74, 76) and which flourished from the mid-first century B.C. through the first century A.D. (Sealey 1985: 64); or even the Lamboglia 2, or Dressel 6, rims of Augustan date discussed by Desbat and Martin-Kilcher 1989. One of a group of three rims attributed to Dressel 6 amphorae from Well 18 at Paphos are also dated to the Augustan period (Hayes 1991: 180, 186 (no. 74), fig. 44:74–76. No. 76 is the closest to the Kom Hadid fragment. Also possibly related is the Apulian(?) rim discussed by Hayes on page 86 (no. 21, fig. 37:7).

Fig. 3.2:16 and 17 are less easy to document although the former may be related to Phoenician or Punic forms that often share the swollen upper neck,[41] while 3.2:17 is reminiscent of some of the imitation Koan amphorae from Paphos published by Hayes (1991:86 no. 20, fig. 37:9).

More Complex Rims

Thicker or more complex amphora rims from the Kom Hadid assemblage are included in this discussion (fig. 3.3:1–5). Although they are numerically the smaller group, they do seem to reflect greater geographic and chronological diversity than is the case with the simpler forms.

Fig. 3.3:1 is a rim fragment from an example of Dressel's type 1 amphora and, more specifically, Dressel type 1B of Lamboglia's (1955: 252–60) subdivision of the original form since it exhibits much more verticality in the profile of the collar rim than the slightly in-turning rim of his type 1C. Peacock and Williams included the Dressel 1B with their Class 4 amphorae[42] and assigned to it an approximate date from the second quarter of the first century B.C. to the last decade of that century (1986: 90).

The rim illustrated in fig. 3.3:2 may be associated with Class 16 in the taxonomy of Peacock and Williams[43] who have isolated five sub-types based primarily on the shape of the body and the presence of a vertical, median furrow on the handle, both of which are lacking on the Kom Hadid fragment. The profile of the rim and the degree to which it is outsplayed is paralleled in their type A (1986: fig. 30:A) for which they have assigned a first century B.C. date and a decidedly western and northern distribution. This shape appears to have been made in many workshops and in many different fabrics (1986: 119).[44]

The thickest amphora rims in the Hadid *corpus* are shown in fig. 3.3:4 and especially fig. 3.3:5. They both display a round, rolled, or bead rim that, given their thickness, is difficult to parallel in deposits contemporary with most of the other amphorae from the site. Some similarities with examples of Peacock and Williams' Class 20 can be seen, but the two groups differ markedly in fabric and, although the shape was exported to the east (as far as Benghazi), it does not appear to predate the early first century A.D.[45] Perhaps a better parallel would be the bulbous first century B.C. amphorae from the Brinidisi area that bear the stamp of *M. Tuccius Galeo*, at least one of which had reached the markets of Alexandria (Cipriano and Carre 1989: 74–77 and the distribution map, fig. 8).

Convincing comparanda for the neck and rim fragment with elliptical (in section) handle illustrated in fig. 3.3:8, are difficult to find.

The distinctive profile of Kom Hadid figs. 3.3:9 and 3.3:10 indicate that they are both examples of the Greco-Italic amphora included by Peacock and Williams with their Class 2 amphorae.[46] This group of vessels has been closely examined by Will, who isolated five subcategories of the type from an earlier "a" through a later "e" (1982: 343–44). The color of the fabric of the rims from Kom Hadid would fit most closely with the fabric either of her type a2 which had a *floruit* in the early third century B.C. and does not appear to have been exported further east than Carthage,[47] or the redder variant of her second century B.C. form "d" that is said to echo Rhodian prototypes. A stamped example of the latter type has actually been found at Alexandria (Will 1982: 353).[48]

Handles

Six amphora handles of non-local fabric from the excavations at Kom Hadid are illustrated here. Four of these (figs. 3.3:6–7, 11–12) are bifed or double-rolled handles that suggest either Koan manufacture or inspiration. The color(s) of their fabrics and slips fall within the range of fabrics from which

Koan and pseudo-Koan amphorae were crafted and have been noted in the discussion of Peacock and Williams' Classes 10 and 11 (see note 38 and the text cited there), which begin to appear during the first century B.C. Such double handles also appear on examples of their Class 39 (1986: 39) for which an Aegean origin has been suggested and whose major period of popularity seems to have been early in the first century A.D.[49] Double-barreled handles in a wide spectrum of fabrics were common in the material collected by Coulson during his survey of the environs of Naukratis. He also calls attention to their distinctively Koan character (1996: 61, and fig. 31, Type G).

Of the two single-rolled handles, the right angle (joining neck to shoulder) of the amphora shown on fig. 3.3:13 could have originated on a wide variety of amphorae with a considerable range of shapes and dates. In connection with the survey material Coulson noted a vague connection between (long) handles with round cross sections and the island of Rhodes, especially during the third century B.C. (1996: 60, his Type A, and fig. 30). The length and elliptical cross section of fig. 3.3:14 also suggest a Rhodian origin to the present author as do the color(s) of its fabric and slip. Compare its fabric with that of the stamped handle #26 below, that bears a Rhodian eponym.[50]

Toes

Fragments of amphora toes (or spikes) of nonlocal fabric are even more difficult to identify than rims and handles. Even discussion of the physical appearance of the fragments is hampered by the fact that the fabric is often thicker at the toe and may not fire to the same color(s) as did the thinner, upper portion of the vessel, and the slip may have been abraded from frequent securing of the vessel in the sand or other abrasive media. Of all the morphologically diagnostic elements of an amphora it was the toe that suffered most.[51] However, for the sake of completeness a representative selection is offered here. Comparanda for the most part has been limited to the identification of similar pieces from the Naukratis survey.

The amphora represented by the rather solid toe of fig. 3.4:1 appears to be of Thasian manufacture, although a Mendean origin cannot be excluded.[52]

The toes of Chian amphorae similar to those illustrated on figs. 3.4:2–4 were described by Coulson as "having a hollow on (their) underside with a lip that turns back outward forming a narrow cuff" (1996: 53). He dated these to the last quarter of the fourth century B.C. (1996: 53 in reference to his type A toes). During the third century B.C. he saw the hollow of such toes becoming smaller and the cuff becoming more pronounced (1996: 53–54, his type C). Similar features are seen on some of the vessels that Coulson viewed, correctly or incorrectly, as having been derived from Mendean or even possibly Attic prototypes (1996: 58–59 and fig. 29). However, A. Berlin, tentatively supported by M. Lawall (personal communication), sees these toes as Cypriot and that is the attribution that is followed here.[53]

Another group of toes, figs. 3.4:5–7, displays a small collar above the rounded point of termination. It is instructive to see how this amphora was fashioned (pl. 3:20a and b) since the present (or latest) band and lower projection of the toe had been formed by the addition of a separate piece of clay that was used to cap (or recap?) a preexisting toe that would have presented to the typologist a very different profile. Toes similar to these appear on Knidian and Koan amphorae (both genuine and derivative) and are most probably to be dated to the late second through the first century B.C.[54]

The toe shown in fig. 3.4:9 appears to be a variant of this group in which the height of the collar has been reduced considerably. It thus forms a morphological transition to those toes in which the upper edge of the collar has ceased to exist as a separate unit (figs 3.4:10–12) and the lower edge now represents the only break in the profile. The closest example to this phenomenon in the material from the Naukratis survey is Coulson's Type O3 of Koan inspiration and of first century B.C. date (1996: 55, and fig. 27:1073; see also 96, n. 218 for reference to a similar, but unpublished, Koan amphora from Rhodes that is dated c. 200 B.C.). The shape is also similar to some of the toes from Paphos that were thought to be related to Knidian examples (Hayes 1991:86 [especially no. 6], and fig. 37.3). The origin of the toe illustrated on fig. 3.4:8 can be assigned to Knidos with a bit more certainty.

A distinctly hemispherical toe, fig. 3.4:13, can be paralleled only by a single example from the survey: Coulson's Type ZA (1996: 60, and fig. 30: 1106). This form, he believed, had been derived from an unpublished specimen from the Agora excavations to which had been assigned a date as late as the second or early third centuries A.D. Such a date would be later than that proposed for the majority of the material excavated at Kom Hadid, but no other comparanda are available. [55]

Plain toes/spikes are the most difficult to attribute with any degree of certainty. Fig. 3.4:14 can be compared with a Koan-inspired toe from the survey dated to the first century B.C. (Coulson 1996: 56, his Type P, fig. 27: 1748); the more cylindrical fig. 3.4: 15 is akin to several Rhodian derivatives of the late third–second centuries B.C. (*inter alia*, Coulson 1996: 57, Type X, and fig. 28:207); the more rounded fig. 3.4:18 is the standard Rhodian toe of apparently the same date. Fig. 3.4:17 is too amorphous to elicit convincing parallels while the spikes shown on figs. 3.4:16 and 19 do not appear to have parallels among the material from the Naukratis survey. The possibility exists that they may be from Italian Dressel 2–4 (Sealey 1985: 28, fig. 7), a form that has been subsumed by Peacock and Williams under their Class 10 (see note 71), and of which Sealey noted the "infinite typological variety within the class (1985: 27).[56]

22. Amphora toe showing method of construction (pl. 3.20 a, b)

Locus 7609   N.III.76.27   MC# 1200

Fabric: Well-levigated clay. Sand-sized mica and white grit frequently to 1 mm (rarely to 2 mm). Fabric (top) 7.5YR 7/4 (Pink) to 7/6 (Reddish Yellow); (bottom) 7.5YR 6/4 (Light Brown) to 6/6 (Reddish Yellow). Slip in/out 10YR 8/2–8/3 (Very Pale Brown).

Date: 2nd–1st century B.C.(?)

Discussion: This fragment illustrates a method of completing the toe of an amphora by capping it with an extension in clay. The profile thus obtained suggests a Koan or Knidian origin (or inspiration) for the piece.

Stamped Handles (fig. 3.5)[57]

23. Amphora handle fragments with stamp (fig. 3.5:1)

Locus 7608   N.III.76.33   MC #70

   rectangular

   Rhodian eponym

   220–180 B.C.

Fabric: Extremely well-levigated clay. Occasional sand-sized white grit and micaceous inclusions. Fabric between 5YR 6/6 (Reddish-Yellow) and 7.5YR 6/6 (Reddish-Yellow). Exterior slipped 10YR 8/4 (Very Pale Brown); interior, 7.5YR 8/4 (Pink).

*Fig. 3.3. Naukratis (Kom Hadid) Pottery Corpus: Imported Amphora Neck/Rims (1-5, 8-10)
and handles (6, 7, 11-14)*

No.	Pottery Bag	Locus	Field no.	Description
	Imported Amphora Neck/Handles			
1	N.III.76.16	7603	621	Very well-levigated clay. Sand-sized white grit and micaceous inclusions. Fabric/core 5YR 7/6–6/6 (Reddish Yellow). Thin slip in/out 7.5YR 8/2 (Pinkish White) appearing 7.5YR 8/4 (Pink) where thinnest.
2	N.III.76.25	7604	1294	Well-levigated clay. Sand-sized white grit and micaceous inclusions. Fabric c. 5YR 6/6–6/8 (Reddish Yellow) with thin core of 7.5YR 6/6 (Reddish Yellow). Slipped in/out 10YR 8/3 (Very Pale Brown) where thick, 5YR 8/4 (Pink) where thin.
3	N.III.76.05	7603	352	Well-levigated clay. Sand-sized white grit and micaceous inclusions to 1mm, frequent straw casts to 2–3 mm. Same fabric as #996. Very thin white slip turns surfaces in/out 5YR 7/4 (Pink).
4	N.III.76.16	7603	623	Well-levigated clay. Occasional white grit c. 1 mm. Fabric and interior surface 5YR 6/6–6/8 (Red). Exterior slipped 10YR 8/2 (White) through 8/4 (Very Pale Brown).
5	N.III.76.27	7609	1173	Exceptionally well-levigated clay. Occasional sand-sized white grit and micaceous inclusions. Very rare pink grit to 5 mm. Fabric/core 10YR 8/3 (Very Pale Brown). Slip out and over rim 10Yr 8/4 (Very Pale Brown). Interior as fabric.
6	N.III.76.27	7609	1197	Well-levigated clay. Frequent white grit and sand-sized micaceous inclusions to 1mm, rarely to 2 mm. Core of c. 5YR 6/3 (Light Reddish Brown) blends through 5YR 7/4 (Pink) to fabric color of 5YR 7/6 (Reddish Yellow). Slipped 10YR 8/4 (Very pale Brown),
7	N.III.76.06	7603	501	Very well-levigated clay. Frequent sand-sized micaceous inclusions and occasional sand-sized white grit. Fabric between 2.5YR 6/6 Light Red) and 5YR 7/6 (Reddish Yellow). Slipped 10R 8/2 (White) to 8/3 (Very Pale Brown).
8	N.III.76.58	7609	3347	Very well-levigated clay. Sand-sized mica and white grit, occasionally to 1 mm. Fabric/core 7.5YR 7/4 (Pink). Slipped 10YR 8/3–8/4 (Very Pale Brown) in/out.
9	N.III.63.11	6305	4139	Well-levigated clay. Sand-sized white grit and micaceous inclusions infrequently to 1 mm. Fabric/core between 2.5YR 6/6 and 6/8 (Red). Slip in/out 10YR 8/2 (White) to 8/3 (Very Pale Brown).
10	N.III.76.50	7603	6751	Very well-levigated clay. White grit sand-sized to 1 mm, few to 3 mm. Fabric/core 2.5YR 6/6 (Light Red). Slipped in/out 10YR 8/2 (White) to 8/3 (Very Pale Brown). In places (where slip thinner ?) surfaces nearer to the color of the fabric.
11	N.III.76.58	7609	3362	Very well-levigated clay. Sand-sized white grit and micaceous inclusions. Fabric/core between 2.5YR 6/6 and 6/8 (Light Red). Slipped 10YR 8/3–8/4 (Very pale Brown).
12	N.III.76.50	7603	1769	Very well-levigated clay. Sand-sized micaceous inclusions only. Fabric/core c. 5YR 8/4 (Pink). Exterior slipped c. 2.5Y 8/2 (White); interior as fabric.
13	N.III.76.16	7603	625	Well-levigated clay. Occasional white grit c. 1 mm. Fabric and interior surface 5YR 6/6–6/8 (Red). Core (c. 3 mm.) 2.5YR 6/8 (Light Red). Exterior slipped 10YR 8/2 (White) through 8/4 (Very Pale Brown).
14	N.III.62.19	6207	3285	Very well-levigated clay. Occasional sand to 1 mm. Fabric/core 5YR 7/6–6/6 (Reddish Yellow). Exterior slipped 10YR 8/2 (White) that appears c. 5YR 7/4 (Pink) because it is so thin.

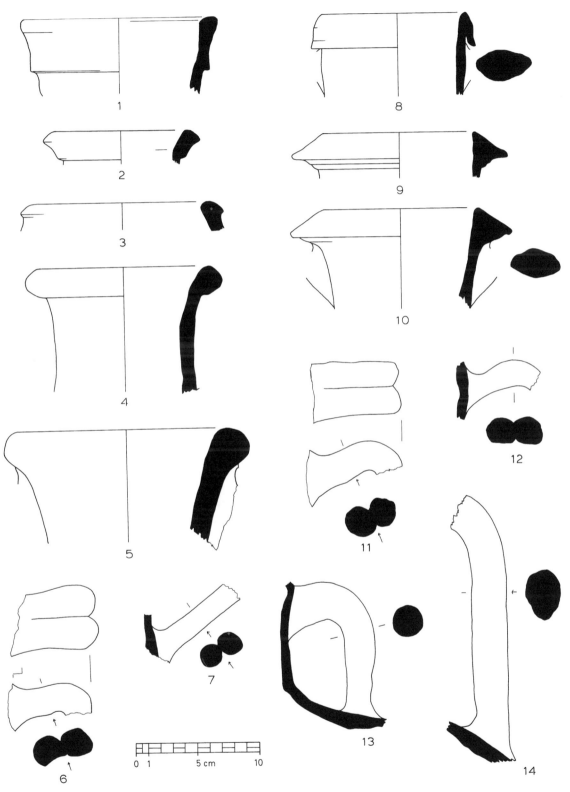

Fig. 3.3. Naukratis (Kom Hadid) Pottery Corpus: Imported Amphora Neck/Rims (1–5, 8–10) and Handles (6, 7, 11–14).

Fig. 3.4. Naukratis (Kom Hadid) Pottery Corpus: Imported Amphora Toes

Amphora Toes

No.	Pottery Bag	Locus	Field no.	Description
1	N.III.62.46	6205	4170	Moderately well-levigated clay. Frequent sand-sized white and white, very frequent micaceous inclusions. Fabric/core between 2.5YR 5/6–5/8 (Red). Thin slip 5YR 7/3–7/4 (Pink).
2	N.III.63.07	6304	3718	Well-levigated clay. Sand-sized micaceous inclusions, fine straw casts and occasional white grit to 1 mm. Fabric/core c. 2.5YR 6/6–6/8 (Light Red). Exterior slipped 5YR 7/4–7/6 (Reddish Yellow).
3	N.III.76.10	7605	658	Well-levigated clay. Sand-sized white grit and micaceous inclusions. Fabric 5YR 6/6–6/8 (Reddish Yellow). Slipped c. 5YR 8/4 (Pink).
4	N.III.76.55	7605	1832	Moderately well-levigated clay. White and gray grit sand-sized to 1 mm, frequently to 2 mm. Fabric/core 5YR 7/6–6/6 (Reddish Yellow). Exterior slipped(?) as fabric.
5	N.III.62.19	6207	3304	Very well-levigated clay. Sand-sized white and gray grit to 1 mm, fine straw casts. Fabric 5YR 7/6–6/6 (Reddish Yellow). Exterior slipped 10YR 8/3 (Very Pale Brown), interior 5YR 7/6 (Reddish Yellow).
6	N.III.63.05	6304	3669	Very well-levigated clay. Sand-sized white grit and micaeous inclusions. Fabric/core interior 2.5YR 6/8 (Light Red), outer between 5YR 7/4 (Pink) and 7/6 (Reddish Yellow). Slipped, exterior only, c. 2.5Y 8/2 (White) where thick, nearer 5YR 8/3–8/4 (Pink) where slip is thin. Interior as inner core.
7	N.III.76.27	7609	1200	Very well-levigated clay. Sand-sized mica and white grit frequently to 1mm (rarely to 2mm.). Fabric (top) 7.5YR 7/4 (Pink) to 7/6 (Reddish Yellow); bottom 7.5YR 6/4 (Light Brown) to 6/6 (Reddish Yellow). Slip in/out 10YR 8/2–8/3 (Very Pale Brown).
8	N.III.130.04	13002	1424	Well-levigated clay. Occasional 1 mm white grit, some straw casts to 3 mm. Fabric and surfaces 5YR 7/4 (Pink) to 7/6 (Reddish Yellow).
9	N.III.76.15	7601	759	Moderately well-levigated clay. Frequent white grit and micaceous inclusions, sand to 1 mm. Fabric/core 2.5YR 5/8 (Red). Thick slip (exterior only) does not adhere well, 2.5Y 8/4 (Pale Yellow).
10	N.III.76.05	7603	363	Well-levigated clay. Sand-sized white grit and micaceous inclusions to 1mm. Fabric/core 5YR 7/4 (Pink). Exterior slip 10YR 8/2(White) to 8/3 (Very Pale Brown); interior slip 5YR 8/4–7/4 (Pink).
11	N.III.76.95	—	381	Exceptionally well-levigated clay. Occasional sand and white grit to 1 mm. Fabric c. 2.5 YR 6/6 (Light Red). Exterior slipped between 10YR 8/3 (Very Pale Brown) and 2.5Y 8/4 (Pale Yellow). Interior slipped 5YR 7/4 (Pink).
12	N.III.76.58	7609	3358	Well-levigated clay. White grit to (Reddish Yellow).
13	N.III.76.15	7601	757	Very well-levigated clay. Sand-sized white grit (rarely to 1 mm) and micaceous inclusions. Fabric 5YR 6/4 (Light Reddish Brown), core 5YR 6/6 (Light Reddish Brown). Thin slip in/out 10YR 8/3 (Very Pale Brown) to 7.5 YR 8/4 (Pink).
14	N.III.76.02	7601	271	Well-levigated clay. Frequent white, red, and gray grit to 1 mm. Fabric inner 5YR 7/6 (Reddish Yellow); outer 10YR 7/4–8/4 (Very Pale Brown). Exterior slipped between 10YR 8/4 (Very Pale Brown) and 2.5Y 8/4 (Pale Yellow). Interior plain, color as inner fabric.
15	N.III.62.06	6201	3121	Well-levigated clay. Occasional sand-sized white grit. Fabric 5YR 6/6 (Reddish Yellow). Exterior slipped c. 2.5Y 8/2 (White) -8/4 (Pale Yellow).
16	N.III.76.03	7602	254	Well-levigated clay. Occasional white grit to 1 mm, fine straw casts. Fabric/core 2.5YR 6/6 (Light Red). Interior slipped c. 2.5YR 6/6 (Light Red), exterior slipped 2.5Y 8/2 (White).
17	N.III.76.58	7609	3361	Well-levigated clay. White sand-sized grit and micaceous inclusions. Fabric 5YR 7/6–7/8 (Reddish Yellow). Exterior slipped(?) 5YR 7/4 (Pink) to 7/6 (Reddish Yellow). Exterior abraded.
18	N.III.76.27	7609	1145	Fabric description missing.
19	N.III.63.12	6305	4292	Very well-levigated clay. White grit c. 1 mm and sand-sized micaceous inclusions. Fabric 5YR 7/4 (Pink) to 7/6 (Reddish Yellow). Exterior slipped(?) 5YR 8/3–8/4 (Pink), interior slipped(?) 5YR 8/4 (Pink).

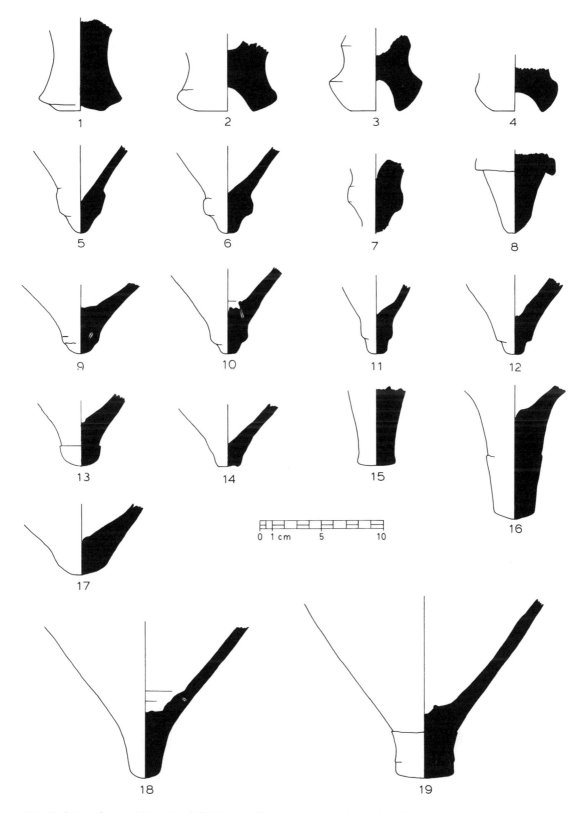

Fig. 3.4. Naukratis (Kom Hadid) Pottery Corpus: Imported Amphora Toes.

Discussion: Stamps with this eponym usually include a month or device. It is unclear whether this piece had either since it is incomplete. This type also occurs at Rhodes (Lindos), Delos, Pergamon, Nea Paphos, Samaria, Ophel, Alexandria, Histria.

Comparanda: Schuchhardt and Fabricus 1895: 435–37 nos. 775–96; Nilsson 1909: 352 no. 8; Grace 1952: 528, 1953: 122; Canarache 1957: 237 no. 534; Crowfoot 1957: 380; Sztetyllo 1975: 172 no. 38, 1976: 31 no. 23.[58]

24. Amphora handle fragments with stamp (fig. 3.5:2)

Locus 7608   N.III.76.42   MC #92

    rectangular

    Rhodian eponym

    220–180 B.C.

Fabric: Very well-levigated clay. Occasional sand-sized white grit and micaceous inclusions. Fabric/core between 5YR 6/6 (Reddish-Yellow) and 7.5YR 6/6 (Reddish-Yellow). Exterior slipped 10YR 8/3 (Very Pale Brown) on bottom and sides to 10YR 8/4 (Very Pale Brown) on top of handle and exterior rim; interior 7.5YR 8/4 (Pink).

Discussion: This type also occurs at: Rhodes (Lindos), Pergamon, Athens, Nea Paphos, Gezer, Ophel, Samaria, Alexandria, Carthage, Siracuse, Histria.

Comparanda: Schuchhardt 1895: 456–58 nos. 980–96; Nilsson 1909: 410 no. 65b; Reisner 1924: 314 no. 40; Grace 1934: 226 no. 42, 1953: 122; Canarache 1957: 244 nos. 561–62; Gentili 1958: 56 no. 78; Sztetyllo 1975: 179 nos. 62–63, 1976: 41 no. 76.[59]

25. Amphora handle fragments with stamp (fig. 3.5:3)

Locus 6303   N.III.63.03   MC #2

    circular with rose

    Rhodian fabricant

    225–200 B.C.

Fabric: Exceptionally well-levigated clay. Occasional sand-sized white grit and micaceous inclusions. Fabric between 5YR 6/6 (Reddish-Yellow) and 7.5YR 6/6 (Reddish-Yellow). Exterior slipped 10YR 8/3 (Very Pale Brown); interior 7.5YR 8/4 (Pink).

Discussion: This type also occurs at Rhodes (Lindos), Delos, Athens, Salamine, Samaria, Ophel, Alexandria, Carthage, Siracuse, Histria.

Comparanda: Nilsson 1909: 419 no. 191; Reisner 1924: 311 no. 33; Grace 1934: 238 R87, 1952: 526; Canarache 1957: 231 no. 518; Crowfoot 1957: 383; Calvet 1972: 21 no. 24; Sztetyllo 1975: 167 nos. 14–15.[60]

26. Amphora handle fragments with stamp (fig. 3.5:4)

Locus 7609   N.III.76.27   MC #61

    rectangular

    Rhodian eponym

    150–100 B.C.

Fabric: Extremely well-levigated clay. Occasional sand-sized and micaceous inclusions and rare, sand-sized white grit. Fabric 7.5YR 7/6–6/6 (Reddish-Yellow). Exterior slipped with thin 2.5YR 8/2 (White) to 10YR 8/3 (Very Pale Brown), where very thin, c. 7.5YR 8/4 (Pink); interior 10YR 8/3–8/4 (Very Pale Brown).

Discussion: This type also occurs at Rhodes (Lindos and Villanova), Delos, Samaria, Tel Istabah.

Comparanda: Nilsson 1909: 421 no. 200; Reisner 1924: 314 no. 43; Grace 1952: 529, 1953: 123 no. 78; Crowfoot 1957: 381.[61]

27. Amphora handle fragments with stamp (fig. 3.5:5)
Locus 7618   N.III.76.73   MC #148
    rectangular
    Rhodian fabricant
    220–180 B.C.
Fabric: Exceptionally well-levigated clay. Rare, sand-sized micaceous inclusions only. Fabric/core 5YR 7/6 (Reddish-Yellow). Exterior slipped c. 10YR 8/2 (White); interior c. 5YR 8/4 (Pink).
Discussion: This type also occurs at Rhodes (Lindos), Delos, Pergamon, Samaria, Tell Sandhannah, Ophel, Alexandria, Carthage, Siracuse, Histria.
Comparanda: Schuchhardt 1895: 460 no. 1019; Macalister 1901: 38–39 no. 110; Nilsson 1909: 427 no. 225; Reisner 1924: 312 no. 40; Grace 1952: 527, Crowfoot 1957: 383; Gentili 1958: 63 no. 104; Sztetyllo 1975: 181 no. 74; Landau 1979: 156 no. 26.[62]

28. Amphora handle fragments with stamp (fig. 3.5:6)
Locus 7605   N.III.76.55   MC #114
    rectangular
    Rhodian fabricant
    220–180 B.C.
Fabric: Extremely well-levigated clay. Rare sand-sized white grit and micaceous inclusions. Fabric: 7.5YR 7/6–6/6 (Reddish-Yellow). Exterior slipped 10YR 8/3–8/4 (Very Pale Brown) to 5YR 8/4 (Pink) where thin. Interior vessel wall not preserved.
Discussion: Also occurs at Rhodes (Lindos), Pergamon, Nea Paphos, Salamine, Samaria, Tell Sandhannah, Ophel, Gezer, Siracuse, Histria.
Comparanda: Schuchhardt 1895: 479–80 nos. 1207–12; Macalister 1901: 132–33 no. 220 and 396 no. 327; Nilsson 1909: 494 no. 422; Macalister 1912: 362 no. 463; Reisner 1924: 312; Grace 1950: 141 no. 33; Canarache 1957: 266, no. 651; Crowfoot 1957: 384; Gentili 1958: 78 no. 154; Sztetyllo 1976: 53 no. 136; Calvet 1972: 27 nos. 44–45.[63]

29. Amphora handle fragments with stamp (fig. 3.5:7)
Locus 6202   N.III.62.20   MC #33
    circular with rose
    Rhodian eponym(?)
Fabric: Extremely well-levigated clay. Rare sand-sized white grit and micaceous inclusions. Fabric 7.5YR 7/5 (Reddish-Yellow) with inner (3 mm) core of 5YR 6/6 (Reddish-Yellow). Exterior/interior slipped 10YR 8/2 (White), very abraded.
Discussion: The inscription is incomplete but is considered to be Rhodian because of the month, the common Rhodian device (the rose), the handle profile, and the fabric and slip.[64]

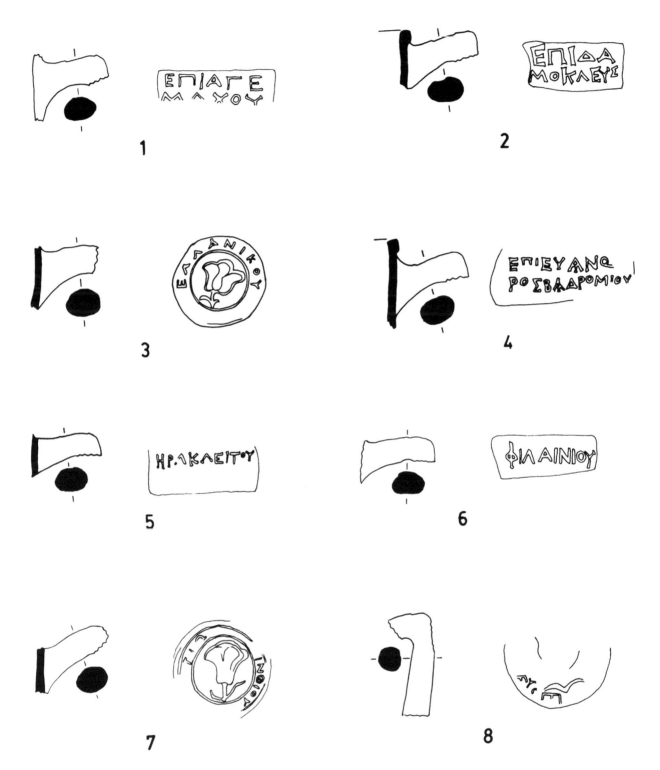

Fig. 3.5. Stamped handles as imported amphorae. The scale of the impression is 1:1; that of the profile is 1:4.

30. Amphora handle fragments with stamp (fig. 3.5:8)

Locus 7609   N.III.76.78   MC#168

  circular with rose

  Rhodian

Fabric: Very well-levigated clay. Occasional sand-sized white grit and very fine straw casts, some sand-sized micaceous inclusions. Fabric/core 7.5 YR 7/6–6/6 (Reddish-Yellow). Possible, very thin white slip or exterior and interior slightly lighter than fabric color.

Discussion: The inscription is incomplete but most probably Rhodian because of the common Rhodian device (the rose), the fabric, and the slip.[65]

Other Ceramics

31. Pot Stand(?) with Incised Letters (pl. 3.21:a and fig. 3.6:1, 3)

Locus 7613   NIII.76.44   No MC# assigned

Technique: Wheelmade. The letters ΠΕ had been incised on the underside of the stand before it had been fired.

Fabric: Well-levigated clay. The core of the fabric ranges from 7.5R 4/4 (Weak Red) to 10R 4/6 (Red) below surfaces c. 7.5R 5/6 (Red) to 10R 5/4 (Weak Red). Sand-sized to 1 mm grit temper in white, gray, and red, with frequent micaceous inclusions of similar size. Unslipped.

Description: A fragment of a low, thick-walled ring stand with a finished foot. The basal, internal surface had been incised with two letters while the clay was still soft and before the piece had been fired in the kiln.

Date: Ptolemaic Period.

Discussion and Comparanda: A total of fifteen fragments of pot stands were registered during the excavations at Kom Hadid of which only two (here 31 and 32) had been incised before firing.[66] These low stands constitute one of the few ceramic forms that were not encountered during our excavations at Kom Ge'if, but four examples (one incised) were recovered during the survey of Naukratis and its environs where they form Coulson's corpus of type B stands (Coulson 1996: 79–80, registration numbers 1359, 1427, 1542, and 1239 [incised]). Coulson felt that his type B stands were "not paralleled elsewhere in Egypt" (Coulson 1996: 79) and therefore assigned to them the same date as he gave to his taller, type A stands late second to fifth centuries A.D. Berlin, however, citing parallels at Coptos, the Bucheum and Tell el-Maskhuta (Chapter 2), offers a Hellenistic date that seems to be more in line with the rest of the pottery from Kom Hadid than does the rather late date suggested by Coulson.

As for the function of these pieces, Berlin (Chapter 2) has suggested that they were intended to support amphorae and/or round-bottom jars in a household or domestic setting. This is probably the case, but an alternate hypothesis would interpret them as stacking rings designed to separate individual pots during the firing process. This is the function that Edwards assigned to two similar pieces from the Pnyx whose diameters exactly matched the stacking circles of several of the Megarian bowls in the same deposit.[67] Such an industrial function might account for the extreme discoloration of #32. The objects from the Pnyx are dated to the third to second centuries B.C. (Edwards 1956: unnumbered introductory page).

32. Pot Stand with Incised Letters (pl. 3.21:b and fig. 3.6:2, 4)

Locus 7608   NIII.76.43   No MC# assigned

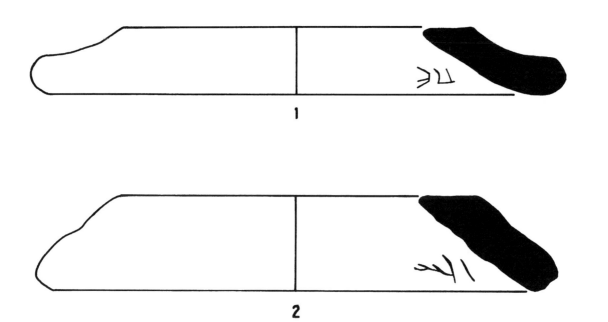

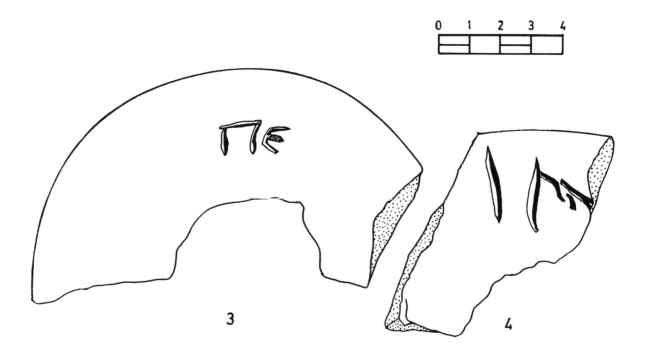

Fig. 3.6. Terracotta "Stands" (1 and 3: # 31; 2 and 4: # 32), incised before firing.

Technique: Wheelmade. The letters had been incised on the underside of the stand before it had been fired.

Fabric: Well-levigated clay. The core of the fabric ranges from 7.5R 4/4 (Weak Red) to 10R 4/6 (Red) below surfaces c. 7.5R 5/6 (Red) to 10R 5/4 (Weak Red). Sand-sized to 1 mm grit temper in white, gray, and red, with frequent micaceous inclusions of similar size. Traces of smoothed slip on both surfaces evidently of similar color to that of the fabric but fired (secondarily?) through shades of reddish gray to dark gray or black on the incised surface.

Description: A very small fragment of a low, thick-walled ring stand with a finished foot. The basal, internal surface had been incised with two letters while the clay was still soft and before the piece had been fired.

Date: Ptolemaic Period.

Discussion: See #31 above.

33. Fragments of a Vessel with Bichrome Decoration (pl. 3.22 and fig. 3.7)
Locus 7603   N.III.76.04   MC#29
Technique: Wheelmade.

Preservation: Four (nonjoining) sherds considered to be from same vessel.

Fabric. Very well-levigated clay. 10R 5/4 (Red) to 7.5YR 4/2 (Weak Red) fabric with frequent white, gray, and red grit temper (to 1 mm) and occasional sand-sized micaceous inclusions. Slip(?) of same color as fabric in/out. Bichrome decoration in white/cream (no Munsell) to 7.5YR 4/2 (Pinkish White) as Fabric IC, and c. 5YR 3/2 (Dusky Red) to black (no Munsell).

Date: A.D. 400–600?

Discussion: Although crafted in a fabric similar to the basic red Delta silt so frequently encountered at Naukratis (Fabric I, Mineral Tempered Red Ware), this piece differs markedly from the rest of the ceramic repertoire known from the site. The vessel appears to be a low, open form with sharply out-splayed sides, that would make the elaborate decoration difficult to view when the piece was placed on a horizontal surface. The decoration itself presents us with one of the few representations of an anthropomorphic theme in the entire pottery corpus. Two fragments present a horizontal band with diagonal slashes of color. The other two fragments (if they should be as closely juxtaposed as they are presented here) seem to provide us with a horizontal metope pattern, in one frame of which is an individual holding an object above shoulder height at his/her right side. The question of whether a human or a deity is represented cannot be answered at this time. It is tempting to interpret the figure as Apollo holding his lyre, or even an element of Christian iconography.

With great trepidation, the piece is here (tentatively) attributed to the (post-Meroitic) Nubian X-Group (Ballana Culture) and dated (following Bourriau 1981: 110–11) c. A.D. 400–600, sometime in the period bracketed by the compulsory Christianization of Egypt by Theodosius I in A.D. 390 and the advent of Islam in A.D. 641 Some of the wheelmade pottery of the Ballana culture can be of a red silt fabric with decoration in cream and black,[68] but neither the form nor the decoration can find a satisfying parallel in Adams' definitive corpus of medieval Nubian ceramics (1986 passim).

Whether the above attribution is correct or not, the piece is included here for the sake of completeness. It certainly seems to be about the latest piece of pottery from the site. Unfortunately it comes from an open, topsoil locus, which presents a wide range of possibilities.

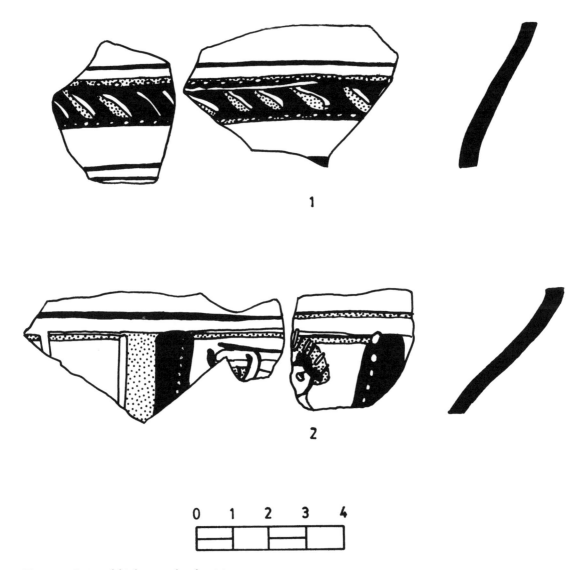

Fig. 3.7. Painted bichrome sherd # 33.

Faience

The manufacture and use of the "glazed" wares popularly referred to as faience has had a strong association with the site of Naukratis ever since the early work of Petrie at the site (1886: especially 5a, 36–37, 40; and Webb 1978 passim) and can, in fact, be traced back to the Egyptian Predynastic Period of the fourth millennium B.C. (Lucas and Harris 1962: 155; and the very technical treatment by Kaczmarczyk and Hedges 1983). Many loci from our excavations at Kom Hadid, as well as from our work at Kom Ge'if (Leonard 1997: figs. 7.11 and 7.12), produced many tiny bits of faience that were simply too small to reconstruct the shape, or even the size of the original vessel, and the presence of such morphologically nondiagnostic pieces has simply been noted in the Locus Summaries. In other instances, however, the wet soils of Naukratis had been less cruel, and the fragments were large enough that they could be drawn and reconstructed on paper. These pieces are presented below and related, where possible, to similar forms in the ceramic repertoire to which appeal is usually made for their date.[69] If one follows the general trend "from a yellowish toward a cleaner whiter paste" noticed by Thompson (1973: 11) as having been completed by the reign of Ptolemy IV Philopator (murdered in 205 B.C.), this would provide the Kom Hadid corpus with a *terminus post quem* toward the end of the third century B.C.

Monochrome Faience Vessels

Twenty-two morphologically diagnostic sherds comprise the Kom Hadid *corpus* of monochrome faience tableware. This number includes small dishes with internally thickened rims (fig. 3.8:6, 8–12; fig. 3.9:10–12, 14, 15),[70] vessels with straight rims (fig. 3.9:13 and variants fig. 3.8:7, 11), and the distinctive echinus bowls with incurved rim (figs. 3.8:5; fig. 3.9:9).[71] A single vessel exhibited a simple, rounded base without a distinct foot (fig. 3.8:1), but most pieces presented a ring base or elevated foot (fig. 3.8:2–4; fig. 3.9: 6–8).[72] All of these features can be paralleled in the pottery assemblage from the site (see above, Chapter 2).

Decorated Faience Vessels

Five of the faience fragments (three body sherds and two rims) exhibit traces of decoration that had been executed in a second (or third) color. A small body sherd (fig. 3.9:1) with yellow surfaces has been enhanced with a light green band on the interior and a light brown design on the exterior. A second vessel (fig. 3.9:2; pl. 3.23b)[73] was decorated on what appears to have been the exterior of the vessel with a light blue floral(?) pattern against a very pale blue background. This floral element is very reminiscent (to the author at least) of the Mycenaean Flower that often appears on the shoulders of Aegean stirrup jars that were traded widely around the eastern Mediterranean during the Late Bronze Age, and were actually imitated—in faience—in Egyptian workshops.[74] A third body sherd (fig. 3.9:3, pl. 3.24) has been given a slightly three-dimensional scale pattern, the raised portions of which appear lighter in color than the interstices in which more of the blue-green glaze has accumulated. A similar design was excavated at Samaria (Reisner 1924: 326, no. 5a).

Of the rim sherds, one (fig. 3.9:4; pl. 3.25) displays a dark brown band within which a cable pattern appears in reserve allowing the band to contrast with the white color of the surface. The interior of the other rim was embellished with a dark brown petal design radiating from the center of the white interior surface. Similarly decorated fragments are also known from Samaria (Reisner 1924: 327, nos. 1b and 2a).

34. Base (fig. 3.8:1)
Locus 4803   N.III.48.04   MC#2
Fabric: Faience.
Dimensions: Restored diameter of base: 5.8 cm.
Date: Ptolemaic Period.
Description: White core. Medium blue in/out.

35. Base (fig. 3.8:2)
Locus 6207   N.III.62.19   MC#36
Fabric: Faience.
Dimensions: Restored diameter of base: 5.1 cm.

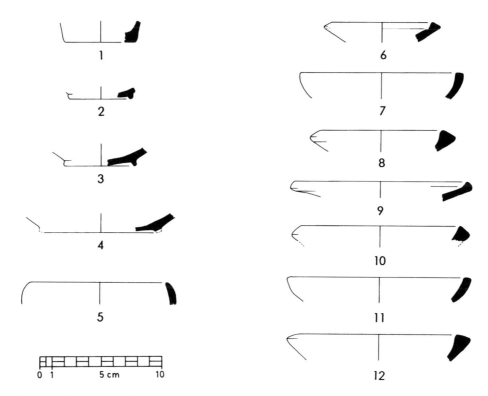

Fig. 3.8. Faience vessel fragments.

Date: Ptolemaic Period.
Description: White core. Light blue in/out.

36. Base (fig. 3.8:3)
Locus 6305   N.III.63.111   MC#34
Fabric: Faience.
Dimensions: Restored diameter of base: 5.8 cm.
Date: Ptolemaic Period.
Description: White core. Light blue-green in/out.

37. Base (fig. 3.8:4)
Locus 6305   N.III.63.15   MC#50
Fabric: Faience.
Dimensions: Restored diameter of base: 10.1 cm.
Date: Ptolemaic Period.
Description: Light yellow core with surfaces of the same color.

38. Rim (fig. 3.8:5)
Locus 6203   N.III.62.12   MC#16
Fabric: Faience.
Dimensions: Restored diameter of rim: 12.2 cm.

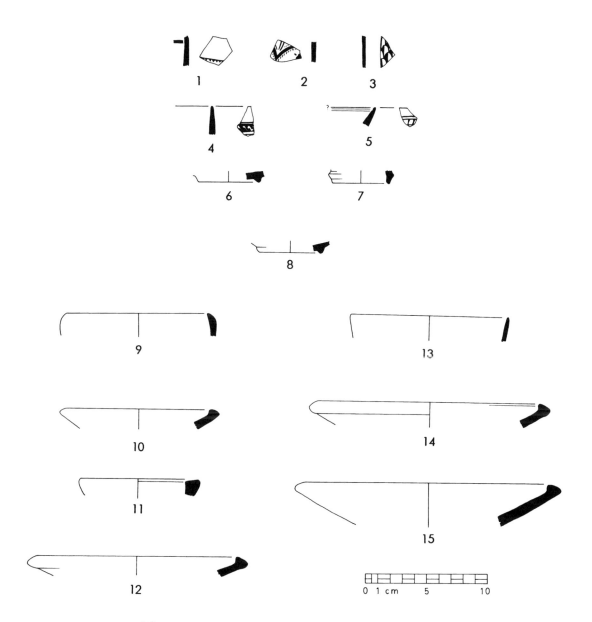

Fig. 3.9. Faience vessel fragments.

Date: Ptolemaic Period.
Description: White core. Greenish yellow in/out.

39. Rim (fig. 3.8:6)
Locus 7605   N.III.76.05   MC#13a
Fabric: Faience.
Dimensions: Restored diameter of rim: 7.8 cm.
Date: Ptolemaic Period.

Description: White core. Light blue in/out.

40. Rim (fig. 3.8:7)
Locus 7613   N.III.76.65   MC#125b
Fabric: Faience.
Dimensions: Restored diameter of rim: 13.2 cm.
Date: Ptolemaic Period.
Description: White core. Traces of blue in/out. Same vessel as **44** (fig. 3.8:11)?

41. Rim (fig. 3.8:8)
Locus 4803   N.III.48.09   MC#7
Fabric: Faience.
Dimensions: Restored diameter of rim: 9.2 cm.
Date: Ptolemaic Period.
Description: White core. Light blue in/out.

42. Rim (fig. 3.8:9)
Locus 7603   N.III.76.05   MC#13b
Fabric: Faience.
Dimensions: Restored diameter of rim: 14.2 cm.
Date: Ptolemaic Period.
Description: White core. Traces of light blue in/out. Very worn.

43. Rim (fig. 3.8:10)
Locus 7606   N.III.76.13   MC#27
Fabric: Faience.
Dimensions: Restored diameter of rim: 13.1 cm.
Date: Ptolemaic Period.
Description: White core. Light blue in/out.

44. Rim (fig. 3.8:11)
Locus 7613   N.III.76.64   MC#125a
Fabric: Faience.
Dimensions: Restored diameter of rim: 14.8 cm.
Date: Ptolemaic Period.
Description: White core. Light blue in/out. Same vessel as **40** (fig. 3.8:7)?

45. Rim (fig. 3.8:12)
Locus 6304   N.III.63.09   MC#18
Fabric: Faience.
Dimensions: Restored diameter of rim: 12.9 cm.
Date: Ptolemaic Period.
Description: White core. Light blue in/out.

46. Body sherd (fig. 3.9:1)
Locus 6207   N.III.62.19   MC#36b

Fabric: Faience.
Dimensions: 2.2 × 2.4 cm.
Date: Ptolemaic Period.
Description: White core. Yellow in/out. Light green band in; light brown decoration out.

47. Body sherds (one [pl. 3.23a] is not drawn here) (pl. 3.23a,b and fig. 3.9:2)
Locus 7613   N.III.76.70   MC#140d
Fabric: Faience.
Dimensions: 2.3 × 1.8 cm.
Date: Ptolemaic Period.
Description: White core. Very pale yellow-green on interior(?), exterior decorated with light blue floral(?) pattern against a very pale blue background.

48. Body sherd (pl. 3.24 and fig. 3.9:3)
Locus 7605   N.III.76.32   MC#69
Fabric: Faience.
Dimensions: 1.0 × 2.1 cm.
Date: Ptolemaic Period.
Description: White core. Light green surfaces. Blue-green design on exterior.

49. Rim (pl. 3.25 and fig. 3.9:4)
Locus 6215   N.III.62.38   MC#71
Fabric: Faience.
Dimensions: 1.2 × 2.1 cm. Restored diameter of rim uncertain.
Date: Ptolemaic Period.
Description: Yellow core. White surfaces with brown design on exterior.

50. Rim (pl. 3.26 and fig. 3.9:5)
Locus 6207   N.III.62.19   MC#36a
Fabric: Faience.
Dimensions: 1.3 × 1.4. Restored diameter of rim uncertain.
Date: Ptolemaic Period.
Description: White core. Very pale blue in/out. Dark brown decoration out.
The photograph on pl. 3.26 was taken after joins were made that do not appear in the drawing (fig. 3.9:5).

51. Base (fig. 3.9:6)
Locus 6207   N.III.62.19   MC#36c
Fabric: Faience.
Dimensions: Restored diameter of base: 4.6 cm.
Date: Ptolemaic Period.
Description: White core. Light blue in, pale yellow out.

52. Base (fig. 3.9:7)
Locus 7613   N.III.76.70   MC#140c

Fabric: Faience.
Dimensions: Restored diameter of base: 4.2 cm.
Date: Ptolemaic Period.
Description: White core. Light blue in/out.

53. Body sherd (fig. 3.9:8)
Locus 7613   N.III.76.70   MC# 140a
Fabric: Faience.
Dimensions: Restored diameter of base: 5.0 cm.
Date: Ptolemaic Period.
Description: White core. Very pale green out and as ground on interior. Design on interior in pale blue.

54. Rim (fig. 3.9:9)
Locus 7603   N.III.76.41   MC#95
Fabric: Faience.
Dimensions: Restored diameter of rim: 11.3 cm.
Date: Ptolemaic Period.
Description: White core. Light yellow-green in/out.

55. Rim (fig. 3.9:10)
Locus 6304   N.III.63.10   MC#12
Fabric: Faience.
Dimensions: Restored diameter of rim: 10.2 cm.
Date: Ptolemaic Period.
Description: White core. Light blue in/out.

56. Rim (fig. 3.9:11)
Locus 7613   N.III.76.70   MC#140b
Fabric: Faience.
Dimensions: Restored diameter of rim: 9.7 cm.
Date: Ptolemaic Period.
Description: White core. Pale blue in/out.

57. Rim (fig. 3.9:12)
Locus 7605   N.III.76.55   MC#117b
Fabric: Faience.
Dimensions: Restored diameter of rim: 16.0 cm.
Date: Ptolemaic Period.
Description: White core. Green in/out. Worn. Same vessel as #59 (fig 3.9:14)?

58. Rim (fig. 3.9:13)
Locus 7608   N.III.76.33   MC#98
Fabric: Faience.
Dimensions: Restored diameter of rim: 12.9 cm.

Date: Ptolemaic Period.
Description: White core. Blue in/out.

59. Rim (fig. 3.9:14)
Locus 7605　　　　　N.III.76.55　　　　　MC#117a
Fabric: Faience.
Dimensions: Restored diameter of rim: 17.8 cm.
Date: Ptolemaic Period.
Description: White core. Bluish-green mottled to yellow in/out. Same vessel as #57 (fig 3.9:12)?

60. Base (fig. 3.9:15)
Locus 7603　　　　　N.III.76.05　　　　　MC#15
Fabric: Faience.
Dimensions: Restored diameter of base: 19.7 cm.
Date: Ptolemaic Period.
Description: White core, blue in/out.

Lithics

61. Fragment of a *kouros* statue(?) (pls. 3.27, 3.28)
Locus 14403　　　　　N.III.144.08　　　　　MC#6
Material: White, coarse-grained marble.
Dimensions: 9.0 × 6.0 × 6.0 cm.
Date: 6th century B.C.(?).
Description: A fragment interpreted as representing the nape of the neck of a *kouros* statue. One side exhibits a series of parallel cuttings perhaps indicating plaited hair (pl. 27). A rust-stained dowel-hole(?) is partially preserved at break (pl. 28).
Discussion: Because of the paucity of fine stone in the Western Delta, all such pieces encountered during our excavations at Kom Hadid were registered. This piece had been registered simply as a miscellaneous piece of imported marble. Subsequent study of the photographs of the piece (after it was no longer available for firsthand study) has suggested the present identification. Although the piece is too fragmentary for further attribution, an Archaic stone statue would not be out of place at the site.

62. Fragment of a ringstand[75] (pl. 3.29 and fig. 3.10:A)
Locus 6305　　　　　N.III.63.18　　　　　MC#44
Material: White limestone.
Dimensions: H. 5.5 cm, W. 2.9 cm. Reconstructed external diameter c. 20 cm.
Date: Uncertain (Ptolemaic?).
Description: A segment of a limestone ringstand.

63. Fragment of a column (pl. 3.30 and fig. 3.10B)
Locus 13002　　　　　N.III.130.04　　　　　MC#4
Material: White limestone.
Dimensions: Preserved H. c. 6.0 cm, W c. 10 cm. Reconstructed diameter c. 25 cm.

Date: Ptolemaic(?).

Description: Fragment of fluted column in soft white limestone.

Discussion: The reconstructed diameter (c. 25 cm) of this fragment is smaller than either of the two fluted drums that Hogarth encountered in the cemetery of Naukratis (Hogarth 1898/99: 23). It is also smaller in diameter than any of the drums discovered during the survey in a very secondary position built into a bench in the modern village of Kom Ge'if (Coulson 1996: 14–16, fig. 7 and pl. VII–VIII), some of which were also fluted.

64a. Fragment of stone[76] (pl. 3.31a)

Locus 6205   N.III.62.23   MC#57

Material: White marble.

Dimensions: 12.0 × 12.3 × 1.5 cm.

Date: Ptolemaic.

Description: Broken piece of gray and white marble with traces of plaster adhering to one flat side.

Discussion: Although pieces of such stone "veneer" could have been employed to decorate either the walls or floor of a structure, they most probably indicate the presence of a building with an *opus sectile* pavement at the site.

64b. Fragment of stone (pl. 3.31b)

Locus 6301   N.III.63.02   MC#25

Material: Red porphyry.

Dimensions: 9.2 × 6.0 × 1.3 cm.

Date: Ptolemaic.

Description: Broken piece of red porphyry.

Discussion: As is the case with 64a above, this fragment of porphyry most probably indicates the presence of a structure decorated with a flooring of *opus sectile* (or the more specific *opus alexandrinum* employing only red and green stones) somewhere in the vicinity. This would have been a luxurious touch to a building at Naukratis since stone of any kind is very scarce in the area.

65. Two fragments of aggregate pavement[77]

65a. Locus 7619   N.III.76.71   MC#135   (pls. 3.32a, 3.33a)

65b. Locus 7619   N.III.76.72   MC#149   (pls. 3.32b, 3.33b)

Material: Mixed composition.

Dimensions: 65a: 8.6 × 8.1 cm; 65b: 6.0 × 6.1 cm.

Description: These fragments appear to illustrate the individual stages in the construction of pavement as described by Pliny, Vitruvius and other ancient authors.[78] A basal layer of coarse, gray lime mortar (the *ruduss*) containing inclusions of iridescent white shell, gray stone, red brick/ceramic, and kiln waste (averaging 3–5 mm but occasionally as large as 1 cm). The bottom of this layer bore a series of concave impressions including those of sticks and branches (average diameter c. 2.5 cm) perhaps representing the subfloor, bedding layer (the *statumen*). Above this layer of coarse mortar had been added a second layer of gray, lime mortar (the *nucleus*) that exhibited frequent, but smaller (sand-sized to 1 mm), inclusions of red (ceramic or brick) binder. Field observation and description noted that into this upper layer a number of unworked, white pebbles of limestone or marble had been set and subsequently

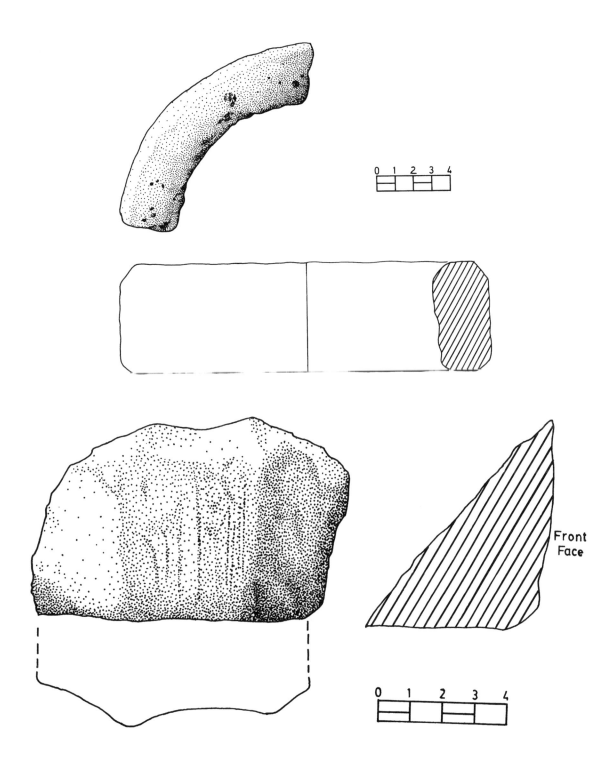

Fig. 3.10. A) Fragment of a limestone ringstand(?) (#62); B) Segment of a fluted limestone column (#63).

grouted with a thin (and slightly finer) coating of the same material. However, it is not impossible that this layer of grouting was actually an example of the layer identified by Moore (1968) as the *supra-nucleus* and that the stones had been set into it and not into the *nucleus*.

Date: Ptolemaic Period.

Discussion: These fragments are presented here simply as pieces of aggregate pavement in spite of the fact that, in the field, they had been registered as portions of a pebble mosaic. This change in nomenclature has been made for two reasons. The first is to avoid their confusion with pebble mosaics in the sense of those at Pella, Olynthos, and other sites in the Greek World (von Lorentz 1937) in which water-smoothed stones have been set in an eye-pleasing design or pattern; the second reason is to remove them from any discussion of the origin and development of the true (or tessellated) mosaic, and the attendant argument over the exact meaning and ramifications of the passage in the *Deipnosophistai* (v. 207c) by Athenaeus (of Naukratis) that related the gift of the *Syracusia*, a mosaic-decked(?) yacht, by Hieron II of Syracuse to Ptolemy III (Euergetes) who quickly renamed it the *Alexandris*.

A major champion of the theory for an early- to mid-third century B.C. invention of the tessellated mosaic in Sicily and its subsequent diffusion throughout the Mediterranean world is Kyle Phillips, whose views are based substantially on the presence of the tessellated Ganymede and Eagle mosaic in Room 3 of the House of Ganymede at Morgantina (Phillips 1960). This mosaic stands stylistically in sharp contrast to the pavements in Rooms 1 and 2 of the same structure where irregular bits of stone had been set into the flooring.[79] On the other hand, note that Dunbabin (1994: 26, and n. 2) no longer sees Athenaeus' story of the *Alexandris* as having any bearing on the development of the tesselated mosaic, objecting in part to the degree of emphasis placed on the Ganymede Mosaic to the exclusion of *terrazzo*, *opus signinum*, and other pavement types that appear in the same house (1994: 28–29). These latter pavement types were quite widespread throughout the area and especially in the Punic World where their use can be traced back into the first half of the third century B.C. (1994: 32–39).

These two terms, *terrazzo* and *opus signinum*, were also considered to describe the Kom Hadid fragments, but were abandoned because of the incredible amount of flexibility that is apparent in the use of these two descriptors. For instance, *terrazzo* is often used to describe a pavement that is similar to a modern terrazzo floor where pebbles or other bits of stone have actually been incorporated into the *nucleus* and not individually set into it; while the term *opus signinum* has been employed to define a variety of pavement types including those in which some (or even most) of the inclusions are bits and pieces of terracotta.[80] Although Dunbabin uses both the terms *terrazzo* and *opus signinum*, she considered them both to be unsatisfactory, preferring instead a term such as a "cement pavement" or "pavement of aggregate" (1994: 30–31 and n. 14). This latter term seems best to describe the Kom Hadid fragments, and a so a variant of it, "aggregate pavement," has been utilized here.[81]

Regardless of the terminology employed, however, one thing is clear: The main difference between the Kom Hadid fragments and others with which they might be compared is that that the primary intention of the artisans at Naukratis was the creation of a proper, functioning use-surface or pavement, and not to produce an artistic embellishment or decoration for the building. The question of whether such decorated floors existed at Naukratis has not yet been answered, nor can we postulate whether the simplicity of the Hadid fragments reflects the function of the structure, the economic status of the owners, or even the lessened importance of the hinterland as power and prestige became more and more concentrated in the port city of Alexandria.

Glass

66. Fragment of an Ingot or palette of blue-green glass (pl. 3.34)
Locus 6301   N.III.63.01   MC#26
Material: Blue glass.
Dimensions: c. 3.5 × 3.8 cm.
Decription: Fragment of a blue-green glass plaque or ingot with longitudinal grooves.
Date: Uncertain Ptolemaic(?).
Discussion: Because of the small size of this fragment, identification of its function is difficult. An ingot or other piece of bulk glass would not seem out of place at a site so close to Alexandria that has been described as "one of the greatest glass-manufacturing centres of antiquity" (Lucas and Harris 1962: 184), while the use of the cosmetic palette to grind *kohl* is a tradition that extends back thousands of years into the Predynastic period. The blue-green color of Ptolemaic glass was most probably achieved by the addition of copper compounds as coloring agent(s) rather than the cobalt of earlier periods or the iron of later periods (Lucas and Harris 1962: 188–89).[82]

Metal

On the whole, metal objects were fewer and less well preserved at Kom Hadid than at Kom Ge'if, perhaps due to the height of the present water table at Hadid. Five copper coins were retrieved (from Loci 6202, 6305, 7606, 7608, and 7613), but heavy corrosion and other metal disease(s) had completely removed their original surfaces and they could not be identified even after meticulous cleaning and stabilization by conservator Weber. Short pins in copper or copper alloy (from Loci 7603 and 7606) and an iron pin with a copper(?) head (from Locus 7613) were also found. Iron nails (also very corroded) that had been so prevalent at Kom Ge'if were encountered in only two deposits at Kom Hadid (Loci 6205 and 7603). Several small and indistinguishable lumps of copper/bronze were recorded elsewhere (Loci 6203, 6207, 6209, 7618, and 13002).

Plaster

Two-dimensional

During his tenure at Naukratis, Petrie noted "frescoed Roman brickwork" in association with the slag heaps at Kom Hadid (references in Coulson and Leonard 1982: 363); and Hogarth encountered traces of several floors of "hammered earth overlaid with fine plaster" (1898/99: 33) that had been decorated in a variety of colors of which he noted crimson, brilliant blue, and yellow. These colors occurred in both solid and striped patterns.[83] Small, fragmentary bits of decorative plaster, also in very poor condition, were encountered in many of the archaeological deposits during our work at Kom Hadid; those that were large or distinctive enough to be registered separately are discussed below. Unfortunately, their secondary archaeological contexts do not allow us to comment on whether they had originally been used to decorate walls, floors, or even ceilings. However, the impressions of chaff and other vegetal matter on the backs of #74 and #79 could suggest that some were originally part of a floor (from a second story?), while the beveled imitation of drafted-margin orthostats of #76 suggest that other pieces had originally been part of a wall decoration.

Material. Samples of plaster from both Kom Ge'if and Kom Hadid were tested for composition on a random basis by conservator Gail Weber. She found that over 90% of the pieces represented lime plaster (calcium carbonate, $CaCO_3$) and that none of them could be proven to be gypsum (calcium sulphate, $CaSO_4$).[84] In fact, Weber noted that the two samples that did not react to hydrochloric acid were definitely *not* calcined gypsum. At first, this might seem strange, given Egypt's long history of using decorated gypsum plaster to embellish the walls of its buildings and tombs (Lucas and Harris 1999: 76), and the bountiful supplies of gypsum that occur naturally in the Mariout region to the west of Alexandria (Lucas and Harris 1999: 78, with references). Furthermore, the temperatures required to produce a plaster from gypsum (c. 130°C) is only about 15% of that which is needed to obtain a similar product from limestone (c. 900°C).[85] The production of lime plaster in the western Delta, an area in which trees have always been a scarce commodity, would have required a substantial amount of fuel.

The Delta potters of the Ptolemaic Period, however, never seem to have had trouble finding a sufficient supply of fuel to fire the huge quantity of pottery that they produced, a fact that was especially apparent at Kom Hadid whose surface was carpeted with kiln waste and furnace product, the material that had been identified by Petrie as metal slag. Today, in the modern village of Kom Ge'if, the collection of dung is a major industry and an absolutely essential task if even a minimum level of sanitation is to be maintained. The material thus collected is formed into patties and air dried for later use as for building materials and fuel (see also Miller 1984, Miller and Smart 1984). Viewed in such a context the consumption of large amounts of fuel by the Ptolemaic lime slakers was probably just as important to the life of the community as was the work of the potters.[86]

Because the use of lime plaster, which appears to have several distinct advantages over gypsum plaster, cannot be documented before the Ptolemaic Period, it is thought by many to have been a Greek practice that was introduced to Egypt in the wake of Alexander's conquest.[87] Evidently, if the new technique was good enough for the builders of the new capital, it would have been sought after by the citizens of Naukratis who for centuries had considered their city to have been the only Hellenic presence in the country.

Technique. Several of the plaster fragments from Kom Hadid include preparatory layers (i.e., multiple layers or coats of plaster placed one upon the other). Some of these represent base (or buildup) layers of coarse plaster that had been smoothed in preparation for a final finish (or face) coat. Other fragments, however, give clear indication of distinct phases of decorating or redecorating. In the latter instances a finished and decorated surface had been covered by another coat of coarse plaster and then given a second finish coat that would have been subsequently painted with a new design. The most complex fragment from Hadid is #69 (pl. 3.37; fig. 3.11:C), which preserves five distinct layers that include two face coats.[88]

In every case where multiple layers are present, there is a noticeable increase in the quality and fineness of the plaster from the base coat(s) to the face coat, with decreasing amounts of temper in the plaster as one moves towards the face coat. Examining this material under magnification, conservator Weber noted the presence of charcoal as well as "sand and gravel of a fluvial origin" in these substrata. Quite often the river gravel was large enough to be seen by the unaided eye and occasionally larger lithic inclusions (c. 1.0–1.5 cm) were also encountered. In addition to the grit-temper, the layers of undercoating also contained bits of grog (ground potsherds and fired brick) which, according to both Pliny and Vitruvius, was especially desirable in buildings situated in damp locations (Ling 1976: 212). The proximity of Naukratis to the Nile canal would seem to support their views. Although the reddish grog was usually confined to the basal layers, a sufficient amount of the material had occasionally been mixed into the face coat(s) to give them a distinctly pinkish hue.

As noted above, the finished surface (or face coat) of each fragment was always the finest (least tempered) of the preparatory layers and could exhibit smoothing, painting, and/or sculpting (see Pratt 1976: 227):

1. The surface could simply be smoothed, evidently with a board (or "float") in the same manner as a modern mason would finish a cement slab;
2. The surface could be painted, either solid monochrome or in decorative patterns such as vegetal garlands (#67) or the veining of marble (#70).[89] According to conservator Weber, the colors of the Kom Hadid fragments (see Table 3.1)[90] had been applied when the surface was dry (*al secco*) rather than when it was still wet (*al fresco*);[91]
3. The plaster could be sculpted while it was still wet in order to give the surface the three-dimensional appearance of blocks with drafted margins (#76) or other elements of an architectural facade (#83).

String courses representing marginally drafted blocks of stone (in both solid colors and *faux* marble), articulated by means of lines inscribed in the plaster as well as by color separation, strongly link the Kom Hadid fragments with other structures decorated in the so-called Masonry Style.[92] The presence of similar Masonry Style decoration on at least one of the walls of the Wardian Tomb in nearby Alexandria suggests an approximate date of the second century B.C.,[93] and we know from the ruins at Pompeii that the popularity of the style extended into the first century B.C. (Laidlaw 1985). In discussing the fragments of painted (*al secco*), lime-plaster from the walls of Herod's Palace at Jericho, Rozenberg (1966: 123–25, and 128) noted several differences between the decorated walls of the Hasmonean/Hellenistic Period and those that had been executed after the beginning of Herod's building activity in the region (i.e., shortly after c. 30 B.C.).[94] These differences included the fact that

1. Hellenistic (pre-Herodian) paintings had fewer layers of plaster, since fewer layers would be required when painting al secco as opposed to al fresco where the pigment is applied directly to the surface of the rapidly drying wall;
2. linear patterns were less regular in Hasmonean than in Herodian work;
3. relief devices of incised or inscribed lines and beveled features (as well as molded architectonic elements such as #83 to be discussed below) that had been so common in Hasmonean and other Hellenistic buildings did not continue their popularity in the Herodian period.[95]

These features are also to be found in the plaster fragments from Kom Hadid and combine with other evidence at the site to reinforce a date for them in the second–first century B.C., sometime before Augustus incorporated Egypt into the Roman orb.

Plaster Fragments (Figs. 3.11 and 3.12)

67. Plaster Fragment (pl. 3.35 and fig. 3.11:A)
Locus 6210   N.III.62.29   MC#58
Preservation: 6.6 × 6.1 × 0.8 cm.
Description: Fragment of gray-white, lime (CaCO$_3$) plaster with a 10R 3/6–4/6 (Dark Red) design that appears to be part of a floral or vegetal pattern. Two layers of plaster (top 5 mm, bottom 2–3 mm).
Date: 2nd century–first half of first century B.C.

Discussion: See above.

68. Plaster Fragment (pl. 3.36 and fig. 3.11:B)
Locus 6301   N.III 63.01   MC#79
Preservation: 4.8 × 5.0 × 1.8cm
Description: Fragment of lime plaster consisting of three coats. A white surface coat sandwiching a 5YR 8/2 (Pinkish White) coat with traces of a second coat of white plaster on the back (cf. pl. 3.41a for sandwich). All three layers have sand-sized to 0.1 cm red (terracotta) grit/grog and fine straw casts. Front face has thin (c. 0.4 cm) stripe of green-black color paralleled by a wider (preserved to 1.0 cm) stripe of c. 2.5YR 5/4 (Reddish Brown) to 5/6 (Red).
Date: 2nd century–first half of first century B.C.
Discussion: See above.

69. Plaster Fragment (pl. 3.37 and fig. 3.11:C)
Locus 6301   N.III.63.01   MC#28
Preservation: c. 8.0 × 5.2 × 1.8 cm
Description: Fragment of lime plaster consisting of a total of five layers of plaster representing at least two finished and color-decorated surfaces (faces 1 and 2) with associated makeup layers. Plaster of two grades: a finer white finish coat for face 1 that has sand-sized to (occasionally) 1–2 mm red grit/grog inclusions; and a coarser, 5YR 7/2 (Pinkish Gray), makeup coat for face 2 with sand-sized to 1 mm red (terracotta) grog and fine air bubbles. Decoration on face 1 is 2.5YR 4/6–5/6 (Red) on 10 YR 8/3 (Very Pale Brown) background; decoration on face 2 is 7.5YR 6/6 (Reddish Yellow) to 4/6 (Strong Brown) on a 10YR 8/3 (Very Pale Brown) background.
Date: 2nd century–first half of 1st century B.C.
Discussion: See above.

70. Plaster Fragments (pl. 3.38a–c and fig. 3.11:D)
Locus 13009   N.III.130.12   MC#17
Preservation: Fragment A: 10.6 × 10.1 × 1.4 cm; Fragment B: 3.0 × 3.5 × 1.5 cm; Fragment C: 3.5 × 3.6 × 1.6 cm.
Description: Fragments of decorated lime plaster (representative 3 of 8 pieces are illustrated).
Fragment A (left): Exterior surface decorated with a pattern imitating veined marble in c. 10YR 6/1 (Gray) and 10YR 7/1 (Light Gray) pigment.
Fragment B (upper right): Composition as Fabric A, but with one stripe nearing the color green (no Munsell).
Fragment C (lower right): Composition as Fabric A. Color differentiation is less distinct on the actual pieces themselves than on the drawing.
Date: 2nd century–first half of 1st century B.C.
Discussion: See above.

71. Plaster Fragments (pl. 3.39a–c and fig. 3.12:E)
Locus 13003   N.III.130.08   MC#13
Preservation: Fragment A: 6.1 × 6.9 × 0.5 cm.; Fragment B: 3.3 × 3.5 × 0.05 cm; Fragment C: 2.1 × 3.4 × 0.5 cm.

Table 3.1. Plaster Background and Decoration

Color of Background	Color of Decoration	Catalogue Number
White or Gray-White	Red	#67, #79, #80
White or Gray-White	Blue	#78, #79
White or Gray-White	Gray	#70A, #70C, #71C, #81
White or Gray-White	Green	#70B, #82D
White or Gray-White	Red and Green	#68
White or Gray-White	Gray and Green	#71B
Dark Gray	Yellow	#73 face 2
Pinkish White/Gray	Red	#82B, #82E
Pinkish White/Gray	Yellow	#75 face 1
Pinkish White/Gray	None	#76 A–C
Very Pale Brown	Red-Yellow	#69 face 2
Very Pale Brown	Red	#69 face 1
Reddish yellow	Dark Red-Gray	#75 face 2
Reddish yellow	Red	#74A
Yellow	None	#74B
Red	None	#77, #82A
Red	White/Pale Brown	#71A, #72

Table 3.2. Plaster Two- and Three-Dimensional Decoration

Design	Catalogue Number
Two-Dimensional Decoration:	
Undecorated Surface(?) Coat	#77 (red), #78 (blue), #80 (red), #82a (red)
Abstract (Linear/Curvilinear Motives)	#68, #70, #71, #72, #73, #74, #82c–e
Representational (Vegetal/Floral Motives)	#67, #69 faces a and b, #82b
Miscellaneous	#75 (spots), #79 (fugitive color)
Three-Dimensional Decoration:	
Beveled	#76 A–C
Crown Molding	#83

Description: Three fragments of lime plaster.

Fragment A (left): (The bottom 0.1 cm may represent another layer/phase of plaster). Surface decorated with 10R 4/4 (Weak Red) to 4/6 (Red) background against which linear/curvilinear designs were added in 10YR 8/2 (White) to 8/3 (Very Pale Brown).

Fragment B (center): With distinct 0.1 cm bottom layer. Surface decorated with 10YR 4/1 (Dark Gray) stripes roughly alternating with streaks of light green (no Munsell).

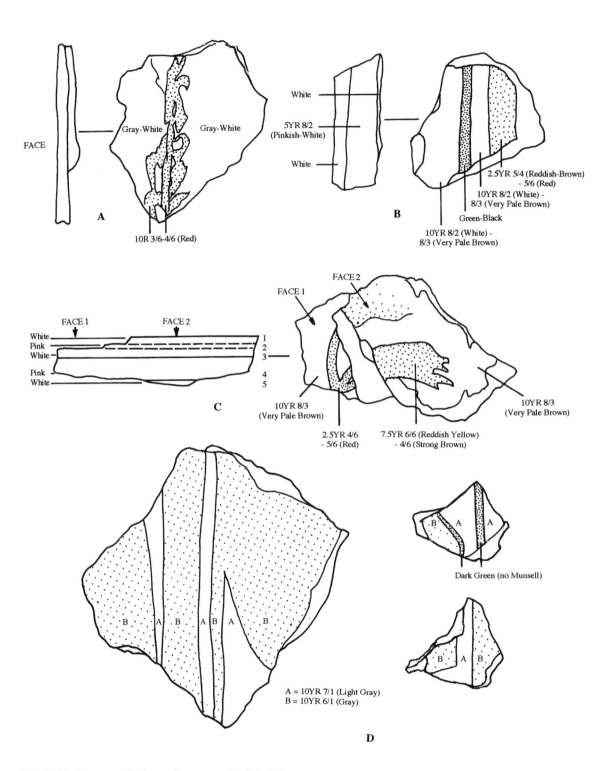

Fig. 3.11. Decorated plaster fragments (# 67–70)

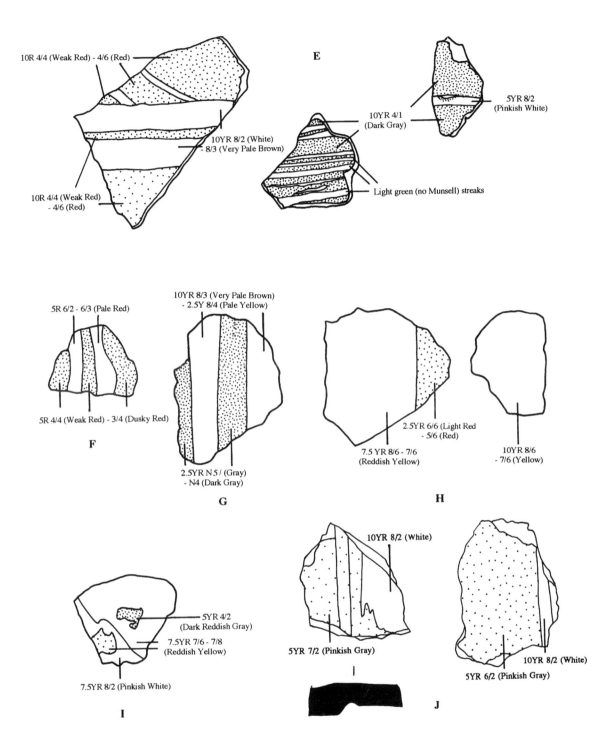

Fig. 3.12. Decorated plaster fragments (# 71–76).

Fabric C (right): Consisting of at least three distinct layers. Top (face): c. 0.04 cm white plaster; middle: c. 0.01 cm c. 5YR 8/2 (Pinkish White) with sand-sized and slightly larger, red (terracotta) grit/grog; bottom: c. 0.1 cm pink (as middle) with similar inclusions; surface of face coat patterned with the same dark green color as the center sherd (fragment B).

Date: 2nd century–first half of 1st century B.C.

Discussion: See above.

72. Plaster Fragment (fig. 3.12:F)

Locus 13007   N.III.130.14   MC#20

Preservation: c. 4.1 × 4.5 × 0.5 cm.

Description: Fragment of fine, white lime plaster with some straw casts. Surface color between 5R 4/4 (Weak Red) and 3/4 (Dusky Red) with white linear/curvilinear design. The white appears as 5R 6/2–6/3 (Pale Red), but is probably a white pigment that was applied thinly enough to allow some of the red to show through from below.

Date: 2nd century–first half of 1st century B.C.

Discussion: See above.

73. Plaster Fragment (fig. 3.12:G)

Locus 7603   N.III.76.20   MC#106

Preservation: 5.3 × 4.0 × 0.7 cm.

Description: Fragment of lime plaster decorated with vertical stripes. Note: the 6–7 cm thickness includes three distinct layers: an inner, basal layer c. 1 cm white bonded to a middle layer 2 cm of pink (comparable to 10R 6/3–6/4 [Pale Red]) with an earlier undecorated surface (face 1); and a third (final) layer of white (2 cm) with a second finished surface (face 2). The matrices of all three layers have sand-sized terracotta inclusions (grog). The outermost finished surface (face 2) of 2.5YR N5/–N4/ (Dark Gray) is decorated with stripes (c. 1 cm wide) of a color between 10YR 8/3 (Very Pale Brown) and 2.5Y 8/4 (Pale Yellow).

Date: 2nd century–first half of 1st century B.C.

Discussion: See above.

74. Plaster Fragments (fig. 3.12:H)

Locus 6302   N.III.63.06   MC#13B

Preservation: Fragment A: 3.6 × 2.9 × 08 cm; Fragment B: 4.8 × 5.1 × 1.0 cm.

Description: Two fragments of decorated lime plaster. Impressions on the basal layer indicate that the plaster had been applied to an uneven surface. Thickness: c. 1.0 cm: inner 0.2 cm layer of white plaster with air bubbles; middle 0.4/0.5 cm layer of 5YR 7/2 (Pinkish Gray) to 7/3 (Pink) with gray grit and terracotta (grog) sand-sized to 0.2 cm; and outer 0.3 cm layer of 5YR 8/2 (Pinkish White) with air bubbles, white and gray grit, and red terracotta grog from sand-sized to 2 mm.

Fragment A: Surface color between 7.5YR 8/6 and 7/6 (Reddish Yellow) decorated with stripe between 2.5YR 6/6 (Light Red) and 5/6 (Red) (fig. 3.12:H left).

Fragment B: basal layer not preserved. Surface color 10R8/6–7/6 (Yellow) (fig. 3.12:H right).

Date: 2nd century–first half of 1st century B.C.

Discussion: See above.

75. Plaster Fragment (fig. 3.12:I)

Locus 6205   N.III.62.21   MC#40 (Fragment B)

Preservation: 6.2 × 4.1 × 0.8 cm.
Description: Fragment of lime plaster, consisting of two layers, with smooth inner surface (face 1) of 7.5YR 8/2 (Pinkish White), a spot of yellow decoration close to 10YR 8/6–7/6 (Yellow) changing to darker 7.5YR 7/6–7/8 (Reddish Yellow) where pigment is thicker, and another surface of 7.5YR 7/6–7/8 (Reddish Yellow) with a spot of 5YR 4/2 (Dark Reddish Gray).
Date: 2nd century–first half of 1st century B.C.
Discussion: See above.

76. Plaster Fragments (pl. 3.40a–c and fig. 3.12:J, two fragments illustrated)
Locus 6210   N.III.62.48   MC#78
Preservation: Ave. 4.5 × 5.0 cm. Thickness 0.5 cm.
Description: Three fragments of white lime plaster, each consisting of at least three layers. Top (face) coat, c. 0.4 cm of white plaster; middle c. 0.1 cm coat of 5YR 6/2–7/2 (Pinkish Gray) with sand-sized to 1mm terracotta (red) grog.; bottom c. 0.1 cm coat of the same color as middle coat with similar, but larger, inclusions. Bottom layer may represent another (earlier) phase of plastering. Exterior surfaces (5YR 7/2 Pinkish Gray) of two have been beveled to represent a drafted-margin orthostat block or other architectural feature.
Date: 2nd century–first half of 1st century B.C.
Discussion: See above.

77. Plaster Fragment (not illustrated)
Locus 4803   N.III.48.09   MC#6   K
Preservation: 5.4 × 4.2 × 1.1 cm.
Description: White lime plaster fragment, red exterior surface.
Date: 2nd century–first half of 1st century B.C.
Discussion: See above.

78. Plaster Fragment (not illustrated)
Locus 7604   N.III.76.24   MC#43   L
Preservation: 3.1 × 2.0 × 0.6 cm.
Description: Fragment of gray-white lime plaster decorated with light blue color, slightly fugitive.
Date: 2nd century–first half of 1st century B.C.
Discussion: See above.

79. Plaster Fragments (not illustrated)
Locus 7609   N.III.76.27   MC#51   M
Preservation: Range from 3.0 × 4.0 cm to 10 × 10 cm.
Description: Several large fragments of decorated lime plaster, consisting of as many as three preparatory layers of gray plaster, finished with a smoothed white exterior surface, that had been decorated with either a fugitive blue or red pigment. The innermost (i.e., basal) surface preserves impressions of straw(?) and what appears to have been a coarser surface to which the plaster had been applied.
Date: 2nd century–first half of 1st century B.C.
Discussion: See above.

80. Plaster Fragment (not illustrated)
Locus 7618   N.III.76.76   MC#164   N

Preservation: 4.1 × 4.5 × 0.8 cm.
Description: Small fragment of white lime plaster, traces of red pigment on exterior surface.
Date: 2nd century–first half of 1st century B.C.
Discussion: See above.

81. Plaster Fragment (not illustrated)
Locus 13010   N.III.130.13   MC#19
Preservation: 6.8 × 4.4 × 2.2 cm.
Description: Four small fragments of gray lime plaster with darker 10YR 6/1 (Gray) stripes on a lighter gray (no Munsell) ground.
Date: 2nd century–first half of 1st century B.C.
Discussion: See above.

82. Plaster Fragments (pl. 3.41 a–e)
Various topsoil loci.
Preservation: 5.5 × 5.2 × 1.0 cm.
Description: Miscellaneous plaster fragments from open *loci* are added here in order to give a wider impression of the range of painted decoration found at the site.
Date: 2nd century–first half of 1st century B.C.
Discussion: See above.

Three-dimensional

83. Fragment of architectural relief [96] (pl. 3.42 and fig. 3.13)
Locus 7605   N.III.76.53   MC#111
Preservation: 5.8 × 4.0 × 2.6 cm.
Description: Fragmentary crown molding with ovolo, decorated with egg-and-dart motive, in which the dart appears to be abnormally isolated from the eggs. The molding was constructed in two stages: a coarse inner layer of plaster (indicated by stippling on the drawing) was first applied to the wall; this was followed by a finer, whiter face coat of plaster that bore the three-dimensional decoration. The upper surface of both layers of plaster appears to have been flattened as if it had been shaped against a firm surface (a wooden form or a previously dried, plaster surface?).

Because of its fragmentary condition, this molding is difficult to understand. Even its original stance cannot be ascertained with any degree of certainty, and a change in the stance would obviously bring about a corresponding change in the profile. Therefore, for the sake of presentation, two stances are offered here (fig. 3.13):

1. Stance A that treats the fragment as a more canonical crown molding;
2. Stance B that presents a less typical profile, but one that takes into consideration the (apparently) flattened upper surfaces of the two layers of plaster.

Date: 2nd century–first half of 1st century B.C.
Discussion: Among the moldings presented by Shoe, the closest parallel for the profile of the Kom Hadid fragment, as presented in Stance A, is a sixth century B.C. ovolo in terracotta from Miletus (1936: 13, and pl. III:10). This belongs to her Ovolo Type IC (with the bottom deeper than the top), the same group to which she has assigned the epistyle crown from the first Temple of Apollo at Nau-

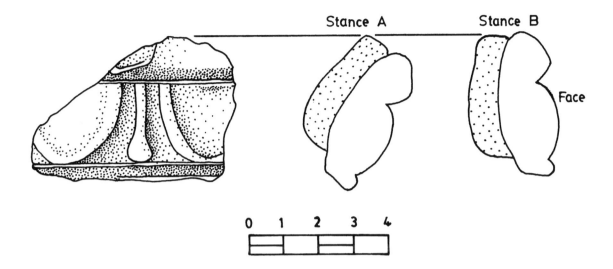

Fig. 3.13. Three-dimensional architectural relief in plaster (# 83).

kratis (Shoe 1936: 13, and pl. III:2).[97] There are also similarities between it and the profile of the ovolo on the crown of the altar on the south frieze of the later sixth century B.C. Siphnian Treasury at Delphi (Shoe 1936: 15–16, and pl. VI:12) which she assigned to her Ovolo Type IE (oval) category that also included the epistyle crown from the later temple of Apollo at Naukratis (Shoe 1936: 17, and pl. VI:14).[98]

The closest parallel for the profile of the piece as presented in Stance B, comes from the epistyle of the West Agora Gate at Ephesus, a structure that is dated to the end of the second century B.C. In discussing this piece Shoe remarked that, in the original publication, the chief molding on this structure had been identified by the excavators as an ovolo, but that there was no doubt in her mind that it should be considered to be a *cyma reversa* (1936: 63, and pl. XXVIII:31, her *Cyma Reversa* IV) and, in fact, it does seem to represent a rather hybrid creation.[99]

Three-dimensional, architectural moldings in sculpted plaster also occur at Jericho in a variety of profiles that appear to have come from the upper portion of the walls, since some of the fragments even displayed the impression of reeds and other wooden elements of the structure. According to Rozenberg, the most commonly appearing features were variations on the egg-and-dart pattern of which she illustrates several (1996: 126 and figs. 22–23). These closely resemble the fragment from Kom Hadid. In addition to Jericho, she also noted similar pieces of egg and tongue at Cypros, Herodion and Masada, as well as at Hellenistic sites such as Tel Anafa (1996: 126, and note 28, 29 with references). Weinberg (1971: 97–98) has published an elaborate egg-and-dart molded border from Tel Anafa that he assigned to the second phase of architecture at the site, the end of second century and first half of the first century B.C.[100] Such a date would be very much in keeping with Rozenberg's suggestion that "the local Hellenistic tradition of using molded architectonic elements as the most important part of the decoration had already gone out of use" by the time of Herod's elaborate building program (1996: 128); and it would also agree with the *floruit* of the representation of marginally drafted blocks of stone through the use of inscribed lines.

In summary then, while with Stance A we may be morphologically closer to sixth century B.C. Ionic forms that actually existed in limestone at Naukratis, with Stance B we are nearer to structures that are closer, chronologically, to the majority of the pottery and other elements of material culture that have been excavated at Kom Hadid. It is not impossible that the earlier pieces of sculpted stone may still have been visible to, and have served as the model or inspiration for, a Hellenistic artist attempting to duplicate them from plaster in the Masonry Style, the fashionable medium of the day.

Notes

[1] The author wishes to thank Dr. Irene Bald Romano for her helpful comments (based on photographs) on many of these figurines and plaques, and for directing the author to many very useful references. Errors and omissions are, of course, the author's.

[2] For coroplastic material found at Naukratis that is illustrative of the ancient Greek theater, see the following works by Webster. For tragedy and satyr plays: a terracotta mask (male?): ET7 (Webster: 1967: 66, cf. Gutch 1898/99: 96, no. 322); the terracotta head of a satyr figurine: ET16 (Webster: 1967: 67 [= B.M. C638]); and two satyr heads from clay braziers: AV50 and AV51 (Webster 1967: 53; cf. Conze 1890: 130, no. 814, 816 [= B.M. C889 and C891]); For Old and Middle Comedy: a terracotta (male?) mask: AT120, possibly of Attic fabric (Webster 1969b: 127, 221 = Webster 1969a: 100, UT12); and New Comedy: a terracotta mask of a young man: ET11 (Webster 1969a: 103); terracotta heads of male slaves: ET41, ET42, ET 43, and possibly ET 44 (Webster 1969a: 107–8 [cf. Petrie 1886: fig. 14, pl. 15]; and Walters 1903: cat. no. 261).

[3] For other terracotta figurines from Naukratis, in addition to those published by Petrie (1886), Gardner (1888), and Gutch (1898/99), see also Higgins (1969: 404–7) for nine pieces in the British Museum (nos. 1542–1550) that, for the most part, predate the material presented here, and Dunand (1990: 74-75 [no. 142] and 108 [no.252]). It is unfortunate, but understandable, that Gutch illustrated only about twenty percent of the figures with which he dealt.

[4] The fabric that is here referred to as "Delta silt" is the same material that very often in the past has been referred to as "Nile mud." Cf. Higgins 1967: 56, 93.

[5] Much of the basis for Webster's classification, however, was based on vagaries of hair and beard styles. These features, unfortunately, are not preserved on the Naukratis piece.

[6] In this respect, the mask resembles the faces of Ba'al that were associated with earlier Canaanite and Punic cults. Cf. Yadin 1970: 221–22 and fig. 14; Bieber 1961b: 11, figs. 66–69; and Karageorghis 1993:107 (seventh–fourth century B.C.). For (both tragic and comic) masks and masked actors from the Alexandrian cemeteries, cf. Breccia 1930: 63–65.

[7] For a grotesque with sidelock and lotus-bud crown carrying the infant Harpocrates, cf. Perdrizet 1921: 114, no. 292.

[8] Thompson et al. 1987: 45, no. 17; Breccia 1912: 137–38, pl. LXXI:212; Adriani 1961: 19 (inv. no. 25747), pl. VIII:5); Higgins 1967: 102, pl. 43E; Bell 1981: 190–94 nos. 484–534, 166 nos. 283, 285; Schürmann 1989: 312, 314,

319, nos. 1172, 1173, 1180–81, pls. 196–98; and Breccia 1930: 82, Tav. XIII:8.

[9] Higgins 1986: 123.

[10] For Harpocrates with a similar wreath (but without his finger in his mouth), cf. Bayer-Niemeyer 1988: 145, no. 168, Taf. 34:4. Such wreaths, however, usually culminate in a miniature Double Crown of Upper and Lower Egypt, an element that cannot be confirmed on the Naukratis piece since the top of the figure is abraded.

[11] Comparable human/divine female figurines exhibiting surplus bits of clay around the mouth or at lips, include *inter alia*, Bell 1981: 182, 184; Schurmann 1989: 242–43, no. 909, 914, Taf. 150, 151.

[12] Related are figures shown in the same pose, but where the subject wears platform shoes of varying height, usually with an anklet on each leg: Laumonier 1956: 152–53, nos. 441–44, pl. 43.

[13] Perdrizet 1921: 83–86, and the figure of no. 199 on p. 85.

[14] Also generically similar, but probably not related, are the curls of hair on a herm from Athens (invert the Naukratis fragment; Thompson, et al. 1987: 434; cf. pl. 58, T1566), the protrusions on a fragment of a thorn *kantharos* from second century B.C. Corinth (Edwards 1975: 87–88, pl. 54 no. 524, page 87 n. 82 references a similar piece in the contemporary Chatby cemetery in Alexandria), or the pyramidal bosses (termed *bosettes* by Courby 1922: 334, 386) on some imprecate bowls (Edwards 1975: 157–58 pl. 65 no. 783), but note the similarities between the pyramidal bosses on a pine cone vessel (no. 1375) and the slightly rounder bosses on the bunch of grapes (no. 1376) published side-by-side in Laumonier (1956: 284, pl. 102).

[15] The piece does not, however, find ready parallels among the large group of Hellenistic molds from the Athenian Agora (Grandjouan et al. 1989).

[16] For a visual impression of the high quality of these pieces, see the equally well-finished Bes in Dunand (1990: 21, no. 34 [color]).

[17] If the Naukratus fragment is inverted, there are some similarities between it and the sides of some plaques showing Harpocrates leaning against a column(?). Cf. *inter alia*, Bayer-Niemeyer (1988: 94, no. 100, Taf. 20:1 etc.).

[18] The first attempt to classify the Greco-Roman lamps of Egypt was made by Petrie 1905 based primarily on the tremendous number of lamps found during his excavations at Ehnasya (Herakleopolis Magna). Subsequent schemes have

been presented by Osborne 1924, Robins 1939a and b, and recently Daszewski 1987, the last of which has been the most useful to this study. Excellent discussions of the development of the various types of lamps are given by Bailey 1975 in connection with the examples in the British Museum, and by Hayes 1980b in his discussion of the lamps in the Royal Ontario Museum. Although it has been noted that, at least during the Hellenistic period, Egyptian lamp production was more influenced by events and trends in the eastern Aegean and eastern Mediterranean (Shier 1978), the *corpora* of lamps from the Athenian Agora (Howland 1958), Corinth (Broneer 1930), and Isthmia (Broneer 1977) remain indispensable to any study of the form. Also exceedingly valuable is the treatment by Shier 1978 of the lamps from the site of Karanis in the Egyptian Fayoum.

[19] The collections of the British Museum have several wheelmade lamps that are said (or believed) to come from Naukratis. See Bailey 1975 Volume I: Q20, Q22, Q52, Q81, and Q90 (from Athens ?); Q147, Q150, Q152–Q154 (from Ephessos and/or Southern Ionia); and Q365–Q370 (from Rhodes?). Lamps numbered Q513, Q524, Q533, Q537, and Q539, also found at Naukratis, appear to be wheelmade, local (i.e. Egyptian) lamps that follow non-Egyptian prototypes. For these lamps Bailey offers earlier (and/or) original publication(s).

[20] On lamps from Naukratis, cf. also Shier (1978: 4 with n. 33, 21 with n. 172, 32 with n. 279, and 40).

[21] The Egyptian lamps, however, are also very similar in style to lamps of the moldmade Agora Type 29 (A and B), which Howland considered to be related to the wheelmade Type 25 (1958: 94).

A case might also be made for including the Naukratis lamp with the wheelmade poor relations of Howland Type 33A (1958: 101; see also Bruneau 1965: 26, nos. 275–87, pl. 5, and Michelucci 1975: 24, no. 32 [his type VIII], pl. III).

[22] Note also similarities with Thompson's Type A41, which he noted was one of the two most popular lamp types in the Chatby Cemetery at Alexandria, and was most probably the type of lamp that many of the earliest settlers must have carried with them to the new commercial center (Thompson et al. 1987: 22–23, fig. 7: A41).

[23] Several moldmade lamps of Egyptian fabric are in the collections of the British Museum (cf. Bailey 1975: Q555, Q558, Q566*bis*, Q574, Q580, Q594, Q 609, and Q618).

[24] Howland (1958: 143) also calls attention to the fact that the lamp type is similar to Tarsus Group IV lamps (Goldman 1950: 89), which are dated to the end of the third and the beginning of the second centuries B.C.

[25] Hayes (1980a: 19) isolated four major wares/fabrics in the Ptolemaic moldmade lamps in the collections of the Royal Ontario Museum the first of which, a non-micaceous buff clay, he assigned to Alexandria. Most of the lamps from Naukratis would fall into his categories 3 and 4.

[26] The author wishes to thank Andrea Berlin and Mark Lawall for discussing many of the following pieces with him either in person and/or in correspondence. Their help was in-

valuable and their suggestions were heeded in most cases. However, the author bears full responsibility for any errors that appear here.

[27] The author is aware of the difficulties in (and vagaries of) creating and comparing categories of pottery through the use of Munsell colors (different people on different days under different lighting conditions; but the fact that the present author personally Munselled *every* sherd excavated at both Kom Ge'if and Kom Hadid (as well as the stamped handles published by Rehard in Coulson 1996) in indirect sunlight at approximately the same time of day for three seasons, should solve some of the potential problems. In any case, the advantages of using the Munsell Chart certainly do more than outweigh the pitfalls of reporting through such color descriptors as beige and fawn. For the importance of adding the examination of the fabric to other methods of studying amphorae see, *inter alia*, Peacock 1977, and the excellent section by Peacock in Sealey 1985: 153–66. In retrospect, this study should have contained a petrological component, but only a limited amount of material was allowed out of Egypt for study, and we simply did not have the resources to conduct such studies in the field.

[28] It should be noted that the band of red paint is not an exclusively Rhodian embellishment but can also appear on amphorae from Chios, Clazomenae and elsewhere (Coulson 1996: 47, n. 171 with references to Dupont 1982). Lawall offers the caveat that the traces of red paint may be less related to the manufacturing process and more to the packing and retailing process (personal communication).

[29] See also the similar profile of two amphorae attributed to a Rhodian manufacturer by Grace (1934: 306, pl. II:4 and 5). Note that she had somewhat modified her third century B.C. date for these pieces after that plate had been made. Coulson (1996: 63) saw a decline in the importation of amphorae from Rhodes and other (presumably Greek) cities in the first century B.C. that he felt reflected the growing Roman intervention in the Aegean area during that time.

[30] Such a groove appears on some pseudo-Koan amphorae from Cyprus (Hayes 1991: 86 [no. 16], and fig. 37:2), but it is uncertain whether or not these features carried any typological or chronological significance. There is also some similarity between the grooved rim of the vessels illustrated on figs. 3.2:11 and 12 with the rim of the Gauloise 5 amphora (Peacock and Williams 1986: 148 [their Class 30]) that appears in the second half of the 1st century A.D., but the necks of these later forms are much shorter than the Kom Hadid pieces.

[31] Coulson would date these pieces as late as the second century A.D. on the basis of unpublished material from the Athenian Agora (1996: 51, and fig. 24).

[32] Peacock and Williams assign the Dressel 20 amphora to their Class 25 which also includes Beltrán V, Ostia I, and Callender 2 (1986: 136–40, and especially the evolutionary chart on fig. 65). Note that the form does reach the markets of the eastern Mediterranean (especially) during the early Empire period (1986: 136; with references to Riley and to Will).

[33] The Oberaden 83 is grouped by Peacock and Williams (along with Haltern 71 and Dressel 25) in their Class 24 (1986: 134–35). Note, however, the profile on some of the Cam 184 amphorae at Colchester Sheepen (Sealey 1985: figs. 6:50 and 7:63). At least one of the fabric variants of the Cam 184 has been attributed to Rhodes (Sealey 1985: 51, 55–56) and it is believed to have evolved "from its Hellenistic predecessors by the late first century A.D." (1985: 56, citing V. Grace).

[34] At least two of the Dressel 2–4 fabrics have been attributed to Rhodes, but the other five are still unassigned to a specific area. In addition to Rhodes, derivatives of "Koan" Dressel 2–4 (Class 10) amphorae, complete with bead rim and double-barreled handle, were made at a minimum of seven ateliers in the eastern Mediterranean including Cos, Knidos, and even the Lac Mariout district behind Alexandria (Empereur and Picon 1989: 225–31 [with references] and figs. 2–4b).

[35] The author also sees a similar, embryonic concavity of the inner profile of the rim on Peacock and Williams' Class 1 amphorae (1986: 82–83) that includes examples of the Brindisi amphora and the Ostia LXVI. Examples of this type, which can occur in a 5YR 7/6 (Reddish Yellow)—7.5YR 7/4 (Pink) fabric similar to some of the Kom Hadid vessels, were widely distributed in the eastern Mediterranean region from the late second century B.C. to the mid-first century B.C.

[36] Andrea Berlin, however, suggests (personal communication) that a Rhodian or even a Cypriot origin for these pieces cannot be excluded. On Cypriot amphorae and their distribution, see Calvet 1986.

[37] Coulson's description of the fabric as "almost uniformly yellowish red . . . and the slip a creamy white color" (1996: 47) is not unlike the fabric of the Hadid examples.

[38] Their Class 9 amphorae includes forms known under other terms: Rhodian Type, Ostia LXV, Camulodunum 184, and Callender 7 (Peacock and Williams 1986: 102). Several similar rims identified as Koan were encountered by Coulson during the Naukratis Survey (1996: 47–49, and fig. 23). Morphological similarities also exist between the present fig. 3.2:7 and chronologically earlier rims attributed to an atelier on Chios (Grace 1934: 301–302, pl. II.1).

[39] In other systems, Peacock and Williams' Class 10 amphorae may appear as "Koan Type" (from the bifed handles), Dressel 2–4, Ostia LI, Camulodunum 182–183, Callender 2, and Benghazi ER amphora 4 (1986: 105). These rounded rims from Kom Hadid also share similarities with Peacock and Williams' slightly later (first–second century A.D.) Class 11 or "pseudo-Koan" amphorae of unknown origin but which share the bifed handles (1986: 107–8). For a detailed discussion of the typology of the Dressel 2–4 amphora, see Fariñas del Cerro et al. 1977; and for the problem of differentiating the origins, especially of "Rhodian" (Dressel 2–4) amphorae, see Peacock (1977: especially 266–70).

[40] Compare, however, the rim profiles of imitation(?) Koan amphorae from Paphos (Cyprus) complete with bifed handles (Hayes 1991: 86, and fig. 37:1), and the internally

bevelled rims of Naukratis Survey no. 1484 (Type G2) and no. 826 (Type F) also said to be of Koan inspiration (Coulson 1996: 47 and fig. 23).

[41] It should be noted that both A. Berlin and M. Lawall (personal communication) question whether the sherd is correctly drawn.

[42] For the subdivisions of the Dressel 1 and the makeup of their Classes 3 through 6, see Peacock and Williams (1986: 86–95).

[43] 1986: 117–19. Their Class 16 also includes Dressel 7–11, Beltrán I, and Paunier 435. Their Class 17 which also included some examples of Beltrán I (and was traded at least far east as Benghazi) is morphologically similar in concept, but it is much more attenuated than examples of Class 16 and the Kom Hadid piece (Peacock and Williams 1986: 120–21).

[44] See also the series of forms from Cerro de los Mártires in southern Spain (Lloris 1997: 105–6, figs. 4–10); and those published as Dressel 7–13 from Lunì by Siena (1977: 213–14, and figs. 18–19).

[45] 1986: 126–27. Class 20 also included pieces assigned to Dressel 14, Beltrán IVA, and Ostia LXII categories.

[46] Their Class 2 is said to include those amphorae also termed Republicaine 1 and Lamboglia 4 (1986: 84–85).

[47] Will does cite, however, two vessels in the British Museum that may have originated in a Near Eastern context (1982: 343). Grace also mentions similar pieces in the British Museum (1971: 55–56, and 88).

[48] The small ridge(s) below the point of greatest diameter on these pieces is also seen on a rim from Paphos (Hayes 1991: fig. 38:7, not discussed in text?). See also Coulson's Type U2, nos. 1035 and 1042 (1986: 50, and fig. 24) from the Naukratis Survey.

[49] See Panella and Fano 1977 for a classification of the amphora with bifed handles found at Pompeii.

[50] Lawall, however, does not think that a Rhodian origin for 3.3:14 is likely (personal communication).

[51] At Naukratis it was very often difficult to gain a correct impression of the *original* shape of the toes/spikes since they had suffered so much from chipping and breakage.

[52] See, for instance, the amphorae identified as Mendean derivatives from the Naukratis Survey (Coulson 1996: 58 and fig. 29).

[53] Note the ridge on the stem of fig. 3.4–3, possibly a Cypriot feature, also appears on a toe from the Naukratis Survey (Coulson 1996: 58 and fig. 29:436).

[54] Coulson's method of distinguishing the chronology of his pieces by the degree to which the hollow interior of the vessel protrudes into the toe does not seem to be internally consistent (1996: 54–55 and fig. 27), and does not work with the Kom Hadid examples. At Paphos note the similarities of the Chian related and imitation Koan toes to the Hadid pieces (Hayes 1991: 86, no. 15, fig. 37:4, and no. 17, fig. 37:2).

[55] Possibly related is a toe from Paphos thought to be Cypriot fabric (Hayes 1991: 95 no. 45, and fig. 37:8).

[56] See also the toes on some of the amphorae discussed by Farinas del Cerro, et al. in their typology of the Dressel 2–4

amphorae (1977, especially nos. 19, 31, 57, and 92). Note, however, the evidence for a third century A.D. atelier for the Dressel 2–4 amphorae in Egypt (Empereur 1986).

[57] For a fuller treatment of the stamped amphorae from the Kom Hadid excavations, see Coulson, Wilkie, and Rehard 1986, and Rehard in Coulson 1996: 147–61. The latter work became available to the present author after this section was written.

[58] See Rehard in Coulson 1996: 148, no. 1, fig. 57:1, pl. xix:1; and Coulson, Wilkie, and Rehard 1986: 540, no. 1.

[59] See Rehard in Coulson 1996: 150, no. 5, fig. 57:5, pl. xix:5; and Coulson, Wilkie, and Rehard 1986: 540, no. 5.

[60] See Rehard in Coulson 1996: 150, no. 6, fig. 57:6, pl. xix:6; and Coulson, Wilkie, and Rehard 1986: 540, no. 6.

[61] See Rehard in Coulson 1996: 150, no. 7, fig. 57:7, pl. xix:7; and Coulson, Wilkie, and Rehard 1986: 540, no. 7.

[62] See Rehard in Coulson 1996: 150, no. 8, fig. 57:8, pl. xix:8; and Coulson, Wilkie, and Rehard 1986: 540, no. 8.

[63] See Rehard in Coulson 1996: 152, no. 15, fig. 58:15, pl. xx:5; and Coulson, Wilkie, and Rehard 1986: 541, no. 15.

[64] See Rehard in Coulson 1996: 150, no. 10, fig. 58:10, pl. xix:9.

[65] See Rehard in Coulson 1996: 153, no. 19, fig. 59:19.

[66] For the thirteen unincised stands see Berlin Chapter 2 and fig. 2.51:1–13.

[67] Edwards 1956: 88–89 and 108, nos. 121 and 122. The former is closer in shape to the examples from Kom Hadid.

[68] Bourriau 1981: 11, no. 222; and Emery 1967: 311, fig. 49:18, 23–25. See also the earlier(?) Meroitic vessels from Faras illlustrated in color in Wildung (1996: pl. 420).

[69] On the corpus of similar pieces from Samaria, Reisner stated, "Nearly all the forms were clearly imitations of the black-glazed or of other Greek and Hellenistic pottery vessels" (1924: 326).

[70] Cf. from Samaria, Reisner (1924: 327, nos. 13a, 14a, and 15a).

[71] Compare from Corinth, Edwards (1975: 30 note 14, and 211), and Romano (1994: 97, nos. 115 and 116, pl. 31), and from Samaria, Reisner (1924: 327, no. 3392, fig. 12a).

[72] Compare From Samaria, Reisner (1924: 327, nos. 13a, 15a, and 16a).

[73] Plate 3:23 contains a second sherd (23a) that was not drawn in the field. It is assumed that both pieces come from the same vessel since they were excavated and put in the same pottery bag.

[74] For the "Mycenaean Flower" motive, see Furumark (1941: 284–98) and Mountjoy (1986: 68–69). For the popularity of vessels decorated with this motive (FM 18), see Leonard (1994: 152–54). For stirrup jars in faience, see Foster (1979).

[75] A similar stand in faience in the Harper Family Trust Collection is dated to the Third Intermediate Period (715 B.C.; Scott 1992: 23, no. 7).

[76] In addition to the two pieces presented here as #64a and #64b, similar pieces of stone were found in the following deposits: Locus 13001 (N.III.130.01, MC#1): a small piece of white, coarse-grained marble; Locus 6301 (N.III.63.02, MC#1): several pieces of marble(?), including one piece that had been blackened secondarily by fire (evidence for Petrie's lime-slaking activity in the area?); and Locus 6302 (N.III.63.06, MC#13a): two small pieces of gray-white marble (1.3 cm and 2.0 cm thick respectively).

[77] Similar fragments of pavement were encountered in neighboring Locus 7613 (N.III.76.70, MC#144), and Locus 7618 (N.III.76.64, MC#155, and N.III.76.74, MC#156). This last fragment (MC#156) contained a single (honey-colored) pebble that was identified as alabaster by conservator Weber.

[78] See, *inter alia*, Fischer 1971, Neal 1976, and Sear 1976.

[79] Phillips 1960: 243–45. Is his phrase "irregularly shaved pieces" a typographical error for "irregularly shaped pieces" of stone (1960: 244)? For background on this topic see also Blake (1930) and Levi (1947).

[80] For the description of fourteen different grades of *opus signinum* in a single villa, along with the type(s) of weight and traffic that each might carry and the possible function of the areas of which they were a part (most dating to the first century B.C.), see Cotton and Métraux (1985: 87–88, 123–25, and 127–28).

[81] Note that Dunbabin distinguishes between surfaces whose inclusions are mixed throughout the pavement layer and those where they are set into the pavement to form a surface of adjoining pieces (1994: 36). The Kom Hadid pavement actually seem to have been executed in a manner that combines these two techniques.

[82] The later Roman glass from the site of Karanis in the Fayoum Oasis has been fully published by Harden (1936) but, unfortunately, there are no parallels to the Kom Hadid piece.

[83] Hogarth 1898–1899: 33, Rooms 11, 19, and 20; and von Bissing 1951: 52, 75.

[84] The present author understands the term lime plaster to represent calcium carbonate ($CaCO_3$). Note that, in discussing the antecedents of related stuccowork of Roman date, Ling (1976: 209) differentiates between plaster made from gypsum and that made from lime (meaning calcium oxide, CaO). However, he does discuss the process by which the calcium oxide (CaO) is turned back into calcium carbonate ($CaCO_3$) in a form that can then be used by the builder or decorator. On this topic see also Ling (1972: 23–25).

[85] Following Lucas and Harris (1999: 78–79).

[86] During his tenure at Naukratis Petrie believed that he had found evidence of post-Roman, lime-slaking activity in the area of his Great Temenos by which means he believed the Ptolemaic entryway to that structure had finally been destroyed (1886: 9, 34). Our project never found supporting evidence for this event, although a small piece of marble with traces of secondary burning was excavated in Locus 6301.

[87] Ling (1972: 24), referencing Harris and Lucas (1999: 74–78.)

[88] For both Pliny and Vitruvius the number and composition of the substrata were, in theory, an important and complicated matter but, in practice, it seems that many builders felt at liberty to take short cuts and to reduce the number and complexity of these layers. (See Ling 1976: 213–14).

[89] The colors preserved on the Kom Hadid fragments compare well with the reds, green/grays and other colors of the garlands and decorative features including *faux* marble in the second century B.C. Wardian Tomb in nearby Alexandria (Venit 1988).

[90] Munsell descriptors are presented with the appropriate entry in the Locus Summaries. The red and reddish brown pigments were thought by Weber to have been derived from ocher. Analysis of the other colors was not attempted. For the range of pigment options available to the Ptolemaic craftsmen, see Lucas and Harris (1989: 338–51), and Pratt (1976: 224–27).

[91] For the method of application of the paint to walls of the Roman period, see now the results of the work conducted by the *Istituto Centrale dell' Restauro* in Rome described by Pratt (1976: 227–29).

[92] This style has been knowned by a number of names, *inter alia*, Pompeian First Style, Romano-Campanian First Style, Encrustation Style, Structural Style, and Greek Masonry Style. For a discussion on the origin(s) of the style, see Bruno (1989) and Laidlaw (1985).

[93] Venit 1988: 78, and fig. 11. References to similar string courses in the House of the Tritons on Delos are referenced in n. 20.

[94] Rozenberg follows Netzer's dates (1975: 93 and n. 18) that are slightly lower than that proposed by the original excavators of the site (Kelso and Baramki 1955: 1–49). Since

Herod was a staunch ally of Marc Antony and Cleopatra, and subsequently also of Octavian/Augustus, the Hasmonean period in Egyptian terms can be equated with the last half of the Ptolemaic Period.

[95] The representation of string courses on the plaster walls of Alexandrian tombs go back to the third century B.C. (Venit 1988: 89 and especially n. 68).

[96] Fragments of architectural sculpture in both limestone and marble were found during the early excavations at Naukratis, most of which are presently in the British Museum. These fragments were assembled and discussed primarily by Pryce (1928: 170–79, the first [limestone] temple of Apollo [B 391–B 404]; the second [marble] temple of Apollo [B 405–B 4330]; and a few miscellaneous blocks [B 434–B 436]). See also Shoe (1936: 12–13, 47, 153–55, 171–72, and 180). Gardner recorded finding "a piece of egg-molding in limestone, probably from the earliest temple of Hera, but its forms (were) not remarkable enough to be worth detailed description" (Gardner 1888: 61). Nor, evidently, did he consider it to have been worth illustrating. The piece from the Hera temple does not appear to be any of those discussed by Pryce.

[97] This piece is British Museum B 47 (Pryce 1928: 174 and fig. 13).

[98] This piece is British Museum B 409 (Pryce 1928: 176).

[99] The suggested similarities between the plaster fragment from Naukratis and the epistyle from Ephesus are confined to the upper portion of the molding.

[100] A doctoral dissertation on the Tel Anafa wall decoration was completed by Robert Gordon under the direction of Saul Weinberg (Gordon 1977).

Appendix 1:
Field Pottery Fabric Types

Albert Leonard, Jr.

> How much further can the process of parceling out the motley fabrics of Naukratis among her equally motley population be carried? —H. L. Lorrimer, *Naukratis 1903*

The Fabrics[1]

Although a small number of imported sherds were found during our four seasons of excavation, the vast percentage of the ceramic material represented plainer wares, the majority of which are considered to have been of relatively local production. The amount of well-excavated and well-published comparative material for the pottery that we excavated at Kom Ge'if was quite limited during the years that we were in the field. It therefore was considered best to register this pottery according to a number of individual fabric types, with the understanding that the divisions and differences between them may not always have been intentional or desired. These fabrics, however, formed the basis for all work on the pottery during our seasons at Naukratis and they are included in the present publication in the hopes that our material might be assimilated more easily into corpora of pottery from other sites in the Nile Delta and beyond.

The plain wares from Naukratis, presented below, can readily be divided into two subgroups: those predominantly tempered with mineral inclusions, and those tempered with organic matter. The mineral-tempered fabrics, discussed first, appear to be a basically homogeneous group with minor, internal variations such as the presence or absence of a slip and/or color variants that were presumably the result of differences in kiln temperatures or other vagaries of the manufacturing process.

Following discussions with Mike Rodziewicz, and later with Andrea Berlin, however, it seemed best to discuss the pottery in the final publication according to the recognized terminology of the 1990s. Through resource to photos, fabric descriptions, and actual samples, the following correlations between our field fabrics and the more recent terminology were made, but it was felt that a great deal of information would be lost if the details of our original groupings were not presented. Note that in the captions to the pottery drawings both sets of information are included, for instance: "Delta silt (IA)" is the fabric recorded in the field as Fabric IA (Mineral-tempered Red Ware: with a Red Slip). Such a fabric, however, is now more recognizeable to many scholars simply as Delta Silt. Imports, local amphorae, and sherds that did not fit readily into one of these specific fabrics were given a more formal and specific description, and these are included in the captions to the figures.

Delta Silt Fabrics

Field Fabric I

Plain Mineral-tempered Red Ware. This fabric consisted of a well-levigated clay, which in its basic version was unslipped. The core ranges from 7.5YR 4/2 (Weak Red) to 10R 5/8 (Red) below a surface generally in the range of 7.5R 5/6 (Red) or 10R 5/4 (Weak Red). Temper consisted of finely ground (sand-sized to 1 mm) white, gray and red grit with the white being the predominant material. Micaceous inclusions of similar size were also quite frequent. All the vessels in this fabric were wheel-made with deep finger corrugation frequently visible on the interior of the vessel, while the exteriors of many vessels were scored by the potter's fingernails.

Field Fabric 1A

Mineral-tempered Red Ware, with Red Slip.   On some (predominantly the open) forms of this variant, a 7.5YR 4/6 (Red) to 3/6 (Dark Red) slip had been added. This slip had often been burnished while it was still turning on the wheel in 1 to 2 mm wide horizontal bands, usually spaced from 1 to 1.5 cm apart. A preference to restrict the slip to the upper portions of the vessel was noted on the exterior of many pieces, and the slip was often allowed to drip down the sides in an irregular pattern.

Field Fabric IB

Mineral-tempered Red Ware, with Orange Slip.   The fabric of this subtype was also similar to that of the main fabric with the addition of an orange slip between 10R 6/8 (Light Red) and 5/8 (Red). In some instances the slip appeared to have been used to completely cover the interior and/or exterior of the vessel, while in other examples it has been applied decoratively in a band on the upper surface of the vessel or allowed to drip down the sides of the vase. Randomly spaced wheel-burnishing was frequently noted on this fabric.

Field Fabric IC

Mineral-tempered Red Ware, with White Painted Band(s).   This subtype was recognized in only one example (Leonard in Coulson and Leonard 1981a: fig. 8:30). Its fabric is similar to that of the main type, but the exterior surface had been decorated with an undulating band of 7.5YR 8/2 (Pinkish White) paint.

Field Fabric ID

Mineral-tempered Red Ware, with Red Painted (Bands).   This subtype is definitely a variant of the main type but with the addition of a painted band of 7.5YR 5/2–4/2 (Weak Red) or 10R 4/4 (Weak Red) wash(?).

Field Fabric IE

Mineral-tempered Red Ware, with Painted Designs.   A variant of the main Mineral Tempered Red Ware with the addition of designs in 7.5YR 5/2–4/2 (Weak Red) or 10R 4/2–4/3 (Weak Red) and/or 5YR 8/4–8/3 or 10YR 8/2 (White). Examples of this fabric may simply have been more elaborately decorated examples of Fabrics IC and ID.

Field Fabric II

Plain Mineral-tempered Brown Ware.   This fabric must be considered as a (firing?) variant of the main Field Fabric I, being similar in the method of manufacture, as well as in the type and size of the inclusions. It differs, however, in the color of its core, which is sometimes gray, often 10R 5/8 (Red), but most frequently 5YR 4/6 (Yellowish Red). The interior and exterior surfaces are un-slipped and vary in color from 5YR 6/3 (Light Reddish Brown) to 5/3 (Reddish Brown).

Field Fabric IIA

Mineral-tempered Brown Ware, with Brown Slip. This subtype is identical in fabric to the main Fabric II ware, except that it has been covered with a slip of, or fired to the same color as, the fabric. As in the A variant of the Mineral-tempered Red Ware, this slip can exhibit randomly spaced bands of wheel burnishing.

Field Fabric IIB

Mineral-tempered Brown Ware, with Orange Slip. As with Field Fabric IB, this subtype exhibited a slip that was used either to cover the whole vessel or to highlight specific portions of the form. The slip varied in color between 5YR 7/6 and 6/6 (Reddish Yellow) and was placed directly on the brown fabric of the main Fabric II.

Field Fabric IIC

Red or Brown Mineral-tempered Ware, Mottled. The existence of this category reinforced the relationship between the red and brown mineral tempered wares, as well as supported the suggestion that the color differences between the two wares were the product of vagaries in the firing stage of the vessels' manufacture. The pieces included here had either red or brown as their predominant color but were mottled through a full spectrum of earth colors to a dark gray and very occasionally black. This appeared to be the result of the primary firing, and not, as in the class of cooking pots, the result of secondary burning associated with the use of the vessels. In most cases, parallels for the shapes could be found readily among the vessels of Fabrics I and II.

Field Fabric IID

Mineral-tempered: Fired Black. The last variant of the Red (Field Fabric I) and Brown (Field Fabric II) mineral-tempered wares was that in which the surfaces had been completely fired to black. Again, it should be noted that this is the result of primary, not secondary, firing.

Field Fabric III

Cooking Pot Ware. Many of the cooking pots or casseroles from our excavations at Naukratis had been fashioned from a fabric that shares many similarities with the red mineral-tempered ware to which it must be directly related. The clay of the cooking pots is as well-levigated as that of any of the other fabrics, and the grit inclusions remain about 1 mm rather than the larger, more heat conductive, pieces that are often found in vessels with this function. Whereas the examples of Field Fabric IIC were randomly mottled from their position or time in the kiln, the cooking pots exhibited gray to black discoloration on the lower portions of the body, below the slightly projecting handles, and other on areas that would be in close proximity to the heat of a secondary fire. Many of the pots had been given the same, thin, horizontally burnished bands noted above in some examples of Field Fabric I and Field Fabric II.

Field Fabric IIIA

Cooking Pot Ware: Variant. This subfabric was represented in the Naukratis catalogue by only two pieces. Both of these fragments were from similar necked jars and differ only in their size. Although they closely resembled the Field Fabric I Ware, the fabric appeared to be much more completely levigated, and the vessels were fired to a hardness paralleled only by the cooking pots discussed above. The exteriors, and portions of the interiors, of the two certain examples were covered with a 7.5R 4/6 (Red) Slip, as are the Fabric I pieces. Where abraded, the Fabric IIIA sherds reveal a surface close to 10R 6/8 (Light Red), the color seen on decorated examples of Fabric IB.

Chaff-Tempered Fabrics

Field Fabric IV

Chaff-tempered Pink Ware. While the first three field types were characterized by mineral temper, the Fabric IV fabric, and its variants, rely heavily on straw and chaff temper.

The clay of Fabric IV vessels was poorly, or at best moderately, levigated. That it is related to the fabrics of Fabrics I–III can be seen by the presence of red, white, and gray grit averaging c. 1 mm, but the mineral inclusions were in the minority. As shown by the casts, the major tempering agent was straw (c. 3–5 mm in length and c. 1 mm in diameter) and chaff (up to 1 cm in length and 2–3 mm in diameter), both of which were used in large quantities. Although in most cases the vessels had been fired at a temperature sufficient to burn away most of this organic material, the cores of some of the fragments showed the temper itself rather than the casts. The low temperature of the kiln was also evidenced by the color of the core, which ranges from black on the thicker pieces through 7.5R 5/4–4/4 (Weak Red) on some of the thinner sherds. The interior and exterior surfaces of all examples of this type had been heavily coated with a slip that ranged from 2.5YR 6/4 (Light Reddish Brown)–6/6 (Light Red) to a 10R 6/4 (Pale Red)–6/6 (Light Red), but this slip was as rich in organic inclusions as the fabric. Hence the surfaces were heavily pocked by the casts of the temper. This slip was very thick, up to 2–3 mm, and readily adhered to the surface corrugation resulting from the formation of the pot. Only a single example (an unillustrated ring-base fragment) varied from this norm, exhibiting a thick 10YR 8/2 (White) slip on the interior surface. In all other respects, however, it was the same as the standard Fabric IV.

Field Fabric IVA

Chaff-tempered Brown Ware. As with the mineral-tempered wares, the chaff-tempered fabrics also had color variants that were most probably the result of differing kiln conditions. Examples of Fabric IVA had cores of 5YR 5/3–4/3 (Reddish Brown) with surface between 7.5YR 6/4 (Light Brown) and 5/4 (Brown), but in other respects they were the same as the major Fabric IV. A small base (Leonard in Coulson and Leonard 1981a: fig. 5:7) was the exception; both its core and its surface have 5YR 7/8 (Reddish Yellow).

Field Fabric IVB

Chaff-tempered Mottled Ware. Fabric IVB was a version of the chaff-faced wares with surface colors mottled between those of Fabrics IV and IVA.

Field Fabric IVC

Chaff-tempered Red Ware. Three sherds (unillustrated) of a fabric similar to that of Fabric IV, but covered on the exterior with a 7.5R 6/8 (Light Red) slip, stood out sharply from the rest of the assemblage. Unfortunately, these were all body sherds and thus did not contribute to our knowledge of the shapes of this variant. They are included here because of their distinctive nature and for the sake of completeness.

Field Fabric IVD

Chaff-tempered Black Ware. Although the colors of the chaff-tempered class did vary and mottling did occur, only one example had been fired completely black. It was assigned a special subfabric in order to balance the Fabric IIC of the mineral-tempered ware and to hold a position in the corpus for future occurrences of the type.

Field Fabric IVE

Chaff-tempered Painted Ware. Only one example of chaff-tempered ware had been noted that bore a painted decoration. This is, unfortunately, a body sherd, which shows a broad (4 cm) band of 5YR 8/3–7/3 (Pink) paint around the body of the vessel, bordered above and below by a c. .06–.07 cm band of 5YR 6/2 (Pinkish Gray) paint.

Coarse Fabrics

Field Fabric VA

Smooth-slipped Coarse Ware. Coarse wares appeared in the Naukratis assemblage in two very distinct subtypes: Fabric VA (Smooth-slipped Coarse Ware) whose use of chaff tempering formed a bridge between the chaff-faced wares of Fabric IV and the very rudimentary Fabric VB (Coarse Ware) to be discussed below. Morphologically, Fabric VA vessels consisted basically of low, thick-walled bowls or platters. The fabric was poorly levigated, and the large (1.0–1.5 cm) pieces of chaff temper often appeared in clumps in the thick gray and/or 10R 5/4 (Weak Red) sections. The interior and exterior surfaces of these vessels had been covered with a thick slip, which corresponded in color to the various subtypes of the chaff-faced group. Surprisingly, compared with the Fabric IV fabrics, much more care has been taken to remove the large organic temper from the slip. It was replaced by small (sand-sized to .01 cm) white and gray mineral temper. Admittedly, the surfaces, on occasion, are broken by the casts from the small organic tempering agents that remained, but, on the whole, the slip presented a much better appearance than the chaff-tempered wares and recalled the slips of the mineral-tempered vessels. This fact can, perhaps, be used to argue the relative homogeneity of the local fabrics at Naukratis during this period.

Field Fabric VB

Coarse Ware. Fabric VB consisted of the truly coarse vessels of the assemblage. Forms had thick walls and simple shapes. Large pieces of chaff, to 1.50 cm in length and up to 3 mm in diameter, were frequent in the poorly levigated fabric, and thick gray cores are common. Most fabric colors range from 2.5YR 5/4 (Reddish Brown) to 6/6 (Light Red) and slips, when present, were the same color as the fabric but broken by the chaff casts. To judge from the marks on the preserved surfaces, some of the vessels were apparently smoothed with a handful of chaff before they were fired.

One vessel, illustrated by Leonard (Coulson and Leonard 1981a: fig. 13.B:2), appeared from its charred interior and fenestrated body to have functioned as a type of brazier. Two other fragments also had traces of holes through their wall, but neither was sufficiently preserved to give any indication of its original shape. The remainder of the Fabric VB coarse-ware sherds come from low bowls and platters.

Local Amphora Fabrics

Field Fabric VI

Amphorae. Fragments from amphorae constituted our Field Fabric VI. Although it is readily admitted that this is equivalent to changing typological horses in midstream, it was thought best to keep fragments of such a distinctive form together in one section.

The most common amphora type had a long neck and slightly outsplayed rim. The fabric was moderately well-levigated, containing mineral temper similar to, but larger (up to 2 mm) than, the mineral-tempered fabric, Fabric I, and its variants. The thin (c. 3 mm) cores range from gray to 7.5YR 5/2 (Brown), usually sandwiched by a 10R 6/6 (Light Red)–5/6 (Red) fabric. Traces of a very thin slip appeared on the exterior of most of the examples. Where relatively thick, this slip was approximately 10YR 8/3–8/4 (Very Pale Brown), but where thinner, it approached 5YR 8/3–8/4 (Pink). It is here considered that this is the same slip and that the color of the pinker variant is simply a result of the overlapping of a thin layer of whitish slip over the reddish fabric. The slip was entirely missing from some parts of these vessels, especially near the rim and in the handle zone, where raised ridges of clay had been left after paring or hand-smoothing the junction of these features to the main form.

Although morphologically similar to the other amphorae of Fabric VI, the neck fragment illustrated by Leonard (Coulson and Leonard 1981a: fig. 12:4) differed completely in terms of fabric and temper. It was made of a poorly levigated fabric with a thick black core and surface colors not unlike the redder variants of the amphorae previously discussed (5YR 6/3 [Light Reddish Brown]–5/3 [Reddish Brown]). It was the temper, however, seen also in some of the amphora toes, that caused it to stand out so sharply from the other vessels of this form, for it is closely related to the chaff-tempered fabrics of Fabric IV and its variants. In fact, this similarity might, at first, suggest that it was a local version of an imported form were it not for the fact that the temper and levigation of the majority of the amphorae gave the impression of being related to the mineral-tempered wares of Fabric I. It is here considered, therefore, that almost all of the amphorae from Naukratis that were included in Fabric VI represented relatively local products, with the mineral-tempered being the norm and the chaff-tempered forming an evidently not-too-successful variant.

Field Fabric VIA

Amphora with Pink Paint/Slip. The only variant to the local amphorae noted in the assemblage was the upper portion of a small vessel illustrated by Leonard (Coulson and Leonard 1981a: fig. 12:8). The fabric was 7.5YR 5/2 (Brown), as the standard amphorae considered above, and the well-levigated clay showed only sand-sized white grit and micaceous inclusions. The exterior surface, however, had been covered with a 5YR 7/4 (Pink) to 7/6 (Reddish Yellow) slip/paint, which had been carried over the rim to form a horizontal band c. 3 cm wide on the interior. That this paint was extremely fluid when applied is illustrated by the way that it had dripped down into the interior of the vessel.

Delta Silt Slipped and Burnished Ware

Field Fabric VII

Red Burnished, Drip-painted Ware. Three sherds from the corpus had a 10R 5/6 (Red) paint applied in drips on their exterior surfaces. The fabric, temper, and color of these fragments were all similar to Fabric IIA, with which they are probably to be grouped, but at this embryonic stage in the development of the present corpus they are best kept as a separate entity. That they should be considered among the finer wares is evidenced by the randomly spaced, horizontal band-burnishing that appeared on the interior surface of the fragments (illustrated by Leonard in Coulson and Leonard 1981a: fig. 12.7).

Miscellaneous Fabrics

Field Fabric VIII

Red Slipped Closely-burnished Ware. Although the use of randomly spaced band-burnishing has been previously noted, examples of the burnishing of the entire exterior surface of a vessel to a high luster are quite rare. Three of these fragments were body sherds, while the remaining four offered minimal information about their complete forms. The fabrics of two sherds appeared to be related to the mineral-tempered wares, while one fragment might suggest a relation with the chaff-tempered class.

Perhaps to be included in this category was an (unillustrated) body fragment of a well-levigated and well-fired fabric. The color of the fabric was within the range of the Fabric I clays, 10R 6/8 (Light Red)–5/8 (Red), but the burnishing strokes (applied after the vessel had been removed from the wheel) were vertical rather than horizontal and closely spaced. The possibility that it was an import to Naukratis would not be excluded.

Field Fabric IX

White Smooth-slipped Ware.[2] The vessels included in this category were made of a moderately well-levigated fabric resembling, in color, Field Fabric I (Mineral Tempered Red Ware). It contained white and gray grit temper averaging 1–2 mm, and fine straw casts could be present, but were infrequent. One surface was left as the fabric, while the other surface was covered by a smooth coat of 7.5YR 8/2 (Pinkish White) or white (no Munsell equivalent) slip. Below the slip, the color of the core could range from 7.5YR 7/4 (Pink) to 5YR 7/4 (Pink). Where the slip was applied more thinly, the surface often took on the pinkish hue, but even where thinly applied the slip was unbroken by the mineral inclusions of the fabric with the result that the surface was always smooth. The range of shapes in this fabric is limited at Naukratis, and it may have been an import. Perhaps the minute fragment of a double amphora handle in this fabric would point to an East Greek origin.

Field Fabric IXA

White Gritty-slipped Ware. This ware was characterized by a slip approximating 10YR 8/2 (White) that was slightly gritty to the touch. The clay was well-levigated and tempered with sand-sized to 1 mm white grit and fine straw. The firing of the individual vessels varied as did the color of the cores, which could range from the color of the slip through 5YR 7/3 (Pink). The range of vessel types was larger than that of Fabric IX from which the presence of the gritty slip definitely sets it apart. The shape of the baggy base (Leonard in Leonard and Coulson 1981a: fig. 13A:7) and internally grooved rim (Leonard in Coulson and Leonard 1981a: fig. 13A:6) might suggest that we are dealing here with products of a local workshop.

Field Fabric IXB

White-slipped Coarse Ware. The two, rather abraded, sherds (Leonard in Coulson and Leonard 1982: fig. 13A:12, and one unillustrated fragment) of this category were definitely from amphorae; but, because the shapes are completely different from the more standard amphora of Fabric VI, and since they may be related by fabric to Fabric IX, they were classified as a separate entity. The fabric was well-levigated with c. 1 mm white grit, which was surprisingly fine for vessels of this size. The core was approximately 5YR 5/3 (Reddish Brown) below a fabric of 5YR 7/4 (Pink). The interior surface of the amphora toe had been given a coating of a 5YR 7/3–7/4 (Pink) slip, while the exteriors of both sherds had been covered with a slip between 5YR 8/2 (Pinkish White) and 7.5YR 8/2 (Pinkish White). This category is considered to be an import at Naukratis, and its similarities to Fabric IX may suggest an East Greek origin.

Field Fabric X

Pink-slipped Ware. Although there was some variety within Fabric X, the common denominator was the presence of a thick slip ranging in color from 5YR 8/3–8/4 (Pink). In some cases the color of the slip appears to be the result of how thickly it had been applied, since it can vary through 5YR 8/3 (Pink) to 10YR 8/2 (Pinkish White) on the same fragment. The fabric was well-levigated and tempered with c. 1 mm white, gray, and occasionally red temper. The core was gray on the thicker fragments, sandwiched between the 2.5YR 6/4 (Light Reddish Brown) of the fabric, but in the thinner sherds the color of the fabric predominates throughout the entire section. Although Fabric X contained more variety than other types noted here, it was definitely distinct from them and, in that sense at least, warranted consideration as a separate class.

Terra Nigra Fabrics

A significant quantity of "Black Glazed" or Terra Nigra sherds were encountered during the excavations at Naukratis. In the field I separated such pieces into seven groups, which appeared to me to represent five different and distinct fabrics. The surface appearance of a given piece was recorded on a simple, tripartite scale: dull, shiny, or lustrous.

Terra Nigra 1

Terra Nigra 1, as defined in the field, is the equivalent to our standard Fabric IID (Mineral-tempered Ware: Black) whose fabric and surface color appear to have occurred during the firing process.

Terra Nigra 2

Examples of Terra Nigra 2 differ from the above fabric in that a lustrous black slip has been applied over extremely well-levigated and (usually temperless) fabrics of distinctive color that range from c. 2.5YR 6/6 (Light Red) to 5YR 6/6 (Reddish Yellow). Such pieces appear to have been genuine imports from the Greek World.

Terra Nigra 3

The fabric of Terra Nigra 3 is fired throughout to a light to medium gray, often approaching 5YR 6/1 (Gray). There is no distinct core.

Terra Nigra 4

Consists of a group of three, visually-related, gray-brown fabrics that may be variants of each other. In the field these were separated into three subgroups (4A through 4C).

Terra Nigra 4A

A fabric c. 10YR 3/2 (Very Dark Grayish Brown) that can range to 10YR 4/3–3/3 (Dark Brown). It does not exhibit any distinct core. The surfaces are usually shiny to lustrous.

Terra Nigra 4B

A fabric c. 10YR 3/2 (Very Dark Grayish Brown) that can range to 10YR 4/3–3/3 (Dark Brown). It differs from the above fabric in that it exhibits a very distinct gray or black core. In addition there seem to be minute pieces of lithic temper in the slip. Surface appearance is shiny to lustrous.

Terra Nigra 4C.

Gray-brown fabric with red or red and gray core. A c. 10YR 3/2 (Very Dark Grayish Brown) to 10YR 4/3–3/3 (Dark Brown) fabric, with a distinct c. 5YR 4–8 (Red) or 7.5YR 3/6–3/8 (Dark Red) core. An evidently related variant of this fabric (recognized and recorded but not isolated in the field) displayed a c. 7.5YR N5/ (Gray) central core within a red (as above) sandwich. Surfaces were usually at least shiny to lustrous.

Terra Nigra 5

A fabric that has been fired c. 7.5YR N6/–N5/ (Gray) almost completely through the section, except just below the slip where there is a very thin sandwich in the gray-brown range of the Terra Nigra 4 series (c. 10YR 3/2 [Very Dark Grayish Brown] to 10YR 3/3 [Dark Brown]) and may, in fact, actually be related to that group. There are traces of fine organic temper in the slip. Surfaces are usually dull, although sometimes dull to shiny.

Notes

Epigraph was also quoted by Price (1924: 181), and answered in a somewhat different manner.

[1] This appendix was originally published as part of the Kom Hadid report (Leonard 1997), It is repeated here for the sake of accessibility to this volume.

[2] The description of this fabric differs slightly from that presented after it had been isolated during our initial season of excavation (Leonard in Coulson and Leonard 1981a). This fuller description is the result of the examination of the tremendous quantity of sherd material during subsequent seasons.

Appendix 2:
Environmental and Medical Problems
Encountered during the 1980 Season

Morris Weiss, M.D.

The fellow who coined the phrase, "He who tastes water of the Nile shall return" might well have added, "and be certain to have a bottle of Lomotil tablets." This appendix is a summary of the environmental difficulties experienced in the summer of 1980 while excavating and living at the village of Kom Ge'if, the site of the ancient Greek city of Naukratis.[1]

As a cardiologist whose avocation is archaeology, I joined the expedition as a volunteer. In anticipation of a harsh environment, the directors requested that I include a number of basic medicines in my baggage. No one, however, could have envisioned the series of traumatic events we would have to overcome to maintain the health of the group. Almost every hardship one could imagine in such a setting occurred; but, with the cooperative efforts of the entire staff, that first season at Naukratis was nonetheless extremely fruitful. Nothing we experienced was unique, but it would be worth reviewing those obstacles that can prevent an excavation from being productive.

Kom Ge'if is an Egyptian farming village, consisting primarily of mudbrick buildings with surrounding fields. The way of life is quite simple and, except for an occasional tractor, the sights resemble scenes painted on the walls of ancient tombs and temples. In this pastoral environment, the basic necessities of food, water, and sanitation became major logistical problems for the group.

A four-room farmhouse with dirt courtyard facing a shallow irrigation canal served as excavation headquarters. One room was converted into a kitchen, another used for a dining room, a third for storing materials, and the last as a haven from the intense afternoon heat. The volunteers pitched their one- and two-person tents in the courtyard for sleeping while several larger screen houses were used for processing artifacts. We were naive in the ways of Egyptian village life; we did not fully anticipate the hazards of living in a farm enclosure where humans and animals cohabit. The natives bring cows and water buffaloes into the farmhouses at night, and the excrement is dried and used as fuel for cooking and heating. This provides perfect breeding conditions for flies, of which there is always a dense population, both inside and outside the buildings. In addition, our farmhouse and courtyard were heavily infested with fleas from the dogs, chickens, and other animals that inhabited the area. Our advance party arrived several days earlier than the rest of the group and was soon covered with flea bites after sweeping straw, dung, and debris from the farmhouse. The dust and straw in the courtyard where the tents were pitched were also heavily infested. Soon, every tent, along with our clothing and bedding, was flea-ridden. Our initial efforts to eliminate the fleas were unsuccessful. After two weeks we managed to obtain some spray guns and a malodorous local flea spray. After watching the villagers sweep down their courtyards, we adopted the idea, cleansed our own facility of straw and sprinkled the area with flea spray. This successfully kept down the pest problem.

Water also proved to be a major problem. The immediate water supply was a hand-pumped well only 5.0 m from the toilet. Since the water table in the Delta is in places only 3.5 m below the surface, the well was undoubtedly contaminated. We secured an adequate supply of water for cooking and drinking by bringing "clean" water in five-gallon containers from a pump in a neighboring village that was on the water line from the provincial capital.

A constant supply of "clean" water is an absolute necessity, for a person must drink, in addition to his usual daily intake of two to three liters, 14–16 extra 8-ounze (250 cc) glasses of water each day in order to survive the heat of the Delta. He also must take four to eight salt tablets per day to keep up strength. To encourage drinking, a vat of water, to which we added an Egyptian brand of concentrated orange-flavored extract, was always available in the kitchen. Periodically, volunteers cleaned the containers with boiling water, since they would rapidly become contaminated.

Although unsafe for drinking, our well water could be used in several different ways. A 20-gallon (80-liter) galvanized tank was secured on top of the farmhouse, fittings were attached and brought through the roof, and a closet off one of the rooms thus became a shower. To prevent fungus infection of the feet, a pan of water with added Clorox was placed outside the shower, and everyone was required to walk through this before drying his/her feet. Another galvanized tank, fitted with spigot, was placed in the courtyard. We made an attempt at purification by adding Halozone tablets, and we could then use the water from the second tank for washing hands and face before meals.

General sanitation was another logistical stumbling block. Mess kits served as dishes. These were kept on a table and covered with window screening to keep away the flies. Dish washing involved scrubbing loose food particle off the utensils with boiled "clean" water and detergent, then dipping them in boiling water and allowing it to air dry on the screen-covered table.

The only indoor toilet was one of Turkish style in a closet off one of the rooms. In the closet were kept a ladle and a large ceramic jug filled with well water which was used for flushing in conjunction with a scoop of powdered lime. Soap and a tub of "clean" water for washing hands were also available nearby. A single Turkish toilet was obviously inadequate for the entire staff of 24 people. Accordingly, we dug a trench latrine near the campsite. Toilet seats were purchased in Cairo and a commode was constructed over a trench measuring 1.0 m. in width and 2.0 m. in depth, with broken pottery at the bottom to facilitate the percolation of waste. This trench latrine was only a short distance from the tents, but to reach it required a dash across the courtyard, followed by a leap across the irrigation canal. When the "Kom Ge'if gallop" or the "Damanhur dance" struck, even the speediest and most agile of us risked disaster if we tried to run too hastily, especially in crossing the canal.

The kitchen area was made off-limits to everyone except the volunteer cook and his/her helpers for that day. We covered the windows with screening and eliminated flies with a local bug spray. Two-burner stoves fueled by bottled gas served for cooking. No refrigeration, however, was available during the first season owing to the nine-month wait required for the purchase of refrigerators in Egypt, so basic staples had to be bought daily from local vendors.

Egyptians fertilize their fields with "night soil" (human excrement). Consequently all vegetables and most fruits must be thoroughly cooked, and no salad items can be eaten raw. The American gastrointestinal tract is not prepared to cope with the parasites and bacteria with which the Egyptian has learned to live. The delicacies of our rural area included unpasteurized water buffalo butter, goat's milk and goat yogurt, all of which we had to avoid. A local sausage, thoroughly recooked, was our main meat source. Only the orange, with its thick outer skin, was safe to eat fresh.

The menus were devised to provide adequate fluid volume, salt, and calories for people performing hard manual labor in a hot humid environment. Our day began at 4:00 a.m. with a quick breakfast of hot tea, local bread, and jelly. At 9:00 a.m. we ate a second breakfast, much the same as the first, but with some hard cheese added. The noon meal included soup for volume and pasta for calories. Supper was a lighter meal of soup, pasta, or eggs. Large quantities of salt were added to all prepared foods, and, to increase caloric intake, cheese, jelly, bread, and, if available, peanut butter, were provided with each meal. Volunteers from the group did all the cooking as well as the washing of the dishes. All pots were scrubbed in boiled "clean" water and air dried in the same manner as the mess kits.

The medical problems we faced also seem worthy of review. Fortunately, all the illnesses which occurred could be treated at camp. The most serious skin problems, with which everyone was afflicted to some degree, were from flea bites. Two types of reaction occurred, the milder being a small puncture lesion requiring only a local application of Calamine lotion to control the itching. The more serious reaction produced a swelling and redness around bite areas, and the resultant itching was severe. This discomfort caused loss of sleep, and soon fatigue and irritability occurred. A topical steroid ointment controlled some of the redness and swelling, but oral Benadryl, an antihistamine, was necessary for the incessant itching. Nothing, however, was totally effective in controlling the allergic-like reaction. Oral steroid therapy did not seem justified because of potential harmful side effects. This problem can only be solved with the total elimination of the fleas.

The only other minor skin problems encountered were one case of infected hair follicles from a dirty beard and a mild case of acne on the chest wall that was due to heat and dirt. Both of these were soon eliminated with cleansing and a mild topical antibiotic ointment. Wind, sand, and dust caused frequent irritation of the eyes. There was one case of a foreign body in the eye, consisting of a dust particle that was easily removed from the upper lid; another person required topical eye antibiotic for the treatment of mild conjunctivitis. Contact lenses should not be worn in such an environment.

One of the volunteers came to the excavation with a flu syndrome and several others developed similar symptoms during the next five to seven days. These consisted of 24 hours of fever as high as 102.6°F (39.2°C) with muscle aching. The illness rapidly resolved itself with adequate fluids and aspirin for the control of the pain and fever. Two of the flu cases developed transient mild bronchitis with coughing for 24–36 hours, which cleared spontaneously without the use of antibiotics.

Fortunately, no serious cases of injury occurred and all minor abrasions were quickly treated with cleansing, first-aid cream, and a simple Band-Aid.

Disorders of the gastrointestinal tract were with us from the time the group arrived in Cairo until we left Egypt. Most volunteers had some mild form of disorder, even from drinking the water in Cairo. Symptoms usually involved one to three days of lower abdominal cramping with diarrhea or loose stools which, to my knowledge, were never bloody, and associated at times with slight nausea but with no vomiting. Many developed a more severe form of this disorder while at camp. Those most seriously affected were the individuals who failed to keep all the sanitary rules and at times broke the dietary warnings concerning raw fruit, vegetables and salads, especially during the weekend rest periods in Alexandria. Those whose diarrhea did not abate in 24–48 hours were watched carefully and their fluid intake increased. A bland diet was recommended, but no antibiotics were prescribed for this short-term illness. If the diarrhea persisted for five days, the individual started antibiotics and usually saw improvement within 48 hours. There were only two who were treated in this manner, and they were prescribed Vibramycin.

Every attempt was made to prevent dehydration. We spiked the water with the orange concentrate already mentioned in order to make it more enticing to those reluctant individuals who did not appreciate the dehydrating effects of the Delta environment. Extra canteen water was carried to the site each today, and frequent breaks for water with added salt tablets were encouraged.

For several days one group of volunteers conducted a surface sherding survey of a large, unshaded area, and several of them became quite dehydrated. They all developed the earliest signs of dehydration, including irritability, marked fatigue, and a feeling of weakness. It was calculated that as many as 25 additional 8-ounze (250cc) glasses of fluid per day would have been necessary to keep these people well-hydrated in this type of environment.

An occasional excavator, against advice, would try to work when afflicted with abdominal cramps, nausea, and diarrhea and subsequently became severely dehydrated, developing marked nausea and vomiting with an intense headache. In two such cases, Compazine suppositories were prescribed to control the nausea and vomiting. These patients were also given small sips of water every few minutes along with frequent salt tablets, and usually within eight to twelve hours, they began to respond.

The volume of urine passed during a twenty-four hour period is a good indication of one's state of hydration. If one passes less than 750cc per day, a negative fluid balance is occurring. Each person was advised to watch carefully his/her urine volume and to drink more water if not producing at least 250cc three times a day.

Our problems were further compounded by the nature of the campsite. The courtyard where the tents were pitched was unprotected from the sun, so that the tents were much too hot to enter until the evening hours. Only two small rooms were available where individuals could read or write letters. Sleep was virtually impossible during off hours from 2:00 to 5:00 p.m. because of the crowded conditions, intense heat, and incessant flies. As a result, those fatigued by dehydration were made worse by poor afternoon rest conditions, often compounded by a lack of sleep at night due to fleas.

Most of us arrived at Naukratis thinking the Egyptian scorpion and asp would be our greatest enemies. Everyone carried camping cots with legs at least six inches high. We discovered, however, that the villages had effectively eliminated scorpions and snakes from their immediate environment. These, of course, are a much greater hazard when excavating in areas which are not inhabited. Instead, fleas, flies, and fluid balance became our foes. Subsequent seasons at Naukratis have not been as difficult, since more living space has been available and a greater variety of foods could be purchased in Alexandria. But, scrupulous attention to sanitation, pest control, and fluid balance remain essential to any successful excavation in this part of the world.

Notes

[1] This section is offered here as an appendix to the main work not only because of its intrinsically didactic value, but also because it supplies the human backdrop against which the labors of our very dedicated staff and volunteers must be viewed.

Bibliography

Adams, W. Y.

    1986   *Ceramic Industries of Medieval Nubia: Vol. 1. Memoirs of the UNESCO Archaeological Survey of Sudanese Nubia.* Lexington: University of Kentucky.

    n.d.   Pottery Wares of the Ptolemaic and Roman Periods at Qasr Ibriim: Preliminary Ware Descriptions. Provisional Report of the Qasr Ibrim Expedition, Department of Anthropology, University of Kentucky. Lexington: University of Kentucky.

Adan-Bayewitz, D.

    1993   *Common Pottery in Roman Galilee. A Study of Local Trade.* Ramat-Gan: Bar-Ilan University.

Adan-Bayewitz, D., and Perlman, I.

    1990   The Local Trade of Sepphoris in the Roman Period. *Israel Exploration Journal* 40: 153–72.

Adriani, A.

    1940   Fouilles et Découvertes-Alexandrie. *Annuaire du Musée Gréco-Romain II* (1935–1939): 65–135.

    1952a   Nouvelles Découvertes dans la Nécropole de Hadra. *Annuaire du Musée Gréco-Romain III* (1940–1950): 1–27.

    1952b   Nécropole et ville de Plinthine. *Annuaire du Musée Gréco-Romain III* (1940–1950): 140–59.

    1961   *Reportorio d'arte dell' Egitto greco-romano, I–II.* Palermo: Fondazione "Ignazio Mormio" del Banco di Sicilia.

Amiran, R.

    1969   *Ancient Pottery of the Holy Land.* New Brunswick, NJ: Rutgers University.

Ariel, D.

    1990   *Excavations at the City of David 1978–1985, Directed by Yigal Shiloh.* Vol. II. *Imported Stamped Amphora Handles, Coins, Worked Bone and Ivory, and Glass.* Qedem 30. Jerusalem: Institute of Archaeology, Hebrew University of Jerusalem.

Bailey, D. M.

    1975   *A Catalogue of the Lamps in the British Museum.* Vol. 1: Greek, Hellenistic, and Early Roman Pottery Lamps. London: The British Museum.

    1985   *Excavations at Sidi Khrebish Benghazi (Berenice).* Vol. 3, Part 2: The Lamps. Libya Antiqua Supplement 5. Tripoli: Department of Antiquities.

Bayer-Niemeier, E.

    1988   *Griechisch-Römischer Terrakotten.* Liebieghaus-Museum Alter Plastik Bildwerke der Sammlung Kaufmann, Band I. Melsungen: Gutenberg.

Bell, M.

    1981   *The Terracottas.* Morgantina Studies. Vol. 1. Princeton: Princeton University.

Berlin, A.

    1997   *Tel Anafa.* Vol. 2, I. *The Hellenistic and Roman Pottery: The Plain Wares.* Journal of Roman Archaeology Supplementary Series 10.2.1. Ann Arbor: Kelsey Museum of the University of Michigan.

Bieber, M.

    1961b   *The History of the Greek and Roman Theater.* 2nd ed. Princeton: Princeton University.

Birmingham Museum

    1968   *Ancient Life in Miniature: An Exhibition of Classical Terracottas from Private Collections in England.* Birmingham: Birmingham Museum and Art Gallery.

Blake, M. E.

    1930   The Pavements of the Roman Buildings of the Republic and Early Empire. *Memoirs of the American Academy in Rome* Vol. 8: 1–159.

Bol, P. C., and Kotera, E.

    1986   *Bildwerke aus Terracotta aus Mykenischer bis Römischer Zeit.* Liebieghaus-Museum Alter Pastik Antike Bildwerke, Band III. Melsungen: Gutenberg.

Bourriau, J.

    1981   *Umm el Gaʿab: Pottery from the Nile Valley before the Arab Conquest.* Catalogue of an exposition. Cambridge: Fitzwilliam Museum.

Breccia, E.

1912   *La Necropoli di Sciatbi.* Catalogue général des antiquités égyptiennes (Musée d'Alexandrie) nos. 1–624. Cairo: Institut française archéologique orientale.

1930   Monuments de L'Égypte Gréco-Romaine, II:1. *Terrecotte figurate Greche e Gréco-Egizie del Museo di Alessandria.* Bergamo: Officine dell'Istituto italiano d'arti grafiche.

1978   *Le Musée gréco-romaine d'Alexandrie* (1931–1932) Vol. 2. Reprint. Rome: Bretschneider.

Broneer, O.

1930   *Corinth. Vol. IV, Pt. II, Terracotta Lamps.* Cambridge: American School of Classical Studies at Athens and Harvard University.

1977   *Terracotta Lamps, Isthmia Vol. III.* Princeton: American School of Classical Studies.

Bruneau, P.

1965   *Les Lampes.* Exploration Archéologique de Délos faite par L'École française d'Athènes. Fascicule XXVI. Paris: Éditions E. de Boccard.

1970a   *Exploration archéologique de Délos XXVII. L'îlot de la Maison des Comediens.* Paris: École française d'Athènes.

1970b   Tombes d'Argos. *Bulletin de Correspondance Héllenique* 94: 437–531.

Bruno, B.

1989   Lombardia: Ricerche in Corso. Pp. 642–44 in *Amphores romaines et histoire économique: dix ans de recherche,* eds. M. Lenoir, D. Manacorda, and C. Panella. Collection de l'ecole française de Rome 114. Rome: École française de Rome.

Budge, E. A. W.

1972   *From Fetish to God in Ancient Egypt.* New York: Benjamin Bloom.

Callaghan, P.

1981   The Little Palace Well and Knossian Pottery of the Later Third and Second Centuries B.C. *Annual of the British School at Athens* 76: 35–58.

Callaghan, P., and Jones, R. E.

1985   Hadra Hydriae and Central Crete: A Fabric Analysis. *Annual of the British School at Athens* 80: 1–17.

Calvet, Y.

1972   *Salamine de Chypre III: Les Timbres Amphoriques.* Paris: E. de Boccard.

1986   Les amphores chypriotes et leur diffusion en Méditerranée orientale. Pp. 505–14 in *Recherches sur les Amphores Grecques,* eds. J.-Y. Empereur and Y. Garlan. *Bulletin de Correspondence Hellenique Supplement* XIII. École française d'Athenes. Athens: Diffusion de Boccard.

Canarache, V.

1957   *Importul Amforelor Stampilate la Istria.* Bucharest: Editura Acadamiei Republicii Populare Romine.

Charlesworth, D.

1969   Tell el-Fârâ'în: The Industrial Site, 1968. *Journal of Egyptian Archaeology* 55: 23–30.

Cipriano, M. T., and Carre, M.-B.

1989   Production et typologie des amphores sur la côte adriatrique de l'Italie. Pp. 67–104 in *Amphores romaines et histoire économique: dix ans de recherche,* eds. M. Lenoir, D. Manacorda, and C. Panella. Collection de l'ecole française de Rome 114. Rome: École française de Rome.

Corbett, P. E.

1955   Palmette Stamps from an Attic Black-Glaze Workshop. *Hesperia* 24: 172–86.

Cotton, M. A., and Métraux, G. P. R.

1985   *The San Rocco Villa at Francolise.* Rome: British School at Rome.

Coulson, W. D. E.

1996   *Ancient Naukratis, Vol. 2: The Survey at Naukratis and Environs. Part 1: The Survey at Naukratis.* Oxbow Monograph No. 60. Oxford: Oxbow Books.

Coulson, W. D. E., and Leonard, A. Jr.

1979   A Preliminary Survey of the Naukratis Region in the Western Nile Delta. *Journal of Field Archaeology* 6: 151–68.

1981a   *Cities of the Delta, Part 1.* Naukratis. American Research Center in Egypt Reports, Vol. 4. Malibu: Undena.

1981b   Excavations in the South Mound at Naukratis, 1981. *Muse* 15: 39–45.

1982   Investigations at Naukratis and Environs, 1980–1981. *American Journal of Archaeology* 86: 361–80.

1983   The Naukratis Project, 1983. *Muse* 17: 64–71.

Coulson, W. D. E., and Wilkie, N. C.

1986   Ptolemaic and Roman Kilns in the Western Nile Delta. *Bulletin of the American Schools of Oriental Research* 263: 61–75.

Coulson, W. D. E., Wilkie, N. C., and Rehard, J. W.
  1986   Amphoras from Naukratis and Environs. Pp. 535–50 in *Recherches sur les Amphores Grecques,* eds. J.-Y. Empereur and Y. Garlan. Bulletin de Correspondence Hellénique, Supplément XIII. Athens: Diffusion de Boccard.
Coulson, W. D. E., Leonard, A. Jr., and Wilkie, N. C.
  1980   The Naukratis Project, 1980. *American Research Center in Egypt Newsletter* 112: 49–50.
  1982   Three Seasons of Excavations and Survey at Naukratis and Environs. *Journal of the American Research Center in Egypt* 19: 73–109.
  1983   The 1982 Campaign at Naukratis and its Environs. *American Research Center in Egypt Newsletter* 122: 51–58.
  1984   The Naukratis Project, 1983. *American Research Center in Egypt Newsletter* 125: 28–40.
Courby, F.
  1922   *Les vases grecs à reliefs.* Bibliothèque des écoles françaises d'Athènes et de Rome. Paris: E. de Boccard.
Crowfoot, G., Crowfoot, J., and Kenyon, K.
  1957   *Samaria-Sebaste: Reports of the Expedition in 1931–33 and of the British Expedition in 1935.* 3 vols. London: Palestine Exploration Fund.
Crowfoot, J.
  1957   *The Objects from Samaria.* London: Palestine Exploration Fund.
Daszewski, W.
  1987   Les lampes égyptiennes d'époque hellénistique. *Les lampes de terre cuite en Méditerranée,* eds. T. Ozoil and A. Justinien. Travaux de la Maison de l'Orient 13. Lyon: Maison de l'Orient.
Desbat, A., and Martin-Kilcher, S.
  1989   Les amphores sur l'axe Rhône-Rhin à l'époque d'Auguste. Pp. 339–65 in *Amphores romaines et histoire économique: dix ans de recherche,* eds. M. Lenoir, D. Manacorda, and C. Panella. Collection de l'ecole française de Rome 114. Rome: École française de Rome.
Dever, W. G., and Lance, H. D.
  1978   *A Manual of Field Excavation: Handbook for Field Archaeologists.* Cincinnati: Hebrew Union College.
Dore, J.
  1989   The Coarse Pottery. Pp. 87–248 in *Excavations at Sabratha 1948–1951.* Vol. 2, part 1. *The Finds: The Amphorae, Coarse Pottery, and Building Materials,* eds. M. Fulford and M. Hall. Society for Libyan Studies, Monograph 1. London: Society for the Promotion of Roman Studies.
Dothan, M.
  1971   *Ashdod 2–3. The Second and Third Seasons of Excavations 1963, 1965.* 'Atiqot 9–10 (English series). Jerusalem: Israel Antiquities Authority.
  1976   Akko: Interim Excavation Report First Season, 1973/4. *Bulletin of the American Schools of Oriental Research* 224: 1–48.
Dray, E., du Plat Taylor, B. A., and du Plat Taylor, J.
  1951   Tsambres and Aphendrika: Two Classical and Hellenistic Cemeteries in Cyprus. *Report of the Department of Antiquities, Cyprus,* 1937–1939: 24–123.
Drower, M.
  1985   *Flinders Petrie: a Life in Archaeology.* London: Gollancz.
Dunand, F.
  1990   *Catalogue des terres cuites gréco-romaines d'Égypte.* Musée du Louvre, département des antiquités égyptiennes. Paris: Réunion des musées nationaux.
Dunbabin, M. D.
  1994   Early Pavement Types in the West and the Invention of Tessellation. Pp. 26–40 in *Fifth International Colloquium on Ancient Mosaics,* Part 1, eds. P. Johnson, R. Ling and D. J. Smith. Journal of Roman Archaeology Supplementary Series No. 9. Ann Arbor: Journal of Roman Archaeology.
Dupont, P.
  1982   Amphores commerciales archaïques de la Grèce de l'Est. *La parola del passato* 37: 193–209.
Edwards, G. R.
  1956   *Hellenistic Pottery.* Pp. 79–112 in *Small Objects from the Pnyx: II,* eds. L. Talcott, B. Philippaki, G. R. Edwards and V. R. Grace. *Hesperia* Supplement 10. Princeton: American School of Classical Studies at Athens.
  1975   *Corinthian Hellenistic Pottery.* Corinth: Results of Excavations Conducted by the American School of Classical Studies at Athens. Vol. 7, part 3. Princeton: American School of Classical Studies at Athens.
Emery, W. B.
  1967   *Lost Land Emerging.* New York: Charles Scribner's Sons.

Empereur, J.-Y.
1986   Un atelier de Dressel 2–4 en Égypte au IIIe siècle de notre ére. Pp. 599–608 in *Recherches sur les Amphores Grecques*, eds. J.-Y. Empereur and Y. Garlan. Bulletin de Correspondence Hellénique Supplément XIII. École Française d'Athènes. Athens: Diffusion de Boccard.

Empereur, J.-Y., and Garlan, Y., eds.
1986   *Recherches sur les Amphores Grecques. Bulletin de Correspondence Hellénique* Supplément XIII. École Française d'Athènes. Athens: Diffusion de Boccard.

Empereur, J.-Y., and Picon, M.
1989   Les régions de production d'amphores impériales en Méditerranée orientale. Pp. 223–48 in *Amphores romaines et histoire économique: dix ans de recherche*, eds. M. Lenoir, D. Manacorda, and C. Panella. Collection de l'ecole française de Rome 114. Rome: École française de Rome.

Enklaar, A.
1985   Chronologie et Peintres des Hydries de Hadra. *Bulletin Antieke Bescharing* 60: 106–51.

Fariñas del Cerro, L., Fernandez de la Vega, W., and Hesnard, A.
1977   Contribution à l'établissement d'une typologie des amphores dites "Dressel 2–4." Pp. 179–206 in *Méthodes classiques et méthodes formelles dans l'étude des amphores (Actes du colloque de Rome, 27–29 Mai 1974)*, ed. G. Vallet. Collection de l'ecole française de Rome 32. Rome: École française de Rome.

Fischer, M.
1989   Hellenistic Pottery. Pp. 177–87 in *Excavations at Tell Michal, Israel*, eds. Z. Herzog, G. Rapp, and O. Negbi. Minneapolis: University of Minnesota.

Fischer, P.
1971   *Mosaic: History and Technique.* New York: McGraw-Hill Book Company.

Foster, K.
1979   *Aegean Faience of the Bronze Age.* New Haven: Yale University.

Fraser, P. M.
1972   *Ptolemaic Alexandria.* 3 vols. Oxford: Oxford University.

Fulford, M. G.
1986   The Pottery from Pit 2 (Context Y.1.xxv/24): Amphorae [and] The Other Coarse Wares. Pp. 183–98 in *Excavations at Sabratha 1948–1951*, by P. M. Kenrick. Journal of Roman Studies Monograph 2. London: Society for the Promotion of Roman Studies.

Furumark, A.
1941   *The Mycenaean Pottery: Analysis and Classification.* Stockholm: Svenska Institutet I Athen.

Gardner, E.
1888   *Naukratis II.* Egypt Exploration Fund Memoir 6. London: Egypt Exploration Fund.

Gempeler, R. D.
1992   *Die Keramik römischer bis fruharabischer zeit.* Elephantine 10. Mainz: von Zabern.

Gentili, G. V.
1958   I Timbri amforari Rodii nel Museo Nazionale di Siracusa. *Archivo Storico Siracusano* 4: 18–95.

Giddy, L., Smith, H., and French, P.
1992   *The Anubieion at Saqqâra II. The Cemeteries.* Excavation Memoir 56. London: Egypt Exploration Society.

Gill, D.
1986   Attic black-glazed pottery. Pp. 275–98 in *Excavations at Sabratha 1948–1951*, by P. M. Kenrick. Journal of Roman Studies Monograph 2. London: Society for the Promotion of Roman Studies.

Goldman, H., ed., et al.
1950   *Excavations at Gözlü Kale, Tarsus.* Vol. 1. Princeton: Princeton University.

Gordon, R. L.
1977   *Late Hellenistic Wall Decoration of Tel Anafa.* Ph.D. dissertation, University of Missouri–Columbia.

Grace, V.
1934   Stamped Amphora Handles Found in 1931–1932. *Hesperia* 3: 197–310.
1950   The Stamped Amphora Handles. Pp. 135–48 in *Excavations at Gözlü Kule, Tarsus.* Vol. 1, ed. H. Goldman. Princeton: Princeton University.
1952   Timbres amphoriques trouvés à Délos. *Bulletin de Correspondence Hellenique* 76: 514–40.
1953   The Eponyms Named on Rhodian Amphora Stamps. *Hesperia* 22: 116–28.
1956   Stamped Wine Jar Fragments. Pp. 113–89 in *Small Objects from the Pnyx: II.* Hesperia Supplement X, ed. L. Talcott et al. Princeton: American School of Classical Studies at Athens.

1962   Stamped Handles of Commercial Amphoras. Pp. 106–30 in *Excavations at Nessana 1*, ed. H. Dunscombe Colt. Princeton: Princeton University.

1971   Samian Amphoras. *Hesperia* 40: 52–95.

1985   The Middle Stoa Dated by Amphora Stamps. *Hesperia* 54: 1–54.

Graindor, P.

1939   *Terres cuites de l'Égypte gréco-romaine*. Antwerp: de Sikkel.

Grandjouan, C., Markson, E, and Rotroff, S.

1989   *Hellenistic Relief Molds from the Athenian Agora. Hesperia* Supplement 23. Princeton: American School of Classical Studies.

Grataloup, C.

1991   Karnak. Temple d'Amon-Rê, 1990. *Bulletin de Liaison du Groupe International d'Étude e la céramique égyptienne* 15: 22–27.

Gratien, B., and Soulié, D.

1988   La Céramique de Tell el-Herr. Campagnes 1986 et 1987. Étude préliminaire. *Cahiers de recherches de l'Institute de papyrologie et d'égyptologie de Lille* 10: 23–55.

Grose, D. F.

1989   *Early Ancient Glass.* New York: Hudson Hills.

Gutch, C.

1898/99 Excavations at Naukratis. The Terracottas. *Annual of the British School at Athens* 5: 67–97.

Harden, D. B.

1936   *Roman Glass from Karanis found by the University of Michigan Archaeological Expedition in Egypt, 1924–29.* Ann Arbor: University of Michigan.

Hayes, J. W.

1976a   Pottery: Stratified Groups and Typology. Pp. 47–123 in *Excavations at Carthage 1975 Conducted by the University of Michigan.* Vol. 1, ed. J. H. Humphrey. Tunis: Cérès Productions.

1976b   *Roman Pottery in the Royal Ontario Museum: A Catalogue.* Toronto: The Royal Ontario Museum.

1980a   *Ancient Lamps in the Royal Ontario Museum I: Greek and Roman Clay Lamps: A Catalogue.* Toronto: The Royal Ontario Museum.

1980b   Problèmes de la céramique des 7ᵉ–9ᵉ siècles ap. J.-C. à Salamine et à Chypre. Pp. 375–80 in *Salamine de Chypre Histoire et Archéologie: État des Recherches.* Colloques Internationaux du Centre National de la Recherche Scientifique; No. 578. Paris: Centre National de la Recherche Scientifique.

1983   The Villa Dionysos Excavations, Knossos: The Pottery. *Annual of the British School at Athens* 78: 97–169.

1986   Sigillate orientali. Pp. 1–96 in *Enciclopedia dell'arte antica. Classica e Orientale. Atlante delle forme ceramiche* II. *Ceramica fine roman nel bacino mediterraneo (tardo ellenismo e primo impero).* Rome: Istituto della enciclopedia italiana.

1991   *Paphos.* Vol. III: *The Hellenistic and Roman Pottery.* Nicosia: Department of Antiquities of Cyprus.

Hellström, P.

1965   *Labraunda: Pottery of Classical and Later Date, Terracotta Lamps and Glass.* Swedish Excavations and Researches 2.1. Lund: CWK Gleerup.

Hennessy, J.

1970   Excavations at Samaria-Sebaste, 1968. *Levant* 2: 1–21.

Herodotus

1954   *The Histories.* Trans. A. de Selincourt, from Greek. Baltimore: Penguin Books.

Higgins, R. A.

1967   *Greek Terracottas.* London: Methuen.

1969   *Catalogue of the Terracottas in the Department of Greek and Roman Antiquities*, British Museum, Vol. 1 (Greek: 730–330 B.C.). London: The British Museum.

1986   *Tanagra and the Figurines.* London: Trefoil Books.

Hogarth, D. G.

1898–99 Excavations at Naukratis. *Annual of the British School at Athens* 5: 26–46.

Hogarth, D. G., Lorrimer, H. L., and Edgar, C. C.

1905   Naukratis, 1903. *The Journal of Hellenic Studies* 25: 105–36.

Holladay, J. S., Jr.

1982   *Cities of the Delta, Part 3*: Tell el-Maskhuta. American Research Center in Egypt Reports, Vol. 6. Malibu: Undena.

Hölscher, U.
1954   *The Excavation of Medinet Habu V: Post-Ramessid Remains.* Oriental Institute Publications 66. Chicago: The
        Oriental Institute.

Hope, C. A.
1987   *Egyptian Pottery.* Aylesbury: Shire Publications.

Howland, R. H.
1958   *The Athenian Agora IV: Greek Lamps and Their Survivals.* Princeton: American School of Classical Studies at
        Athens.

Jacquet-Gordon, H.
n.d.   From the Twenty-First Dynasty to the Ptolemaic Period. Unpublished manuscript prepared for the Manual of
        Ancient Egyptian Pottery.

Jones, F.
1950   The Pottery. Pp. 149–296 in *Excavations at Gözlü Küle, Tarsus.* Vol. 1, ed. H. Goldman. Princeton: Princeton
        University.

Kamal, A.
1904–5 *Stèles ptolémaiques et romaines.* Catalogue Général des Antiquités Égyptiennes du Musée du Caire, nos. 22001–
        22208. Cairo: L'Institut français d'archéologie orientale.

Karageorghis, V.
1993   *Coroplastic Art of Ancient Cyprus.* Volume 3. Nicosia: A. G. Leventis Foundation.

Kaufmann, C. M.
1915   *Graeco-Ägyptische Koroplastik. Terrakotten der griechisch–romischen und koptischen Epoche aus der Faijum-Oase
        und anderen Fundstätten.* Leipzig: Heinrich Finck.

Kaczmarczyk, A., and Hedges, R. E. M.
1983   *Ancient Egyptian Faience: An Analytical Survey of Egyptian Faience from Predynastic to Roman Times.* Warminster:
        Aris and Phillips.

Keay, N.
1989   The Amphorae. Pp. 5–86 in *Excavations at Sabratha 1948–1951.* Vol. 2. *The Finds.* Part 1. *The Amphorae, Coarse
        Pottery, and Building Materials,* eds. M. Fulford and M. Hall. Society for Libyan Studies, Monograph 1. London:
        Society for the Promotion of Roman Studies.

Kelley, A.
1976   *The Pottery of Ancient Egypt: Dynasty I to Roman Times.* Toronto: Royal Ontario Museum.

Kelso, J. L., and Baramki, D. C.
1955   Excavations at New Testament Jericho and Khirbet En-Nitla. *Annual of the American Schools of Oriental Research*
        29–30: 1–49.

Kenrick, P.
1985   *Excavations at Sidi Khrebish Benghazi (Berenice),* Vol. 3, Part 1: *The Fine Pottery.* Libya Antiqua Supplement 5.
        Tripoli: Department of Antiquities.

Kleiner, G.
1984   *Tanafgrafiguren. Untersuchungen zur hellenistischen Kunst und Geschichte,* revised edition. Berlin: W. de Gruyter.

Köster, A.
1926   *Die Griechischen Terrakotten.* Berlin: Hans Schoetz.

Koehler, C. G.
1979   *Corinthian A and B Transport Amphoras.* Ph.D. Dissertation, Princeton University.

Kraus, B. S., and Jordan, R. E.
1965   *Human Dentition Before Birth.* Philadelphia: Kimpton.

Laidlaw, A.
1985   *The First Style in Pompeii: Painting and Architecture.* Archaeologica 57. Rome: G. Bretschneider.

Lamboglia, N.
1955   Sulla cronologia delle anfore romane de età republicana. *Rivista Studi Liguri* 21: 252–60.

Landau, Y.
1979   Tel Istabah, Beth Shean: The Excavations and the Hellenistic Jar Handles. *Israel Exploration Journal* 29: 152–59.

Lapp, P. W.
1961   *Palestinian Ceramic Chronology, 200 B.C.–A.D. 70.* New Haven: American Schools of Oriental Research.

Laubenheimer, F.
1989   Les amphores gauloises sous l'Empire. Recherches nouvelles sur leur production et leur chronologie. Pp. 105–
        138 in *Amphores romaines et histoire économique: dix ans de recherche,* eds. M. Lenoir, D. Manacorda, and
        C. Panella. Collection de l'ecole française de Rome 114. Rome: École française de Rome.

Laumonier, A.
 1956 *Delos XXIII. Les figurines terre cuite.* Exploration archeologique de Delos faite par L' École François d'Athènes, fasc. 23. Paris: E. de Boccard.

Lenoir, M., Manacorda, D., and Panella, C., eds.
 1989 *Amphores romaines et histoire économique: dix ans de recherche.* Collection de l'École française de Rome 114. Rome: École Française de Rome.

Leonard, A., Jr.
 1994 *An Index to the Late Bronze Age Aegean Pottery from Syria-Palestine.* Studies in Mediterranean Archaeology 114. Jonsered: Paul Åströms.
 1997 *Ancient Naukratis* Vol. 1: *Excavations at a Greek Emporium in Egypt.* Part I: *The Excavations at Kom Ge'if.* Annual of the American Schools of Oriental Research 54. Boston: ASOR.

Levi, D.
 1947 *Antioch Mosaic Pavements.* Princeton: Princeton University. Reprint, 2 vols. Rome: L'Erma di Bretschneider, 1971.

Ling, R.
 1972 Stucco Decoration. *Papers of the British School at Rome* XL: 11–57.
 1976 Stuccowork. Pp. 209–21 in *Roman Crafts,* eds. D. Strong and D. Brown. London: Duckworth.

Lloris, M. B.
 1977 Problemas de la morfología y del concepto histórico geográfico que recubre la noción tipo. Aportaciones a la tipología de las ánforas beticas. Pp. 97–131 in *Méthodes classiques et méthodes formelles dans l'étude des amphores (Actes du colloque de Rome, 27–29 Mai 1974),* ed. G. Vallet. Collection de l'ecole française de Rome 32. Rome: École française de Rome.

Lloyd, A. B.
 1975 *Herodotus Book II. Volume 1, Introduction.* Leiden: E. J. Brill.
 1988 *Herodotus Book II. Volume 3, Commentary 99–182.* Leiden: E. J. Brill.

Lucas, A., and Harris, J. R.
 1962 *Ancient Egyptian Materials and Industries,* 4th edition. London: Edward Arnold.

Lurker, M.
 1980 *The Gods and Symbols of Ancient Egypt.* New York: Thames & Hudson.

Macalister, R. A. S.
 1901 Amphora Handles with Greek Stamps from Tell Sandahannah. *Palestine Exploration Fund Quarterly Statement:* 25–43; 124–44.
 1912 *The Excavations of Gezer,* 1902–1903 and 1907–1909, Vol. 2. London: John Murray.

Majcherek, G.
 1992 Alexandria, Kom el-Dikka, 1990–1991. *Bulletin de Liaison du Groupe International d'Étude de la céramique égyptienne* 16: 1–4.

Majcherek, G., and Shennawi, A.
 1991 Tell el-Haraby. A newly discovered kiln-site. *Bulletin de Liaison du Groupe International d'Étude de la céramique égyptienne* 16: 1–4.

Michelucci, M.
 1975 *La Collezione di lucerne del Museo Egizio di Firenze.* Accademia Toscana di scienze e lettere, Studi XXXIX. Firenze: Lep S. Olschki.

Miller, N. F.
 1984 The Use of Dung as Fuel: An Ethnographic Example and an Archaeological Application. *Paléorient* 10(2): 71–79.

Miller, N. F., and Smart, T. L.
 1984 Intentional Burning of Dung as Fuel: A Mechanism for the Incorporation of Charred Seeds into the Archaeological Record. *Ethnobiology* 4: 15–28.

Mond, R., and Myers, O.
 1934 *The Bucheum,* Vol. 1. *The History and Archaeology of the Site.* Egypt Exploration Society Memoir 41. London: Egypt Exploration Society.

Moore, R. E.
 1968 A Newly Observed Stratum in Roman Floor Mosaics. *American Journal of Archaology* 72: 57–68.

Mostafa, I.
 1988 Tell Fara'on-Imet. *Bulletin de Liaison du Groupe International d'Étude de la céramique égyptienne* 13: 14–18.

Mountjoy, P. A.
 1986 *Mycenaean Decorated Pottery: A Guide to Identification.* Studies in Mediterranean Archaeology 73. Göteborg: Paul Åströms.

Netzer, E.
  1975   The Hashmonean and Herodian Winter Palaces at Jericho. *Israel Exploration Journal* 25: 89–100.
Nicholson, P., and Patterson, H.
  1985   Ethnoarchaeology in Egypt: The Ballâs Pottery Project. *Archaeology* 38/3: 52–59.
Nilsson, M.
  1909   *Timbres Amphoriques de Lindos.* Explorations archéologique de Rhodes 5. Copenhagen: Bianco Luno.
Ochsenschlager, E.
  1967   The Excavations at Tell Timai. *Journal of the American Research Center in Egypt* 6: 32–51.
Osborne, A.
  1924   *Lychnos et Lecerna; catalogue raisonné d'une collection de lampes en terre cuite trouvées en Égypte.* Alexandria: Société archéologique d'Alexandrie.
Panella, C.
  1989   Le anfore italiche del II secolo D.C. Pp. 139–78 in *Amphores romaines et histoire économique: dix ans de recherche,* eds. M. Lenoir, D. Manacorda, and C. Panella. Collection de l'ecole française de Rome 114. Rome: École française de Rome.
Panella, C., and Fano, M.
  1977   Le anfore con anse bifide conservate a Pompei: contributo ad una loro classificazione. Pp. 133–77 in *Méthodes classiques et méthodes formelles dans l'étude des amphores, Actes colloque de Rome, 27–29 Mai 1974.* Collection de l'école française de Rome. Palais Farnèse (École Française de Rome).
Peacock, D. P. S.
  1977   Roman Amphorae: Typology, Fabric and Origins. Pp. 261–78 in *Méthodes classiques et méthodes formelles dans l'étude des amphores (Actes du colloque de Rome, 27–29 Mai 1974),* ed. G. Vallet. Collection de l'ecole française de Rome 32. Rome: École française de Rome.
Peacock, D. P. S., Bejaoui, F., and Belazreg, N.
  1989   Roman Amphora Production in the Sahel Region of Tunisia. Pp. 179–222 in *Amphores romaines et histoire économique: dix ans de recherche,* eds. M. Lenoir, D. Manacorda, and C. Panella. Collection de l'ecole française de Rome 114. Rome: École française de Rome.
Peacock, D. P. S., and Williams, D. F.
  1986   *Amphorae and the Roman Economy.* London: Longman.
Pemberton. E.
  1985   Ten Hellenistic Graves in Ancient Corinth. *Hesperia* 54: 271–307.
  1989   *Corinth: The Sanctuary of Demeter and Kore: The Greek Pottery.* Corinth XVIII, Part I. Princeton: American School of Classical Studies at Athens.
Perdrizet, P.
  1921   *Les terres cuites Grecques d' Égypte de la collection Fouquet.* Strasbourg: Berger-Levrault.
Petrie, W. M. F.
  1885   Al-Tanis I (EEF Memoir 2).
  1886   *Naukratis, Part I.* London: The Egypt Exploration Fund.
  1888   Tanis II (EEF Memoir 5).
  1889   *Tanis.* London: Trübner & Co.
  1891   *Ten Years Digging in Egypt, 1881–1891.* London: The Religious Tract Society.
  1904   *Methods and Aims in Archaeology.* New York: Macmillan.
  1905   *Roman Ehnasya (Herakleopolis Magna).* 1904. *Plates and Text Supplementary to Ehnasya.* London: The Egypt Exploration Society.
  1909   *Memphis I.* Egyptian Research Account Volume 15. London: British School of Archaeology in Egypt.
Petrie, W. M. F., Mackay, E., and Wainright, G.
  1910   *Meydum and Memphis (III).* Egyptian Research Account Volume 18. London: British School of Archaeology in Egypt.
  1911   *Roman Portraits and Memphis (IV).* Egyptian Research Account, Volume 20. London: British School of Archaeology in Egypt.
Philipp, H.
  1972   *Terrakotten aus Ägypten im Ägyptischen Museum Berlin.* Bilderhefte der Staatlichen Museen Preussischer Kulturbesitz, Heft 18/19. Berlin: Gebr. Mann.
Phillips, K. M., Jr.
  1960   Subject and technique in Hellenistic-Roman Mosaics: A Ganymede Mosaic from Sicily. *The Art Bulletin* 42(4): 243–62.

Pratt, P.
 1976 Wall Painting. Pp. 223–29 in *Roman Crafts,* eds. D. Strong and D. Brown. London: Duckworth.
Pryce, F. N.
 1928 *Catalogue of Sculpture in the Department of Greek and Roman Antiquities of the British Museum.* Volume 1, Part 1: Prehellenic and Early Greek. London: The British Museum.
Reisner, G.
 1924 *Harvard Excavations at Samaria* I. Cambridge: Harvard University.
Riley, J.
 1979 The Coarse Pottery from Berenice. Pp. 91–466 in *Excavations at Sidi Khrebish Benghazi (Berenice).* Libya Antiqua Supplement 5.2. Tripoli: Department of Antiquities.
Robins, F. W.
 1939a *The Story of the Lamp.* London: Oxford University.
 1939b Graeco-Roman Lamps from Egypt. *Journal of Egyptian Archaeology* 25: 48–52.
Rohde, E.
 1968 *Griechische Terrakotten.* Monumenta Actis Antiquae, Band 4. Tübingen: Ernst Wasmuth.
Romano, I. B.
 1994 A Hellenistic Deposit from Corinth, Evidence for Interim Period Activity (146–44 B.C.). *Hesperia* 63: 57–104.
Rotroff, S.
 1984 The Origins and Chronology of Hellenistic Gray Unguentaria. *American Journal of Archaeology* 88: 258.
 1997 *Hellenistic Pottery. Athenian and Imported Wheelmade Table Ware and Related Material.* 2 vols. *The Athenian Agora 29.* Princeton: American School of Classical Studies at Athens.
Rotroff, S. I., and Oakley, J. H.
 1992 *Debris from a Public Dining Palace in the Athenian Agora. Hesperia* Supplement 25. Princeton: American School of Classical Studies.
Rozenberg, S.
 1996 The Wall Paintings of the Herodian Palace at Jericho. Pp. 121–38 in *Judaea and the Greco-Roman World in the Time of Herod in the Light of Archaeological Evidence,* eds. K. Fittschen and G. Foerster. Abhandlungen der Akademie der Wissenschaften in Göttingen, Phil.-hist. Klasse, Series 3, Number 215. Göttingen: Vandenhoeck and Ruprecht.
Samartzidou, S.
 1988 Recent Finds from the Cemeteries of Ancient Amphipolis. Pp. 327–35 in *First Workshop on Archaeology in Macedonia and Thrace.* Thessaloniki: University of Thessaloniki.
Schuchhardt, C., and Fabricus, E.
 1895 *Altertümer von Pergamon Vol. III, 2: Die Inschriften von Pergamon.* Berlin: Spearman.
Schürmann, W.
 1989 *Katalog der Antiken Terrakotten im Badischen Landsmuseum, Karlsuhe.* Studies in Mediterranean Archaeology 84. Göteborg: Paul Åström.
Scott, G. D., III
 1992 *Temple, Tomb and Dwelling: Egyptian Antiquities from the Harer Family Trust Collection.* San Bernadino: California State University, University Art Gallery.
Sealey, P. R.
 1985 *Amphoras from the 1970 Excavations at Colchester Sheepen.* B.A.R. British Series 142. Oxford: B.A.R.
Sear, F.
 1976 Floor Mosaics. Pp. 231–40 in *Roman Crafts,* eds. D. Strong and D. Brown. London: Duckworth.
Seger, J. D.
 1971 *Handbook for Field Operations.* New York: Hebrew Union College.
Seton-Williams, M. V.
 1967 The Tell el-Farâ'în Expedition, 1967. *Journal of Egyptian Archaeology* 53: 146–55.
 1969 The Tell el-Fârâ'în Expedition, 1968. *Journal of Egyptian Archaeology* 55: 5–22.
Shier, L. A.
 1978 *Terracotta Lamps from Karanis Egypt.* University of Michigan, Kelsey Museum of Anthropology Studies No. 3. Ann Arbor: Kelsey Museum of Anthropology Studies.
Shoe, L.
 1936 *Profiles of Greek Mouldings.* Cambridge: Harvard University for the American School of Classical Studies at Athens.
Slane, K. W.
 1986 Two Deposits from the Early Roman Cellar Building, Corinth. *Hesperia* 55: 271–318.

Sparkes, B.
1962   The Greek Kitchen. *Journal of Hellenic Studies* 82: 121–37.
Sparkes, B., and Talcott, L.
1970   *Black and Plain Pottery of the 6th, 5th, and 4th centuries B.C.* 2 vols. *The Athenian Agora* 12. Princeton: American School of Classical Studies at Athens.
Sztetyllo, Z.
1975   Timbres amphoriques grecs des fouilles polonaises à Alexandrie (1962–1972). *Études et Travaux* 8. Le Group de Recherche d'Histoire Romaine de l'Université des Sciences Humaines de Strasbourg. Strasbourg: Association pour l'etude de la civilisation Romaine.
1976   *Nea Paphos I: Les Timbres Cérmaiques.* Warsaw: Editions Scientifiques de Pologne.
Talcott, L., Philippaki, B., Edwards, G. R., and Grace, V. R.
1956   *Small Objects from the Pnyx: II. Hesperia* Supplement 10. Princeton: American School of Classical Studies at Athens.
Tcherikower, V.
1937   Palestine under the Ptolemies. A Contribution to the Study of the Zenon Papyri. *Mizraim* 4–5: 9–90.
Thompson, D. B.
1963   *Troy. The Terracotta Figurines of the Hellenistic Period.* Excavations Conducted by the University of Cincinnati, Supplementary Monograph 3. Princeton.
1973   *Ptolemaic Oinochoai and Portraits in Faience, Aspects of the Ruler-Cult.* Oxford: Clarendon.
Thompson, H. A.
1934   Two Centuries of Hellenistic Pottery: *Hesperia* 3: 310–480.
Thompson, H. A., Thompson, D. B., and Rotroff, S. I.
1987   *Hellenistic Pottery and Terracottas.* Princeton: American School of Classical Studies at Athens.
Tufnell, O.
1961   'These were the Potters' . . . Notes on the craft in southern Arabia. *Annals of the Leeds University Oriental Society* 2: 26–36.
Vallet, G., ed.
1977   *Méthodes classiques et méthodes formelles dans l'étude des amphores (Actes du Colloque de Rome, 27–29 Mai 1974).* Collection de l'École française de Rome 32. Rome: École français de Rome.
Venit, M. S.
1988   The Painted Tomb from Wardian and the Decoration of Alexandrian Tombs. *Journal of the American Research Center in Egypt* 25: 71–91.
von Bissing, F. W.
1951   Naukratis. *Bulletin Societe Royale d'Anthropologie d'Alexandrie* 39: 33–82.
von Lorentz, F.
1937   ΒΑΡΒΑΡΩΝ ΥΨΑΣΜΑΤΑ. *Bulletino Dell'Istituto Archeologico Germanico Sezione Romana* 52: 165–222.
Vossen, R.
1984   Towards Building Models of Traditional Trade in Ceramics: Case Studies from Spain and Morocco. Pp. 341–97 in *The Many Dimensions of Pottery,* eds. S. E. van der Leeuw and A. C. Pritchard. Amsterdam: University of Amsterdam.
Waagé, F. O.
1948   Hellenistic and Roman Tableware of North Syria. Pp. 1–60 in *Antioch-on-the-Orontes.* Vol. 4.1: *Ceramics and Islamic Coins.* Princeton: Princeton University.
Walters, H. B.
1903   *Catalogue of the Terracottas (British Museum).* London: The British Museum.
1914   *Catalogue of the Greek and Roman Lamps in the British Museum.* London: The British Museum.
Webb, V.
1978   *Archaic Greek Faience, Miniature Scent Bottles and Related Objects from East Greece, 650–500 B.C.* Warminster: Aris & Phillips.
Weber, W.
1914   *Die Ägyptisch-Griechischen Terrakotten.* Mitteilungen aus der Ägyptischen Sammlung, Königliche Museum zu Berlin Band II. Berlin: Verlag von Karl Curtius.
Webster, T. B. L.
1967   *Monuments Illustrating Tragedy and Satyr Play.* Bulletin of the Institute of Classical Studies, Supplement 20. London: University of London.

1969a   *Monuments Illustrating Old and Middle Comedy.* Bulletin of the Institute of Classical Studies, Supplement 23. London: University of London.

1969b   *Monuments Illustrating New Comedy.* Bulletin of the Institute of Classical Studies, Supplement 24. London: University of London.

Weinberg, S. S.
1971   Tel Anafa: The Hellenistic Town. *Israel Exploration Journal* 21: 86–109.

Whitcomb, D. S., and Johnson., J. H.
1979   *Quseir al-Qadim 1978. Preliminary Report.* American Research Center in Egypt: Cairo.

1982   *Quseir al-Qadim 1980. Preliminary Report.* American Research Center in Egypt Reports, Vol. 7. Malibu: Undena.

Wildung, D.
1996   *Sudan. Antike Königreiche am Nil.* Tübingen: Wasmuth.

Wilkie, N. C.
1981   Kom Dahab. Pp. 73–77 in *Cities of the Delta, Part 1, Naukratis,* eds. W. D. E. Coulson and A. Leonard, Jr. Malibu: Undena.

Will, E. L.
1982   Greco-italic amphoras. *Hesperia* 51: 338–56.

1989   Relazioni mutue tra le anfore romane. I ritrovamenti in Oriente, alla luce dei dati ottenuti nell'Occident. Pp. 297–309 in *Amphores romaines et histoire économique: dix ans de recherche,* eds. M. Lenoir, D. Manacorda, and C. Panella. Collection de l'ecole française de Rome 114. Rome: École française de Rome.

Williams, C. K.
1978   Corinth 1977, Forum Southwest. *Hesperia* 47: 1–39.

Wilson, K.
1982   *Cities of the Delta II.* Mendes. American Research Center in Egypt Report no. 7. Malibu: Undena.

Wright, K. S.
1980   A Tiberian Pottery Deposit from Corinth. *Hesperia* 49: 135–77.

Yadin, Y.
1970   Symbols of Deities at Zinjirli, Carthage and Hazor. Pp. 199–231 in *Near Eastern Archaeology in the Twentieth Century,* ed. J. A. Sanders. Garden City: Doubleday.

Zayadin, F.
1966   Early Hellenistic Pottery from the Theater Excavations at Samaria. *Annual of the Department of Antiquities of Jordan* 11: 53–64.

Plates

Plate 1.1. Photomosaic map of Ancient Naukratis showing the relative position of the South Mound at Kom Ge'if and the area locally known as Kom Hadid (Mound of Iron). North is to the right (G. Johnson).

Plate 1.2. Kom Hadid. The undulating modern surface showing tagged excavation areas: Area 48 in the foreground; Area 62/63 in the middleground (scale on Wall 7612/6212); and Area 76 in the background. Photo from the east (A. Leonard, Jr.).

Plate 1.3. Kom Hadid. Area 76 showing east–west, mudbrick Wall 7612 in the southeastern corner of the square. Rising ground water fills the probes made against the near (north) face of the wall. Photo from the north (A. Leonard, Jr.).

Plate 1.4. Kom Hadid. The foreground shows Area 62 on the right with the northern face of east–west Wall 7612/6212, and on the left Area 63 without any trace of the wall. Subsequent excavation of the (1 m) balk between the Areas 62 and 63 (see location of the scale) found the missing southern face of the wall. In the background, Area 76. Photo from the east (A. Leonard, Jr.).

Plate 1.5. Kom Hadid. Area 76 in the foreground showing Wall 7612 (scale) after it was traced eastward (as Wall 6212) into Areas 62 and 63. Photo from the west (A. Leonard, Jr.).

Plate 1.6. Kom Hadid. Areas 62 and 63 showing east–west Wall 7612/6212. Photo from the south(west) (A. Leonard, Jr.).

Plate 1.7. Kom Hadid. Area 48 showing the extension of Wall 7612/6212 from Area 62/63 on the right (west) to Area 48 on the left (east). Photo from the north (A. Leonard, Jr.).

Plate 1.8. Kom Hadid. Bipod photography over Area 76. Photo from the east (G. Johnson).

Plate 1.9. Kom Hadid. Bipod photograph of east–west Wall 7612/6212 (scale) in Area 62/63 (G. Johnson).

Plate 1.10. Kom Hadid. Bipod photograph of east–west Wall 7612/6212 in Area 62/63 to the left (west) and Area 48 (scale) to the right (east) (G. Johnson).

Plate 3.1. Fragment of a miniature, terracotta theatrical mask (#1), perhaps representing an old man in Greek Comedy (A. Leonard, Jr.).

Plate 3.2. Fragment of a miniature, terracotta theatrical mask (#2) representing a character in ancient Greek drama (A. Leonard, Jr.).

Plate 3.3. The upper portion of a terracotta figurine of the god Harpokrates as a child with an elaborate coiffure (#3), wearing the Double Crown of Upper and Lower Egypt (A. Leonard, Jr.).

Plate 3.4. Head from a terracotta figurine of the god Harpokrates (#4) shown as a youth with sidelock of hair (A. Leonard, Jr.).

Plate 3.5. Head of a terracotta figurine of a female (#5), perhaps the goddess Aphrodite (A. Leonard, Jr.).

Plate 3.6. Head of a terracotta figurine of young male (#6) (A. Leonard, Jr.).

Plate 3.7. Head a terracotta figurine of young male (#7) wearing a pointed hat(?) (A. Leonard, Jr.).

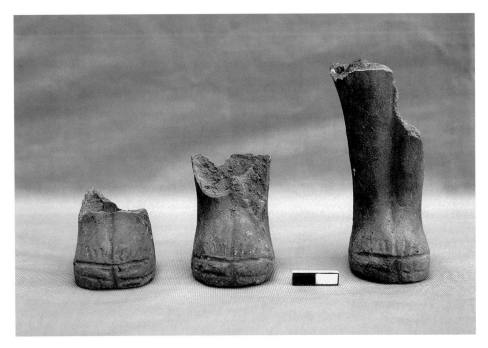

Plate 3.8. The lower extremities, of three very similar terracotta figurines of the hybrid deity Isis-Aphrodite (#8–#10), possibly from the same workshop or mold (A. Leonard, Jr.).

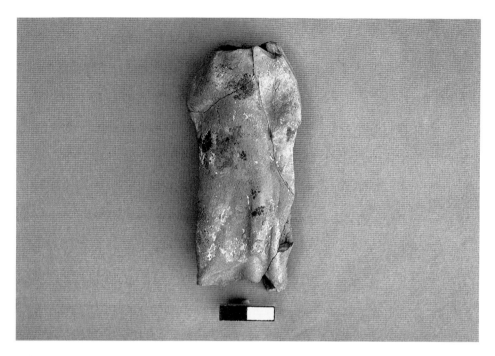

Plate 3.9. Fragment of a terracotta figurine of a young man (#11) wearing a himation (A. Leonard, Jr.).

Plate 3.10. Fragment of a terracotta vessel or figurine (#12) in the shape of a bunch of grapes (A. Leonard, Jr.).

Plate 3.11. Fragment of a terracotta figurine (#13) representing drapery (A. Leonard, Jr.).

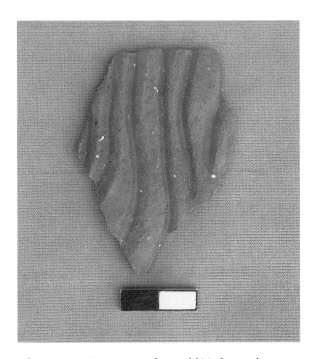

Plate 3.12. Fragment of a mold(?) for a plaque or figurine (#14) depicting curls of hair or drapery (A. Leonard, Jr.).

Plate 3.13. Fragment of a mold(?) for a plaque or figurine (#15) depicting drapery (A. Leonard, Jr.).

Plate 3.14. Two (non-joining) fragments of a terracotta plaque or plaques (#16a and b). Subject matter unidentified (A. Leonard, Jr.).

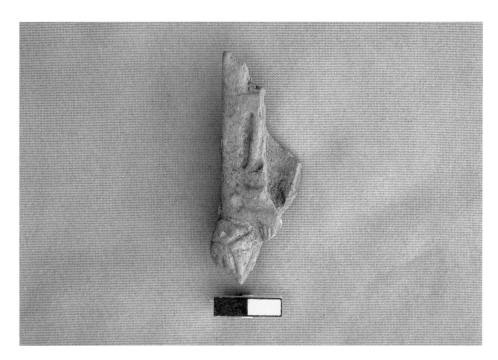

Plate 3.15. Fragment of a terracotta plaque (#17) with architectural(?) elements (A. Leonard, Jr.).

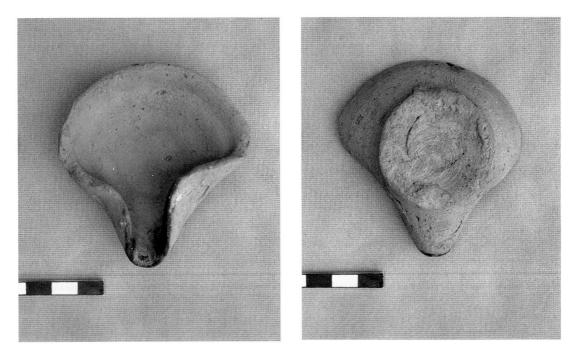

Plate 3.16. (a, b) Wheelmade, terracotta saucer lamp (#18) (A. Leonard, Jr.).

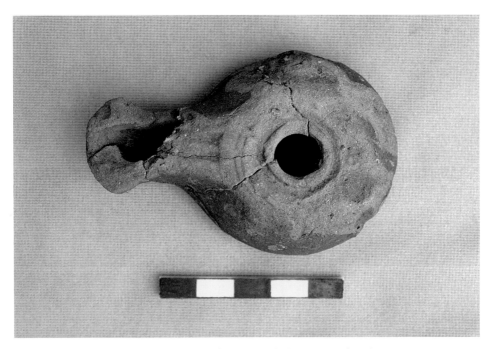

Plate 3.17. Wheelmade, terracotta lamp (#19) (A. Leonard, Jr.).

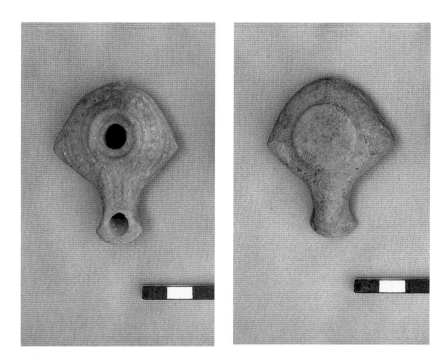

Plate 3.18a, b. Moldmade, terracotta lamp (#20) (A. Leonard, Jr.).

Plate 3.19. Moldmade, terracotta lamp (#21) (A. Leonard, Jr.).

Plate 3.20a, b. Toe of imported amphora (#22) showing how it was made (A. Leonard, Jr.).

Plate 3.21. Terracotta pot stands or stacking rings (#31 and #32), incised before firing (A. Leonard, Jr.).

Plate 3.22. Fragments of an open vessel with polychromatic decoration (#33), possibly from the Nubian X-Group (Ballana) culture (A. Leonard, Jr.).

Plate 3.23. Body sherds of a white faience vessel (#47) with blue floral(?) design (A. Leonard, Jr.).

Plate 3.24. Body sherd of a (closed?) faience vessel (#48) bearing a scale pattern in two shades of blue (A. Leonard, Jr.).

Plate 3.25. Rim fragment of a white faience cup/bowl (#49) decorated on the exterior with a cable pattern in brown-black (A. Leonard, Jr.).

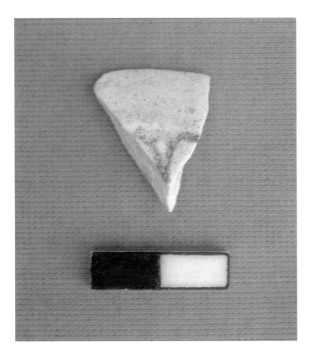

Plate 3.26. Rim fragment (after joined) of a white faience bowl (#50) decorated on the interior with a floral(?) pattern in blue (A. Leonard, Jr.).

Plate 3.27. Fragment of white marble (#61), perhaps representing the plaited hair of a kouros statue (A. Leonard, Jr.).

Plate 3.28. Fragment of white marble (#61), perhaps from a kouros *statue (A. Leonard, Jr.).*

Plate 3.29. Segment of a limestone ringstand(?) (#62) (A. Leonard, Jr.).

Plate 3.30. Fragment of a fluted limestone column (#63) (A. Leonard, Jr.).

Plate 3.31. Fragment of gray and white marble (#64a, left); fragment of red porphyry (#64b, right) from an opus sectile pavement (A. Leonard, Jr.).

Plate 3.32. Two fragments of aggregate pavement (#65 a and b), showing the "pebbled" walking surface (A. Leonard, Jr.).

Plate 3.33. Two fragments of aggregate pavement (#65a and b), showing the impression of the sub-floor, bedding layer (statumen) for the pavement (A. Leonard, Jr.).

[268]

Plate 3.34. Fragment of blue-green glass plaque or ingot (#66) (A. Leonard, Jr.).

Plate 3.35. Fragment of wall plaster (#67), perhaps depicting a garland of floral pattern (A. Leonard, Jr.).

Plate 3.36. Fragment of wall plaster (#68) showing a green stripe on a gray ground, perhaps in imitation of drafted masonry (A. Leonard, Jr.).

Plate 3.37. Fragment of wall plaster (#69) showing two successive "face" coats each with a painted decoration (A. Leonard, Jr.).

Plate 3.38. *Fragments of wall plaster (#70) mottled (gray-on-gray) to produce a faux marble pattern (A. Leonard, Jr.).*

Plate 3.39. *Fragments of wall plaster (#71) illustrating the range of patterns that decorated the walls (and/or floors) of the building(s) at Kom Hadid (A. Leonard, Jr.).*

Plate 3.40. Fragments of gray, wall plaster (#76). Each has been inscribed to represent a string course utilizing marginally drafted blocks of stone (A. Leonard, Jr.).

Plate 3.41. Miscellaneous fragments of decorated wall plaster (#82) from Kom Hadid (A. Leonard, Jr.).

Plate 3.42. Fragment of plaster architectural molding (#83) with egg and dart/tongue motif (A. Leonard, Jr.).